PN 2287 .D2823 T83 2014

Tucker, David C., 1962-

Joan Davis

DATE DUE

JOAN DAVIS

*America's Queen of Film, Radio
and Television Comedy*

David C. Tucker

McFarland & Company, Inc., Publishers

Jefferson, North Carolina

ALSO BY DAVID C. TUCKER AND FROM MCFARLAND

*Eve Arden: A Chronicle of All Film, Television,
Radio and Stage Performances* (2012)

*Lost Laughs of '50s and '60s Television:
Thirty Sitcoms That Faded Off Screen* (2010)

Shirley Booth: A Biography and Career Record (2008)

*The Women Who Made Television Funny:
Ten Stars of 1950s Sitcoms* (2007)

Frontispiece: Joan Davis, entering her
Universal Studios dressing room, in 1944.

LIBRARY OF CONGRESS CATALOGUING-IN-PUBLICATION DATA

Tucker, David C., 1962–
Joan Davis : America's queen of film, radio
and television comedy / David C. Tucker.
p.   cm.
Includes bibliographical references and index.

ISBN 978-0-7864-7784-5 (softcover : acid free paper) ∞

ISBN 978-1-4766-1502-8 (ebook)

1. Davis, Joan, 1912–1961.   2. Actresses—United States—
Biography.   3. Comedians—United States—
Biography.   I. Title.
PN2287.D2823T83 2014   792.02'8092—dc23   [B]   2014006085

BRITISH LIBRARY CATALOGUING DATA ARE AVAILABLE

On the cover: Joan Davis, early 1950s publicity photograph

Manufactured in the United States of America

*McFarland & Company, Inc., Publishers
Box 611, Jefferson, North Carolina 28640
www.mcfarlandpub.com*

To Ciro Barbaro, Joan's greatest fan...
and in memory of our beloved Jenny

Acknowledgments

Two individuals deserve special thanks for going above and beyond the call of duty in contributing to this book. Ciro Barbaro, one of Joan's most devoted and knowledgeable fans, shared much valuable information with me. His efforts to preserve copies of her *I Married Joan* episodes have done much to ensure that they are not lost to future generations. Patricia Dollisch, an accomplished genealogist, spent a number of hours tracing the previously unknown background of Joan's family, as well as researching her true date of birth.

Research was also furthered by the efforts of several talented people drawing on the collections of various institutions. Mark Fletcher, a Los Angeles–based researcher, successfully mined the depths of the UCLA Film and Television Archive and the Margaret Herrick Library. I am grateful to Ned Comstock for access to materials in the University of Southern California's Cinema Arts Library, and to graduate students Jordan Wolf and Emily McNish, who skillfully reviewed the Harry Crane papers at UCLA. Access to materials from the Minnesota Historical Society added greatly to my understanding of Joan's life and background; my thanks to librarian Hampton Smith.

James Robert Parish was, as always, generous with his advice and contacts, and author Lynn Kear continues to be a source of inspiration and ideas, as well as a friend I value greatly. As always, I appreciate the support of my colleagues at the DeKalb County Public Library, including Interlibrary Loan Librarian Sara Lagree, my faithful reader Brad Mathura, and the staff of the Processing Center.

Last but never least, my thanks to my mother, Louise Tucker, and to Ken McCullers.

Contents

Preface

Her career lasted more than thirty years, and encompassed a popular television comedy series, an Emmy nomination for Best Comedienne, roles in more than forty motion pictures, and a radio career that made her, in the mid–1940s, the highest-paid female performer in that medium. Yet information about Joan Davis' life and career remains difficult to come by, more than fifty years after her death in 1961.

What little information has been made available does not always flatter her memory. For many, the title of Joan's television series, as well as its timing (debuting in the fall of 1952), mark it a rip-off of *I Love Lucy*, and this is how it is often dismissed when television historians write about it. The version of the opening titles seen on most syndicated episodes of *I Married Joan*, in which it is described as "America's favorite comedy show," and Joan as "America's Queen of Comedy," strike many viewers unfamiliar with her lengthy motion picture and radio career as an unwarranted display of egotism on the star's behalf.

The memoirs of her *I Married Joan* leading man, Jim Backus, painted an unflattering picture of her as self-centered, ego-driven, and running roughshod over colleagues' feelings. Ben Ohmart, who wrote a brief biography of Joan Davis in 2006, was able to find few firsthand sources to interview forty-five years after her death; the two chief sources of information were the first two husbands of Joan's daughter Beverly, both long divorced from her and holding their former mother-in-law in low esteem. Joan's own death at the age of forty-eight, followed by the deaths in a house fire of much of her remaining family two years later, meant that other voices who might have helped perpetuate her memory were silenced.

Even with the dearth of first-hand information from Joan's co-stars and colleagues, however, there are glimpses of a Joan Davis not described in these works. Abe Burrows, head writer of Joan's radio series *Joan Davis Time*, wrote many years after her death, "I was very fond of her, and we were very close.... She was a fine actress and a good and dear friend."[1] While compiling credits for guest players on *I Married Joan*'s 98 episodes, I noted the names of more than two dozen performers who had previously worked with its star either on radio or in films. Could it be that the star, self-involved as some had depicted her, had gone out of her way to give old friends and colleagues work in her television show?

While her true legacy should be her performances, those too are often frustratingly out of reach. Much of her radio work is lost to the present-day listener, and few of her films have been released on DVD. Episodes of *I Married Joan* are generally available only on poor quality, public domain DVDs, where they are frequently missing scenes chopped out for time in syndicated reruns.

Researching Davis' career proved more difficult than my previous efforts to write about actresses such as Eve Arden and Shirley Booth. Genealogical research and access to public records (birth and death certificates, marriage and military records) ultimately allowed me

1

to track down a substantial amount of information that has not been previously published. I was able to verify her correct date of birth, as well as trace her family background and that of her husband, vaudeville comedian Si Wills. The invaluable archives of the Minnesota Historical Society yielded unexpected treasures: a school registration card, and articles from her high school newspaper in which we can see a teenaged Joan (then called Josephine) enjoying the beginnings of her adult career, and sending cheerful messages home to friends she'd left behind. The papers of veteran comedy writer Harry Crane, part of the Special Collections at the Charles E. Young Research Library at the University of Southern California, Los Angeles, aided in reconstructing storylines, characters, and jokes from her popular radio comedy shows, including *Joan Davis Time* and *Leave It to Joan*, of which only a handful of episodes are still in existence. The UCLA Film and Television Archive provided not only an opportunity to view episodes of *I Married Joan* not included on the bootleg DVD compilations sold online, but also a look at her long-unseen 1956 pilot for an ABC-TV comedy series, *The Joan Davis Show*, which goes unmentioned in most accounts of her career. The archives of *Variety*, and the clippings file maintained on Davis by the Margaret Herrick Library at the Academy of Motion Picture Arts and Sciences, further documented her professional accomplishments.

This book begins with a brief biography of Joan Davis covering both the major events of her personal life—her marriage to and divorce from Si Wills, the birth and career of her daughter Beverly, etc.—and also the high points of a successful career cut short by her early death.

The filmography covers in detail her career in motion pictures. For each film, there is a brief synopsis, along with critical commentary on the film as well as Joan's role within it. Also included is background information on the film's production, notes on other key cast members, and excerpts from reviews (mostly those published at the time of the film's original release).

The radiography provides complete coverage of Joan's successful radio career, starting with her featured role on Rudy Vallee's popular show in the early 1940s, and her subsequent starring roles on CBS between 1945 and 1950. Episode logs have been constructed to the fullest extent possible for *The Rudy Vallee Sealtest Show* and *The Sealtest Village Store* (1942– 45), *The Joan Davis Show* (1945–47), *Joan Davis Time* (1947–48), and *Leave It to Joan* (1949–50). Guest appearances on other popular radio shows are documented as well.

Joan's best-remembered role was as the star of the popular early television comedy series *I Married Joan*, which was originally broadcast on NBC from 1952 to 1955 and seen for many years afterwards in syndicated reruns. This book's videography focuses primarily on *I Married Joan*, documenting its creation, development and broadcast history, and provides the most detailed guide ever compiled to its 98 episodes. Also included is information about Joan's pilots for other series that did not make it to the airwaves—not only her first television attempt with *Let's Join Joanie*, but her efforts to make a comeback between 1956 and 1960.

Another popular radio star of the 1940s, Fred Allen, wrote in his memoirs:

> Whether he knows it or not, the comedian is on a treadmill to oblivion. When a radio comedian's program is finished it slinks down Memory Lane into the limbo of yesteryear's happy hours. All that the comedian has to show for his years of work and aggravation is the echo of forgotten laughter.[2]

Allen's forecast proved unduly gloomy where his own career was concerned. His comedy is still remembered, quoted, and appreciated today. Likewise, Joan Davis deserves to be remembered—not only as a strikingly original and successful comedienne, but also as one who took control of her own career in a way that few female performers of her era were able to do.

I

BIOGRAPHY

"Father rushed into the room to look at me—his first-born child. Then he rushed out and called his insurance company and said—'I want to report an accident.'"—The Life and Loves of Joan Davis, 1944

Like almost everything else in her life, Joan Davis' birth was fodder for comedy. And like so many actors, her real age and date of birth have been subject to question. The date given in official biographies was June 29, 1912, and her mother Nina Mae Davis, who outlived her, would have that year recorded on Joan's gravestone. But previous writers and researchers have also given 1907 as a birth year. Never the typical Hollywood glamour girl, Joan bucked the usual trend: The later of the two dates is correct.

During her lifetime, Joan repeatedly told reporters that her given name was Madonna Josephine Davis, but the name recorded on her birth certificate was Josephine Donna Davis. She was apparently named after her paternal grandmother Josephine Hertogs Davis; Joan would continue the tradition by naming her own daughter Beverly Josephine. Joan was born in St. Paul, Minnesota, on June 29, 1912. Joan's birth certificate is interesting in that it was altered some 32 years after it was originally filed. It has been stamped with a notation along the bottom edge reading, "Amended by State Registrar pursuant to affidavit filed on ____," with the date 2–11–44 written in by hand. Asterisks indicate three areas of the document that were amended. The birth date, originally recorded as July 4, 1912, was crossed out by hand and changed to June 29. No middle name had been recorded on the original document; "Donna" was subsequently written between the first and last names, with a caret to indicate its placement. The spelling of Joan's mother's maiden name was also corrected. The original document was filled out by the midwife Rose Labon, who delivered baby Josephine at the family's residence at 275 Bates Avenue.

Her father, LeRoy Davis, was born on May 24, 1887, in San Francisco, California, to Josephine Hertogs Davis (1868–1949), a native of Australia, and Benjamin Davis, born circa 1860 in California. Josephine, paternal grandmother of the future Joan Davis, emigrated to America with her family as a girl in the late 1870s, after which they settled in Minnesota. LeRoy's parents were married on October 5, 1883, in Minnesota, when Josephine was only fifteen years old; after LeRoy, they would have two other sons, Alfred and Joseph. Although a native Californian, and a resident of Seattle during his teens, LeRoy spent most of his adult life in the St. Paul area. He pursued a career as a railroad man, employed by Northern Pacific. When Joan was born in 1912, he was working as a switchman; he moved up to become a dispatcher.

Joan's mother, the former Nina Mae Sinks, was born in Minnesota on February 28,

1887, the daughter of Harry Clay Sinks (born August 1860) and Mary Hartigan Sinks (1863–1921). Nina had three sisters, Katherine, Myrtle, and Martha. According to the 1900 U.S. Census, Harry reported that he had been born in Wisconsin; his wife Mary was a native Minnesotan whose father had been a native of Ireland. At that time, their household on Fuller Avenue consisted of Mr. and Mrs. Sinks and their four daughters, plus Harry's 67-year-old father-in-law James Hartigan and a 24-year-old servant named Lena Cramer. Although the presence of a servant (possibly a boarder) might suggest otherwise, it was apparently a solidly blue-collar household. Neighbors of the Sinks family worked as policemen, porters, carpenters, and telephone linemen. Harry was employed as a health officer, and Nina's grandfather reported working as a day laborer.

At the time of Joan's birth, her parents had been married for less than two years; Mr. and Mrs. Davis were married in St. Paul on November 23, 1910. Prior to the marriage, Nina was living at home and employed as a store clerk. Joan was to be their only child. The family continued to live in the Bates Avenue house for the next several years; it was still their home in 1917, when LeRoy registered for possible service in World War I. His registration card described him, then 30 years old, as a man of medium height and weight, with light blue eyes and dark brown hair.

Josephine and her parents lived in the Dayton's Bluff community, also home to future Supreme Court Justice Harry A. Blackmun and his family. Reminiscing late in life, Blackmun described the neighborhood as "distinctly lower middle class ... occupied largely by working people—they were good, solid people, but nearly all in modest circumstances."[1] Although there were few indicators in Joan's family background to suggest a future in show business, there was at least a little precedent for her interest in performing: Joan's maternal grandfather Harry Sinks was reported in the 1910 U.S. Census to be employed as a musician in a theater, and by 1920 an orchestra musician.

Joan's own career began at an early age. "The whole thing started," she later recalled, "when Mom began letting me sing and speak pieces in church when I was three. By the time I was seven I was sure (and Dad was willing to be convinced) that I was ready for my 'debut.'"[2] Journalist Paul Harrison described what came next: "One evening she braved an amateur bill to sing a song and do a serious little dance of her own devising. Her performance laid an egg; the silence was thunderous. Instead of going home in tears she went home mad. Next evening she went to another theater and did the song and dance again, but this time for comedy. She won first prize."[3]

Flushed with success, Joan entered every amateur talent show she could find, beginning in the Minneapolis–St. Paul area and eventually branching out. "I'd won 27 straight prizes as an amateur," Joan later explained, "and after I copped an all-star championship in Seattle, we decided that it was about time to cash in on it."[4] She was variously billed as "The Toy Comedienne" or "Cyclonic Josephine Davis" and found success doing her act on the Pantages circuit. When she was eleven, playing an engagement in New York, Joan's father told theater managers she was a midget, so as to avoid trouble with that state's stricter child labor laws.

"I was crazy for an audience," Joan later recalled of those early years. "I still attended school but worked nights and summers. It seemed perfectly natural to go to school and work. My attitude toward other kids was, 'What, you're not working? Pooh!'"[5] Though she began to receive better pay for her performing, she clarified that she was not put to work out of need, as some children were; Joan's father supported the family adequately with his railroad job. When she wasn't on the road, Joan pursued her formal education. She attended elementary school at the Madison School in St. Paul, located at the northeast corner of Tenth and Minnesota streets, graduating in June 1926.

By the time she was in her teens, Joan had decided to give up show business for the time being. By her own account she was a good student, was named valedictorian of Mechanic Arts High School in St. Paul, where she was also a stalwart of the school's debating team, and ran track. Her status as valedictorian is unconfirmed, but she did indeed make an impression on the school, despite spending a relatively short time there.

Mechanic Arts had a large student body; Josephine was one of more than 100 students entering as freshmen in the fall of 1926. For its time, it was an impressively diverse school, with students of varied ethnic and cultural backgrounds. Among those who passed through its doors in the 1920s were the aforementioned Harry Blackmun, as well as a young Roy Wilkins, later to become the longtime executive director of the National Association for the Advancement of Colored People (NAACP). Wilkins recalled in his memoirs that it was a Mechanic Arts teacher who first encouraged him to develop his writing skills; he described it as "the best high school in the city."[6] Its doors remained open until 1976.

Surviving in the archival collections of the Minnesota Historical Society is the registration card Josephine completed upon enrolling as a new student at Mechanic Arts in 1926. By this time, the family had left the house on Bates Avenue; the Davises' home address is given as 625 Central Park Place, with a telephone number of CEdar 6974. The school official completing the pupil card noted under Remarks, "An only child."

Josephine wrote that she wished to be enrolled in "college prepartory [*sic*]" coursework. Asked to specify her favorite subjects in school, she cited arithmetic and civics; her least favorite was drawing. Written in a firmer hand is what appears to be Josephine's initial class schedule at Mechanic Arts, which included history, English, gym, Orchestra (it's noted that she plays the violin), math, and French.

Throughout the first half of 1927, Joan's name appeared frequently on the academic Honor Rolls published in the school newspaper, the *Cogwheel*. In the February 11, 1927, issue, she was included in a list of "Students Having Average of 90 in 3 Solids." She was credited again with Honor Roll standing in March and April of that year.

She also found time to take part in a wide array of extracurricular activities. Not long after enrolling at Mechanic Arts, she was elected as a freshman representative to the Student Council. According to the school yearbook, the "M," the Council's "greatest single accomplishment of the year" was the formation of a Public Service Committee which "reduced loitering about the halls and prevented pupils from going to their lockers during periods; it has directed strangers coming into the building, and has done much to keep the building clean."

Josephine also joined the Girls' Cogwheel Club. The yearbook noted two activities in which she took part: The first was a Washington's Birthday assembly in which she and several other members "danced the minuet in costume." In March, a masquerade party was held. "A short entertaining program was given by Josephine Davis, Shirley Rock, and Elaine Zai Kaner. The party was well attended, and everyone enjoyed it," reported the "M." As a member of the Debating Team, Josephine was one of nine students chosen in February 1927, according to the *Cogwheel*, to prepare for a debate on "the proposed department of education," with matches scheduled for other nearby schools during the spring season.

Although she made quite a splash during that first year at Mechanic Arts, Josephine did not return for her sophomore year in the fall of 1927; an October 21, 1927, article in the *Cogwheel* explained why. She had taken a job in a popular revue, "Hughie Clark's Jazz Boat," which was then playing an engagement at the Palace-Orpheum theater in St. Paul.

"During the summer she danced in Chicago and while there signed up for a forty weeks engagement with this company. Josephine is one of a group of twenty dancers and singers, but appears in two solo numbers during the one hour and ten minutes of the act. This is three times the length of an ordinary vaudeville act. Most of Josephine's dancing is of the acrobatic type, but one of her solos is an eccentric number. Her work has been commented upon very favorably by critics." The troupe had played engagements in Sioux City, Iowa, and Milwaukee in addition to Chicago, and after finishing up in St. Paul was due to tour "all the larger cities on the Eastern and Western Coasts."

She told the *Cogwheel* reporter that she meant to return to Mechanic Arts in the fall of 1928 to finish her high school education. "Josephine said she would like to be going to school now but when she received such an advantageous offer, she thought it wiser to accept it." After finishing her education, she intended to pursue a full-time dancing career.

In Reading, Pennsylvania, the local newspaper described the Hughie Clark company's revue thusly:

> This company has 20 people, all capable artists, each possessing some individual ability in the song, dance, or musical line. Hughie Clark, a fat and jolly sort of fellow, is also winning his audiences with his witty sayings and humorous remarks. He is the conductor of Dick Lucke's Arcadians, a jazz band chuck full of snap, youth and pep.[7]

The show was also well-received in Waterloo, Iowa, where a local critic wrote,

> Headed by Hughie Clark, a rotund singer who acts as master of ceremonies, introducing the numbers with comedy quips, the show consists of clever singing and dancing and several musical numbers by Tommy Monaco's jazz band, which accompanies the performers. The stage elaborate setting represents the foredeck of a battleship.

Praising various featured performers, he added, "Josephine Davis, also a good popular singer who dances, makes another hit with her stuttering comic.... The show is interesting thruout [*sic*] despite the vast amount of dance and song numbers, being finely varied."[8]

Variety (September 19, 1928) caught up with the act in New York and called it "so-so ... for the family trade." Of the featured performers, "Josephine Davis, comedienne of promise, was the individual highlight," decreed the reviewer.

Her stage success meant that Joan's education once again went on the back burner. In February 1929, the *Cogwheel* published on its front page a letter written by Josephine to faculty member Mary Copley, describing her recent experiences as a featured member of a road show:

> I am having a wonderful time as well as an educational trip. At the close of the '28 term, I joined a Chicago show named "The Jazz Boat" as featured commedienne [*sic*]. A few months later as a reward of hard and steady work, I received a raise in salary and another one looks favorable.
>
> This is my second season with this company and I am the only woman member of the original cast left.
>
> After playing Chicago we went towards the South. I saw the blue gass [*sic*] of Kentucky. Last year I had the pleasure of seeing the Kentucky Derby run.
>
> We started east and played New York City, at a Broadway theater a few months. While in New York, I visited Niagara Falls. Although not being on my honeymoon, I enjoyed it as well.
>
> Then we started for Washington, D.C. I was anxious to see the White House. One can't realize the beauty of the District until he has seen it. I would rather make my home there than anywhere else, that is, if there was no St. Paul.

I saw the preserved theater where Lincoln was assassinated. We were playing not far from it, and it was amusing to see the theaters in comparison.

I am going to Buffalo next week and then back to New York.

Josephine finished the letter by providing her address at a hotel on West 45th Street, and promising to answer any friends from Mechanic Arts who wrote to her there.

A few weeks later, Josephine, back in St. Paul, gave the *Cogwheel* an interview describing her time in New York and her work with the Hughie Clark troupe. "I met some very interesting people during my engagement in New York. Billy [*sic*; should be Billie] Dove and Lupe Velez were at a party which I attended.... Miss Dove is as charming in real life as she is in the pictures. Colonel Charles Lindberg[h] was pointed out to me during a performance at a theater at which I played. I did not get a chance to meet him personally."

In the same article, she described the differences between Gotham and her world in St. Paul. "I found that there is a greater distinction of class in New York than there is here in the Middle West. There are three distinct classes: the wealthy and prominent people belong to the first class, the majority of people belong to the second class, and the very poor people belong to the third class."

Whether Joan's hit-and-miss public school education actually resulted in a diploma is uncertain. In April 1929, she told the *Cogwheel* reporter that she would resume her education at Mechanic Arts in the fall; however, her burgeoning career appears to have taken precedence.

After high school, Joan briefly held a job as a clerk in a five-and-dime store, where she managed to find some real-world comedy in the art of selling goldfish, but the teenager was focused primarily on pursuing her show business aspirations.

"As I soon as I finished high school," Joan later recalled, "I decided to go to Broadway. My parents and I talked it over and they reluctantly agreed that at last I was old enough to take care of myself and could go alone. After all, I had bookings, I had an agent—I was a real career woman. I took a room at the Century Hotel in New York City. Two days later there was a knock on the door—Mother. My parents had talked it over again."[9] Eventually, however, Joan prevailed, and was on the road again. Her parents subsequently divorced.

In the fall of 1929, Josephine was onstage in San Antonio, Texas, featured in *Roof Garden Revels*, a "Merry Musical Nonsensical Revue," which also featured Gil Lamb (later to work with Joan on radio), comedian Ralph Whitehead, and tap dance team Barnett and Clark. The *San Antonio Express* (November 25, 1929) singled out Josephine, "comedienne of the Sis Hopkins type," for praise, and said the show "lives up to all advance reports..."

Some time in the early 1930s, she began to use the name Joan Davis professionally, rather than Josephine. No longer with the Hughie Clark troupe, she sought new opportunities for career advancement. She teamed with comedian Ben Blue, not an entirely happy experience. "We did a burlesque adagio dance," she later recalled, "and sometimes he'd catch me and mostly he wouldn't. After the act, Blue would look on the floor, and if there wasn't any blood, it was no good. What a guy!"[10] Tired of her partner's disregard for her safety, Joan decided to move on.

Joan's agent arranged an interview for her with a comedian named Si Wills, who was looking for a female partner. Of that original meeting, a reporter noted, "He had plenty of applicants. For three weeks he interviewed blonds, brunets, and redheads. But he turned them all down. They didn't quite click. Then along came Joan Davis. With a fine regard for consistency, Si, who had made all the other applicants show their routines and ear lobes, hired Joan after two minutes of conversation in the agent's office, without any parade of talent whatsoever!"[11] The new team was paired onstage with a slogan dubbing them "A Youthful Fit of Wit."

The man who would become Joan's husband, vaudeville partner, and father of her child was born Serenus Morgan Williams in Pennsylvania on September 20, 1896, the son of Thomas and Margaret Williams. In addition to his parents, both natives of Wales, Serenus had an older sister named Margarette, and an older brother, Edward, according to the 1900 U.S. Census. Though he would be known professionally as Si Wills, Joan's future husband would resurrect his birth name years later, when he played a character named Serenus on her radio show.

Williams saw military service near the end of World War I, as a private first class starting in February 1918; he was released from the service about a year later. In the 1920 U.S. Census, Serenus was reported living in Philadelphia in a household headed by his apparently widowed mother, brother Edward, and two teenage sisters, Vera and Loretta. Serenus' mother and brother both worked in a cafeteria, as server and baker, respectively, while 23-year-old Serenus was described as an actor in a road show.

For a time in the 1920s, Si was teamed professionally with Bob Robins. Of their fall 1921 booking at the Majestic Theatre in La Crosse, Wisconsin, a reviewer for the local newspaper wrote, "Si Wills and Bob Robins are two names, though bracketed for the first time as a duo, [that] are well known individually. Si Wills is a character comedian who achieved distinction as an impersonator of the type known as the 'Smart Aleck.' Bob Robins has the distinction of being able to sing the deepest bass note of any vocalist on the vaudeville stage."[12] In the summer of 1924 Wills and Robins were in Calgary, Alberta: "Si Wills and Bob Robins are two comedians, nuts, or clowns, whichever the fancy of the spectator likes, but they kept the audience in an uproar for twenty minutes last night. The act is impossible to describe, but it is a howl from start to finish ... an enjoyable set that received a vociferous encore."[13]

More than fifteen years Joan Davis' senior, Si had been onstage for about a decade by the time they met, enjoying modest success as a comedian, though his act prior to their pairing seemed to be lacking something. Reviewing his appearance at the Loew's Orpheum in a nine-minute comedy routine, *Variety* (January 29, 1930) called him a "[f]amiliar type of single gagger, best appreciated by neighborhood audiences. Gab lacks a solid punch. Goes in for some comedy instrument playing on what looks like a prop instrument. Looks like a small oboe and sounds like a bagpipe. Also does hoke crystal gazing, looking into a gray balloon while repeating and answering comedy questions." In the late 1920s, Wills broke into films, appearing in a series of comedy shorts shot at the New York studios of Pathé with comedian Bob Carney. Among their shorts were *One Nutty Night*, *Under the Cock-eyed Moon*, *All for Mabel*, and *Sixteen Sweeties*.

Sixteen Sweeties, a 21-minute short labeled onscreen "A Melody Comedy," was produced, directed, and written by Harry Delmar. It takes the form of a revue, with song-and-dance numbers interspersed with comedy routines. Top-billed Thelma White (best-remembered today for her role in *Reefer Madness*) is joined by Carney and Wills, comedian Harry McNaughton, who serves as the British-accented emcee, and the Eddie Elkins Orchestra. Wills and Carney's main contributions come in the form of brief routines they perform in front of the curtain, interrupting McNaughton as he attempts to introduce each act, and a separate routine in which they impersonate historical figures. Carney takes the role of Paul Revere, while Wills adopts a "sissy" style to play Jesse James, who alibis himself and his brother for those bank robberies with, "Folks say the James boys were just a bit *queer*!"

The latter film was in production on December 10, 1929, when a deadly fire broke out at the Pathé Manhattan lot. The tragedy, which resulted in the loss of several lives among its cast and crew, caused significant changes in New York's fire safety laws, and resulted in criminal charges being filed against studio executives.

Another short featuring Wills, *A Night in a Dormitory*, also had Ginger Rogers and Thelma White in its cast. Of his appearance there, *Variety* (January 1, 1930) noted, "Si Wills does a rube boob in typical vaude[ville] manner, looking like a possibility for screen work." For the time being, however, he would find greater success on stage.

The pairing of Wills and Joan Davis as a comedy team proved beneficial to both. Perhaps the first notice *Variety* took of them together was in the July 7, 1931, issue, where the 15-minute segment of "Wills and Davis" was reviewed under "New Acts." The item noted that Wills' partner was billed merely as Davis, "under the new RKO no first name billing idea." Seemingly getting his first look at the former child comic, the reviewer said of Joan Davis, "Wills has a find in the girl. She is funny and helps him to make this a good attempt to get away from a moth-eaten single.... This act with a few minor cuts of mossy gags will be ready to shoot."

RKO took an ad in the July 21, 1931, *Variety* to announce that Wills and Davis had been booked "for a tour of the entire circuit...," an ambitious schedule indeed. Between late May (beginning in Yonkers, New York) and early August, their stops included Cincinnati, Cleveland, Boston, Nashville, Indianapolis, Sioux City, Minneapolis, Seattle, Portland, Dallas, New Orleans, and Atlanta, before winding up in Birmingham, Alabama. The ad quoted a recent rave review the act had received in that same trade paper, which called them "surefire," adding that Joan "has youth, dynamic energy, personality ... and [d]oes a stuttering song that's a comic gem."

What began as a business relationship quickly turned personal for Joan and Si; she later revealed that he first proposed to her only two weeks after they met. According to a fan magazine account, "Si didn't wait until they had finished rehearsing the new act before he conducted her to the New York license bureau. But Joan was still so undersized that she couldn't convince the clerk she was of marriageable age." Nor did she have her birth certificate at hand. Convinced that this was an omen, Joan refused to listen to Si's ongoing entreaties to marry him until they reached Chicago, where he "invested his entire savings in a circlet of heart-shaped diamonds, set in platinum. The jeweler promised, 'Money back if the girl doesn't accept before you leave Chicago.'"[14]

Variety first reported Joan and Si's impending marriage in July 1931. They took out a marriage certificate in Cook County, Illinois, on August 12, 1931, and were married the following day. Joan was still a teenager; Si was in his mid-thirties. Since they were in the middle of a successful tour, there was only the briefest of honeymoons before Wills and Davis were back on the job.

Variety (October 20, 1931) took note of their engagement at the Palace, which offered "Si Wills and Joan Davis for rough laughs actuated by natural antics of Miss Davis who, however, should wear other gowns." A month later, they were on the bill at the RKO Keith's Theatre in Syracuse, New York, sharing billing with the Marcellus Dancers, the Original Honey Boys, and Carleton James. Of their act, local newspaper critic Chester B. Hahn wrote, "Keith's stage show headlines the frequently funny, generally entertaining Si Wills and Joan Davis; but really folks, do you need those raw brassiere and mumps gags?"[15]

A month or so later, Si and Joan were in Winnipeg, Canada, where they were better received. "[T]he antics and fooleries of the two, and especially those of the young lady, left the patrons gasping. Although Si was the star, he frequently gave the stage to his partner,

Joan and her husband Si Wills, pictured a few months after their 1931 marriage, became popular attractions on the RKO vaudeville circuit.

and she availed herself fully of the chance to get over some eccentric movements and laugh-making quips."[16]

January 1932 found them in Seattle, at RKO's Orpheum Theatre, where vocalists The Five Honey Boys topped the bill. The reviewer for the *Seattle Times* noted, "But there's another honey on the new stage bill. This one is very feminine and pretty—when she wants to be. But Joan Davis, it seems, doesn't give that about being feminine and pretty. She has a perfectly grand time doing a comedy stagger, eccentric dances and other funny things." He added that her rendition of "You Tell Her, I Stutter" "makes her more popular than ever."[17] This routine would find its way into one of Joan's first film appearances, in *Millions in the Air*.

February took them to Oakland, California; in March, Joan and Si hit Salt Lake City, May, the Paramount theater in Des Moines, and that summer, they were at the Palace in Chicago.

Joan's roughhousing occasionally resulted in injuries. "The worst splinter I ever got," Joan later commented, "was from a stage in—of all places on Earth—Grand Rapids, Michigan.... [I]t broke off in me and I'll never forget what a time a doctor had getting it out. He tried a couple of times and I was actually too tough to cut! He had to get out a little whetstone and sharpen his knife! I had hysterics, which was as good as an anaesthetic."[18]

As a team, Joan and Si arrived on the scene too late to reach the top ranks of vaudeville. However, their careers share some parallels with those of the more successful team of George Burns and Gracie Allen. Like George and Gracie, they began performing together with the assumption that the man would have the funny lines; when audiences found the female half of the pair funnier, however, they adjusted the act accordingly. And like George Burns, Si Wills would be credited with behind-the-scenes contributions to the act that solidified his wife's following.

In a 1944 *Silver Screen* profile of Joan, writer William Lynch Vallee described Joan and Si's vaudeville act:

> Wills opened the act with jokes—Joan dashed onstage for a rapid comedy crossfire. Followed songs and dances by both with a finish that had Wills as a burlesque crystal gazer using a silver balloon as a crystal ball. Out among the audience, collecting questions, Joan would pounce on a respectable looking old lady and ask Wills what the customer was thinking. He would surreptitiously break the balloon with his left hand and scornfully ask the old lady if she was sure her question was clean.[19]

Joan and Si attained one of the major goals of vaudeville performers in 1932 when they were offered an engagement at New York's Palace Theatre. As vaudevillian Kitty Doner explained, "It was every actor's ambition to play the Palace.... Monday afternoon was the first show, and the house would be filled with performers from the shows around town.... And all the Broadway talent scouts and agents would come down to catch the first show Monday afternoon, because how you went over determined what your future bookings would be."[20] Of their engagement there, Joan later recalled, "I wore a light blue gown with mink sleeves and collar, very expensive, probably $75 or $100.... I was almost paralyzed, I was so scared, even through the applause, even though we were a hit."[21]

She needn't have been worried. Of their engagement at the Palace, *Variety* (September 13, 1932) reported, "Miss Davis works her audience up to a highly appreciative point, finally threatening to hold up the show with her dancing. She goes into some swell spills.... Wills stands by playing the guitar and singing. He contributes much to the act, working gags, mugging and in other ways strengthening the response, but it's Miss Davis who makes the act big." Unfortunately, within a year, even the Palace, a major destination for vaudeville performers, would cut back on live performances in favor of movies.

As the Associated Press' Hubbard Keavy noted in 1938, "Joan had been a success for years and years, as anyone who remembers the halcyon days of vaudeville will testify. She and her husband, Cy [*sic*] Wills, had an act and they worked the year around. That is, they did until there wasn't any more vaudeville. Three years ago, when there were so few bookings that it cost the Willses more to travel than to stay home, they came here [Hollywood] to live."[22] They would soon learn, however, that their success in vaudeville did not provide an easy entrée to work in the motion picture industry.

Another factor in the couple's desire to stay home was the birth of daughter Beverly in Los Angeles on August 5, 1933. "It was because of her that we decided to give up the stage and try motion pictures so that she might have a real home," Joan explained. "Taking a youngster on tour isn't all that it's cracked up to be."[23] Joan would later claim that she had quickly realized that Beverly was destined to follow in her footsteps. "Beverly is a born ham," she told an interviewer in 1956. "When she was a baby the first word she said was 'Mama'—in a cracked voice just like mine. I heard that and I said, 'Oh, boy, here we go.'"[24] Indeed, Beverly, who first found her way onstage when she made an unexpected entrance in the middle of someone else's act, would grow up to pursue a career as a comic actress, and would work with her mother on her radio show and later on *I Married Joan*.

Newly settled in California, Joan and Si set about finding jobs in the burgeoning motion picture industry. Although they had previously worked as a team, they would not do so in Hollywood. The fact that they had been popular on the vaudeville stage meant little in the motion picture world, however. One of her first breaks came when Mack Sennett cast her in a comedy short, *Way Up Thar*, a hillbilly comedy with music that allowed her to incorporate some of her most successful stage routines. After shooting, Sennett reportedly commented of Joan, "Watch that girl. She's got something."[25]

Si, too, found some work, both as an actor and as a screenwriter. In the late 1930s, he played character roles in films such as Warner Brothers' *Penrod and Sam* (1937) and Universal's *The Devil's Party* (1938). Sometimes his roles were small enough that he did not receive screen credit, and eventually it became evident that his Hollywood acting career was to achieve no great heights.

Though audiences, and prospective employers, had had the chance to see in her action in the Sennett short, Joan continued to seek out opportunities to display her comic gifts on film. She did a small role as a specialty performer for family friend Ray McCarey in the Paramount comedy *Millions in the Air*, released in late 1935. Her brief appearance achieved its purpose when Joan found studios suddenly interested in signing her to a contract. Joan had already enjoyed a profitable association with RKO in her vaudeville days, which factored into her decision to sign with that studio. Describing her as "Joan Davis, brilliant young stage and screen comedienne," RKO announced her signing to a contract in the spring of 1936, noting that she attracted notice with her "electrifying personality and talent"[26] in *Millions in the Air*.

Though apparently eager to sign her to the contract roster, RKO executives didn't seem to know what to do with their new player once they had her. Joan had a small role in one RKO picture, *Bunker Bean*, and after that mostly sat idle, though the studio was turning out features and shorts in which she might well have found a niche. Unable to make headway at RKO, she asked for and received a release from her contract before the year was out. Having done so, she promptly signed with 20th Century–Fox.

If Joan had been frustrated by the lack of work she found at RKO, the same would hardly be true of her four-year stint at Fox. Over the next several years, she worked almost constantly, playing featured roles in numerous pictures. In 1937 alone, she would be seen in ten Fox films.

According to a studio press release, "Miss Davis, recruited from vaudeville, scored heavily with studio projection-room audiences when scenes from her first picture, Jane Withers' *The Holy Terror*, were being inspected, and every producer on the 20th Century–Fox lot started bidding for her services. Attractive enough to take romantic roles, she prefers comedy, believing that the comedienne has a longer career than the leading lady."[27] Fox would find her useful both to play small comic parts in A pictures, as well as assuming larger roles in B movies shot at the studio's Western Avenue lot, under the supervision of producer Sol Wurtzel.

As Lynn Bari (1913–1989), also a B-movie stalwart who appeared in several of the same pictures as Joan, would later recall, the workload could be intense. "You started work an hour before the 'A' pictures did," she noted. "Six days a week. No laws allowing breaks for lunch, dinner, or between-calls. You just worked till you dropped."[28] No stranger to hard work, Joan not only survived, but thrived.

Pleased with the first flushes of cinematic success, and the attendant publicity, in 1937, Joan told a reporter, "Of course I'll start a clipping book. But if I get snooty, Si has threatened to train another girl to be funnier than I. He's got me scared, all right."[29]

After several years on the road, Joan enjoyed the opportunity to establish a permanent home, and both she and Si were doting parents to Beverly. Nonetheless, signs of marital troubles were observed not long after she began to enjoy the first flush of movie success, leaving Wills feeling slighted. In the summer of 1937, syndicated columnist Harrison Carroll

Studio pose of Fox contract player Joan Davis in 1939, looking not much like the madcap characters she typically played on-screen.

reported, "The other day, Wills decided he could take it no longer and moved out. After a day's separation, however, they decided they couldn't get on without each other. Hope the happy ending sticks."[30] It did—for a time.

Joan's film work in 1938 found her playing bigger featured roles at Fox, often centering on the strenuous, knockabout comedy for which she was becoming well-known to filmgoers. Supposedly the many injuries she had sustained over the course of her years in comedy did have a silver lining, according to the *Los Angeles Times*. "During treatment at Cedars of

Lebanon for a wrenched back, it was discovered her vertebrae possess the resiliency of those of a 12-year-old. Dr. C.A. Fayworth ascribed this phenomenon to her many years of falling on the vaudeville stage which kept her framework conditioned for such blows. She has sustained twenty-one slight injuries since her debut in films."[31]

During a 1939 personal appearance tour, Joan and Si revived some of their old routines and made a sentimental stop in Chicago. "They worked in the Palace Theater there, the same house in which they were performing when they were married seven years ago last August. To heighten the 'second honeymoon' flavor, the couple stopped at the Bismarck Hotel, where they stayed as bride and groom, and visited all the restaurants where they used to dine."[32]

Although Joan's four-year association with 20th Century–Fox benefitted her career in many ways, the studio clearly did not intend to groom her for stardom. Syndicated columnist Jimmie Fidler, a big fan of Joan, described her as "one of the funniest feminine clowns that ever faced a camera," but said in late 1939 that he opposed her being promoted from the featured roles that audiences so enjoyed. Noting that star comediennes like Martha Raye and Marie Wilson had burned out quickly at other studios, he was happy to learn that Joan had renewed her contract with 20th Century–Fox as a character player. "Because her zany antics are one of my chief movie delights," Fidler wrote, "I hope she will continue to resist every effort made by her studio to pad her roles. I hope she will be content to play hilarious bits, let her salary grow slowly, and leave stardom to the serious emotionalists to whom it properly belongs."[33]

When a census taker visited the Wills-Davis household on North Beverly Drive in May 1940, he found five people in residence. In addition to Joan, Si, and six-year-old Beverly, there was a married couple, Arthur and Mable Wilson, who functioned as chauffeur and maid-cook, respectively. Joan was reported to have worked an average of 60 hours per week, with an yearly income said to be in the $5,000-plus range—an understatement to be certain, as she could surely have added another zero. Si, whose current status was listed as "seeking work" (as he had been doing for 20 weeks), reported that he had been employed ten weeks in 1939, taking home about $1,000 for his efforts.

In 1941, Joan declined to renew her contract as a featured player at Fox, preferring to freelance. After a few worrisome months of little screen work, she was cast in a strong featured role in Universal's Abbott and Costello comedy *Hold That Ghost*. Her role of Camille Brewster represented a step up from some of the forgettable parts she'd played at Fox. It was followed not long afterwards by her first starring role in a B comedy, Columbia's *Two Latins from Manhattan*.

That was also the year that Joan began to make herself known as a radio performer, beginning with a couple of well-received guest appearances on Rudy Vallee's Thursday night NBC show. Joan's adjustment to radio wasn't an immediate one. "Radio performers had always stood decorously close to the mike to read their lines. Joan couldn't do that; her whole training was against it. She had to be an animated jack-on-strings or she couldn't get warmed up. So, between her lines she moved about, kicked, waved her arms, as she would have done on a vaudeville stage. A harried assistant producer had to follow her with a portable mike."[34]

While Joan's career was thriving, her personal life was not. In the fall of 1941, Joan and Si filed paperwork to legally separate. Columnist Jimmie Fidler reported, "By arrangement made through attorneys, Miss Davis and Wills have agreed to live apart for three months, during which period they will decide whether to resume their marital status or take steps toward permanent separation or divorce.... Meanwhile personal friends of the couple are

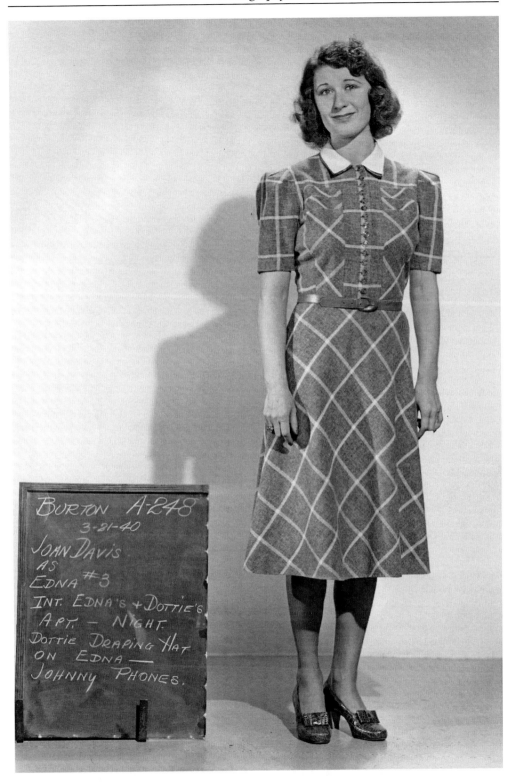

Joan Davis doing wardrobe tests for the role of Edna in *Manhattan Heartbeat* (1940).

attempting to effect an earlier reconciliation."[35] Mr. and Mrs. Wills did in fact reconcile, at least for the time being. They also moved out of the house they had occupied since relocating to California several years earlier. The *Los Angeles Times* reported on the new domicile in Bel Air:

> Joan Davis (Mrs. Si Wills) waited all day in vain for her husband to mention the fact that it was their eleventh wedding anniversary and was surprised and puzzled at dinner time to be invited for an auto ride. Five minutes of bewilderment followed before the car drew up before a house in Bel Air. Entering, Joan found guests assembled to offer congratulations and to watch her surprise when Si presented her with the deed to her new home.[36]

By early 1942, Joan had become a favorite of Rudy Vallee's radio listeners, and they sent letters of complaint any week that she didn't appear. Publicly, Vallee dubbed her "the radio find of 41-42-43-44," and she soon signed on as a regular on his show, joining John Barrymore. Although the trio was popular, the format had to change before long. Barrymore's death in the spring of 1942 left the show more dependent on Joan's contributions. *Radio Mirror* (April 1943) described the show's revamped format: "Take a general store in a small town (where anything can happen and usually does), add to this a proprietor who considers himself quite a ladies' man, a love-struck assistant who says of herself, 'What has Rita Hayworth got that I couldn't have remedied?' and a beautiful village girl who basks in the sunshine of Rudy's smile.... Joan Davis casts wistful and hopeful glances at all the handsome men who happen to be around..."

In 1943, when Vallee took a leave of absence to serve in the Coast Guard, the show was revamped to place Davis front and center. Vallee would later say ruefully, "I didn't realize how easily I could be replaced. Joan Davis took over the show with scarcely a ripple on the entertainment scene."[37] Despite some initial sponsor skepticism, *The Sealtest Village Store*, with top-billed Joan supported by Jack Haley, was a ratings winner for NBC from 1943 through 1945.

Her radio success also boosted her stock as a film actress. "Though she's such a clever comedienne," commented columnist Virginia Vale in 1942, "her [film] roles just seemed to be getting smaller and smaller. Then Rudy Vallee asked her to guest star on his program a few times, and she was such a hit that he made her a regular. Whereupon the film studios began to wake up to what they'd been missing, and she's in demand once more."[38]

In many ways, 1945 was the year in which Joan was at her peak. Aside from a thriving movie career (she even wangled a part for Beverly in *George White's Scandals*), she had become radio's most popular comedienne. After two highly successful seasons as the star attraction on the Sealtest program, Joan's agents at the William Morris agency were guiding her toward her next career move: her own show. Given the high ratings of her show with Jack Haley, there were multiple sponsors interested in awarding her a contract more lucrative than the one she had with National Dairies. The deal being sought was for Joan as a solo act, and did not include any other performers or elements associated with the Sealtest show. Her popularity also won her a multi-page spread in *Life* magazine.

After some months of negotiations, Joan signed a lucrative deal for her own series. *The Joan Davis Show* made its bow on CBS's Monday night schedule in the fall of 1945, under the sponsorship of Lever Brothers, hawking its Swan Soap. The advertising agency overseeing the show, Young and Rubicam, assembled an expensive promotional campaign, with numerous ads in top magazines. Joan brought along her producer from the Sealtest show, Dick Mack, to oversee the new one. Joan herself owned the series, under the banner of Joan Davis

Joan encouraged her daughter Beverly's show business aspirations, and helped win her this early appearance as a young version of Joan's character in *George White's Scandals*.

By the mid–1940s, Joan was top-billed in comedies like Universal's *She Gets Her Man*.

Enterprises, and it was she who employed cast members Harry Von Zell, Andy Russell, Verna Felton, and Shirley Mitchell, as well as a writing staff that included Si Wills. The sponsor was paying out approximately $1 million annually for the package, causing several sources to report that Joan herself was banking a seven-figure salary. Still, the deal made her radio's highest-paid female performer, surpassed by only a few male stars, among them Bob Hope and Jack Benny.

Joan was also a strong box office name in the movie world, though her films generally lacked big budgets, top co-stars, or strong critical acclaim. She made pictures at multiple studios, among them RKO, Columbia, and Universal. The latter gave her top billing in two comedies tailored to her gifts, *She Gets Her Man* and *She Wrote the Book*. By this time, she could command $75,000 per picture. Still, fans and industry observers alike noticed that the scripts she was given weren't always top-drawer, as columnist Jimmie Fidler noted: "Hollywood's best commedienne [*sic*] makes you wonder why she isn't given Class A breaks."[39]

As time passed, it looked less certain that Joan's move from Sealtest for her own radio series had been the right choice. The high ratings she'd enjoyed in the spring of 1945 had brought top money for *The Joan Davis Show*, but also an intense level of pressure to deliver commensurate ratings to her new sponsor, despite the fact that her show now aired on a different night and a different network. In 1947, Joan's sponsor exercised an option to drop her show, although her contract still had two years to run. Joan was back on the air that fall nonetheless, the show revamped and retitled *Joan Davis Time*, using a then-innovative system that allowed her show to be sponsored by multiple entities in different cities.

Signed as head writer of *Joan Davis Time* was Abe Burrows, then best-known for his contributions to the popular and well-regarded radio comedy *Duffy's Tavern*. Burrows, familiar with Joan's previous work, noted, "I was startled when I first met her in person; she was a poised and very attractive woman." Thirty-odd years after their radio collaboration, he noted, "There's a picture of Joan on my office wall, and people keep saying to me, 'Who's that beautiful blonde?'"[40] Inspired by his new perspective on Joan Davis, Burrows took a different, subtler approach in writing her show.

Columnist John Crosby noticed a discernible change in Joan's show when Burrows took over: "[T]he Burrows dialogue has succeeded in softening some of her bleaker outlines and, more importantly, in demonstrating that the Davis talent consists of something more than the ability to open her mouth a great distance and make loud noises. The torturous plots that used to afflict that show have been straightened out to a considerable degree, the characters have been sharpened and a good deal of pleasant satire has been pumped into the middle of the show, once occupied exclusively by dim jokes and basket-weaving."[41]

When not at work on a radio show or film, Joan's hobbies included sports; she was an avid golfer and fisherwoman, and regularly attended prizefights in Hollywood. She also was said to be an avid reader whose shelves at home were filled with novels and biographies. A dog lover, she owned a bulldog and a poodle at different times in her life.

Whenever her schedule allowed, Joan visited her hometown of St. Paul, where residents were proud of her accomplishments. "Applause all the way down the line of march greeted Joan Davis, the St. Paul girl who made good in Hollywood by cashing in on her own characteristic type of comedy," reported a local newspaper in 1947, printing a photo of the star riding in a parade.[42] Her parents had by this time divorced, and by the mid–1940s Nina had relocated to Hollywood, where she would live for the remainder of her life. Back in Minnesota, her father was now married to second wife Florence.

The dynamic between Joan and her mother Nina, as adults, is difficult to ascertain after so many years have passed. Two of Beverly's ex-husbands would tell Joan's biographer Ben Ohmart that the star's treatment of her mother was shabby. Joan, they said, gave her mother an extremely modest stipend on which to live (apparently she was receiving no alimony from ex-husband LeRoy, for reasons unknown), and relegated the senior Mrs. Davis to a cheap apartment where she lived alone.

Joan, it would seem, was primarily a daddy's girl. As for Nina, whatever grievances Joan

Joan and comedian Eddie Cantor seemed a natural pair in movies like *Show Business*, so much so that rumors swirled about their off-camera relationship.

might have had against her are unclear. There are a few indications that Nina may have envied her daughter's stardom, and craved her own moment in the spotlight. A photo of Joan and her mother appeared alongside a profile of the star in the November 1954 issue of *Women's Home Companion*; the caption, purportedly supplied by Joan, read, "My mother always says she'll take over for me any time I want to quit—and she's always on the set shooting days." Another article asserted, "It was Mrs. Davis who taught the star of *I Married Joan* vaudeville tricks when the latter was only 7 and mother and daughter appeared in an act called 'The Toy Comedienne.' Now, Mrs. Davis insists upon handling Joan's fan mail."[43] If Nina had in fact appeared on-stage opposite her daughter, it had gone unreported in previous accounts of Joan's career.

In films and radio, Joan Davis was firmly established as the girl who could never land her man. According to multiple sources, however, Joan was romantically involved in the mid–1940s with Eddie Cantor, with whom she co-starred in two films, *Show Business* and *If You Knew Susie*. At the least, the two comedians admired each other's work, having known each other since they both toiled at Fox in the 1930s, and said so publicly. However, their *Show Business* co-star Constance Moore told Cantor's biographer, "Eddie and Joan were mad for each other. It's hard to say exactly when their relationship began, but it soon became obvious.... We tried to pretend they were studying the script, but there was very little doubt they were having a physical relationship. They spent so much time in his trailer."[44] Cantor was not only a married man, but one whose wife Ida and five daughters were frequently referenced in his public persona.

In light of their rumored relationship, Joan and Eddie's joint appearance on *Command Performance* in the summer of 1947 was bold. Promoting the forthcoming release of *If You Knew Susie*, in which they played husband and wife, they teamed up for a skit in which she supposedly believed they were now married in real life. "Oh, look, Joan, let's be sensible about this," Eddie pleads, per the script, as she plans their happy life together, oblivious to the fact that he already has a family at home. Eventually, he buys her off with the promise of a $5,000 fur coat, but it seems that she and Ida have a little surprise in store for Cantor.

With *Susie* in the can, Joan checked into Cedars of Lebanon Hospital for a week-long stay that October. "Just a week's rest," she told columnist Harrison Carroll. "I had a little sacroiliac trouble and I'm getting my back massaged so I can take bows. Just nodding your head is no satisfaction."[45] By then it was also no secret that Joan's marriage was on the rocks.

In November 1947, Joan filed for divorce from Si after sixteen years of marriage, citing cruelty. Though Wills had worked on her radio writing staff for the past several years, and played a small featured role on *The Joan Davis Show*, she placed her career that fall in the hands of new head writer Abe Burrows; the resulting revamp of her show, as *Joan Davis Time*, left no room for Si's participation as either writer or performer.

A few weeks later, she appeared before Superior Court Judge Thurmond Clarke to obtain a divorce from Si. Joan told the court that her husband had taken to being absent from the house until the wee hours. "He would say he had been hunting and fishing."[46] According to *Newsweek*, that wasn't her only complaint: "Miss Davis testified that Wills wrote her radio show and then criticized it."[47] Unexpectedly, Si revived his acting career when he accepted a role in Frank Seltzer's *The Gay Intruders*, his first picture assignment in seven years.

If the timing of Joan's divorce was connected to her rumored affair with Cantor, his marital status remained intact nonetheless (as it would until Ida's death in 1962). Joan and Eddie's second film together, *If You Knew Susie*, was only a modest box office success, and by then their personal relationship had also cooled. As Cantor's biographer Herbert G. Goldman noted, "Cantor and Davis, who had seemed like soulmates for four years, were never close again."[48]

The cancellation of Joan's weekly CBS radio show, *Joan Davis Time*, in the spring of 1948, plus the lukewarm public reception to *If You Knew Susie*, left her at loose ends professionally. Syndicated columnist Erskine Johnson reported in May that Joan had her eye on a Broadway show that she and Beverly, now a teenager, could do together, but nothing came of this, or of her efforts to secure a radio sponsor for the 1948-49 season.

Out from under the strains of a weekly show, however, and newly single, Joan devoted more time to her private life. In the summer of 1948, she accepted an engagement ring from Danny Elman, described by columnists as a Chicago lumber tycoon. An engagement party for the couple was held at the home of actress Esther Williams, whose husband Ben Gage was featured in Joan's radio series. Joan told Hedda Hopper, "Danny was very cute when he put the ring on my finger. But he says it's too personal to talk about."[49] The couple planned to be married in a few months, when her divorce from Si was final. Elman relocated from Illinois to California in expectation of marrying Joan.

Joan received her final divorce decree from Si in December 1948. They had agreed to share custody of Beverly, with each to have the 15-year-old for six months out of the year. By this time, Beverly was enjoying her own radio success with a featured role as Fuffy Adams, sidekick to teenager Judy Graves, on the Saturday morning comedy series *Junior Miss*. Beverly also nabbed a featured part in the film comedy *Mickey*. By all accounts, Joan took pleasure in her daughter's burgeoning career, and opened doors for her when she could. After a dry period in the motion picture world, Joan closed a deal late that year to produce and star in a Western comedy for Columbia Pictures (ultimately released as *The Traveling Saleswoman*), and would devote much of her time in 1949 to the project.

In August 1949, columnist Erskine Johnson reported that "the marriage date is just around the mink" for Joan and Danny, noting that they'd been spotted shopping together at a prominent furrier's.[50] Within a few months, though, the relationship apparently hit a rough patch. "Joan Davis and Danny Elman have broken their engagement via transatlantic phone," reported Dorothy Kilgallen in May 1950. "His new love is Wendy Evans, the model."[51] That didn't prove to be the end of the relationship, however; Elman would continue to be in Joan's life into the 1950s, though they would never marry. Not to be outdone, Si was reported by Louella Parsons in 1948 to be seriously involved with a younger woman, Betty Todhunter, whom he would later marry.

Joan launched her final radio series in 1949, CBS's *Leave It to Joan*, which continued through a summer run in 1950. By then, radio ratings and budgets were dropping, as the popularity of television grew, and the show was only moderately successful. Joan was being seriously eyed for her own television show, however, and soon left radio behind, though she appeared occasionally as a guest star on *The Big Show*, the top-budgeted NBC variety show hosted by Tallulah Bankhead. Her 1950 pilot for a half-hour television comedy series for CBS, *Let's Join Joanie*, which featured her radio supporting player Joseph Kearns, did not attract a sponsor, causing her to do some rethinking about how her video format should be different from what had worked well on radio.

As a single mother, Joan was also raising a teenage daughter. In the early 1950s, Beverly was involved with a young man named William Bast, who would subsequently become a screenwriter, and through Bast met his aspiring actor friend James Dean. In Bast's view, Joan was suspicious of any young men who expressed an interest in Beverly, thinking them opportunists who were more interested in the family money than in her daughter's charms. His own account does little to dispel the notion: "As Jimmy and I were broke," Bast wrote, "we spent most of our time swimming in Beverly's (or, more accurately, Joan's) pool; eating Beverly's (or, more accurately, Joan's) food; drinking (quite definitely Joan's) booze; and watching Beverly's own personal television in her bedroom..."[52]

Joan gets ready to dish up another turkey on radio's *Leave It to Joan.*

Received into Joan's personal quarters, Bast found it a memorable experience. "[Her bedroom] turned out to be a Hollywood movie set where Joan spent most of her time gossiping on the phone in her enormous and terribly impressive king-size bed—a rarity at that early date—propped up by great downy pillows and a powdery pink-feathered bed jacket.... I got the impression that she rarely got out of bed, except occasionally to play golf or to be entertained by producers or studio executives courting her for a possible picture, radio series, or a guest-star appearance."[53] According to Bast, Beverly confirmed her mother's relationship with Eddie Cantor a few years earlier.

After dating Bast, and briefly being engaged to him, Beverly took up with his buddy, James Dean. Joan was reportedly not impressed by the future movie star, whom she found uncouth. After Dean's untimely death in 1955, Beverly would be among several people who claimed to have occupied a special place in the late actor's heart, saying that they had been in love and nearly gotten married.

While her public reputation depicted her as virtually unbreakable, Joan experienced some health problems as the 1950s dawned. In November 1950, Erskine Johnson reported, "Joan Davis' medics are telling her to take it easy. Her recent hospital visit was one of those stitch-in-time actions to ward off a nervous breakdown."[54]

Nonetheless, Joan was about to embark on three of the busiest years of her life, as star of her own NBC-TV sitcom, *I Married Joan*. As with her later radio shows, Joan served as executive producer of the show, which was mounted under the auspices of her Joan Davis Enterprises. A domestic sitcom in which Joan played the zany wife of a prominent municipal judge, the series featured actor Jim Backus (1913–1989) as her patient spouse, Brad. Premiering one year after Lucille Ball's top-rated *I Love Lucy*, Joan's show was viewed by many as NBC's attempt to replicate the popular CBS sitcom; in fact, an early review of *I Married Joan* in *Newsweek* dubbed her "Lucy's TV Sister." Although never a Top Ten hit, *I Married Joan* would enjoy a three-year run on Wednesday evenings for sponsor General Electric, and a healthy afterlife in reruns.

Joan clowns for reporters on her return from an overseas trip in the spring of 1950.

While up to her ears in work on the forthcoming show, set to premiere in the fall of 1952, Davis was dismayed to learn that Beverly, still a teenager, had eloped to Carson City, Nevada, with a fireman from Pasadena named Lee Bamber (1927–2005). "When I catch my breath I suppose I'll be able to say what I think about it," Joan told the press. "After all I only met the boy once and then only for a few seconds."[55] Beverly's marriage followed only a few months on the heels of her broken engagement to William Bast. The new Mr. and Mrs. Bamber had to wait for a honeymoon until Beverly completed her scenes in MGM's *Small Town Girl*.

A few days after the ceremony, Joan admitted she was still "peeved" about the unexpected marriage: "I guess I'm at what you'd call the cooling-off stage. I just couldn't believe it. I made her repeat it five times. I thought it was some sort of a gag."[56] By September, though, Joan told columnist Harrison Carroll that she and Beverly had made their peace. "I held out for two weeks, but you can't stay mad at your own kid."[57] In 1953, Joan cast

Chosen to play Joan's TV husband on *I Married Joan* was Jim Backus, later to be famous as the voice of Mr. Magoo, and as wealthy Thurston Howell III on *Gilligan's Island*.

her daughter in a recurring role on her TV sitcom, the star's daughter cast as her college-aged sister onscreen.

The marriage, however, did not prove to be a happy one. Less than a year after the wedding, as Beverly was beginning her featured role on *I Married Joan*, Carroll reported, "The marriage of Joan Davis' daughter and Lee Bamber, former city fireman, has hit the rocks. They have been separated for several weeks, Bamber told me, and he doesn't know whether there will be a divorce."[58] Before long, there was.

Although she relished the success of *I Married Joan*, its star admitted that her years of comedy acclaim led people to expect someone other than the person she was off-camera. "People expect me to be funny all the time," she said in 1952. "I walk down an aisle and if I don't land on my face they're disappointed. I sit in a chair and if it doesn't collapse I'm letting them down. When I sit quietly, listening to others tell funny stories, they ask, 'Are you feeling all right?' or 'What's the matter, Joan, sick?' And if you don't glad hand everybody, they call you stuck up."[59]

Joan and her steady date, Palm Springs city councilman Jerry Nathanson, were photographed at a performance of the Ice Capades in 1956.

Though her work on *I Married Joan* was demanding, Joan hoped to remain active in film work as well. "I intend to go on making pictures," she told journalist Howard McClay in 1953. "Perhaps not as many as I used to, but enough to keep in touch with the moviegoer. Frankly, I came across a lot of pretty sad material during some of my film chores. Now I can be a bit more selective, make—I hope—better film comedies."[60]

In truth, Joan's motion picture career was over after the 1952 release of *Harem Girl*. During 1952 and 1953, Joan was under contract to Columbia to deliver her next film comedy, to be titled *Jungle Joan*, aided by the same writer and producer (Edward Bernds and Wallace MacDonald, respectively) responsible for *Harem Girl*. In July 1953, however, *Daily Variety* reported, "All ties between Columbia and Joan Davis have been severed and future pix for the actress cancelled by mutual consent."[61] No reason was given for the termination of Joan's Columbia deal. In exchange for dissolving the pact, Joan reimbursed the studio for monies paid out for the original screenplay.

In April 1954, Joan announced Beverly's engagement to Army Second Lieutenant Alan Norton Grossman (born 1932), whom she had met on a blind date arranged by mutual friends. In light of the forthcoming marriage, which took place that July, Beverly gave up her featured role in *I Married Joan*, planning to relocate for the next several months to the Washington state base where her new husband was stationed. The new Mr. and Mrs. Grossman appeared together in one episode in the spring of 1955, when Beverly returned for a visit. Later that year, Beverly announced that she was expecting her first child; she gave birth to Joan's first grandchild, Guy Steven Grossman, in mid–December. Although this marriage would last long enough to give Joan two grandsons, Guy and Larry, it too would ultimately end in divorce, with Beverly resuming her acting career while Grossman went on to a career as a schoolteacher.

Joan herself took her sitcom off the air at the end of its third season, though her sliding ratings opposite ABC's popular *Disneyland* series made it unlikely that the sponsor would have renewed for a fourth year regardless. Popular in afternoon reruns on NBC for a year or so, the show later went successfully into syndication, where it would be seen for years to come.

With more free time on her hands, Joan was more active socially once *I Married Joan* wound down, and she didn't lack for male companionship. In May 1955, columnist Harrison Carroll, who always seemed to keep close tabs on Joan and her clan, reported on rumors that her relationship with Palm Springs City Council member Jerome "Jerry" Nathanson (1911–1994) was becoming serious, and might lead her to the altar, but she denied it. "I'm not dating anybody else," she told Carroll, "but Jerry and I have known each other only seven weeks. We are not engaged and we are going to wait and be sure."[62] A few weeks later, however, Joan attended comedian Joe E. Lewis' opening at the Mocambo with Danny Elman in tow, explaining to Carroll, "I still see Danny and I still see Jerry."[63] Indeed, she was spotted at various events and parties throughout the summer with Nathanson as her escort, although a traffic accident put him in the hospital with a broken back in October 1955.

Nathanson, who served on the Palm Beach City Council from 1950 to 1958, was evidently quite the ladies' man, said to be involved at various times with actresses Anne Francis (*Forbidden Planet*), Patricia Neal (*The Fountainhead*), and Patricia Owens (*The Fly*), whom he would marry in 1960. His relationship with Joan cooled, and by the summer of 1957 another columnist described Nathanson as Joan's "ex-boyfriend." Meanwhile, Joan's ex-husband Si married his longtime lady friend Betty Todhunter in Las Vegas on August 2, 1956. The groom was on the verge of turning sixty; his new wife, at thirty-seven, was seven years younger than Joan. In November, Beverly told columnist Louella Parsons that she would soon have a half-sibling, as the second Mrs. Si Wills was expecting. In March 1957, Si and Betty became the parents of a son, John.

Though the conventional wisdom has been that Joan Davis all but retired professionally once *I Married Joan* ended in 1955, becoming something of a recluse, in truth she would spend the next several years trying to find the right vehicle for her weekly television come-back. In 1956, she signed a lucrative deal with ABC for a new television show. Her *Joan Davis Show* pilot, which co-starred Beverly, didn't find a buyer, nor did the comedy *Joan of Arkansas*, casting her as a female astronaut, pitched to NBC in 1958. In the late 1950s, she was seen with some frequency as a guest star on comedy and variety shows, working alongside Steve Allen, Dinah Shore, and Garry Moore, among others.

Beverly landed one of her best-known film roles as Dolores, trombonist in Sweet Sue's band and roommate to Marilyn Monroe's Sugar Kane, in *Some Like It Hot* (1959). Actress Grace Lee Whitney (born 1930), later to be better-known as Yeoman Janice Rand on *Star Trek* (NBC, 1966–69), played another band member, and recalled in her memoirs that she and Beverly struck up a friendship during the film's location shoot. Whitney, candid about her own addictions, described herself and Beverly as "the true alcoholics in the group," saying that they played hooky from their household responsibilities for some time after the shoot near San Diego ended, ending up on a bender in Tijuana. "When we finally had enough fun and partying," Whitney wrote, "Beverly and I both went home to L.A., sneaked back into our houses, weathered the inevitable storms with our husbands, and resumed our wifely, motherly duties."[64]

As for Beverly's mother, from this point forward, Joan's name would be in the newspaper primarily for what happened in her private life, rather than her career. She raised eyebrows with her romantic involvement with a significantly younger man, safety engineer Budd Stock, to whom she announced her engagement in the spring of 1957. In August 1958, columnist Harrison Carroll reported that he had asked Joan and Budd when they would be getting married, but was told there was not yet a definite date. The relationship came to an unhappy end in early 1959 when an argument between Joan and her beau turned physical, causing her to file misdemeanor assault and battery charges.

The quarrel apparently began when the couple returned to Joan's house in Palm Springs, and she was unable to find her keys. "I had hidden the key somewhere outside the house," Stock, now described as a real estate agent, told reporters. "But when we pulled into the driveway I couldn't find it. When I told Joan the key was missing she hit the windshield of the car with her purse, and I pushed her. That's all there was to it."[65] Joan's account was quite different, saying that Stock had hit her, describing the blow as either a judo or rabbit punch, and she claimed to have the bruises to prove it. Accounts of what happened varied, but she pressed charges against Stock, and he was arrested on January 29, 1959. Within a few days, Joan had thought better of pursuing her claim, dropping the charges against him, but indicated that they had irrevocably ended their relationship.

Although she put her relationship with Stock behind her, Joan had other stresses with which to cope in 1959. In August, she sustained injuries to her face after taking a fall at her home while climbing the stairs. Described by her personal physician as minor, they did not require corrective surgery. Happier family news was the birth of Beverly's second son, Larry, in September.

On the evening of December 20, 1959, Joan's father LeRoy died in the Northern Pacific Benevolent Association Hospital in St. Paul. The cause of death, according to his death certificate, was "carcinoma prostate with metastasis," with a contributing factor being "arteriosclerotic heart disease." He had undergone surgery for his condition several months earlier. LeRoy's obituary in the *St. Paul Pioneer Press*, published on December 23, 1959, reported that he was survived by second wife Florence E. Davis, as well as by Joan, Beverly and her sons, and LeRoy's brother Alfred, then a resident of Seattle.

Although Joan's public appearances were growing infrequent as the 1960s dawned, she was front and center at the U.S. Circuit Court in Honolulu in January 1960, testifying in a lawsuit she'd filed against the Elizabeth Arden corporation. The suit alleged that a beauty salon employee had burned Joan's eye with bleach while styling her hair back in May 1954, and asked $125,000 in damages. The court found in her favor at the conclusion of the six-day trial, but reduced the settlement to $20,000. "Miss Davis, besieged at every recess by autograph seekers, appeared in a filmy, rose-colored dress and wore white, green, and rose-colored shoes," reported a fashion-minded UPI staffer.[66] A few months later, Joan turned up at a Los Angeles nightclub to see her sitcom co-star Jim Backus perform his new act, which he was preparing to take to Las Vegas. Her companion on the outing was a nurse; Backus had already heard rumors that Joan's health was flagging. Still, she signed a new three-year contract with the William Morris agency that summer, authorizing them to represent her in forthcoming film, television, and theater projects.

As if enough trouble hadn't befallen Joan already, her house on Bellagio Road in Bel Air caught fire on the evening of September 5, 1960. Battalion Chief Robert Raedke of the West Los Angeles fire department told reporters the fire began in the master bedroom upstairs. Joan, watching television downstairs, was unaware of the blaze quickly spreading through the second floor of her home.

A passerby, John Bustetter of Encino, on his way to a dinner party with his wife, stopped when Mrs. Bustetter saw smoke coming from the house. Bustetter enlisted the aid of another man to search the house, where they found "the famed actress collapsed on the living room sofa. Together they carried her from the home, then returned to search the lower floor for other persons."[67] The next day, Joan publicly expressed gratitude to the men, whose identities she hadn't learned amid the confusion and excitement of the incident. Joan's house sustained substantial damage, and she lost valuable furs and jewelry. This was not to be the last time that a house fire led to tragedy for Joan's family.

In November, Beverly embarked upon her third and final marriage, tying the knot in Las Vegas with real estate developer Martin Colbert (1922–1994). Colbert was older than his new wife by about ten years.

Though still a relatively young woman, Joan's health took a decided turn for worse in the early months of 1961. Late one May evening, Joan was rushed to the nearby Desert Hospital by her mother Nina after complaining of severe back pain. She had been attended at home by her personal physician Max Levine at around 8 p.m. before being hospitalized. "She was conscious when she was admitted," said a hospital spokesman, "and she seemed to be coming along fine. She was sleeping pretty well. And then at 3 this morning she just went boom—just like that. She just stopped breathing."[68] Hospital staff attempted without success to resuscitate her. Nina was at Joan's bedside when she died on May 22, 1961, as was a Catholic priest. She was 48 years old.

Jim Backus sang her praises in the obituaries that appeared: "We had a very good working relationship, but I hadn't seen her much since the series ended. The last time I saw her was last August [1960]."[69] According to the Associated Press, Backus sent Joan's family a telegram that read, "The nation has lost a great lady and the foremost feminine talent in her field." Joan's death came amidst a flurry of Hollywood passings, less than two weeks after that of actor Gary Cooper, and a few weeks prior to the demise of Jeff Chandler.

A memorial service was held for Joan on Saturday, May 27, at St. Paul the Apostle Church in West Los Angeles, with approximately 100 mourners in attendance. According to the *Los Angeles Times*, "A handful of curious fans and a few celebrities attended the funeral. For the most part only the star's relatives and close friends joined the Rev. Elwood Kieser, a Paulist priest, in offering the Requiem Mass...."[70] Joan was buried at the Holy Cross Cemetery in Culver City, her gravestone giving her birth and death dates and reading simply, "Our Beloved."

Syndicated columnist Bob Foster, recalling a visit with Joan while her sitcom was in production, wrote that she "was probably the most unaffected artist I've met in the 11 or so years I have been writing this column. She was grateful at the time because she was being given a chance to do a television series.... Many times, during the height of the show, she commented how wonderful television had been to her."[71]

In the days following her death in 1961, Joan's TV spouse Jim Backus was gracious in his remarks about her. He would be less so by the time he wrote his memoirs in the early 1980s.

Earl Wilson reported that even in her last months Joan had been craving a return to work: "N.Y. ad agencies were considering two TV series for comedienne Joan Davis when she died."[72] Said *Variety*, "Immediately prior to her death, it was reported she was 'terribly excited' over a script submitted to her by Harold Breecher, of Famous Artists agency, in which Miss Davis would play in a department store comedy format for television opposite George O'Hanlon."[73] Oddly, the same article reported that Joan had "been in virtual retirement at the desert home for the past 10 years," which was anything but true.

Louella O. Parsons wrote that she was "sad to hear of the sudden death of Joan Davis. Her friends know that the last years of Joan's life were not happy, but she always thought, to the end, that that rainbow was just around the next hill."[74]

The disposition of Joan's estate was placed in the hands of her daughter Beverly, in the belief that she would be the principal heir in the absence of a will. However, the estate, with an estimated value in the $1 million range, quickly became the object of a court battle between Beverly and Joan's ex-husband Si Wills. Beverly, now Mrs. Martin Colbert, challenged the November 24, 1941, will submitted for probate by her father, in which her mother bequeathed everything to him. Contending that that document had been invalidated by her mother's divorce, Beverly's lawyers produced a more recent will. Si's lawyer, in turn, asked to have Beverly removed as executor of the estate, claiming that she lacked the business experience necessary to fulfill her duties.

The handwritten will submitted by Beverly's lawyers, Barry S. Scholer and Albert G. Bergman, dated back to August 1956. Not meeting all the criteria of a valid will, since it lacked a complete date, it nonetheless was argued by Beverly's attorneys to show her mother's intent. It divided the bulk of the will between Beverly and her son Guy, with bequests also made to Joan's mother Nina, her father (who had since died), and Joan's maid, Lorena Watts. Nina appeared in court to support her granddaughter's claim.

Not until October 1961 did the legal tangle reach resolution. The settlement primarily favored Beverly, in accord with the 1956 will, while Si was given a house in Palm Springs, a car, and an unspecified sum of money. Beverly and her husband took up residence in Joan's Bel Air home with her sons Guy and Larry.

It's been reported that Beverly, upon inheriting the bulk of her mother's estate, lost interest in seriously pursuing her career. However, she did continue to act with some regularity into the early 1960s. In 1961, she had a small role in Jerry Lewis' comedy *The Ladies Man*, and later that year was signed for a guest appearance in NBC's short-lived Western series *The Tall Man*, cast as a mail-order bride. In the summer of 1962, Beverly was among the ensemble cast chosen for a new musical revue, "Chip Off the Old Block." Featured performers were all the children of stars, among them Harold Lloyd, Jr., Mickey Rooney, Jr., Lou Costello's daughter Carol, and Preston Foster's daughter Stephanie. Beverly sang a song titled "I Dig Wigs," and told syndicated columnist Lydia Lane that it was a fitting number for her. "I'm the type that gets bored with myself," Beverly said, "and instead of having to dye my hair for a dramatic change, I just put on a wig. My husband finds it amusing. 'It's like bigamy,' he says."[75] While appearing in the revue, Beverly also had a soap commercial running on TV, causing a viewer to ask *TV Key Mailbag*'s Steven H. Scheuer in July the identity of the young woman "who looks and sounds like a very young Joan Davis."

She appeared in a pilot for a sitcom, *Hooray for Love*, which didn't sell, but aired as an episode of the summer series *Vacation Playhouse* in September 1963. "This is the best of some mighty poor pilots," reported the syndicated *TV Key* column (September 9, 1963) of the show, which starred Darryl Hickman and Yvonne Craig. "The dialogue holds up and Beverly Wills, who reminds you of her mother, Joan Davis, will give you a charge on the show." Beverly also completed another TV pilot, *Shape Up Sergeant*, a spinoff of NBC's short-lived military school sitcom *McKeever and the Colonel*.

Perhaps the only good thing to come from Joan's early death was the fact that she wasn't around to see what happened to the remainder of her family. Tragedy struck in the fall of 1963, when Beverly's Palm Springs house caught fire in the middle of the night. The probable cause of the deadly blaze was Beverly's smoking in bed. Beverly's four-year-old son Larry had crawled into bed with her during the night, and would be found there by firemen. Nina and the older boy, Guy, apparently rushed into Beverly's room in hopes of rescuing the two, but succumbed to the smoke. Not home that evening was Beverly's husband Martin, away on a business trip, or the family dog. Neighbors said the latter, a good watchdog, might well have awakened the family and prevented the tragedy.

"All windows had been blown out of the master bedroom by the time we arrived by the intense heat in the room," reported Palm Springs Assistant Fire Chief Warren Empey.[76] Not until after the blaze was extinguished were firemen able to recover the bodies of Joan's mother, daughter, and grandchildren. Beverly had recently turned thirty years old.

Beverly and her grandmother, Nina, were given a joint funeral ceremony at Our Lady of Solitude Catholic Church in Palm Springs. Beverly's young sons were buried in a private graveside service arranged by their father.

Only weeks after her death, Beverly was seen on television, featured in a November 1963 episode of CBS's *Petticoat Junction*. In early 1964, her last television appearance, a guest role on *Mister Ed* in which she played an old classmate of Carol Post (Connie Hines), aired. Syndicated columnist Mike Connolly reported that Beverly had been on the verge of a career breakthrough at the time of her death, having been offered a regular role in actor John McGiver's forthcoming CBS sitcom. *Many Happy Returns*, as the show was ultimately titled, would have featured Beverly in "the part of a snippy spinster who runs the complaint booth in John's department store.... Beverly was on the way to becoming as big a comedienne as her mother. She was a funny, lovable girl."[77] The series, without Beverly, ran during the 1964-65 season, did not catch on, and was canceled after one year.

Just as had happened with her mother's death two years earlier, Beverly's death resulted in an inheritance quandary. Inheriting the bulk of her mother's estate had left Beverly a very well-to-do woman. Chief beneficiaries under Beverly's will were her two young sons, who also died in the fire. Beverly had also provided in the will for her grandmother. If it could be established that Beverly's children had survived her by any appreciable amount of time, then her ex-husband Alan, father of the two boys, was expected to inherit the estate through them. However, if the deaths were ruled to be simultaneous, then Beverly's estate would go to her current husband, Martin Colbert, previously recipient of a modest bequest in his wife's will. The question was being raised, interestingly, by the bank that had administered not Beverly's estate, but Joan's.

In early February, "Judge Merrill Brown ruled there was not sufficient evidence to prove that the four died other than simultaneously," the *Los Angeles Times* reported. Taken into account in the judge's ruling was the testimony of Palm Springs Fire Chief James Harris, who opined "that there was evidence of an explosion which would have killed anyone in the bedroom where the bodies were found."[78]

According to syndicated columnist Alex Freeman, "Only a few of Beverly Wills' closest pals knew she had planned to obtain a divorce and then marry a handsome Hollywood realtor."[79] Beverly's widower, Martin Colbert, became the husband of actress Patricia Blair (*The Rifleman, Daniel Boone*) in 1965, though they subsequently divorced.

Beverly's father (and Joan's ex-husband), Si Wills would outlive them both by a number of years, surviving into his early eighties. Although he spent his later years mostly out of the public eye, Louella Parsons did report in 1964 that Si was collaborating with writer-producer Bill Bacher on a screenplay based on Joan's life. Parsons noted that the working title, *Laugh, Clown, Cry*, "was pathetically fitting to the story of the comedienne who made so many people laugh—but whose personal story was filled with trouble and tragedy."[80] The project never came to fruition, possibly because Wills' writing partner died a year or so later.

Si Wills died on Monday, October 3, 1977, in Riverside, California, by then so long out of show business that *Variety* failed to note his passing. A death notice appeared in the Palm

Springs community newspaper, the *Desert Sun*, using Si's given name, Serenus Williams, and announcing a memorial service to be held in the Palm Springs Mortuary Chapel on Friday, October 7. Following the service, he was interred at the Riverside National Cemetery. He was survived by second wife Betty, who died in October 2004 at the age of 85, and their son John.

By the 1970s, reruns of Joan's films and television shows were becoming less frequent. While her career achievements were commemorated with two stars on the Hollywood Walk of Fame (one for her radio work at 1716 Vine Street, and another for her films at 1521 Vine Street), she was no longer the household name she once had been. However, when the Christian Broadcasting Network began showing *I Married Joan* in the early 1980s, and films such as *Hold That Ghost* were issued on home video, fans new and old alike had the opportunity to once again see a rare comic talent at work.

Some of those viewers, in a pre–Internet world, wrote to the show business columnists of various newspapers to ask for details on the comedienne whose work they were enjoying, whether she was still alive and what had become of her. One columnist in 1985 received a letter from a puzzled viewer of *I Married Joan* who wrote, "On the reruns, they call her 'The Queen of Comedy.' Where was Lucille Ball at that time?" In response, he noted that both ladies became popular sitcom stars in the 1950s, then added, "But before TV, Joan Davis starred in dozens of movie comedies and was certainly the leading comic film actress."[81]

Today, more than fifty years after her untimely death, a small but select fan base remembers Joan by posting clips of her best work on YouTube, collecting bootleg or public domain copies of her films and TV shows, and laughing at the lady who gave them so many hours of pleasure, sometimes at the expense of her own. To them, if not the world at large, she still retains her crown as "America's Queen of Comedy."

II

FILMOGRAPHY

Note: All of Joan Davis' films were in black-and-white.

Way Up Thar (1935)

Joan Davis (*Jennie Kurtz*), Myra Keaton (*Molly Kurtz*), John W. Jackson (*Jimmy Higgins*), June Gittelson (*Sophie Graham*), Al Lydell (*Sam Higgins*), Richard Cramer (*Graham*), Louise Keaton (*Lyddie*), Sons of the Pioneers (*Hillbilly Band*)

Director: Mack Sennett. Educational Pictures; released November 8, 1935. 19 minutes.

In the Ozarks, young Jimmy Higgins enjoys singing with Ma Kurtz's hillbilly band, and has fallen in love with Ma's daughter Jennie. But Jimmy's storekeeper father Sam pressures him to instead marry dumpy, whiny Sophie Graham, daughter of a well-to-do local man. Plotting to secure the engagement of Jimmy to Sophie, Sam forges a proposal note from his son to accompany a gold watch, while fashioning an insulting message to send to Jennie. When the two packages are exchanged accidentally, Jennie happily accepts Jimmy's proposal, but the feud isn't settled so easily. The unexpected radio success of Ma's musical troupe helps settle things.

Joan made her film debut in this musical comedy short. Director Mack Sennett allows her to use some of the well-received material from her vaudeville act, including her dish-juggling act, and a routine in which she cures her stuttering with a sock to her own jaw. Buster Keaton's mother Myra and sister Louise are also featured.

In a *Silver Screen* interview some years later, Joan explained how she landed her first movie role. "In 1934, Hughie Cummings, a pal of Si's, wrote a movie short ... that seemed tailor-made for me. He brought his boss, Mack Sennett, out to our house to see me.... I clowned like mad and the stooges we'd been careful to ask in, howled and rolled on the floor in delight. Sennett admitted I was funny, but said that I was too old."[1] Undaunted, Joan visited Sennett's office the next day, dressed in the most schoolgirlish fashion she could muster, and won him over.

Millions in the Air (1935)

John Howard (*Eddie Warren*), Wendy Barrie (*Marion Keller*), Robert Cummings (*Jimmy*), Eleanore Whitney (*Bubbles*), Benny Baker (*Benny*), Willie Howard (*Tony Pagano*), George Barbier (*Calvin Keller*), Halliwell Hobbes (*Theodore*), Catherine

Doucet (*Mrs. Waldo-Walker*), Samuel S. Hinds (*Col. Edwards*), Dave Chasen (*Dave*), Alden [Stephen] Chase (*Gordon Rogers III*), Bennie Bartlett (*Kid Pianist*), Inez Courtney (*Miss Waterbury*), Irving Bacon (*Perkins*), Russell Hicks (*Mr. Davis*), Joan Davis (*Miss Stutter*), Billy Gilbert (*Escape Artist*), Ralph Malone (*Chauffeur*), Dolores Casey (*Secretary*), Eleanor Woodford, Ludovicio Tomarcio (*Singers*), Paul Fix (*Hank*), Marion Hargrove (*Blonde*), Paul Newlan (*Charles Haines*), Sam Ash (*Headwaiter*), Elba Evans (*Mary Flynn*), Lillian Leighton (*Fat Lady*), Lillian Drew (*Woman on Street*), Maurice Cass (*Professor Duval*), Marion Ladd (*Sally*), Donald Kerr (*Andy*), Bess Wade (*Tough Girl*), Paddy O'Flynn (*Attendant*), Florence Dudley (*Wisecracking Dame*), Al Burke, Jack Hill (*Motor Cops*), Adrienne Marden (*Girl*), Harry Semels (*Greek*)

    Director: Ray McCarey. *Producer*: Harold Hurley. *Screenplay*: Sig Herzig, Jane Storm. *Associate Producer*: Lewis E. Gensler. *Photography*: Harry Fischbeck. *Music and Lyrics*: Ralph Rainger, Arthur Johnston, Leo Robin, Sam Coslow. *Art Directors*: Hans Dreier, John Goodman. *Film Editor*: Ellsworth Hoagland. *Sound Recording*: Harry Lindgren, Walter Oberst. *Interior Decorations*: A.E. Freudeman. *Assistant Director*: William Tummel. Paramount Pictures; released December 12, 1935. 71 minutes.

Among the contestants vying for a shot at stardom on WOX radio's *Colonel Edwards' Amateur Hour* are aspiring singers Eddie Warren, currently earning a living as an ice cream salesman, and Marion Keller, who auditions for the show against the wishes of her affluent father Calvin, whose company, Kello Soap, sponsors the program. The working arrangement that develops between the two young singers jeopardizes Marion's relationship with her fiancé Gordon, as does Eddie's eventual discovery of the young lady's real identity.

Millions in the Air capitalized on the real-life popularity of *Major Bowes' Amateur Hour*, which debuted on New York's WHN in 1934 and successfully went nationwide on NBC the following year. The film may also remind modern-day viewers of Chuck Barris' 1970s kitsch hit *The Gong Show*, as a loud gong is struck here any time a contestant is deemed unsuccessful. Joan, playing a character who shares her name, turns up nearly an hour into the film, as one of the radio show's hopefuls. She does a spirited rendition of Billy Rose and Cliff Friend's 1922 song "You Tell Her, I Stutter." She's billed in the closing credits as "Miss Stutter."

Still trying to attract attention in Hollywood, Joan agreed to perform this minor role for director Ray McCarey, a friend. Rather than establish a low price for her screen efforts, she took no salary for her few days' work. The ploy worked in her favor, as she was offered (and accepted) a contract with RKO-Radio Pictures.

In her feature film debut, Joan shares screen credit with several featured players who will again cross paths with her down the road, including Russell Hicks, Irving Bacon, Samuel S. Hinds, and Inez Courtney. Also seen in a small role here is onetime vaudeville comic Dave Chasen (1898–1973), far better known for Chasen's, the popular Hollywood restaurant he later opened.

The *New York Times* (December 12, 1935) noted that Joan "puts over a comic song extremely well...." Associated Press columnist Hubbard Keavy, in a December 1935 column, wrote, "Small part actors are forgotten people when the best performance lists are made up, although their work often contributes immeasurably to the entertainment value of pictures. Very often, too, their performances are remembered when those of the stars are forgotten." With that in mind, Keavy published his list of the top ten scene-stealers for 1935. Coming in at #6 on his list was Joan, for her bit in *Millions in the Air*, of which he noted, "She didn't even have billing [not true] and the studio had to go into a huddle to get me her name."[2]

If executives at Paramount scarcely remembered her, however, the same was not true at RKO. A few months later came the announcement that "Joan Davis, brilliant young stage and screen comedienne, has been signed to a term contract by RKO Radio, following the recent release of the film feature, *Millions in the Air*, in which Miss Davis revealed electrifying personality and talent."[3]

Bunker Bean (1936)

Owen Davis, Jr. (*Bunker Bean*), Louise Latimer (*Mary Kent*), Robert McWade (*John "J.C." Kent*), Jessie Ralph (*Grandmother*), Lucille Ball (*Rosie Kelly*), Berton Churchill (*Prof. Ed Balthazer*), Edward Nugent (*Mr. Glab*), Hedda Hopper (*Mrs. Dorothy Kent*), Ferdinand Gottschalk (*Dr. Meyerhauser*), Leonard Carey (*Kent's Butler*), Russell Hicks (*Al "A.C." Jones*), Sibyl Harris (*Countess Cassandra*), Joan Davis (*Mabel*), Pierre Watkin (*Mr. Barnes*), Richard Abbott (*Metzger*), Maxine Jennings (*Receptionist*), Patricia Wilder (*Jones' Secretary*), Edgar Dearing (*Policeman*)

Directors: William Hamilton, Edward Killy. *Associate Producer*: William Sistrom. *Screenplay*: Edmund North, James Gow, Dorothy Yost. *Film Editor*: Jack Hively. *Art Director*: Van Nest Polglase. *Associate Art Director*: Al Herman. *Musical Director*: Roy Webb. *Recording*: Clem Portman. RKO-Radio Pictures; released June 26, 1936. 67 minutes.

Bunker Bean is a shy young man employed as a stenographer for an aircraft manufacturer. He lacks the confidence to attract women, especially his boss' pretty daughter Mary. When he inherits a valuable patent for a piece of aircraft equipment, Bunker is initially too timid to demand a fair price from his boss, who offers him $100 for the invention. He consults a fortuneteller, Countess Cassandra, who persuades him that his past lives include stints as both Napoleon Bonaparte and an Egyptian pharaoh. Young Mr. Bean grows more confident in his life at work and at play.

This was the third film adaptation of Harry Leon Wilson's 1912 novel *His Majesty, Bunker Bean*, following silent versions released in 1918 and 1925. Both earlier versions used the full version of Wilson's title, as did this film in its British release. Another comedienne-in-the-making, 25-year-old Lucille Ball, is featured in *Bunker Bean*, much more prominently than Joan, who's seen briefly as a receptionist.

After spending some months under contract at RKO, with only this bit part to show for her patience, Joan asked for her release in mid–1936. Not long after, she signed with 20th Century–Fox, where she was kept extremely busy for the next few years, though her first work there wouldn't reach the screen until early 1937.

The Holy Terror (1937)

Jane Withers (*Corky Wallace*), Anthony [Tony] Martin (*Danny Walker*), Leah Ray (*Marjorie Dean*), El Brendel (*Axel "Bugs" Svenson*), Joe [E.] Lewis (*William Wellington "Pelican" Beek*), Joan Davis (*Lili*), Andrew Tombes (*Commander J.J. Otis*), Fred Kohler, Jr. (*Carson*), Victor Adams (*Flandro*), Raymond Brown (*Phelps*), Gloria Roy (*Maria Blair*), Gavin Muir (*Redman*), John Eldredge (*Lt. Commander Wallace*), Steve Pendleton (*Yeoman*), Emmett Vogan (*Squad Commander*), John Bleifer, Lew Harvey, Stanley

Taylor (*Spies*), Bruce Warren (*Sentry*), Henry Otho (*Master at Arms*), Ben Hendricks, Jr. (*Ben*)

Director: James Tinling. *Associate Producer*: John Stone. *Original Screenplay*: Lou Breslow, John Patrick. *Music & Lyrics*: Sidney Clare, Harry Akst. *Dance Staging*: Jack Haskell. *Photography*: Daniel B. Clark. *Art Director*: Albert Hogsett. *Assistant Director*: William Eckhardt. *Film Editor*: Nick De Maggio. *Sound*: W.D. Flick, Harry Leonard. *Musical Director*: Samuel Kaylin. 20th Century–Fox; released February 5, 1937. 68 minutes.

Little Corky Wallace, daughter of a Naval Air Service officer, lives with him on a military base. Lt. Commander Wallace is engaged in top-secret work involving a new airplane prototype that will give the U.S. "the fastest air fleet in the world." Unfortunately, Corky has a way of unwittingly causing mischief on the base that has its commanding officer threatening to have her sent away to school.

Adjoining the base is the Golden Anchor Café, run by pretty Marjorie Dean. Enemy spies are plotting to take over the building housing the café, which offers a perfect vantage point from which to steal the airplane plans. When Marjorie refuses an offer to sell out, the spies take advantage of a rivalry for her affection between enlisted man Danny Walker and a pompous officer. A fight breaks out in the café between the two men, resulting in Marjorie's business being shut down, most of Corky's sailor friends in the brig, and only Corky left to prevent the spies from committing an act of espionage.

Filmed in the fall of 1936, shortly after Joan signed with Fox, this is the first of two pictures in which she supports the popular child star Jane Withers (born 1926). They worked together again a few months later in *Angel's Holiday*. Joan plays Lili, a kitchen helper at the Golden Anchor. She suffers from a periodic stutter, which she sometimes corrects by punching herself in the jaw. Swedish-accented comedian El Brendel (1890–1964) plays a sailor who woos her. Many years later, the two were reunited professionally when Joan hired Brendel to play her father in guest appearances on *I Married Joan*.

As part of the stage show, Joan performs a song-and-dance routine with comedian Joe E. Lewis (1902–1971), better known for his nightclub work, who was making one of his relatively rare film appearances. At the conclusion of her number, she's struck in the face by flying tomatoes from the audience, to which she cracks, "Thanks for taking 'em out of the can."

Reviewer "Mae Tinee," in the *Chicago Tribune*, said of *The Holy Terror*, "This piece should go over well of Saturday afternoons in neighborhood theaters.... Joan Davis shows possibilities of becoming a popular comedienne."

Time Out for Romance (1937)

Claire Trevor (*Barbara Blanchard*), Michael Whalen (*Bob Reynolds*), Joan Davis (*Midge Dooley*), Chick Chandler (*Ted Dooley*), Douglas Fowley (*Roy Webster*), Bennie Bartlett (*Orville Healy*), William Griffith (*Ambrose Healy*), William Demarest (*Willoughby Sproggs*), Lelah Tyler (*Cora Sproggs*), Andrew Tombes (*James Blanchard*), Georgia Caine (*Vera Blanchard*), Vernon Steele (*Count Michael Montaine*), Inez Courtney (*Mabel*), George Chandler (*Simpson*), Fred Kelsey (*Policeman*), Lynn Bari (*Bridesmaid*), Jerry Mandy (*Joe*), Si Jenks (*Old Man*), Hank Mann (*Rube*), Hal Craig (*Motorcycle Cop*), Guy Usher (*Chief of Police*), Caroline Rankin (*Hotel Guest*), Harrison

Greene, Eddie Kane, Grover Ligon, Jack Norton, Larry Wheat (*Crapshooters*), Gloria Roy (*Maid*), Paul McVey (*Ship's Officer*), Billy Wayne (*Gas Station Attendant*)
    Director: Malcolm St. Clair. *Associate Producer*: Milton Feld. *Screenplay*: Lou Breslow, John Patrick. *Original Story*: Eleanore Griffin, William Rankin. *Photography*: Robert Planck. *Art Director*: Lewis H. Creber. *Assistant Director*: Jasper Blystone. *Film Editor*: Al DeGaetano. *Costumes*: Herschel. *Sound*: George Leverett, Harry M. Leonard. *Musical Director*: Samuel Kaylin. 20th Century–Fox; released February 10, 1937. 72 minutes.

Oil heiress Barbara Blanchard, just married to Count Michael Montaine, finds out moments too late that her new husband is a fortune hunter. Going on the lam, she has her hair dyed blonde and drops her roadster into a pond to throw off her pursuers. But she soon finds herself short on funds, and hitchhiking in the middle of nowhere. Unable to catch a lift, Barbara pretends to faint, and is picked up by Bob Reynolds, a member of a caravan driving cars to California under the supervision of grouchy boss Mr. Sproggs. Also along for the ride are camera bug Ambrose Healy and his bratty son Orville, dippy Mrs. Sproggs, a man who calls himself Roy Webster, and the husband-and-wife team of Midge and Ted Dooley.

Because the convoy members are forbidden to pick up passengers, Barbara hides in

Behind the scenes of *Time Out for Romance* (1937), leading man Michael Whalen (center) takes his place on the set, as Joan (at left) observes.

Bob's car so as not to jeopardize his trip to California, where he has a job waiting. When the stowaway is discovered en route, Barbara claims to be Bob's estranged wife, and is allowed to continue on the journey. However, the man traveling under the alias Roy Webster is actually a jewel thief who, when things start getting hot, stashes the gems in Bob's car. Before the caravan reaches California, Barbara thinks Bob is the jewel thief, he thinks she's the criminal's moll, and the resulting pandemonium climaxes with a multi-car chase that gets all and sundry thrown into jail.

Joan is featured as Midge Dooley, an aspiring performer traveling to California with her husband. As Bob explains of the Dooleys, "She's a dancer and he thinks he's going to manage her right into Eleanor Powell's shoes." She's teamed here for the first time with comic actor Charles "Chick" Chandler (1905–1988), also a former vaudevillian, with whom she would work frequently during her time as a Fox contract player. Joan's eccentric dance routines are a comic high point of this mildly amusing comedy, which gives her ample screen time but not the kind of lines or scenes that make a comedienne's job easy.

Leading lady Claire Trevor (1910–2000) acquits herself ably here, but would receive far more attention for another of her 1937 releases, *Dead End*, which netted her an Oscar nomination as Best Supporting Actress. Director Malcolm St. Clair (1897–1952) was no longer at the peak of his career, but had numerous comedy credits directing such luminaries as Buster Keaton, Harold Lloyd, and Laurel and Hardy.

Fox publicity described *Time Out for Romance* as "a riotous romance on wheels, with every speeding second crammed with hilarious, exciting adventure." This modest B movie came and went without attracting much attention, but reviewers did take notice of Joan's gifts, as she began to find a niche for herself at 20th Century–Fox. "Joan Davis paired with Chick Chandler make a good duo, with a continual stream of clowning," *Variety* noted (March 12, 1937).

On the Avenue (1937)

Dick Powell (*Gary Blake*), Madeleine Carroll (*Mimi Caraway*), Alice Faye (*Mona Merrick*), The Ritz Brothers (*Themselves*), George Barbier (*Commodore Caraway*), Alan Mowbray (*Frederick Sims*), Cora Witherspoon (*Aunt Fritz*), Walter Catlett (*J.J. "Jake" Dibble*), Douglas Fowley (*Eddie Eads*), Joan Davis (*Miss Katz*), Stepin Fetchit (*Herman*), Sig Rumann (*Herr Hanfstangel*), Billy Gilbert (*Joe Papaloupas*), E.E. Clive (*Cabby*), Douglas Wood (*Mr. Trivet*), John Sheehan (*Stage Manager*), Paul Irving (*Harry Morris*), Harry Stubbs (*Kelly*), Ricardo Mandia (*Luigi*), Edward Cooper (*Potts*), Paul Gerrits (*Joe Cherry*), Bess Flowers (*Marie*), Edgar Norton (*James*), Dewey Robinson (*Diner Customer*), Frank Darien (*Stage Doorman*)

Director: Roy Del Ruth. *Executive Producer*: Darryl F. Zanuck. *Associate Producer*: Gene Markey. *Screenplay*: Gene Markey, William Conselman. *Music and Lyrics*: Irving Berlin. *Choreographer*: Seymour Felix. *Photography*: Lucien Andriot. *Art Director*: William Darling. *Associate*: Mark-Lee Kirk. *Set Decorator*: Thomas Little. *Assistant Director*: William J. Scully. *Film Editor*: Allen McNeil. *Costumer*: Gwen Wakeling. *Sound*: Joseph Aiken, Roger Heman. *Musical Director*: Arthur Lange. 20th Century–Fox; released February 12, 1937. 89 minutes.

It's opening night for *On the Avenue*, a musical revue written by and starring Gary Blake. The high point of the revue is a sketch lampooning a well-known family of Park Avenue socialites, the Caraways, and their eccentricities. Sitting in the audience is pretty Mimi Caraway, who isn't amused by the public ridicule.

Mimi makes her way backstage and confronts Gary, slapping his face. When he calls her a poor sport, and refuses to change the sketch, she tries a different approach. Arranging a dinner date with him, Mimi finds him charming company, and by the end of the evening they're in love.

Now that he knows Mimi, Gary has second thoughts about the sketch. But Mona Merrick, jealous of Mimi, resents Gary's instructions to tone down the offending sketch, and to his surprise makes it even worse the next night, when the Caraways are once again in attendance. Ready to play hardball, Mimi gets out her checkbook and buys the entire production.

Joan has a minuscule role here as Miss Katz, secretary to theatrical producer Mr. Dibble. She first appears nearly an hour into the film, delivers only half a dozen lines, and is out of the picture in less than ten minutes. Her most noteworthy line, to Madeleine Carroll, is a slightly incredulous: "Did you send for the Ritz Brothers?" This is her first picture with fellow contract player Alice Faye, with whom she will appear frequently for the next few years.

Within the movie, famed Broadway columnist Walter Winchell is referenced numerous times, as are other notable real-life New York columnists of the day (Louis Sobol, future film director Mark Hellinger, and Ed Sullivan). Winchell himself would later work with Joan on two pictures.

Nash and Ross' *Motion Picture Guide* calls *On the Avenue* "one of the funnier musicals of the 1930s ... a rollicking satire of the hoity-toity set."

The Great Hospital Mystery (1937)

Jane Darwell (*Sarah Keats*), Sig Rumann (*Dr. Triggert*), Sally Blane (*Ann Smith*), Thomas Beck (*Dr. David McKerry*), Joan Davis (*Flossie Duffy*), William Demarest (*Mortimer Beatty*), George Walcott (*Allen Tracy/Arthur Smith*), Wade Boteler (*Lt. Mattoon*), Howard Phillips (*Tom Kirby*), Gloria Roy (*Nurse*), Tom Mahoney (*Bank Guard*), Ruth Peterson (*Desk Nurse*)

Director: James Tinling. *Associate Producer*: John Stone. *Screenplay*: Bess Meredyth, William Conselman, Jerry Cady. *Story*: Mignon [G.] Eberhart. *Photography*: Harry Jackson. *Art Director*: Albert Hogsett. *Assistant Director*: Samuel Schneider. *Film Editor*: Nick De Maggio. *Costumes*: Herschel. *Sound*: G.P. Costello, Harry M. Leonard. *Musical Director*: Samuel Kaylin. 20th Century–Fox; released May 14, 1937. 58 minutes.

On a stormy night at Samaritan Hospital, two new patients are admitted: Allen Tracy, who requests the services of pretty nurse Ann Smith, and grouchy Mortimer Beatty, who complains of stomach pains but seems to be just a hypochondriac. The two newcomers are placed in adjoining rooms, 707 and 708. Shortly thereafter, Ann tells her co-worker that Mr. Tracy died of a heart ailment and, with the help of morgue attendant Tom Kirby, has the body immediately removed from the room. Ann's fiancé, Dr. David McKerry, is puzzled when she pleads with him to sign a death certificate, even though he never attended the patient. Sensible, plain-spoken Sarah Keats, the middle-aged night supervisor, decides to check out Mr. Tracy in Room 708, and finds that there is indeed a dead man there—but he's been shot through the heart.

As Police Lieutenant Mattoon tries to unravel the mystery, with more bluster than brains, Miss Keats demonstrates her skills as an amateur detective. She identifies the man who's been shot as a charity ward patient who died earlier in the day, sets a trap for an intruder who breaks into hospital rooms via the fire escape, and deduces the real reasons behind the cryptic behavior of Chief of Staff Dr. Triggert, nurse Ann, and the suddenly nowhere-to-be-seen Tom Kirby.

Joan provides most of the film's laughs in her role as probationer Flossie Duffy, who tries the patience of Sarah Keats while rendering her services as the clumsiest, most jittery

Nurse probationer Flossie Duffy (Joan Davis) simultaneously undermines both health care and criminal justice, to the frustration of Lt. Mattoon (Wade Boteler), in *The Great Hospital Mystery* (1937).

Angel of Mercy in history. First seen taking one of her trademark falls a few minutes into the film, Joan reappears intermittently throughout, slinging thermometers across the room while trying to shake them, scaling down the fire escape to keep a date with a parking attendant, quaking in fear at the idea of visiting Tom Kirby at his office in the morgue, and ultimately winding up needing a major operation herself. She's particularly funny in her first scene with William Demarest as the hapless Mr. Beatty. When he's told she's on probation (as a nurse), he responds, "What were you in for?" Jane Darwell, as the down-to-earth Miss Keats, garners a few laughs herself in her sharp-tongued exchanges with the slow-witted detective, telling him at one point, "What a time a clinic would have with that brain of yours!"

Attesting to Joan's growing popularity with moviegoers was her prominence in newspaper ads for *The Great Hospital Mystery*, despite her fifth billing onscreen. "Wait till you meet this nitwit night nurse with her shriek like an ambulance siren," ads crowed. "She'll have you rolling in the aisles."

Fox's publicity for the film quoted Joan as saying, "It seems to me that any time a girl who can really handle comedy shows up in Hollywood she instantly gets herself a contract and enough money for twenty-four payments on one of those Beverly Hills mansions. She can be young, old or indifferent—as homely as a mud-hen or as beautiful as a rosebud—with the figure of Venus or that of a freight car—but as long as she can deliver 'hoke' comedy, she is certain of success."[4] The article went on to define "hoke" comedy as "a vaudeville term, derived from 'hokum,' and means the complete opposite of sophisticated comedy."

Popular mystery writer Mignon G. Eberhart (1899–1996), whose career spanned nearly 60 years, introduced her nurse-sleuth Sarah Keate in her 1929 debut novel, *The Patient in Room 18.* This film was adapted from Eberhart's short story "Dead Yesterday," originally published in the September 1936 issue of *Pictorial Review.* Sarah Keate first made the transition to movies in 1935, with Warner Brothers' *While the Patient Slept.* Before Jane Darwell assumed the role, for which the last name was changed to Keats, Keate had been played in previous films by Aline MacMahon and Marguerite Churchill. This was Darwell's only performance as the character, which would next be played by Ann Sheridan. Darwell probably came closer to the author's original depiction of the character.

The film delivers a fairly complicated detective-story plot in just under an hour, one that may have been a bit complicated for audiences to follow on a first viewing. Still, as the *Boston Globe* (June 18, 1937) commented, "Crammed with adventure and excitement, *The Great Hospital Mystery* keeps the patrons sitting at the edge of their seats through much of the action."

Angel's Holiday (1937)

Jane Withers (*June "Angel" Everett*), Joan Davis (*Stivers*), Sally Blane (*Pauline Kaye*), Robert Kent (*Nick Moore*), Harold Huber (*Bat Regan*), Frank Jenks (*Cecil "Butch" Broder*), Ray Walker (*Crandall*), John Qualen (*Waldo Everett*), Lon Chaney, Jr. (*Eddie*), Al Lydell (*Gramp Hiram Seely*), Russell Hopton (*Gus*), Paul Hurst (*Sgt. Murphy*), John Kelly (*Maxie*), George Taylor (*Louie*), Cy Kendall (*Chief of Police*), Charles Arnt (*Ralph Everett*), Irving Bacon (*Fingerprint Expert*), Frank Moran (*Tough Man*), Clem Bevans (*Sheriff*), Kernan Cripps, Emmett Vogan (*Radio Officers*), Fred Kelsey (*Conductor*), Buster Slaven (*Copy Boy*), Si Jenks (*Deputy*), Tom London (*Truck Driver*), Wally Maher (*Reporter*), Troy Brown, Sr. (*Porter*), Jack Cheatham (*Fireman*), Virginia Sale (*Woman*)

Director: James Tinling. *Associate Producer*: John Stone. *Original Story and Screen-play*: Frank Fenton, Lynn Root. *Photography*: Daniel B. Clark. *Art Director*: Bernard Herzbrun. *Assistant Director*: Aaron Rosenberg. *Film Editor*: Nick DeMaggio. Costumes: Herschel. *Sound*: G.P. Costello, Harry M. Leonard. *Song*, "They Blew Themselves Out of Breath": Harold Howard, Bill Telaak. *Musical Director*: Samuel Kaylin. 20th Century–Fox; released June 7, 1937. 76 minutes.

Spunky June Everett, known to her friends as "Angel," is aboard a train with her mystery writer father when she stumbles onto a real-life story. A mysterious new passenger, traveling with her loyal maid Stivers in tow, is movie star Pauline Kaye, incognito as part of a publicity stunt dreamed up by her fast-talking agent, Crandall. She holes up at a hotel per his instructions while newspaper headlines proclaim her kidnapped.

Angel's buddy Nick Moore, a newspaper reporter for the *Daily News-Press* who dated Pauline when they were teenagers in a small town, still has a snapshot of them together from when Pauline was known by her real name, Aggie. Tipped off by Angel as to Pauline's whereabouts, Nick publishes a story headlined "Kidnap Hoax Exposed," which is accompanied by the photo Angel purloined from his pocket. Angry, Pauline decides to go on the lam, enlisting the aid of Crandall's dimwitted helper Butch to hide out at her grandfather's remote farm.

Feeling guilty that she interfered in Nick's reunion with his old flame, Angel follows Pauline to the farm, and leaves Nick a map to its location as well. At the farm, bad guy Bat Regan decides to horn in on the kidnapping action, demanding $20,000 for Pauline's safe return.

Supporting child star Jane Withers for the second time, Joan here plays a character who doesn't suffer pushy little girls gladly. When Angel bluffs her way into Pauline's railway stateroom late at night, pretending to be sleepwalking, Strivers indicates the girl disdainfully and tells the conductor, "If *this* comes with the compartment, you can have it back!" Later, when Angel takes offense at being labeled a "squirt" by Stivers, the plain-spoken maid retorts, "Quiet, squirt! I'll put you back in the grapefruit."

Stivers is admiringly eyed by low-grade bad guy Butch, played by Frank Jenks, but she isn't impressed. She's surprised when she sees him getting directions to the hideout:

STIVERS: Don't tell me you can write!
BUTCH: No, but I can draw.
STIVERS: Yeah, flies!

Later, Joan gets to sing a novelty song, "They Blew Themselves Out of Breath," during which she punches herself in the jaw yet again. She also has a little too much fun with the moonshine provided by Pauline's grandpappy. Even asleep, she's getting laughs, as her animated snoring punctuates a tender reunion scene between Nick and his lady friend.

Once again, Jane Withers provides wish fulfillment for stifled little girls everywhere, as she uses tear gas to break prisoners out of jail, blackmails adults into buying her ice cream sodas and taking her to the park, and keeps everyone around enthralled with her late-night readings from detective magazines, to say nothing of her song-and-dance impersonation of Martha Raye (then a popular comedienne at Paramount). Modern audiences may be a little uncomfortable with the relationship between Jane Withers' Angel and her adult friend Nick, on whom she clearly has a crush. Angel asks her friend how old he'll be when she turns eighteen, and responds with jealousy to her "rival" Pauline.

Lovely Sally Blane (1910–1997), the actress sister of Loretta Young, also worked with Joan in *The Great Hospital Mystery*. Lon Chaney, Jr. (1906–1973), has a minor role as one of Bat's dopey henchmen, whose looks Joan cheerfully insults. Poor Troy Brown, Sr. (1901–1944) is unbilled as the wide-eyed African American railway porter who, in the midst of a mix-up, actually has to say, "There's a black boy in the woodpile somewhere!"

Box Office (May 8, 1937) said, "A broad comedy, well cast and well directed, this will find widespread popularity among the Jane Withers fans." *Film Daily* (April 27, 1937) concurred: "First-rate Jane Withers vehicle with snap and action makes an enjoyable comedy." Of Joan's featured role, *The Hollywood Reporter* (undated, 1937) opined, "Joan Davis draws, for the first time, a part totally unworthy of her, yet by addition of individual comedy business makes it outstanding. Anyone who can get the howls she does with a snore deserves high praise."

Sing and Be Happy (1937)

Anthony [Tony] Martin (*Buzz Mason*), Leah Ray (*Ann Lane*), Joan Davis (*Myrtle*), Helen Westley (*Mrs. Henty*), Allan Lane (*Allan Howard*), Dixie Dunbar (*Della Dunn*), Chick Chandler (*Mike*), Berton Churchill (*John Mason*), Andrew Tombes (*Thomas Lane*), Luis Alberni (*Posini*), Frank McGlynn, Sr. (*Sheriff*), Edward Cooper (*Mason's Butler*), Irving Bacon (*Palmer*), Lynn Bari (*Secretary*), Carroll Nye (*Announcer*), Charles Tannen (*Clerk*)

Director: James Tinling. *Associate Producer*: Milton H. Feld. *Screenplay*: Ben Markson, Lou Breslow, John Patrick. *Music and Lyrics*: Sidney Clare, Harry Akst. *Photography*: Daniel B. Clark. *Art Director*: Lewis Creber. *Assistant Director*: Saul Wurtzel. *Film Editor*: Nick De Maggio. *Costumes*: Herschel. *Sound*: E. Clayton Ward, Harry M. Leonard. *Musical Director*: Samuel Kaylin. 20th Century–Fox; released June 25, 1937. 64 minutes.

Singer-bandleader Buzz Mason has a run of bad luck culminating with a disastrous publicity stunt in which he gives a performance while flying above a small California town in his airplane. The resulting chaos causes $3,000 in damages from vehicle wrecks, and nearly lands Buzz in jail. Instead, he turns up at the offices of his father's advertising agency. Hoping to resume a romance with his former college sweetheart and singing partner Ann Lane, Buzz agrees to settle down and forge a career in the business world.

Ann works for her father's advertising agency, which is John Mason's biggest rival. The two agencies compete for several lucrative accounts, among them a million-dollar deal to advertise Mrs. Henty's Pickles on the radio. Ann is considering a marriage proposal from Allan Howard, an executive in her father's company, who happens to be selling corporate secrets to Mason's company. Buzz's unorthodox approach to the advertising game includes giving a career break to window washers Mike and Myrtle, who have composed their own novelty song about Mrs. Henty's Pickles. At the climactic audition to see which agency will win Mrs. Henty's business, Buzz makes the most of every opportunity to bring the competition to a satisfactory conclusion.

Paired once again with Chick Chandler (after *Time Out for Romance*), Joan is showcased more effectively here than she will be in many of her early Fox films, and her character is slightly more pertinent to the main story. Her amazing physical agility makes her perfectly suited to the role of zany window washer Myrtle, who skids along ledges outside (supposedly) high windows, slides through offices with buckets of water, and falls to the floor with a clatter when someone aims a punch at her partner Mike. Her rubber-faced expressions punctuate

Joan (left) and co-stars Dixie Dunbar, Tony Martin, Leah Ray and Allan Lane do their best to live up to the title of *Sing and Be Happy* (1937).

even the slightest scene, and she dishes out dialogue with perfect timing. Passing the time with Mike playing tic-tac-toe in the grimy windows they should be washing, she loses and says, "Oh, you won again! Well, Post Office is my game!"

While all was lighthearted onscreen, no one was laughing when she was hurt during production. Joan was filming the scene in which Myrtle climbs through an office window and then takes a fall on a slippery, wet floor. She performed the scene all too well, taking a fall that earned her an emergency visit to Cedars of Sinai Hospital and a five-day stay to treat her wrenched back. On her first day back on the set, she told director James Tinling she wanted to get the tricky scene in the can immediately. "If I don't do it the very first thing, I'll lose my nerve and it'll have me licked." Gritting her teeth, she performed the stunt in one take, dusted herself off, and said with some satisfaction, "And that's that."[5]

Berton Churchill (1876–1940), seen here as the hero's stuffy businessman father, was not only an established character actor, but one of the founders of the Screen Actors Guild.

Sing and Be Happy followed so quickly on the heels of Joan's previous picture, *Angel's Holiday*, that both were screened simultaneously in some towns. Fox's publicity campaign called it "The love-and-laugh treat of the season!" The *New York Times'* Frank S. Nugent (June 19, 1937) deemed the film "well-nigh plotless," expressing amazement that it could have required the work of three screenwriters. "The picture's chief distinction," he reported, "is the fact that Joan Davis manages to get through it without knocking herself out—an unprecedented feat of self-control."

Wake Up and Live (1937)

Walter Winchell (*Himself*), Ben Bernie (*Himself*), Alice Faye (*Alice Huntley*), Patsy Kelly (*Patsy Kane*), Ned Sparks (*Steve Cluskey*), Jack Haley (*Eddie Kane*), Walter Catlett (*Gus Avery*), Grace Bradley (*Jean Roberts*), Leah Ray (*Café Singer*), Joan Davis (*Spanish Dancer*), Douglas Fowley (*Herman*), Miles Mander (*James Stratton*), Etienne Girardot (*Waldo Peebles*), Barnett Parker (*Foster*), Paul Hurst (*McCabe*), Warren Hymer (*First Gunman*), Ed Gargan (*Murphy*), Charles Williams (*Alberts*), Gary Breckner (*Announcer*), William Demarest, John Sheehan (*Radio Station Attendants*), Elyse Knox (*Nurse*), Eddie Anderson (*Elevator Operator*), Robert Lowery (*Chauffeur*), George Chandler (*Janitor*), Fred Kelsey, Paul Newlan (*Cops*), Franklyn Farnum (*Tourist*), Frank Darien (*Hay Wagon Driver*), Allen K. Wood (*Jones*), Hank Mann (*Eddie's Shill*), Charles Tannen (*Agent*), The Brewster Twins, The Condos Brothers

Director: Sidney Lanfield. *Associate Producer*: Kenneth Macgowan. *Screenplay*: Harry Tugend, Jack Yellen. *Original Story*: Curtis Kenyon. *Based on the Book by* Dorothea Brande. *Music and Lyrics*: Mack Gordon, Harry Revel. *Photography*: Edward Cronjager. *Art Director*: Mark-Lee Kirk. *Associate*: Haldane Douglas. *Set Decorator*: Thomas Little. *Assistant Director*: A.F. Erickson. *Film Editor*: Robert L. Simpson. *Costumes*: Gwen Wakeling. *Sound*: W.D. Flick, Roger Heman. *Musical Director*: Louis Silvers. 20th Century–Fox; released August 23, 1937. 91 minutes.

Small-time vaudevillian Eddie Kane relocates to New York in search of new career advances. Since his sister Patsy works for famed columnist Walter Winchell, Eddie and his partner, Jean Roberts, get favorable publicity that interests agents in signing them—until it develops that Eddie suffers badly from mike fright. A bust at his radio audition, Eddie is quickly abandoned by Jean, and winds up taking a job as a page at the Federal Broadcasting Company headquarters. During one of bandleader Ben Bernie's live broadcasts from the studio, Eddie is inadvertently heard singing to a microphone he doesn't know is live. The unknown singer is a sensation, and newspapers play him up as "The Phantom Troubadour."

At the radio studio, Eddie befriends beautiful performer Alice Huntley, who hosts a self-help show called *Wake Up and Live*. Her sponsor has just dropped her show, calling it dull. Alice acts as Eddie's agent, arranging for him to make subsequent appearances on Bernie's show with remote, anonymous broadcasts from her apartment. Unbeknownst to Eddie, who thinks he is just rehearsing into a phony microphone as a training technique, he becomes the latest source of competition between the always-feuding Winchell and Bernie, both of whom are determined to publicly unmask the Phantom. Also in there pitching is Jean's unscrupulous agent Gus Avery, who persuades her to flatter Eddie into signing a contract with him.

Top-billed Walter Winchell (1897–1972) and Ben Bernie (1891–1943) had garnered laughs from radio audiences with their gag feud, similar to one that took place a few years later between Fred Allen and Jack Benny. Joan shares screen credit here for the first time with actor Jack Haley. Although they don't interact in *Wake Up and Live*, Haley will become one of Joan's most frequent co-stars during the 1940s, both on radio and in film. Haley's singing voice here is provided by popular crooner Buddy Clark (1912–1949), at that time a regular on radio's *Your Hit Parade*. William Demarest, who enjoyed a strong featured role alongside Joan a few months earlier in *The Great Hospital Mystery*, appears very briefly as a radio station worker who tells a nervous Eddie far too much for his own good about the phenomenon of "mike fright."

The film's title (and some of the philosophy espoused by Alice Faye's character) is taken from the 1936 book *Wake Up and Live!* by Dorothea Brande (1893–1948), a bestselling motivational book long before they were in vogue.

The main supporting role for a funny woman is played here not by Joan but by character actress Patsy Kelly (1910–1981), seen as Winchell's brassy, no-nonsense assistant. Also seen briefly, performing a dance routine with his brother, is Nick Condos, who subsequently became the husband and manager of comedienne Martha Raye.

Tenth-billed, Joan plays one of her most minor roles in *Wake Up and Live*, her character not even given a name. Well over an hour into the film, Joan turns up to perform a brief but funny dance routine. Her Spanish dancer, part of a Latin-flavored production number at Ben Bernie's opening night at the Manila Club, stumbles and staggers across the stage, handicapped by a dress with a too-long train, and is conked on the head by one of a pair of maracas. She's onscreen for less than two minutes. Joan will enjoy a far more substantial role in Winchell and Bernie's second film together, *Love and Hisses.*

The *Los Angeles Times* (May 2, 1937) called the film "enormously appealing. It is expert from start to finish in every department and in every detail. Nor, thank heaven, is there too much of anything or anybody.... [S]uch incidental contributors as the Condos Brothers and Joan Davis are brilliant aids in their proper place."

Despite her minimal footage, *Wake Up and Live* apparently marked a turning point in Joan's Fox career. *Daily Variety* (May 6, 1937) headlined her on Page One, "Joan Davis Upped in 20th-Fox Chores," noting, "Joan Davis has been graduated from lesser roles to more important featured spots ... since her click in comic dance routine in *Wake Up and Live*." She was reported to have a "good assignment" forthcoming in *You Can't Have Everything*, as well as a featured role in *Thin Ice.*

Thin Ice (1937)

Sonja Henie (*Lili Heiser*), Tyrone Power (*Prince Rudolph aka Rudy Miller*), Arthur Treacher (*Nottingham*), Raymond Walburn (*Uncle Dornik*), Joan Davis (*Orchestra Leader*), Sig Rumann (*Prime Minister Ulrich*), Alan Hale (*Baron*), Leah Ray (*Singer*), Melville Cooper (*Herr Krantz*), Maurice Cass (*Count*), George Givot (*Alex*), Greta Meyer (*Martha*), Egon Brecher (*Janitor*), Torben Meyer (*Herman*), George Davis, Albert Pollet, Rolfe Sedan (*Waiters*), Hans Herbert (*Otto*), Bodil Rosing (*Otto's Wife*), Hans Fuerberg (*Baron's Secretary*), Lon Chaney, Jr. (*American Reporter*), Emil Hoch (*Watchmaker*), Leo White (*Count's Secretary*), Marcelle Corday (*Emma*)

Director: Sidney Lanfield. *Associate Producer:* Raymond Griffith. *Screenplay:* Boris Ingster, Milton Sperling, from the play *Der Komet* by Attila Orbok. *Music and Lyrics:* Lew Pollack, Sidney D. Mitchell. *Choreographer:* Harry Losee. *Photography:* Robert Planck, Edward Cronjager. *Musical Director:* Louis Silvers. *Film Editor:* Robert Simpson. *Art Director:* Mark-Lee Kirk. *Set Decorator:* Thomas Little. *Costumes:* Royer. *Sound:* W.D. Flick, Roger Heman. *Assistant Director:* William Forsyth. 20th Century–Fox; released September 3, 1937. 79 minutes.

The Grand Hotel Imperial in St. Christophe promises guests "The Best Winter Sports in the Alps," but an unseasonably warm spell threatens to ruin the start of the lucrative skiing season. Pretty Lili Heiser, the hotel skiing instructor, is one of many townspeople whose livelihood is in jeopardy if snow doesn't fall soon. Offered reservations for a diplomatic party that will occupy eighty-one rooms, hotel manager Herr Krantz accepts them eagerly, as he and his staff pray fervently for a change in the weather.

The snow arrives just before the members of the diplomatic party, led by Prince Rudolph. Rudolph, accompanied by his faithful manservant Nottingham, wishes to avoid the ministrations of the many diplomats from other countries in attendance. He chooses to go into hiding, pretending he's too ill to leave his suite while holing up at the modest village inn under the name Rudy Miller. Enjoying the chance to ski, the prince meets Lili on the slopes and they begin to meet daily to ski together. Unaware that her new friend Rudy is royalty, Lili becomes the object of gossip when the prince's car is seen dropping her off at home. She's mystified by her sudden popularity with the hotel manager and the many diplomatic representatives hoping to curry favor with Prince Rudolph. Given the chance to headline a skating revue at the hotel, something she'd previously been denied, Lili proves her abilities but finds her romance with Rudy thrown into jeopardy when her avaricious uncle foolishly plants a newspaper story about the couple.

Though it features one of Joan Davis' best-remembered song-and-dance routines, the hilarious "I'm Olga from the Volga," *Thin Ice* gives her only a few minutes onscreen. Seen as the leader of an all-female band that's part of the floor show at the Grand Hotel Imperial, Joan's character doesn't even get a name, being known simply as "Orchestra Leader." She doesn't interact with any of the principal characters in the film, and has no role to play in the plot. Both of her novelty songs, however, are knockouts, especially Mack Gordon and Harry Revel's "Olga," which is followed by Lew Pollack and Sidney D. Mitchell's "My Swiss Hilly Billy."

This is the first of three times that Joan appears in support of Sonja Henie (1912–1969), former Olympic skater who won gold medals for Norway before becoming a popular Fox leading lady of the late 1930s and early 1940s.

Writing in the *Los Angeles Times*, Alma Whitaker said of Joan's *Thin Ice* routines, "Every gesture, every intonation is sumptuously funny. If you think it's amusing when gentlemen comedians fall around and whack each other, just see what 120 pounds of femininity can do."[6]

Life Begins in College (1937)

The Ritz Brothers (*Themselves*), Joan Davis (*Inez*), Tony Martin (*Band Leader*), Gloria Stuart (*Janet O'Hara*), Fred Stone (*Coach Tim O'Hara*), Nat Pendleton (*George Black*), Dick Baldwin (*Bob Hayner*), Joan Marsh (*Cuddles*), Jed Prouty (*Oliver Stearns, Sr.*), Maurice Cass (*Dean Moss*), Ed Thorgersen (*Radio Announcer*), Marjorie Weaver (*Miss Murphy*), Robert Lowery (*Sling*), Lon Chaney, Jr. (*Gilks*), J.C. Nugent (*T. Edwin Cabot*), Fred Kohler, Jr. (*Bret*), Elisha Cook, Jr. (*Ollie Stearns*), Charles C. Wilson (*Coach Burke*), Frank Sully (*Acting Captain*), Norman Willis (*Referee*), Dixie Dunbar (*Polly*), Martin Turner (*Pullman Porter*), Lynn Bari (*Co-Ed*), Frank Melton (*Suit Customer*), Sarah Edwards (*Teacher*), Jan Duggan (*Telephone Operator*), Hal K. Dawson (*Graduate Manager*)

Director: William A. Seiter. *Executive Producer:* Darryl F. Zanuck. *Associate Producer:* Harold Wilson. *Screenplay:* Karl Tunberg, Don Ettlinger, suggested by a series of stories by Darrell Ware. *Music and Lyrics:* Lew Pollack, Sidney D. Mitchell. *Song,* "Sweet Varsity Sue": Charles Tobias, Al Lewis, Murray Mencher. *Ritz Brothers Specialties:* Sam Pokrass, Sid Kuller, Ray Golden. *Photography:* Robert Planck. *Art Director:* Hans Peters. *Set Decorator:* Thomas Little. *Assistant Director:* Charles Hall. *Film Editor:*

Louis R. Loeffler. *Costumes:* Royer. *Sound:* Arthur Von Kirbach, Roger Heman. *Musical Director:* Louis Silvers. 20th Century–Fox; released October 1, 1937. 80 minutes.

Lombardy College was originally founded to provide higher education to American Indians, but some members of the current student body are none too enthusiastic when Native American George Black enrolls. Bob Hayner, captain of Lombardy's football team, is among those who has no use for his new classmate, especially when George proves to have athletic ability and takes his place as quarterback. Thanks to the team's erratic scoring record, coach Tim O'Hara has been urged to resign by the school's trustees, so that a younger, more energetic man can take his place. Refusing to do so, O'Hara stakes his future on the outcome of Lombardy's game against his former employer, Midwestern University. When a telegram sent in Bob's name reveals George Black's ineligibility to play as an amateur, it looks like defeat for Lombardy's team and for Bob, whose romance with O'Hara's pretty daughter Janet is endangered.

Three-quarters of a century after it was made, *Life Begins in College* hasn't aged especially well, particularly in regards to cultural and ethnic sensitivity. It may take a few minutes for modern viewers to register the fact that the character of Bob Hayner is basically our romantic lead here, as the script calls for him to welcome an American Indian student to campus by hazing, insulting, and embarrassing him. A drinking game based on taking a swig whenever there's a disparaging reference to tepees, moccasins, etc., would leave a player dangerously soused by the end of the film.

The top-billed Ritz Brothers, appearing in what studio publicity termed "the fastest, funniest, tuniest hit that they or anybody else ever made!" perform several specialty routines but aren't especially well integrated into the rest of the film. Purportedly the proprietors of the Klassy Kampus Kleaners, they befriend George when most of the campus is shunning him, but otherwise have little to do with the plot, such as it is. This is the brothers' first starring role at Fox; they will be gone from the studio by 1939, after complaining about the quality of their scripts.

Making her entrance nearly a half-hour into the film, Joan plays Inez, a young lady who inexplicably sets her romantic sights on stolid George, though he fails to share her ardor. He puts her off by saying he could never marry a woman who didn't have an authentic Indian tattoo like his own. When she finally shows him that she, too, has obtained the necessary skin art, George kisses her with such fervor that she has second thoughts about her wish to marry him. Joan plays her character with zest and good cheer here, but will have a much more effective role to play in a college football comedy when she's cast in *Hold That Co-Ed.*

Nat Pendleton (1895–1967), while on the wrong side of forty to play a college student, has some amusing moments as George, though it's hard to laugh when his character expresses his annoyance with Inez by knocking her to the ground. In a fan magazine profile, Joan claimed that her burly co-star didn't know his own strength. "We clinched, he squeezed, I fainted. Of course, he's one of the best wrestlers in the world, but I'm not. After I came to, he apologized and after that he didn't go about things so realistically."[7]

Singer Tony Martin (1913–2012), cast here as a bandleader, performs musically without being given a character to play, despite his prominent billing. Real-life sports commentator and journalist Ed Thorgersen (1902–1997), familiar to moviegoers from Fox's *Movietone News* series, appears as the announcer giving the play-by-play at the climactic football game. Gloria Stuart (1910–2010), who understandably looks a little bored with her bland ingénue role, will support Joan several years later in *She Wrote the Book.*

College co-ed Inez (Joan Davis) inexplicably sets her sights on stolid George Black (Nat Pendleton) in *Life Begins in College* (1937).

Joan is directed here by William A. Seiter (1890–1964), who will be at the helm again a year or so later when she plays a more substantial role in *Sally, Irene and Mary*.

Variety columnist Phyllis Marie Arthur reported some off-camera fun that took place during the making of the film. "Joan Marsh, Dixie Dunbar, Phyllis Brooks and Joan Davis put on impromptu acts between wardrobe tests.... Joan Marsh played the piano.... Joan Davis did an Indian dance. Dixie tapped while playing her own piano accompaniment. Phyllis Brooks burlesqued her own singing voice."[8]

The *Los Angeles Times'* Edwin Schallert (October 14, 1937) found the film "lacks any great inspiration as a comedy. There is a scarcity of real fun in the dialogue, and though the action is well worked out, with a whirlwind football finish, in which the [Ritz] brethren save the day, the going is at times lugubrious.... Joan Davis shines for a moment or two, but is lacking in opportunity." Said Louella O. Parsons, reviewing the film for the *Los Angeles Examiner* (October 14, 1937), "Joan Davis doesn't have a very big role as the co-ed who is out to capture Nat's heart—but she makes every moment count, and her songs and dances are hilarious."

Love and Hisses (1937)

Walter Winchell (*Himself*), Ben Bernie (*Himself*), Simone Simon (*Yvett Guerin*), Bert Lahr (*Sugar Boles*), Joan Davis (*Joan*), Dick Baldwin (*Steve Nelson*), The Peters Sisters, Chilton & Thomas, The Brewster Twins, Ruth Terry (*Specialties*), Douglas Fowley (*Webster*), Chick Chandler (*Hoffman*), Rush Hughes, Gary Breckner (*Announcers*), Charles Williams (*Irving Skolsky*), Georges Renavent (*Count Guerin*), Charles Judels (*Oscar*), Robert Battier (*Gangster*), Hal K. Dawson (*Music Store Clerk*), Charles Tannen (*Desk Clerk*), Ben Welden (*Bugsy*), Hooper Atchley (*Joe Moss*), George Humbert (*Chef*), Donald Haines (*Newsboy*), Edward McWade (*Ticket Seller*)

Director: Sidney Lanfield. *Executive Producer:* Darryl F. Zanuck. *Associate Producer:* Kenneth MacGowan. *Screenplay:* Curtis Kenyon, Art Arthur. *Story:* Art Arthur. *Music and Lyrics:* Mack Gordon, Harry Revel. *Choreography:* Nick Castle, Geneva Sawyer. *Photography:* Robert Planck. *Art Directors:* Bernard Herzbrun, Mark-Lee Kirk. *Set Decorator:* Thomas Little. *Assistant Director:* William Forsyth. *Film Editor:* Robert Simpson. *Costumes:* Royer. *Sound:* W.D. Flick, Roger Heman. *Musical Director:* Louis Silvers. 20th Century–Fox; released December 21, 1937. 82 minutes.

Orchestra leader Ben Bernie returns from a tour raving about his new discovery, French singer Eugenie, whom he has billed as the toast of Europe. His old rival, columnist Walter Winchell, promises to give the young singer a plug on his radio show. Instead, relishing the chance to stick it to his rival, Winchell tells his listening audience that Bernie and his new protégée are both phonies.

To get even with Winchell, Bernie arranges for the columnist to meet Eugenie, under the name Yvett Guerin. Impressed by her singing, and believing her to be an undiscovered newcomer, Winchell takes her under his wing, mentioning her in his column and arranging auditions for her. Bernie is only too happy to have Winchell aiding and abetting Yvett's career, since he doesn't realize she will be headlining the show Bernie is opening soon.

Further complicating matters is aspiring songwriter Steve Nelson, who's fired from his job at Lindy's for giving Bernie a copy of his song "Sweet Someone." Bernie likes the song and plans to have Eugenie sing it in his show. But when Steve, having taken a new job as an elevator operator, hears Eugenie humming his number, he assumes his work has been stolen.

The success of *Wake Up and Live* led to this follow-up effort re-teaming Winchell and Bernie, released only a few months later. Once again, the plot finds them feuding over the discovery of a new, unknown talent. Joan has a featured role as Winchell's secretary, also named Joan, who's conducting a clandestine romance with Bernie's sidekick Sugar Boles.

Joan's casting was announced in an August 1937 studio press release, which noted, "Continuing to advance Joan Davis in importance, Darryl F. Zanuck has assigned her to the featured feminine comedy role in *Love and Hisses*.... Miss Davis first attracted attention with her eccentric comedy dance in *Wake Up and Live*, but in this new picture she rejoins Walter Winchell and Ben Bernie on the screen in a more important role."[9]

One of her best scenes here, just past the half-hour mark, finds Joan delivering a comic song about her infatuation for her boyfriend Sugar, dancing clumsily around her apartment as she gazes adoringly at photos of Bert Lahr. Later, a romantic rendezvous between Joan and her fella comes to an abrupt end when Sugar's boss walks in unexpectedly, causing Joan to fold herself up like a human accordion and take refuge underneath a leaky sink in the washroom.

Simone Simon and Dick Baldwin play a lengthy scene in front of a hugely unsubtle marquee for *Sally, Irene and Mary*, which Fox released approximately three months after this film, with Joan in a co-starring role.

Louella O. Parsons, reviewing *Love and Hisses* for the *Los Angeles Examiner* (December 30, 1937), again singled Joan out for notice: "To me, one of the funniest comediennes on the screen is Joan Davis and, although she has little to do as the Winchell secretary beyond one hilarious song number, she does it so well you keep wishing she would appear again.... Miss Davis's wild infatuation for [Lahr] is one of the funniest things in the picture."

Sally, Irene and Mary (1938)

Alice Faye (*Sally Day*), Tony Martin (*Tommy Reynolds*), Fred Allen (*Gabriel "Gabby" Green*), Jimmy Durante (*Jefferson Twitchel*), Gregory Ratoff (*Baron Alex Zorka*), Joan Davis (*Irene Keene*), Marjorie Weaver (*Mary Stevens*), Louise Hovick [Gypsy Rose Lee] (*Joyce Taylor*), Eddie Collins (*Ship's Captain*), Barnett Parker (*Oscar*), J. Edward Bromberg (*Pawnbroker*), Andrew Tombes (*Judge*), The Raymond Scott Quintet, The Brian Sisters (*Specialties*), Lon Chaney, Jr. (*Policeman*), Leonard Carey (*Butler*), Hank Mann (*Messenger*)

Director: William A. Seiter. *Executive Producer:* Darryl F. Zanuck. *Screenplay:* Harry Tugend, Jack Yellen. *Original Story:* Karl Tunberg, Don Ettlinger, suggested by the stage play by Edward Dowling, Cyrus Wood. *Associate Producer:* Gene Markey. *Music and Lyrics:* Walter Bullock, Harold Spina. *Choreography:* Nick Castle, Geneva Sawyer. *Photography:* Peverell Marley. *Art Directors:* Bernard Herzbrun, Rudolph Sternad. *Film Editor:* Walter Thompson. *Costumes:* Gwen Wakeling. *Set Decorator:* Thomas Little. *Sound:* Arthur Von Kirbach, Roger Heman. *Musical Director:* Arthur Lange. *Vocal Supervisor:* Jule Styne. *Assistant Director:* Charles Hall. 20th Century–Fox; released March 4, 1938. 86 minutes.

Sally, Irene, and Mary are aspiring Broadway singers working various subsistence jobs—manicurist, hat check girl, cigarette girl—while awaiting their big show biz break. Their agent "Gabby" is a low-rent proposition who mostly fails to live up to his promises. While working at the Covered Wagon Café in Greenwich Village, the young ladies meet talented singer Tommy Randall, who's fed up with show business and has resolved to pack it in. Conniving in cahoots with glamorous former showgirl Joyce Taylor, who wields a heavy checkbook after six wealthy ex-husbands, and has the hots for Tommy, "Gabby" mounts a Broadway show, *Soup to Nuts*, which can serve as a showcase for the young singer, while also providing his other clients some gainful employment. But when he learns who financed his Broadway debut, Tommy balks, and unemployment beckons.

Faster than you can say *deux ex machina*, Mary's uncle dies and leaves her a broken-down steamship, the *General Fremont*. Tommy suggests renovating the ship into a floating nightclub where the talents of Sally and her friends can be showcased, but there is still the small matter of the $25,000 or so needed to fix it up. Each wanting to further the other's career, Sally agrees to marry a rich and flamboyant baron if he finances the new show *Rhythm on the River*, while Tommy likewise agrees to wed Joyce. Aware of the sacrifices her pals are making, Irene concocts a plan to solve the problem for good on opening night.

The *Los Angeles Times* announced in the summer of 1936 that Fox had acquired the rights to do a remake of 1925's *Sally, Irene and Mary*, an early triumph at MGM for Joan Crawford. That silent film was, in turn, adapted from a Broadway show that played for more than 300 performances during 1922 and '23. Early predictions that the new version was being eyed as a vehicle for Dixie Dunbar proved false, as did a casting announcement that said Fred Allen's real-life wife Portland Hoffa would play the role of Mary. What ultimately emerged from the remake was first and foremost an Alice Faye film, with the other two female roles reduced to supporting status.

Unlikely as it may sound, Joan is cast here as the character played in 1925 by Crawford,

In case anyone couldn't remember which of the title roles Joan played in *Sally, Irene, and Mary* (1938), she donned a conveniently labeled uniform.

though Davis' Irene doesn't bear much resemblance to the tragic heroine of the earlier version. Joan's comic highlight comes nearly an hour into the film, when she teams with Gregory Ratoff's Baron Zorka for an energetic seduction scene in which she entices him with her version of a gypsy dance. She's also on the receiving end of romantic attention from Jimmy Durante's character, Jefferson Twitchel. As usual, she's able to sum up almost anyone she meets with an appropriate quip, describing nasty Joyce as "you big painted peacock," and gazing appreciatively at a poster of Tony Martin's Tommy while saying, "Wrap your eyelids around *that*!"

Playing featured roles in *Sally, Irene and Mary* are two well-known comedians, though it wouldn't be regarded as a high point in either's career. This was one of only a few film roles for Fred Allen (1894–1956), whose *Town Hall Tonight* was a successful staple of NBC's radio schedule, and still a favorite of radio historians. According to Allen's biographer, the comedian was none too fond of this film, which he privately called *Sally, Irene and Lousy*. His unlikely comic compatriot is Jimmy Durante (1893–1980), cast as a disgruntled street cleaner who buys an ownership stake in "Gabby"'s talent agency for $200. Like Allen, Durante would be often ill-used in movies, which didn't seem to successfully capture his comic persona. Alice Faye and Tony Martin were at this time real-life spouses, though they would divorce in 1941.

According to a studio press release, Joan used a pedometer to estimate the wear and tear on her feet while performing the film's strenuous dance routines. "At the conclusion of one of the numbers she checked the reading on the dial and found that she created enough foot motion to travel a little more than seventeen miles."[10]

Said the *Winnipeg Free Press* (April 9, 1938), "To Miss Davis goes the credit for supplying most of the fun, and her eccentric dancing, for which she is notable, is a veritable knockout." According to the *Los Angeles Times* (March 10, 1938), "Joan Davis gets a chance to exhibit her talents that far outdoes any recent film, and will gain because of this."

Josette (1938)

Don Ameche (*David Brassard, Jr.*), Simone Simon (*Renee LeBlanc*), Robert Young (*Pierre Brassard*), Joan Davis (*May Morris*), Bert Lahr (*Barney Barnaby*), Paul Hurst (*A. Adolphus Heyman*), William Collier, Sr. (*David Brassard, Sr.*), Tala Birell (*Mlle. Josette*), Lynn Bari (*Elaine Dupree*), William Demarest (*Joe*), Ruth Gillette (*Belle*), Armand Kaliz (*Thomas*), Maurice Cass (*Furrier*), George Reed (*Butler*), Paul McVey (*Hotel Manager*), Fred Kelsey (*Hotel Detective*), Robert Kellard (*Reporter*), Robert Lowery (*Rufe*), Lon Chaney, Jr. (*Boatman*), Slim Martin (*Orchestra Leader*), June Gale (*Café Girl*), Ferdinand Gottschalk (*Papa LeBlanc*), Ruth Peterson (*Switchboard Operator*), Lillian Porter (*Cigarette Girl*), Eddie Collins (*Customs Inspector*), Hank Mann (*Charlie*), Mary Healy (*Girl at Ringside*), Edward Keane (*Doorman*), James C. Morton (*Bartender*), Ray Turner (*Mose*), Alice Armand (*Toinette*)

Director: Allan Dwan. *Executive Producer:* Darryl F. Zanuck. *Associate Producer:* Gene Markey. *Screenplay:* James Edward Grant, based upon a play by Paul Frank, Georg Fraser, from a story by Ladislaus Vadnai. *Music and Lyrics:* Mack Gordon, Harry Revel. *Photography:* John Mescall. *Art Directors:* Bernard Herzbrun, David Hall. *Set Decorator:* Thomas Little. *Costume Designer:* Royer. *Film Editor:* Robert Simpson. *Sound:* W.D. Flick, Roger Heman. *Musical Director:* David Buttolph. 20th Century–Fox; released June 3, 1938. 73 minutes.

Brothers David and Pierre Brassard operate the family business in New Orleans, a cannery called Brassard and Sons. Temperamentally they are opposites, as Pierre is a playboy who loves nightclubs and pretty women, while David is a serious businessman who mostly keeps his nose to the grindstone. The brothers join forces, however, when they learn that their widowed father has fallen in love with French nightclub singer Josette, to whom he has impulsively proposed. Sure that their father's new flame is a fortune hunter who doesn't realize that the older man is retired and living on a modest allowance, David and Pierre plot to stop the marriage. Seeing that Josette is about to open at a local club, the Silver Moon Café, the brothers set their plan into motion, sending their father to New York on a business trip to get him out of the way. While David favors a straightforward approach to the gold-digging singer, proposing a cash payout, Pierre thinks it will be cheaper, and simpler, to charm the woman into falling for him, rather than his father.

When David and Pierre show up for Josette's opening night, they are unaware that the singer being spotlighted there is a phony. The woman they meet as Josette is an aspiring singer and wardrobe mistress at the club, Renee LeBlanc. Shoved onstage at the last minute after the real Josette runs away to New York to be with her fiancé, Renee scores a hit, and is persuaded by the club's owner, Mr. Barnaby, to maintain the ruse of being Josette. The real Josette's former assistant, May Morris, is enlisted to act as Renee's companion.

Unbeknownst to the brothers, Renee is aware of their identities, and plays along when Pierre begins romancing her. In truth, however, she is more interested in the quiet, solid David, who is attracted to her in spite of himself. Threatening to complicate matters is A. Adolphus Heyman, an inebriated patron of the Silver Moon, who saw the real Josette perform in Havana and knows this one is a ringer. When the senior Mr. Brassard returns from New York, having finally seen his greedy fiancée (the real Josette) in her true light, he bitterly denounces the folly of taking women seriously, causing David to assume that he, too, has been suckered by Josette.

In her second and final film with Fox starlet Simone Simon (1910–2005), Joan also works again with Bert Lahr, with whom she had been effectively paired in *Love and Hisses*. Studio publicity positioned Lahr and Davis as "filmdom's newest and funniest laugh team.... Hollywood has no more expert exponents of clumsiness than these. And 20th Century–Fox, recognizing their consummate skill, has decided to give the fans a double-order by teaming them up."[11] The teaming, such as it was, didn't last long, as Lahr and Davis worked together only once more, supporting Shirley Temple in *Just Around the Corner*.

Though her importance to the story here is limited, Joan gets several opportunities to garner laughs amidst the romantic comedy. When we first meet her character, May, she's accompanying Josette through Customs, and spars amusingly with an overzealous inspector. Assigned by jittery Mr. Barnaby to keep the soused Heyman too busy to call the police, as he keeps threatening to do, she finally pulls the phone cord out of the wall and does her best impersonation of a telephone operator who *would* put him in touch with the commissioner of police, if the line wasn't busy. Later, when a drunken David tries to buy Renee's affections with multiple fur coats—"one for each day of the week"—May throws him out of her pal's dressing room bodily—but not before stashing away one of the coats for herself. Joan also manages to have fun with some of the props in the star's dressing room, including a curling iron and a perfume atomizer that threaten to get away from her.

This is Joan's only film with popular Fox leading man Don Ameche (1908–1993). Lynn Bari has a minor role in the opening scene as a beautiful substitute secretary who attracts the interest of playboy Pierre, until he learns she's married to one of the burlier men on the

Joan (right) supported baby-faced Fox starlet Simone Simon for a second time in *Josette* (1938).

Brassard and Sons crew. William Demarest garners some laughs in his scene as Joe, a diner owner whose no-nonsense wife doesn't take it kindly when he seems to have a prior acquaintance with Renee.

Josette was warmly received by *Variety* (June 1, 1938): "This is a corking good entertainment.... Smartly written, well directed and deftly acted ... wholly disregarding any pretense at being other than a featherweight farce with an occasional wallop in the abdomen.... When the leads are out of sight, Joan Davis, Bert Lahr and Paul Hurst do their clowning on a slightly broader pattern. Entire troupe is excellent..."

Keep Smiling (1938)

Jane Withers (*Jane Rand*), Gloria Stuart (*Carol Walters*), Henry Wilcoxon (*Jonathan Rand*), Helen Westley (*Mrs. Willoughby*), Jed Prouty (*Jerome Lawson*), Douglas Fowley (*Cedric Hunt*), Robert Allen (*Stanley Harper*), Pedro de Cordoba (*J. Howard Travers*), Claudia Coleman (*Mrs. Bowman*), Paula Rae Wright (*Bettina Bowman*), The Three Nelsons (*Themselves*), Etta McDaniel (*Violet*), Carmencita Johnson (*Brutus*), Mary McCarthy (*Froggy*), Hal K. Dawson (*Casting Director*), Phyllis Cerf (Secretary), Grace Hayle (*Woman at Auction*), Myra Marsh (*Miss Wesley*), Chester Clute (*Morgan, the Auctioneer*), Sarah Edwards (*Governess*), Harold Goodwin (*Taxi Driver*), Hamilton MacFadden (*Director*), Bert Roach (*Prop Man*), Murray Alper (*Shorty*), Robert Dalton (*Leading Man*), Jayne Regan (*Leading Woman*), Perry Ivins (*Writer*), Muriel Kearney

(*Cassius*), Patsy Mitchell (*Girl in Casting Office*), John H. Elliott (*Spence*), Ruth Clifford (*Schoolteacher*), Forbes Murray (*Hanley*), Dick Alexander (*Pete*), Russ Clark, Pat O'Malley (*Policemen at Auction*), Joan Davis (*Herself*)

Director: Herbert I. Leeds. *Associate Producer:* John Stone. *Screenplay:* Frances Hyland, Albert Ray, from an original idea by Frank Fenton, Lynn Root. *Photography:* Edward Cronjager. *Art Directors:* Bernard Herzbrun, Albert Hogsett. *Set Decorator:* Thomas Little. *Film Editor:* Harry Reynolds. *Costumes:* Herschel. *Sound:* George P. Costello, William H. Anderson. *Musical Director:* Samuel Kaylin. 20th Century–Fox; released August 12, 1938. 75 minutes.

Boarding-school student Jane Rand isn't looking forward to another summer "scratching mosquito bites in some old summer camp." On impulse, she decides to pay an unexpected visit to her uncle Jonathan Rand in Hollywood, where he works as a movie director. When she arrives, Jane is disheartened to find out that her uncle has hit the skids—out of money, unemployable, and reduced to living in a shabby boardinghouse. Befriended by Jonathan's former secretary Carol, Jane takes it upon herself to restore her uncle's career. Along the way, she manages to not only champion Jonathan's cause, but also play benefactor to another actor, and get herself a chance to be seen onscreen as well.

A year or so after Joan last played a character role in a Jane Withers picture, she makes an unbilled cameo appearance in her third appearance with the popular child star. Her sole scene comes nearly an hour into the 75-minute film, when Withers' character Jane Rand has gate-crashed the movie studio. On the lam from a studio policeman, Jane is making her way hurriedly across a studio parking lot when she runs into Joan—literally. Jane apologizes to Joan, who's carrying a script and replies politely, "That's all right." On her way out of the shot, Joan does one of her patented stumbles and then promptly vanishes from the film. Also to be found playing a small role in this film is character actress Myra Marsh, who would work often with Joan on *I Married Joan*. Here, she plays the headmistress of Jane's school.

Daily Variety (June 4, 1938) thought the basic story of *Keep Smiling* "unadulterated hokum," but also gave the film credit for offering "the most complete insight into motion picture studio operations yet given the general public."

My Lucky Star (1938)

Sonja Henie (*Kristina Nielsen*), Richard Greene (*Larry Taylor*), Joan Davis (*Mary Dwight*), Cesar Romero (*George Cabot, Jr.*), Buddy Ebsen (*Buddy*), Arthur Treacher (*Whipple*), George Barbier (*George Cabot, Sr.*), Louise Hovick [Gypsy Rose Lee] (*Marcelle La Verne*), Billy Gilbert (*Nick*), Patricia Wilder (*Dorothy*), Paul Hurst (*Louie*), Elisha Cook, Jr. (*Waldo*), Robert Kellard (*Pennell*), The Brewster Twins (*June and Jean*), Charles Tannen (*Saier*), Paul Stanton (*Dean Reed*), Edward Le Saint (*Executive*), Frederick Burton (*Pilsbury*), Arthur Jarrett, Jr. (*Bill*), Kay Griffith (*Ethel*), Cully Richards (*Photographer*), Dora Clement (*Dean's Secretary*), Eddie Conrad (*Gypsy Fortune Teller*)

Director: Roy Del Ruth. *Producer:* Darryl F. Zanuck. *Screenplay:* Harry Tugend, Jack Yellen. *Story:* Karl Tunberg, Don Ettlinger. *Associate Producer:* Harry Joe Brown. *Music and Lyrics:* Mack Gordon, Harry Revel. *Photography:* John Mescall. *Film Editor:* Allen McNeil. *Art Directors:* Bernard Herzbrun, Mark-Lee Kirk. *Set Decorator:* Thomas Little. *Costumes:* Royer. *Sound:* Eugene Grossman, Roger Heman. *Musical Director:* Louis Silvers. 20th Century–Fox; released September 9, 1938. 90 minutes.

Pretty, Norwegian-born Kristina Nielsen works as a clerk at Cabots' Fifth Avenue department store, whose line of women's sportswear isn't selling as well as it should. Seeing Kristina practice her skating one night on the store's icy roof, playboy George Cabot, Jr., persuades his father, the store owner, to employ the young lady in a promotional gimmick: enrolling her as a student at Plymouth University, where she will entrance the entire student body with her display of Cabot sportswear.

Having completed only one year of college before emigrating to the U.S., Kristina eagerly accepts the offer to further her schooling. However, her initial days at Plymouth are rocky, arriving with mountains of luggage to hold the wardrobe she's expected to model. Though she's befriended by her good-natured roommate Mary Dwight and handsome Larry Taylor, the other students take offense at her frequent display of expensive clothes, thinking her snobbish for flaunting wealth that she actually doesn't have.

The highlight of Plymouth's school year is the annual Winter Ice Carnival, for which rehearsals are underway. Nasty, Southern-accented Dorothy, who wants Larry for herself, arranges for Kristina to be publicly embarrassed with a musical number performed by burly college men donning the newcomer's pricey clothing, crooning lyrics like, "She looks like an ad for a fire sale." A humiliated Kristina wants to leave Plymouth. Instead, with Larry's persuasion, Kristina auditions for the carnival, where her skating abilities win her a lead role, and her photo on the cover of *Life* magazine, as well as greater acceptance from her classmates. But a visit from George Cabot, Jr., in the midst of an impending divorce from his golddigging wife Marcelle La Verne, leads to embarrassing headlines when greedy Marcelle paints Krista as her husband's mistress. Expelled from Plymouth, Kristina goes back to New York, with Larry at her side, in hopes of clearing her name. The solution, as it usually is in a Sonja Henie film, lies in an elaborate ice show, here supposedly staged on the fifth floor of the Cabots' store.

Unlike many of her Fox films, *My Lucky Star* provides Joan with a supporting role that makes sense, and is pertinent to the story. Joan's character Mary becomes a friend to Kristina, and is furnished with some funny lines as well. Not overly dazzled by Kristina's extensive wardrobe from Cabots' Fifth Avenue, Mary comments, "I got a sweater there once, but the store detective made me put it back." Joan is billed at the head of the supporting cast for her substantial role.

Playing Joan's love interest is a young Buddy Ebsen (1908–2003), as bucolic Buddy, who operates a taxi service around

Another future TV star, Buddy Ebsen, played Joan's less-than-ardent admirer in *My Lucky Star* (1938).

campus with the help of his horse, Lula. Mary sometimes has occasion to feel that she's competing with Lula for her boyfriend's attention, remarking, "If you paid as much attention to me as you do that horse, maybe I'd have a few things to write in my diary." When Buddy tries to beg off a date with Mary, saying that Lula is tired, Mary responds, "That's okay, I'll relieve her on the hills." In one of the film's highlights, Joan and Buddy team for a comic song-and-dance routine, "Could You Pass in Love?" in which her lyrics bemoan the fact that his romantic technique doesn't quite live up to his book learning.

Young Richard Greene (1918–1985), near the beginning of his film and television career, makes a handsome leading man for Henie, and is even in the right age range to play a college student, something of a rarity in Hollywood films. Greene will later be known as the star of *The Adventures of Robin Hood* (1955–60), a British-made teleseries that also enjoyed a healthy run in America on ABC-TV. Actor-singer Kirby Grant, who will be Joan's leading man a few years later in *She Wrote the Book*, has an unbilled bit as one of the crooning college students. Cesar Romero and Joan will team up again some years later in *Love That Brute* (1950).

According to the *Los Angeles Times* (August 27, 1938), "Joan Davis all but steals the picture for a time...." *Variety* (September 14, 1938) didn't think this the best of Henie's films, but said "it has enough strength to prove adequately entertaining for the masses.... The clowning of Miss Davis clicks smartly."

Hold That Co-Ed (1938)

John Barrymore (*Gov. Gabby Harrigan*), George Murphy (*Rusty Stevens*), Marjorie Weaver (*Marjorie Blake*), Joan Davis (*Lizzie Olsen*), Jack Haley (*Wilbur Peters*), George Barbier (*Maj. Hubert Breckenridge*), Ruth Terry (*Edie*), Donald Meek (*Dean Fletcher*), Johnny Downs (*Dink*), Paul Hurst (*Slapsy*), Guinn Williams (*Mike Wurgeski*), Bill [Billy] Benedict (*Sylvester*), Frank Sully (*Steve Wurgeski*), The Brewster Twins (*Themselves*), Charles C. Wilson (*Coach Burke*), Glenn Morris (*Spencer*), Carroll Nye (*Radio Newscaster*), Doodles Weaver (*Gilks*), Douglas Evans (*Announcer at State-Louisiana Game*), Sam Hayes (*Announcer at State-Clayton Game*), Stanley Andrews (*Belcher*), Bess Flowers (*Miss Sward*), Dora Clement (*Miss Weatherby*), Charles Williams (*McFinch*), Larry Steers (*Architect*), Larry McGrath (*Referee*), Dick Winslow (*State College Bandleader*), Harold Goodwin (*News Photographer*), Fred Kohler, Jr. (*Daly*), Cy Schindell (*Policeman*)

Director: George Marshall. *Associate Producer:* David Hempstead. *Screenplay:* Karl Tunberg, Don Ettlinger, Jack Yellen. *Original Story:* Karl Tunberg, Don Ettlinger. *Photography:* Robert Planck. *Art Directors:* Bernard Herzbrun, Hans Peters. *Film Editor:* Louis Loeffler. *Set Decorator:* Thomas Little. *Costumes:* Royer. *Musical Director:* Arthur Lange. *Sound:* Arthur von Kirbach, Roger Heman. 20th Century–Fox; released September 13, 1938. 80 minutes.

Former All-American quarterback Rusty Stevens arrives at modest State College to coach the football team. Upon arrival, he finds a woefully underfunded team that lacks even the basic equipment needed to play, and learns that Governor Gabby Harrigan, who's running for the Senate, has slashed the athletic budget as "an unnecessary burden on the taxpayers." Rusty and his players march on Capitol Hill, but are unsuccessful in changing the governor's mind. But then the governor realizes that supporting the football team at State will be politically advantageous; before long, he has allocated $10 million for campus improvements and plans to get publicity by matching Rusty's team against some of the biggest college teams around.

While visiting the campus, Governor Harrigan notes the impressive place-kicking skills of co-ed Lizzie Olsen, daughter of a famed football champion, and insists she be allowed to join the team. Dubbed "the only college girl football player in captivity," Lizzie helps the team tie the score in a game with Louisiana. Later, she comes to the assistance of meek governor's aide Wilbur Peters and helps assemble an even stronger lineup for the team's subsequent games, recruiting two bruiser college dropouts who'd been working as professional wrestlers.

With Harrigan's popularity soaring, his rival for the Senate seat, Major Hubert Breckinridge, adopts similar tactics, building up the football team of nearby Clayton College. The outcome of the senatorial race is directly tied to that of the State-Clayton football match by a wager between Harrigan and his opponent. When the wrestlers are disqualified from the State team, State's chances look chancy. With the all-important game playing out in the midst of a terrific windstorm, Coach Stevens loses several key players to injuries, and is forced to put Lizzie into the game in its climactic moments. She does her best to score while fighting off husky opponents and gusts of wind that threaten to cause a wardrobe malfunction with her torn uniform as she pushes her way to the goal line.

Among the players to be found in *Hold That Co-Ed* are two who will be important to Joan's radio career: John Barrymore (1882–1942), her future castmate on Rudy Vallee's NBC show, and Jack Haley (1898–1979), who will work with Joan on *The Sealtest Village Store*. Though there's no romantic subplot here for Joan, Haley's character does give her an appreciative glance, asking for her phone number on short acquaintance. Song-and-dance man George Murphy (1902–1992) may not make the most convincing football coach ever seen on a motion picture screen, but in real life he successfully realized his own ambitions to serve in the Senate.

Joan's own athletic prowess made her a natural to play this rough-and-tumble role, though she admitted she had misgivings at first. She told a reporter that the *Hold That Co-Ed* script arrived while she was still being treated for injuries she received making *My Lucky Star*. "I opened the book at 'Joan Davis pole-vaults into the scene' and just closed it quietly. I hated to look at the finish if the opening was that bad. I'm still expecting to read 'Joan Davis dives 50 feet through a plate-glass window into a dishrag or a cup of milk.'"[12] On-screen, however, Joan plays the role of Lizzie with infectious vigor and enthusiasm, making this one of the most unusual and memorable of her featured roles at Fox.

Noted the *Baltimore Sun*'s Donald Kirkley (October 1, 1938), "All in all, the film is far above the average for collegiate comedies." *Variety* (September 28, 1938) said, "Miss Davis is a near panic all the way, either on or off the football field, and her presence, plus that of Barrymore, saves the picture."

Just Around the Corner (1938)

Shirley Temple (*Penny Hale*), Joan Davis (*Kitty*), Charles Farrell (*Jeff Hale*), Amanda Duff (*Lola Ramsby*), Bill Robinson (*Corporal Jones*), Bert Lahr (*Gus*), Franklin Pangborn (*Mr. Waters*), Cora Witherspoon (*Aunt Julia Ramsby*), Claude Gillingwater, Sr. (*Samuel G. Henshaw*), Bennie Bartlett (*Milton Ramsby*), Paul McVey (*Mr. Black*), Mary Forbes (*Miss Vincent*), Edgar Norton (*Butler*), Marilyn Knowlden (*Gwendolyn*), Billy

Wayne (*Laundry Attendant*), Ethan Laidlaw (*Police Detective*), Hal K. Dawson (*Reporter*), Eddy Conrad (*French Tutor*)

Director: Irving Cummings. *Executive Producer:* Darryl F. Zanuck. *Associate Producer:* David Hempstead. *Photography:* Arthur Miller. *Set Decorator:* Thomas Little. *Art Directors:* Bernard Herzbrun, Boris Leven. *Film Editor:* Walter Thompson. *Musical Director:* Louis Silvers. 20th Century–Fox; released November 11, 1938. 70 minutes.

The Depression has taken its toll on the Hale family. Father Jeff, an architect whose most recent project lost its financing, now works as an electrician and lives in the basement of the hotel where he and his young daughter Penny once occupied a penthouse. Summoned home from the private school she was attending, Penny takes it upon herself to improve the family fortunes. She befriends Milton Ramsby, a rich kid who now lives in the penthouse with his pretty sister Lola, who's in love with Jeff Hale, and his grouchy uncle, industrialist Samuel Henshaw. Hearing that everyone will be better off when "Uncle Sam" is solvent again, Penny takes this to mean that Milton's uncle needs help, and organizes a benefit to raise money for him.

Joan plays Kitty, maid at the Riverview Hotel and a friend to Penny, whose duties include taking care of the residents' rowdy dogs, including one named Corset (because, she explains, "he's tied in all day and they let him out at night."). Her love interest is the good-hearted if slightly addled chauffeur Gus, played by Bert Lahr, who tells her, "Gee, you're

Considered a promising comedic pair in the late 1930s, Joan and Bert Lahr teamed to play key supporting roles in *Just Around the Corner* (1938).

beautiful—just like a re-paint job." Gus means to make his relationship with Kitty permanent as soon as he finishes paying for her ring—"only 36 more installments." Kitty and Gus both work for fussy hotel manager Mr. Waters, known to her as "Ol' Picklepuss." Joan's smallish (though second-billed) role finds her doing shtick with a passel of dogs that pull *her* around by the leash, and taking part in a song-and-dance routine with Shirley Temple, Lahr, and Bill "Bojangles" Robinson, to the tune of "This Is a Happy Little Ditty."

Filmed under the working titles *Lucky Penny* and *Sunnyside Up*, this is Joan's only picture with top Fox star Shirley Temple (1928–2014), and her third teaming with comic Bert Lahr. According to Lahr's son, the comedian was none too happy about playing a supporting role in a Temple film, and even less so when he learned that some of his scenes had been cut, supposedly at the insistence of the young star's mother. Lahr would come to learn, like Joan, that "the comic was incidental to the picture's value. If you're not part of the story and you're put in as comic relief on the periphery of the script, you're the first thing that is cut."[13]

Boxoffice (November 5, 1938) predicted, "That little nine-year-old boxoffice magnet, Shirley Temple, will inject another hypo into ailing grosses with this, her latest starring vehicle. The marvelous moppet has, as usual, been provided with a topflight story, production and supporting cast and, as usual, out-acts, out-dances and out-charms them all." Joan, according to *Daily Variety* (October 29, 1938), "hasn't much of her typical comedy to do but manages laughs with a scene or two as caretaker of the apartment dogs."

The often-acerbic Frank S. Nugent, writing in the *New York Times* (December 3, 1938), didn't bother to conceal his scorn: "Certainly, nothing so aggravating as this has come along before—nothing so arch, so dripping with treacle, so palpably an affront to the good taste or intelligence of the unwary beholder.... Shirley is not responsible, of course. No child could conceive so diabolic a form of torture."

Tail Spin (1939)

Alice Faye (*Trixie Lee*), Constance Bennett (*Gerry Lester*), Nancy Kelly (*Lois Allen*), Joan Davis (*Babe Dugan*), Charles Farrell (*Bud*), Jane Wyman (*Alabama*), Kane Richmond (*Lt. Dick "Tex" Price*), Wally Vernon (*Chick*), Joan Valerie (*Sunny*), Edward Norris (*"Speed" Allen*), J. Anthony Hughes (*Al Moore*), Harry Davenport (*T.P. Lester*), Mary Gordon (*Mrs. Lee*), Robert Lowery (*Sam*), William B. Davidson (*Sales Manager*), Fern Emmett (*Matilda*), Jonathan Hale (*Racing Official*), Harry Rosenthal (*Harrison*), Irving Bacon (*Storekeeper*), Sam Hayes (*Announcer*), Edwin Stanley (*Doctor*), Eddie Dunn (*Eddie*)

Director: Roy del Ruth. *Associate Producer:* Harry Joe Brown. *Screenplay:* Frank Wead. *Photography:* Karl Freund. *Art Directors:* Bernard Herzbrun, Rudolph Sternad. *Set Decorator:* Thomas Little. *Musical Director:* Louis Silvers. *Film Editor:* Allen McNeil. *Costumes:* Gwen Wakeling. *Sound:* Eugene Grossman, Roger Heman. *Technical Directors:* Paul Mantz, Clifford W. Henderson. 20th Century–Fox; released February 19, 1939. 84 minutes.

Pilot Trixie Lee seeks fame and fortune by entering the Powder Puff competition of the National Air Races. Despite crashing in the preliminary Women's Transcontinental race from Los Angeles to Cleveland, Trixie is undeterred, arriving in Cleveland ready to win the Powder Puff prize with help from her loyal mechanic and best friend Babe. Also quite interested in the outcome of the women's race is Navy Lieutenant Dick Price, who met Trixie previously in San Diego and is happy to renew their acquaintance.

Trixie's chance for victory takes a nosedive when spoiled socialite Gerry (pronounced "Gary") Lester joins the competition. Gerry has been flying for only a few months, but her family wealth endows her with a new, custom-engineered plane that can outperform the other ladies' more modest vehicles. Although Trixie and Gerry take an instant dislike to each other, Trixie is unsuccessful in her attempt to persuade her rival to bow out. Also entering the competition is Lois Allen, who competes as a pilot primarily to be around her husband "Speed," a champion aviator.

After much drama in the sky and on the ground, the Powder Puff competition ultimately pits Trixie head to head with Gerry, for whom she is beginning to acquire a grudging respect. As Babe and the others cheer her on, Trixie goes into the final battle with Gerry.

As Babe, Joan has a goodly amount of screen time, and several nice moments in the spotlight, including one where she mocks Constance Bennett's hifalutin pronunciation of "indubitably." When Trixie and her pals invite Gerry to dinner, hoping to give her a good scare with their accounts of the perils of flying, Babe joins in the trumped-up reminiscing about one unfortunate aviatrix, commenting, "You know, Louise had the queerest-lookin' insides I ever saw." After Gerry bids the other ladies adieu, Babe watches her leave, and notes, "She'd make a wonderful stranger."

Would you fly an airplane repaired by Joan Davis? Alice Faye looks uncertain in *Tail Spin* (1939).

Surprisingly, Babe's later entry into a parachuting competition is largely played for suspense, denying Joan the chance to make the most of a natural venue for her physical comedy. Reminded to pull the cord on her parachute at the appropriate moment, Babe cracks, "Yeah, hope I don't pull the zipper on my union suit instead!" According to syndicated columnist Harrison Carroll, it was an edict from studio head Darryl F. Zanuck that resulted in Joan's comedy here being mostly verbal. "Zanuck has blue penciled all Joan Davis' comedy falls in *Tail Spin.* She was in the hospital for weeks after *My Lucky Star.*"[14]

A dramatic crash scene is *de rigueur* in a film of this type, especially when it's called *Tail Spin.* Wead's screenplay gives us several, including a couple that take place off-screen. One of them affords Nancy Kelly the opportunity to play her most dramatic scenes.

This is an atypical role for musical comedy star Alice Faye, though she does manage to sneak in one song. Playing another pilot is up-and-coming featured player Jane Wyman (1917–2007). Charles Farrell (1901–1990), a former silent screen matinee idol playing a relatively minor role here as mechanic Bud, would later have a career resurgence in early television, playing the second lead in *My Little Margie* during the same years Joan toplined *I Married Joan.*

Though she's billed below the title in *Tail Spin,* Joan's name and face featured prominently in Fox newspaper ads, which described the film as "a zooming story of courageous coeds of the skies that hits with the impact of a cyclone!"

Screenwriter Frank "Spig" Wead (1895–1947), himself a former aviator, turned to writing as a second career after suffering a paralyzing injury in 1926 (though not related to a plane crash). The opening titles credit "the splendid help and cooperation by the committee and those others at the National Air Races in Cleveland which made possible this film." When *Tail Spin* began playing, Joan teamed with husband Si for a 12-week personal appearance tour, beginning with an engagement in Chicago.

The *New York Times'* Frank S. Nugent (February 11, 1939) termed this "a thoroughly competent job of movie-making. It is constructed on a simple formula: every time the picture is about to crash, Mr. Zanuck crashes a couple of planes instead." Added the *Los Angeles Times* (January 28, 1939), "Joan Davis pretty well romps away with the comedy, as is her wont. She has some unusually laughable lines to recite."

Too Busy to Work (1939)

Jed Prouty (*John Jones*), Spring Byington (*Mrs. John Jones*), Ken Howell (*Jack Jones*), George Ernest (*Roger Jones*), June Carlson (*Lucy Jones*), Florence Roberts (*Granny Jones*), Billy Mahan (*Bobby Jones*), Joan Davis (*Lolly*), Chick Chandler (*Joe "Cracker" McGurk*), Marjorie Gateson (*Mrs. Randolph Russel*), Andrew Tombes (*Wilbur Wentworth*), Marvin Stephens (*Tommy McGuire*), Irving Bacon (*Al Gilligan*), Helen Ericson (*Betty*), Harold Goodwin (*Raymond*), Hooper Atchley (*Charles Carter*), Sherry Hall (*Armbruster*), George Melford (*Dugan*), Eddie Acuff (*Stage Manager*), Edwin Stanley (*Frazier*), Jack Green (*Policeman*), Dave Morris (*Baxter*), Eddie Dunn (*Truck Driver*), George Watts (*Jailer*)

Director: Otto Brower. *Screenplay:* Robert Ellis, Helen Logan, Stanley Rauh, based upon *The Torchbearers* by George Kelly and *Your Uncle Dudley* by Howard Lindsay, Bertrand Robinson. *Based Upon Characters Created by* Katharine Kavanaugh. *Associate Producer:* John Stone. *Photography:* Edward Cronjager. *Film Editor:* Fred Allen. *Set*

Decorator: Thomas Little. *Art Directors:* Richard Day, George Dudley. *Costumes:* Helen
A. Myron. *Musical Director:* Samuel Kaylin. *Sound:* Eugene Grossman, William H.
Anderson. 20th Century–Fox; released November 17, 1939. 65 minutes.

John Jones, in his second term as mayor of Maryville, is kept so busy with receptions, committee work, and other ceremonial duties that he's neglecting both his family and his drugstore business. Having promised wife Louise that he will scale back his civic activities, John
can't resist getting involved with a fundraising drive when he learns there's a chance for the
small town to have its own hospital. At her mother-in-law's suggestion, Louise decides to
give her husband a taste of his own medicine. When her old college friend Madge Russel,
an actress-turned-producer, passes through town, Louise agrees to play the female lead in a
local production of the play *Life's Problem*, with all proceeds to benefit the new hospital.
John stews with jealousy watching Louise play scenes with her leading man Wilbur Wentworth, whose drugstores compete with the one that John operates, and grows frustrated
with Louise's neglect of her household chores.

    With Mrs. Jones too busy with the play to spend much time at home, housekeeping
duties at the Jones household fall to visiting cousin Lolly ("Uncle Philbert's girl"), who arrives
unexpectedly for a visit. Lolly is also pressed into service providing props and sound effects

"Uncle Philbert's girl" Lolly (Joan, center) arrives to visit the Jones family in *Too Busy to Work* (1939), with Spring Byington (left) and Florence Roberts.

for Louise's play, a move that almost turns disastrous when she borrows the proceeds of the hospital fundraiser to use as prop money in the stage show.

Joan's early scenes as Lolly provide ample room for her routines, as she mistakes John for a burglar and shoves him into a closet, nearly takes a backward topple down the staircase in the Jones house, shatters dishes, and otherwise wreaks household havoc. As Granny Jones says shortly after meeting Lolly, "If you sent her to Ripley, I'll bet *he* wouldn't believe her!"

Too Busy to Work was a late entry in Fox's successful "Jones Family" series of B films, with only two more entries to follow before the series came to a close in 1940. This installment is an amalgam not only of the usual Jones Family elements, but also two popular plays: George Kelly's *The Torch-Bearers*, which had already been adapted into the 1935 comedy *Doubting Thomas*, starring Will Rogers and Billie Burke, and the Howard Lindsay-Bertrand Robinson 1929–30 Broadway comedy *Your Uncle Dudley*, which likewise had been turned into a 1935 film starring Edward Everett Horton.

Cast here as Joan's love interest is character actor Irving Bacon (1893–1965), playing an inept policeman who's tired of eating his meals off the local lunch wagon, and might be in the market for a wife. Joan's frequent co-star Chick Chandler turns up as an escaped safecracker who's on the loose in Maryville.

Variety's review (November 1, 1939) pronounced *Too Busy to Work* "above par in the recent Jones series releases," and presumed that the character of Lolly would recur in future installments. "Arrival of Joan Davis as permanent guest of the household, and her attempts to handle duties of hired girl, provide some broad and elemental knockabout comedy. Looks like addition of Miss Davis to the series will provide low comedy of slapstick type to contrast with motivation of the family affairs." *The Hollywood Reporter* (October 28, 1939) said, "[T]he laughs come thick and fast. If they come out a little too much on the hokey side, no audience is going to mind very much." Despite the positive response to Lolly, this was Joan's only appearance in the series.

Day-Time Wife (1939)

Tyrone Power (*Ken Norton*), Linda Darnell (*Jane Norton*), Warren William (*Bernard Dexter*), Binnie Barnes (*Blanche*), Wendy Barrie (*Kitty Fraser*), Joan Davis (*Miss Applegate*), Joan Valerie (*Mrs. Dexter*), Leonid Kinskey ("*Coco" Anderson*), Mildred Gover (*Melbourne*), Renie Riano (*Miss Briggs*), Marie Blake (*Western Union Operator*), Mary Gordon (*Scrubwoman*), Robert Lowery (*Architect*), Frank Coghlan, Jr. (*Office Boy*), Otto Han (*Dexter's Houseboy*), David Newell (*Party Guest*)

Director: Gregory Ratoff. *Executive Producer:* Darryl F. Zanuck. *Associate Producer:* Raymond Griffith. *Screenplay:* Art Arthur, Robert Harari. *Story:* Rex Taylor. *Photography:* Peverell Marley. *Art Directors:* Richard Day, Joseph C. Wright. *Set Decorator:* Thomas Little. *Film Editor:* Francis Lyon. *Costumes:* Royer. *Sound:* Arthur von Kirbach, Roger Heman. *Musical Director:* Cyril J. Mockridge. 20th Century–Fox; released November 24, 1939. 72 minutes.

Young wife Jane Norton is only mildly perturbed when her husband Ken forgets their second wedding anniversary. Soon after, though, she finds out that he also lied to her about working late at the office, and that his secretary keeps some expensive perfume in her desk. Though she's reluctant to believe that her husband is cheating on her, Jane tells her oft-divorced buddy Blanche, "I'm going to find out just what it is that secretaries have—that wives haven't!" Without her husband's knowledge, Jane takes a job as secretary to architect Bernard Dexter, a married man. Dexter is a middle-aged wolf who quickly becomes enamored of his pretty new secretary, and wants their relationship to be more than strictly professional.

Unbeknownst to Jane, her husband Ken happens to be working on a business deal with Mr. Dexter, and it becomes increasingly awkward for Jane to avoid being seen by her husband at her job. When Ken invites his wife to a romantic evening out, she's ready to give up the whole charade and forgive him. But when Mr. Dexter insists on getting together in a night-club that same evening to discuss their deal, Jane is angry enough to accompany her boss. Ken is shocked when he shows up with his pretty secretary, with whom he's had a mild flirtation, to discover that his wife Jane seems to be acting out the same relationship with her own boss.

Teenage Linda Darnell (1923–1965), seen here in her second film as a Fox contract player, is working for the first time opposite Tyrone Power, with whom she will ultimately co-star in four pictures. This is Joan's second picture with Wendy Barrie, who previously starred in *Millions in the Air*.

Joan has a smallish role as Miss Applegate, receptionist in the office of Bernard Dexter, Inc. We first meet her when Jane shows up to apply for a job, while Miss Applegate is in the midst of stuffing a pile of envelopes. Though Mr. Dexter refused to buy her a machine to aid with this task, he bought her a box of chocolates—so that she could alternate between

Joan (right) explains the facts of office life to Linda Darnell in *Day-Time Wife* (1939).

licking stamps and chomping candy. More experienced in the business world than Jane, Miss Applegate correctly predicts that the boss will take a liking to her. Tempted momentarily to offer Jane a hint about what kind of man Mr. Dexter is, Miss Applegate reconsiders, telling her new friend, "You know, a girl learns plenty around here that you don't find in seed catalogues." Present in only a handful of scenes, Joan drops out of the film not long after the halfway point.

A likable cast and a brief running time make *Day-Time Wife* a pleasant if unexceptional outing. The screenplay hovers on the edge of smarminess, and in lesser hands than Tyrone Power's the husband character would be pretty unappealing.

Most reviews took little notice of Joan's minor role, though *The Hollywood Reporter* (November 11, 1939) said, "Joan Davis is swell in a part which is little more than a bit." *Daily Variety* (November 11, 1939) wrote that Davis "holds the spectators with her fast, humorous comments during brief period she's on the screen."

Free, Blonde and 21 (1940)

Lynn Bari (*Carol Northrup*), Mary Beth Hughes (*Jerry Daily*), Joan Davis (*Nellie*), Henry Wilcoxon (*Dr. Hugh Mayberry*), Robert Lowery (*Dr. Stephen Greig*), Alan Baxter (*Mickey Ryan*), Katherine [Kay] Aldridge (*Adelaide Sinclair*), Helen Ericson (*Amy McCall*), Chick Chandler (*Gus*), Thomas E. Jackson (*Inspector Saunders*), Joan Valerie (*Vickie*), Elyse Knox (*Marjorie*), Dorothy Dearing (*Linda*), Herbert Rawlinson (*John Crane*), Kay Linaker (*Mrs. John Crane*), Richard Lane (*Lt. Lake*), Tom McGuire (*Edgar*), Harry Strang (*Sgt. Martin*), Lenita Lane (*Mrs. Whitman*), Hooper Atchley (*Mr. Payne*), Don Forbes, John Wald (*Radio Announcers*), Edward Cooper (*Crane's Butler*), George Meeker (*Drunk*)

Director: Ricardo Cortez. *Executive Producer:* Sol M. Wurtzel. *Screenplay:* Frances Hyland. *Photography:* George Barnes. *Art Directors:* Richard Day, George Dudley. *Set Decorator:* Thomas Little. *Film Editor:* Norman Colbert. *Costumes:* Herschel. *Sound:* Joseph E. Aiken, William H. Anderson. *Musical Director:* Samuel Kaylin. 20th Century–Fox; released March 29, 1940. 67 minutes.

The Hotel Sherrington is a residence for women only, and most of the young ladies who live there are preoccupied with either their careers or their marital prospects, especially the latter. Beautiful, sophisticated Carol Northrup acts as surrogate den mother to the other ladies in the hotel, and tells a friend, "I live here because I find it interesting. It's like watching a revue that never quite gives the same show twice. You know, every revue has pretty girls, music, excitement—but this one has its own special blend of comedy, drama, and unfortunately a tragedy thrown in now and again."

A recent arrival, beautiful young blonde Jerry Daily, has just been dumped by her married lover, Wall Street executive John Crane. Vengeful Jerry fakes a suicide attempt with sleeping pills that lands her in the hospital but, much to her disappointment, doesn't result in any embarrassing headlines for Crane and his wife. While there, Jerry meets young resident Dr. Stephen Greig, a good-hearted, honorable man who falls in love with her. Carol begins seeing the owner of the hospital, Dr. Hugh Mayberry.

Though Jerry happily encourages Dr. Greig's attentions, she quickly grows disillusioned with his low salary and long working hours. Behind his back, she takes up with another man, shady Mickey Ryan. When her new man is shot while holding up a café, Jerry persuades Dr.

Greig to operate on him, telling the medico that Mickey is her brother. When Mickey dies on a makeshift operating table, it appears that both Dr. Greig and his superior, Dr. Mayberry, will be implicated in a murder case.

Joan plays Nellie, night maid at the Hotel Sherrington. Unlike some of the less-than-capable working women Joan played, Nellie is kept busy helping the many residents iron their clothes, color their hair, and otherwise maintain their busy social lives. Her double negatives and less-than-perfect speech belying her humble background, Nellie is nonetheless a good friend to the young ladies in the hotel. Admiring a *chic* new hat loaned to her by one of the girls, Nellie says, "That's the chickest [rhymes with 'sickest'] thing I ever saw!"

Once again, Joan is teamed romantically with Chick Chandler, here cast as Gus, a taxi driver who doesn't earn much money ferrying the financially precarious Sherrington ladies around town. Her first scene finds her in the backseat of Gus' cab, where he's pitching woo with such hearty enthusiasm that Nellie protests, "You gotta take it easy. After all, I'm just a kid!" Ultimately, she's forced to cool his ardor by delivering her best right hook to his chin. Featured quite prominently in the film's first fifteen minutes, Joan then vanishes for quite a long stretch, resurfacing near the end to give some moral support to Carol in a time of need.

Free, Blonde and 21 is a quasi-sequel to Fox's *Hotel for Women* (1939), which starred Ann Sothern and Linda Darnell, taking place in the same hotel though introducing a new set of characters. Busy contract players Lynn Bari, Chick Chandler, and Kay Aldridge are veterans of the first film as well, but are cast as different characters. Fox remade *Free, Blonde and 21* in 1944 as *Ladies of Washington*, with African American actress Ruby Dandridge taking the place of Joan as Nellie.

Daily Variety's review (February 9, 1940) noted, "While Misses Hughes and Bari have fattest roles, and handle them with histrionic ease, it is Joan Davis, cast as chambermaid, who romps away with the honors. With Chick Chandler, her taxi-driving fiancé, as her foil, she not only provides the comedy, but garners the artistic honors."

Sailor's Lady (1940)

Nancy Kelly (*Sally Gilroy*), Jon Hall (*Danny Malone*), Joan Davis (*Myrtle*), Dana Andrews (*Scrappy Wilson*), Mary Nash (*Miss Purvis*), Larry [Buster] Crabbe (*Rodney*), Katherine [Kay] Aldridge (*Georgine*), Harry Shannon (*Father McGann*), Wally Vernon (*Goofer*), Bruce Hampton (*Skipper*), Charles D. Brown (*Captain Roscoe*), Selmer Jackson (*Executive Officer*), Edgar Dearing (*Chief Master-of-Arms*), Edmund MacDonald (*Barnacle*), William B. Davidson (*Judge Hinsdale*), Bert Moorhouse (*Paymaster*), Lester Dorr (*Assistant Paymaster*), George O'Hanlon (*Sailor*), Matt McHugh (*Cabby*), Peggy Ryan (*Ellen*), Ward Bond (*Shore Patrolman*), Bernadene Hayes (*Babe*), Barbara Pepper (*Maude*), Steve Pendleton (*Information*), Eddie Acuff (*Guide*), Edward Earle (*Navigator*), Pierre Watkin (*Captain*), Emmett Vogan (*Medical Officer*), Ruth Clifford (*Maid*), Kane Richmond (*Lt. Wood*), Dick Rich (*Beany*), Cyril Ring (*Lt. Commander of U.S.S.* Arizona), George Walcott (*Telephone Man*), Charles Waldron (*Commander-in-Chief*)

Director: Allan Dwan. *Executive Producer:* Sol M. Wurtzel. *Screenplay:* Frederick Hazlitt Brennan. *Additional Dialogue:* Lou Breslow, Owen Francis. *Story:* Frank Wead. *Photography:* Ernest Palmer. *Art Directors:* Richard Day, Lewis Creber. *Set Decorator:* Thomas Little. *Film Editor:* Fred Allen. *Costumes:* Herschel. *Sound:* Eugene Grossman,

William H. Anderson. *Technical Advisor:* Lt. Commander A.J. Bolton, U.S.N. *Musical Director:* Samuel Kaylin. 20th Century–Fox; released July 5, 1940. 67 minutes.

Sally Gilroy and her friends Myrtle and Georgine are excited when the U.S.S. *Dakota*, carrying their sailor boyfriends, docks and its men get shore leave. Sally and her beau Danny Malone are about to get married, but she doesn't know how to tell him about the infant she's taken in while he was at sea: Margaret "Skipper" Lane, daughter of Sally's friend who was killed in a traffic accident. Danny's freewheeling buddy Scrappy Wilson, who's none too fond of Sally, thinks Danny is jumping into marriage too quickly and decides to disrupt the impending ceremony.

Sally and Danny host a party to impress Miss Purvis, their staid neighbor appointed by a judge to look after the baby's welfare. Scrappy manages to turn the affair into a raucous brawl that puts the prospective parents in the worst possible light. An angry Sally gives

Wally Vernon plays Joan's love interest, the aptly named Goofer, in *Sailor's Lady* (1940).

Danny his engagement ring back, allowing an opportunity for another sailor, Rodney, to put the moves on her. Faced with losing custody of Skipper, Sally impulsively agrees to marry Rodney to give the baby a father, but a fistfight between him and Danny leaves the little girl's future more uncertain than ever. Out of options, Sally stows the baby away on the departing *Dakota*, with an explanatory note that says, "First division is responsible for this little girl," and resigns herself to spending time in jail rather than disclosing Skipper's whereabouts.

Joan plays the featured role of Sally's pal Myrtle. For once, she's not avidly chasing men, since Myrtle has already won the heart of Danny's doofus buddy, Goofer (played by Wally Vernon, who'd appeared along with Joan in *Tail Spin*). Unfortunately, Joan's footage is brief, and her chances to shine are few. She squeezes out a few laughs where she can—grimacing when Dana Andrews' Scrappy pulls a telephone cord tautly across her neck, or disclosing her beauty regimen to a curious onlooker ("Dutch cleanser!"), but she's largely left to her devices in a script that treats her as an afterthought.

This is Joan's second picture supporting leading lady Nancy Kelly, another veteran of *Tail Spin*. It also marks the second feature film appearance of up-and-coming Dana Andrews (1909–1992), cast as Danny's irresponsible pal Scrappy. Buster Crabbe (1908–1983), former Olympic swimmer and star of the *Flash Gordon* serials, abandons his heroic stance for the minor role of Sally's erstwhile suitor Rodney.

Fox publicity termed *Sailor's Lady* "one of the most hilarious pictures to come out of Hollywood this year ... romance ashore and fun afloat."[15] The reviewer for the *Los Angeles Times* (July 3, 1940) begged to differ: "The film was undoubtedly made some little while ago, but that is no reason why it shouldn't find a quiet resting place on the shelf. Its entertainment value is next to nothing."

Manhattan Heartbeat (1940)

Robert Sterling (*Johnny Farrell*), Virginia Gilmore (*Dottie Haley*), Joan Davis (*Edna Higgins*), Edmund MacDonald (*Spike*), Don Beddoe (*Preston*), Paul Harvey (*Dr. Bentley*), Irving Bacon (*Sweeney*), Mary Carr (*Grandma in Music Store*), Ann Doran (*Shopgirl's Friend*), James Flavin (*Truck Driver*), Edgar Dearing (*Policeman*), Jan Duggan (*Wife*), Harry Tyler (*Husband*), Steve Pendleton (*Tony*), Edward Earle (*Official*), Murray Alper (*Mechanic*), Dick Winslow (*Bus Driver*), George Reed (*Porter*), Louise Lorimer, Ruth Warren (*Nurses*), Emmett Vogan (*Doctor*), Lenita Lane (*Bentley's Nurse*), Harry Hayden (*Pawnbroker*), Cecil Weston (*Mrs. Cunningham*), Jill Dennett (*Shop Girl*), Margaret Brayton (*Ginger*), George Chandler (*Hawker*), Milton Kibbee (*Mr. Gruen*), Cecil Weston (*Mrs. Gruen*), Dick Winslow (*Bus Driver*), Bob Hoffman (*Tired Boy*), Frances Morris (*Tired Girl*), Harry Denny (*Brakeman*), Forbes Murray (*E.J.*)

Director: David Burton. Producer: Sol M. Wurtzel. Photography: Virgil Miller. Set Decorator: Thomas Little. Costumes: Herschel. Film Editor: Alex Troffey. Art Directors: Richard Day, George Dudley. Musical Director: Cyril J. Mockridge. Sound: Joseph E. Aiken, Harry M. Leonard. Assistant Director: Sam Schneider. 20th Century–Fox; released July 12, 1940. 72 minutes.

Dottie Haley, salesgirl in a department store, is returning by train from a vacation at Camp Mohawk with her friend and co-worker Edna Higgins. While Edna has attracted the attention of another camper, Spike, Dottie makes the acquaintance during the return trip of fellow passenger Johnny Farrell. Their relationship gets off to a rocky start, as Johnny professes to have no use for women or for the institution of marriage.

With the help of her buddy Edna, who leads Johnny to believe that Dottie is romantically involved with her boss Mr. Preston, Dottie manages to make Johnny realize that he cares for her, and they are married. But when Dottie finds herself pregnant only a few months after the wedding, she worries that the news will not sit well with Johnny. Johnny is determined to have Dottie treated by the well-known Dr. Bentley, although the physician's rates are beyond their means.

Manhattan Heartbeat was the second film adaptation of *Bad Girl*, a 1928 novel by Viña Delmar that was subsequently adapted into a Broadway play by Delmar and Brian Marlow; the play opened in 1930 but ran for only a few weeks. In the 1931 film version of *Bad Girl*, directed by Frank Borzage, Joan's character of Edna was played by Minna Gombell. *Manhattan Heartbeat* represented a career break for leading man Robert Sterling (1917–2006), playing his first important role after performing numerous small parts. Best known to modern audiences as fun-loving ghost George Kerby of the 1950s TV sitcom *Topper*, Sterling was judged a promising newcomer by reviewers, as was leading lady Gilmore, who later became the wife of Yul Brynner.

Joan is romantically paired here with character actor Edmund MacDonald (1908–1951), who'd previously appeared in *Sailor's Lady*. Don Beddoe, seen as Dottie and Edna's boss, turns up in several episodes of *I Married Joan*, as do a fair number of other actors seen in Joan's Fox films.

Newspaper ads proclaimed, "A boy and a girl ... and the kind of courage that makes a go of marriage on nothing a week!"

The reviews were mixed, though Joan was frequently singled out for praise. *The Hollywood Reporter* (May 29, 1940) said, "Here is a charming and delightful picture that won't cause any great stir at the box office, but will be sure to please its audiences wherever it is shown.... Joan Davis contributes much with her fine comedy that evokes countless hearty laughs." The *Los Angeles Times* reviewer (May 29, 1940) noted, "The role of ... wise-cracking Edna, who is always on hand with help when it is needed, is ably played by Joan Davis who provides laughs at all the right moments...." *Variety* (June 5, 1940) thought Joan's comedy bits among the few saving graces of a picture its reviewer described as "a slow and uninteresting tale of romance and marriage trials.... Joan Davis overcomes scripting handicaps with several wisecracks and comedy routines..."

For Beauty's Sake (1941)

Ned Sparks (*Jonathan B. Sweet*), Marjorie Weaver (*Dime Pringle*), Ted North (*Bertram Erasmus Dillsome*), Joan Davis (*Dottie Nickerson*), Pierre Watkin (*J.B. Middlesex*), Lenita Lane (*Dorothy Sawter*), Richard Lane (*Mr. Jackman*), Lotus Long (*Anna Kuo*), Glen Hunter (*Rodney Blynn*), Lois Wilson (*Mrs. Lloyd Kennar*), John Ellis (*Lloyd Kennar*), Olaf Hytten (*Father McKinley*), Tully Marshall (*Julius H. Pringle*), Phyllis Fraser [Cerf] (*Julia*), Isabel Jewell (*Amy Devore*), Nigel De Brulier (*Brother*), Janet Beecher (*Miss Merton*), Margaret Dumont (*Mrs. Franklin Evans*), Helena Phillips Evans (*Mrs. Jellicoe*), Carl Faulkner (*Policeman*), Cyril Ring (*Hotel Clerk*), Ruth Warren (*Nurse*), Matt McHugh (*Taxicab Driver*), Lelah Tyler (*Mother*), Fred Walburn (*Boy*), Robert Conway (*Doctor*)

Director: Shepard Traube. *Screenplay:* Wanda Tuchock, Ethel Hill, Walter Bullock. *Original Story:* Clarence Budington Kelland. *Associate Producer:* Lucien Hubbard. *Photography:* Charles Clarke. *Art Directors:* Lewis H. Creber, Richard Day. *Set Decorator:* Thomas Little. *Film Editor:* Nick De Maggio. *Costume Designer:* Herschel McCoy. *Sound:* George Leverett, Harry M. Leonard. *Musical Director:* Emil Newman. 20th Century–Fox; released June 6, 1941. 62 minutes.

Young Bertram Dillsome leads a cloistered life as professor of astronomy at St. Vincent's College. Upon the death of his aunt Dimity Sprig, Dillsome inherits her exclusive beauty salon. In a recording played by her attorney at the reading of her will, the late Aunt Dimity says, "All my nephew knows about a woman's charms he learned in biology, cutting up frogs...." She leaves him the business, which nets $100,000 a year, on the condition that he run it himself for the next two years, an experience she believes will do him good. "You'll take your head out of the stars and look at a flesh-and-blood female every day of the week for the next two years."

Bertram reluctantly takes over the operations of Dimity Sprig, Inc., with the help of his late aunt's longtime associates Dottie Nickerson and Dorothy Sawter. Pretty, well-to-do Dime Pringle, who took a shine to the shy Bertram when her class visited St. Vincent's, decides to help him out, enlisting the aid of her grandfather's top PR man, Jonathan B. Sweet, to win the salon fame and fortune.

Operating the salon proves to be more complex than Bertram had anticipated, despite Sweet's best efforts to publicize him as an exclusive European beauty expert. He's faced with a $250,000 lawsuit from actress Amy Devore, who alleges that her face was scarred by a sunburn treatment she received there. Further complications ensue when a final recording from Aunt Dimity warns Bertram of another crisis brewing at the salon, which somehow involves wealthy client Mrs. Lloyd Kennar, who unexpectedly jumps to her death from the salon window. Soon it becomes evident that some of the salon's socially prominent clients have been confiding their own peccadilloes far too freely while being beautified, leaving them vulnerable to a blackmail scheme.

The *Los Angeles Times* reported in April 1940 that Fox had purchased the rights to Clarence Budington Kelland's six-part magazine serial "For Beauty's Sake," which ran in *The American Magazine* from July to December 1938. "When a woman-hater inherits a swank beauty salon full of glamorous, clamorous cuties and finds a red-hot murder mystery tossed in his lap, the result is fun and thrills galore,"[16] studio publicity men optimistically promised. Running just over an hour, *For Beauty's Sake* has far too many disparate plot elements and twists, most of which hang together none too well. Once again playing the unwillingly single girl, Joan does her best with the sporadic opportunities she's given to liven things up, including a bit where she struggles to answer several phones simultaneously. Her climactic encounter with the bad guys finds her stranded in an elevator gone awry. Her character Dottie is inexplicably attracted to cigar-chomping, obnoxious Jonathan Sweet, and springs into action when he's targeted for elimination by the bad guys.

The great Margaret Dumont (1882–1965), remembered for her many appearances with the Marx Brothers, has a single, memorable scene here as an obstreperous client of the salon. This was the final feature credit in the brief filmography of director Shepard Traube (1907–1983), who enjoyed far more success as a Broadway producer and director. The thriller *Angel Street*, which he produced and directed, opened in 1941 and became a huge hit, running for more than three years.

Public relations man Jonathan B. Sweet (Ned Sparks) finds Dottie Nickerson (Joan Davis) to be bad news in *For Beauty's Sake* (1941).

By the time *For Beauty's Sake* hit theaters in the summer of 1941, Joan had already ended her association with 20th Century–Fox. It had sat on the shelf for the better part of a year after shooting, and may well have been a factor in Joan's decision to pull up stakes and move on. It's hard to disagree with *Daily Variety*'s *For Beauty's Sake* review (June 25, 1941): "Ineptly written, directed and played, its comedy falls flat and the pace makes the 62 minutes' running time seem longer." A few weeks later, moviegoers would see Joan Davis much more effectively showcased in *Hold That Ghost*, her first picture as a freelancer.

Hold That Ghost (1941)

Bud Abbott (*Chuck Murray*), Lou Costello (*Ferdinand Jones*), Richard Carlson (*Dr. Jackson*), Joan Davis (*Camille Brewster*), Mischa Auer (*Gregory*), Evelyn Ankers (*Norma Lind*), Marc Lawrence (*Charlie Smith*), Shemp Howard (*Soda Jerk*), Russell Hicks (*Bannister*), William Davidson (*Moose Matson*), Ted Lewis and His Orchestra, the Andrews Sisters (*Themselves*), Thurston Hall (*Alderman Birch*), Milton Parsons (*Harry Hoskins*), Harry Hayden (*Jenkins*), Janet Shaw (*Birch's Girl*), Nestor Paiva (*Glum*), Frank Penny (*Snake Eyes*), Edgar Dearing (*Iron Dome*), Edward Pawley (*High Collar*), William Ruhl (*Gas Station Customer*), Chuck Hamilton (*Police Car Driver*), Don Terry (*Strangler*), William Forrest (*State Trooper*)

Director: Arthur Lubin. *Screenplay:* Robert Lees, Fred Rinaldo, John Grant. *Original Story:* Robert Lees, Fred Rinaldo. *Associate Producers:* Burt Kelly, Glenn Tryon. *Photography:* Elwood Bredell. *Film Editor:* Philip Cahn. *Art Director:* Jack Otterson. *Associate:* Harold H. MacArthur. *Musical Director:* H.J. Salter. *Musical Numbers Staged by* Nick Castle. *Dialogue Director:* Joan Hathaway. *Assistant Director:* Gilbert J. Valle. *Set Decorator:* R.A. Gausman. *Gowns:* Vera West. *Sound Supervisor:* Bernard B. Brown. *Technician:* William Fox. Universal Pictures; released August 8, 1941. 86 minutes.

Hapless gas station attendants Chuck Murray and Ferdie Jones find themselves unwitting witnesses to a shootout between police and gangster Moose Matson. Fatally shot, Matson is found to be carrying a copy of his will, which provides that whoever is present at the moment of his passing will inherit his run-down roadhouse, the Forrester's Club.

Taking a bus to see their new property, Chuck and Ferdie, along with their fellow passengers, end up stranded for the night at the spooky old house, in the midst of a driving rainstorm. A series of unnerving events during the long night make a nervous Ferdie fear that the house is haunted, though no one else witnesses his bedroom's abrupt changeover into a gambling casino, or a lighted candle that floats in the air of its own accord. Subsequent events demonstrate that the real culprits behind the eerie happenings are Matson's gangster associates, who hope to locate the fortune that they think their late pal stashed somewhere on the premises.

Hold That Ghost was Bud Abbott and Lou Costello's third starring feature to land in theaters, following on the heels of the highly successful service comedies *Buck Privates* and *In the Navy.* Known during production as *Oh, Charlie!,* the film was shot primarily during January and February 1941. Because *Buck Privates* had been such a phenomenal success, however, executives at Universal decided to give audiences Abbott and Costello in another military picture next, going into production on *In the Navy* that same spring. Once that film was in the can, and awaiting release, the boys shot a few additional scenes for what became *Hold That Ghost,* notably the musical sequences featuring the Andrews Sisters that bookend the haunted-house comedy.

Hold That Ghost offered Joan a sizable supporting role as radio actress Camille Brewster, whose professional specialty is providing screams in mystery dramas. (In reality, Joan's own radio career was not yet established at the time the film was shot, though it would be in high gear within a couple of years.) Joan's best-remembered scene is undoubtedly the one in which she dances frenetically to the tune of the "Blue Danube Waltz" with Costello.

A studio press release noted an unusual costuming requirement entailed by Joan's dance sequence, which climaxed when she came to rest in a bucket. "As everyone knows, there are buckets and buckets and it was quite essential that Miss Davis should fit in the container when she did her comedy fall without either losing too much skin or on the other hand, rattle around like a bean in a gourd. So the wardrobe department, flanked by an expert tinsmith, took the exact measurements, making due allowance for comfort of fit, and a special bucket was tailored to size. As a tribute to Costello's marksmanship, he planted Miss Davis snugly in the bucket on the first try."[17]

Director Arthur Lubin (1898–1995) may be best-known for his successful "Francis the Talking Mule" series, and for later serving as producer-director of television's *Mister Ed.* Playing the young romantic couple here are two actors who would make multiple forays into straight horror and science fiction roles, Evelyn Ankers (1918–1985), Universal's favorite scream queen of the 1940s, and Richard Carlson (1912–1977), who played lead roles in *It Came from Outer Space* and *Creature from the Black Lagoon,* among many others.

According to a studio press release, "Carrying a rip-roaring story as a means of holding together their zany dialog and gags, and given a far more elaborate mounting than any of their earlier films, *Hold That Ghost* promises to elevate Abbott and Costello to new heights of cinematic popularity."[18]

Variety (July 30, 1941) called the film "a slam-bang and knockabout comedy, silly and ridiculous, but a laugh-creator and audience-pleaser." As for Joan, the reviewer noted, "Miss Davis also clicks in major fashion with her comedic surprise throughout proceedings, and is an excellent laugh teammate for Costello." Other reviewers also noted how effectively Joan worked with Costello, in their one and only appearance together. That they were never re-teamed can probably be attributed to Costello, who showed signs of jealousy at the laughs Joan won in *Hold That Ghost*. According to the reviewer for *The Hollywood Reporter* (July 28, 1941), "Joan Davis is immense with the best role she's had in years and wraps it up for a smash."

Though she never worked with Abbott and Costello again, Joan would soon enough be starring in her own Universal comedies.

Sun Valley Serenade (1941)

Sonja Henie (*Karen Benson*), John Payne (*Ted Scott*), Glenn Miller (*Phil Corey*), Milton Berle (*Jerome K. "Nifty" Allen*), Lynn Bari (*Vivian Dawn*), Joan Davis (*Miss Carstairs*), The Nicholas Brothers (*Themselves*), William Davidson (*Jack Murray*), Almira Sessions (*Nurse*), Mel Ruick (*Jimmy Norton*), Dorothy Dandridge (*Singer*), Chester Clute (*Process Server*), Sheila Ryan (*Telephone Operator*), Ann Doran (*Waitress*), Gary Gray (*Charles*), June Harrison (*Betty Jean*), Lynne Roberts (*Receptionist*), Ralph Sanford (*Doorman*), Dora Clement (*Wife*), William Forrest (*Husband*), Fred "Snowflake" Toones (*Porter*)

Director: H. Bruce Humberstone. *Producer:* Milton Sperling. *Screenplay:* Robert Ellis, Helen Logan. *Story:* Art Arthur, Robert Harari. *Lyrics and Music:* Mack Gordon, Harry Warren. *Choreographer:* Hermes Pan. *Musical Director:* Emil Newman. *Photography:* Edward Cronjager. *Art Directors:* Richard Day, Lewis Creber. *Set Decorator:* Thomas Little. *Film Editor:* James B. Clark. *Costumes:* Travis Banton. *Ski Clothes:* F.A. Picard. *Technical Director of Skiing Sequences:* Otto Lang. *Sound:* Alfred Bruzlin, Roger Heman. 20th Century–Fox; released August 29, 1941. 86 minutes.

Phil Corey and his band are hoping to land a gig playing in Sun Valley, but auditions are being restricted to well-known bands. When established singer Vivian Dawn has a falling-out with her current bandleader, she agrees to sing a number with Phil's band, and they are hired as a team for the job. Phil's pianist Ted Scott is instantly attracted to Vivian, and they become romantically involved.

Shortly before the group leaves for Sun Valley, Ted is notified that he has been approved to host a refugee. The band's publicity agent "Nifty" Allen filled out an application in Ted's name several months earlier, just for the PR value. Expecting a child, Ted is shocked when his refugee turns out to be Karen Benson, a pretty young Norwegian woman. Karen, who says her goal in coming to America was to find a nice man and marry him, decides Ted will fit the bill nicely, notwithstanding his relationship with Vivian. Karen persuades "Nifty" to let her go along on the band's engagement to Sun Valley. At the resort, Ted is impressed by Karen's prowess as a skier and skater. Sensing that she has competition, Vivian decides to

Two future stars of early television, Milton Berle and Joan Davis, teamed up in *Sun Valley Serenade* (1941). In the final cut there was little of her to be seen.

accept Ted's earlier marriage proposal, but Karen devises a scheme of her own to win her man.

Sun Valley Serenade was, according to *Variety* (July 23, 1941), "the spontaneous brain-child of Darryl Zanuck, 20th-Fox production chief, who got the background inspiration during a vacation sojourn at the resort several months ago. Resultant picture ... is an excellent compound of entertaining ingredients ... displaying box office potentialities of high caliber."

Supporting skating star Sonja Henie for the third time, Joan has a very brief and completely unimportant role as Miss Carstairs, a young lady at the ski lodge who's collecting funds for the Skiers' Aid Society. She's first seen making a wisecrack about the fur coat worn by "Nifty" (Milton Berle) as he disembarks from the train. The porter tells "Nifty," "Don't mind her, boss. She meets all the trains. I think she's been kicked in the head by a pigeon." In the second and third of her three scenes, Miss Carstairs successfully solicits a ten-cent donation for her charity from "Nifty," then marks an X on his vest to remember him. All told, Joan is onscreen for less than a minute.

Joan told a reporter that when she saw *Sun Valley Serenade*, the final product disappointed her. "Her part had been sacrificed for footage. Her swan-dance and several other clever antics she performed on the ice were left on the cutting room floor to shorten the picture."[19] Indeed, this is one of the smallest roles she'd played in quite some time, and must have come as a disappointment not only to Joan herself, but to any moviegoers hoping to enjoy more of the gifted comedienne who'd recently made such a strong impression in *Hold*

That Ghost. Despite her featured billing, her role in the film as released is not only minuscule, but completely extraneous to the action, and could easily have been deleted altogether.

Two Latins from Manhattan (1941)

Joan Davis (*Joan Daley*), Jinx Falkenburg (*Jinx Terry*), Joan Woodbury (*Lois Morgan*), Fortunio Bonanova (*Armando Rivero*), Don Beddoe (*Don Barlow*), Marquita Madero (*Marianela*), Carmen Morales (*Rosita*), Lloyd Bridges (*Tommy Curtis*), Sig Arno (*Felipe Rudolfo MacIntyre*), Boyd Davis (*Charles Miller*), John Dilson (*Jerome Kittleman*), Tim Ryan (*Sergeant*), Eddie Kane (*Club Manager*), Antonio Moreno (*First Latin Man*), Bruce Bennett (*Immigration Officer*), Lester Dorr (*Information Attendant*), Dick Elliott (*Sylvester Kittleman*), Tyler Brooke (*Hotel Clerk*), Stanley Brown (*Master of Ceremonies*), Ernie Adams (*Doorman*), Mel Ruick (*Radio Announcer*), Eddie Bruce (*Jed*)
 Director: Charles Barton. *Producer:* Wallace MacDonald. *Screenplay:* Albert Duffy. *Photography:* John Stumar. *Film Editor:* Arthur Seid. *Art Director:* Lionel Banks. *Lyrics and Music:* Sammy Cahn, Saul Chaplin. *Musical Director:* M.W. Stoloff. Columbia Pictures; released October 2, 1941. 65 minutes.

Joan Daley is publicity agent for the Silver Key Club in New York City. She has booked a Cuban sister act, Marianela and Rosita, to make their American debut at the club, promising her boss Mr. Barlow that the singers will be a smash success. After arriving in New York, the sisters are spirited away from the airport by an unknown interloper, and Joan receives a note telling her they have vanished. With opening night looming, Joan persuades her roommates, aspiring singers Jinx and Lois, to take up residence at the Sussex House hotel and impersonate the Cuban sisters. Jinx and Lois are a hit, and quickly become what one newspaper critic labels "the undisputed singing queens of café society." Off-stage, however, Joan and her pals must cope with not only Mr. Barlow, but also Lois' boyfriend Tommy, a mysterious stranger who claims to be the missing singers' brother Armando, and ultimately the untimely return of the real Marianela and Rosita.

Though Joan, top-billed for the first time, plays every scene with her usual high-octane energy, reeling drunkenly into view as if her life depends on it, the script doesn't allow her many good opportunities for physical comedy. She does get to drop a few wry asides that liven up the proceedings. Finding a note pinned to the wall, Joan cracks, "A note? Now who do I know that can write?" Later, when she learns that her roommates have been hauled down to the police station, she muses, "Under arrest? Their act can't be that bad." The finale demonstrates that nobody does the conga quite like Joan.

This is the first of three Columbia features to team Joan with beautiful model-turned-actress Jinx Falkenburg. Free of her Fox contract, Joan found other studios more willing to cast her in substantial roles, even if they were in B movies. Joan told journalist May Mann she was excited about her role in *Two Latins from Manhattan.* "I play a Rosalind Russell type—a fast-talking girl press agent. This is the first time I've played both the comedy lead and the romantic lead and received star billing."[20]

Roly-poly character actor Dick Elliott (1886–1961), unbilled here for his brief appearance as Jinx and Lois' former employer, would turn up over the next several years in Joan Davis movies (*Sweetheart of the Fleet, Yokel Boy*), and also played small roles on *I Married Joan. Two Latins from Manhattan* also provides an early featured role for Lloyd Bridges

(1913–1988), who plays Tommy. Bridges plays straight man to Joan in an amusing scene that finds her unloading groceries as he rhapsodizes about his relationship with Lois. Ostensibly, Joan is only itemizing her purchases aloud, but the timing seems to give her comments an extra meaning:

TOMMY: Lois is swell, isn't she?
JOAN: Mush...
TOMMY: I think she's the most beautiful girl in the world.
JOAN: Corn...
TOMMY: She rates a good husband, and I'm going to make her one, too.
JOAN: Apple sauce...
TOMMY: You know, Joan, it's different with Lois and me. In our case, it was a case of love at first sight.
JOAN: Baloney.

This was the first of three pictures in which Joan was directed by Charles Barton (1902–1981), who enjoyed a lengthy career helming comedies for Abbott and Costello, Joe E. Brown, and Ma and Pa Kettle, among others, before going on to direct the popular TV sitcoms *Hazel*, *Petticoat Junction*, and *Family Affair*.

Studio publicity advised that "patrons should be prepared for some of the heartiest laughs they've ever had ... a tropical heat wave of mirth."[21] *Variety*'s review (October 1, 1941), however, called *Two Latins from Manhattan* "an ineffectual attempt to provide minor league comedy. Script is sophomoric to extreme, and there's little that either the cast or director can do under the circumstances." Nevertheless, the box office success of this picture inspired Columbia to reunite Joan with Falkenburg and Joan Woodbury a year later in *Sweetheart of the Fleet*.

Yokel Boy (1942)

Albert Dekker (*"Buggsie" Malone*), Joan Davis (*Molly Malone*), Eddie Foy, Jr. (*Joe Ruddy*), Alan Mowbray (*R.B. Harris*), Roscoe Karns (*Al Devers*), Mikhail Rasumny (*Amatoff*), Lynne Carver (*Vera Valaize*), Marc Lawrence (*Trigger*), Tom Dugan (*Professor*), James C. Morton (*Sign Painter*), Pierre Watkin (*Johnson*), Marilyn Hare (*Stenographer*), Lois Collier (*Stewardess*), Fern Emmett (*Landlady*), Harry Hayden (*Bank President*), George O'Hanlon (*Teller*), Betty Blythe (*Reporter*), Leonard Carey (*Monroe*), Dick Elliott (*Doctor*)
Director: Joseph Santley. *Producer:* Robert North. *Screenplay:* Isabel Dawn. *Story:* Russell Rouse. *Based on the Musical Play Written by* Lew Brown *and Scored by* Lew Brown, Charles Tobias, Sam H. Stept. *Photography:* Ernest Miller. *Supervising Editor:* Murray Seldeen. *Film Editor:* Edward Mann. *Art Director:* Russell Kimball. *Musical Director:* Cy Feuer. *Orchestrations:* Gene Rose. *Wardrobe:* Adele Palmer. *Dance Director:* Louis Da Pron. Republic Pictures; released March 13, 1942. 69 minutes.

In Hollywood, Mammoth Pictures is on its last legs after too many of its films fail to turn a profit. Sensing the wolf is at the studio's door, executive producer R.B. Harris reads a newspaper story about small-town boy Joe Ruddy, nicknamed "Public Picture Fan #1," an ardent moviegoer who has an amazing ability to predict which pictures will catch on with audiences. Harris brings Joe to Hollywood and puts him on Mammoth's payroll as a consultant just as production is due to begin on the studio's new gangster picture, *King of Crime*.

When the film's leading man walks out rather than work with the studio's talentless ingénue Vera Valaize, Joe suggests recasting the star role with real-life gangster "Buggsie" Malone, who was just released from prison. "Buggsie"'s sister, nightclub torch singer Molly, convinces him to accept the Hollywood offer, as she wants him to "go legit." Upon arrival at Mammoth, "Buggsie" proceeds to rewrite the script (casting himself in a heroic mold), insist that musical numbers be added, and cast his sister in a major role that leaves envious Vera out in the cold. Studio head Mr. Johnson gets wind of the mayhem and pulls the plug on financing *King of Crime*. "Buggsie" offers to kick in a million dollars of his own dough—provided Molly can remember where she stashed it.

Yokel Boy was loosely adapted from the Broadway musical comedy which played from July 1939 to January 1940, starring Judy Canova and Buddy Ebsen. Republic paid $50,000 for the film rights, initially intending to have Canova reprise her stage role. That didn't pan out. Columnist Jimmie Fidler reported in early 1942 that Republic would instead use contract player Betty Kean in the role, until a broken ankle forced her to bow out of what would have been a plum role for her. Ironically, Kean had chosen to sign with Republic over a counter-offer from Fox. "That," Fidler reported, "was because Fox [then] had Joan Davis, much the same type and already a star, thus too much competition."[22]

Heading what Republic optimistically described as "an all-star cast" were Albert Dekker as "Buggsie" and Joan as his sister Molly, in a role that gave her several opportunities to shine. Among the high points are her frenetic dance routine with Eddie Foy, Jr., as the hapless Joe, for whom Molly has fallen, and a knock-down, drag-out catfight with Lynne Carver's Vera, romantic rival for his attentions. Molly's big scene in *King of Crime*, a dramatic deathbed scene that then segues into a high-kicking dance complete with chorus girls, is also quite funny. She's front and center in the climactic scene where, having sustained a blow to the head, she's dizzily transported back to a giddy childhood while her brother and the studio men try in vain to get her to remember where she hid "Buggsie"'s money.

Top-billed Albert Dekker (1905–1968) was not firmly associated with comedy—he's perhaps best known for his starring role as a mad scientist in *Dr. Cyclops* (1940)—so many movie exhibitors played up Joan in ads for the film. Unfortunately, reviews were generally poor. Said *Variety* (March 25, 1942), "[Albert] Dekker and Miss Davis sadly overplay for the comedy."

Sweetheart of the Fleet (1942)

Joan Davis (*Phoebe Weyms*), Jinx Falkenburg (*Jerry Gilbert*), Joan Woodbury (*Kitty Leslie*), Brenda and Cobina [Blanche Stewart and Elvia Allman] (*Brenda and Cobina*), William Wright (*Lt. Philip Blaine*), Tim Ryan (*Gordon Crouse*), George McKay (*Hambone Skelly*), Walter Sande (*Daffy Dill*), Dick Elliott (*Chumley*), Charles Trowbridge (*Commander Hawes*), Tom Seidel (*Bugsy*), Irving Bacon (*Standish*), Lloyd Bridges (*Sailor*), Stanley Brown (*Callboy*), Boyd Davis (*Mayor*), Gary Breckner (*Radio Announcer*)

Director: Charles Barton. *Producer:* Jack Fier. *Screenplay:* Albert Duffy, Maurice Tombragel. *Story:* Albert Duffy. *Additional Dialogue:* Ned Dandy. *Art Director:* Lionel Banks. *Associate Art Director:* Jerome Pycha, Jr. *Photography:* Philip Tannura. *Film Editor:* Richard Fantl. *Musical Director:* Morris Stoloff. *Sound:* Jack Haynes. *Assistant Director:* George Rhein. Columbia Pictures; released May 21, 1942. 65 minutes.

Secretary Phoebe Weyms pines for her boss, publicity agent Gordon Crouse, but he doesn't return her affections. Hoping to impress him, Phoebe dreams up a publicity stunt involving radio singers Brenda and Cobina, heard on the *Blind Date with Romance* program. She arranges for them to make a personal appearance during a USO function at Madison Square Garden. At the event, a benefit for Navy recruiting, they will be "unmasked" for the first time. The plan hits a snag when it turns out that the "Blind Date Girls" are quite homely in person. Undaunted, Phoebe devises a plan to use two of the agency's prettiest models, Jerry Gilbert and Kitty Leslie, as the "Blind Date Girls," lip-syncing while the real singers perform behind a curtain.

The characters of Brenda and Cobina originated on Bob Hope's popular radio show, a spoof by his writers on the real-life debutantes Brenda Frazier and Cobina Wright, Jr. On radio, "Brenda LaFrenzy" and "Cobina Fright" were, in the words of Frazier's biographer, "two crude, man-chasing old hags ... who spoke in rasping Brooklyn accents."[23] A lawsuit filed by Wright eventually forced Hope to stop using the characters, and may account in part for the relative unavailability of this rarely seen film. Character actresses Blanche Stewart (1903–1952) and Elvia Allman (1904–1992) had previously played the characters onscreen in *A Night at Earl Carroll's* (1940), *Time Out for Rhythm* (1941), and *Swing It, Soldier* (1941). Allman will later be seen in several first-season episodes of *I Married Joan* as Joan's Aunt Vera.

According to a studio press release, "Columbia Pictures is extending the invitation and you're invited ... for a lulu of a musical cruise that's jammed with gags and gals and gobs of melody and fun! ... It's light, it's gay, it's timely, and it features two of the loveliest gals [Falkenburg and Woodbury] that ever wore grease paint! ... [T]he cast also boasts such well-known funsters as Joan Davis and that zany radio team of Brenda and Cobina."[24]

Beauty aside, Falkenburg and Woodbury apparently knew they were being upstaged by Joan's comedic antics, according to the *Los Angeles Times*, which quoted the lovely ingénues as complaining, "What does it matter how we look or act? That longneck steals the scene."[25]

The *Los Angeles Times* (January 21, 1943) found this "[a] wacky and thoroughly enjoyable comedy ... with its unpredictable antics and funny twists ... with, of course, Miss Davis scoring heavily as the clowning secretary." A bit less impressed, columnist Jimmie Fidler said, "Good for chuckles, but no salutes."[26]

He's My Guy (1943)

Dick Foran (*Van Moore*), Irene Hervey (*Terry Allen*), Joan Davis (*Madge Davis*), Fuzzy Knight (*Sparks*), Don Douglas (*Charles B. Kirk*), Samuel S. Hinds (*Johnson*), Bill Halligan (*Martin Elwood*), Gertrude Niesen, The Diamond Brothers, The Mills Brothers, Louis Da Pron, Lorraine Krueger, The Dorene Sisters (*Themselves*), Beatrice Roberts (*Secretary*), Rex Lease (*Office Manager*), Harry Strang (*Policeman*)
Director: Edward F. Cline. *Associate Producer:* Will Cowan. *Screenplay:* M. Coates Webster, Grant Garett. *Story:* Kenneth Higgins. *Photography:* John Boyle. *Film Editor:* Fred Feitshans, Jr. *Art Director:* John B. Goodman. *Associate:* Ralph M. DeLacy. *Musical Director:* Charles Previn. *Orchestrations:* Milton Rosen. *Sound Director:* Bernard B. Brown. *Technician:* Jess Moulin. *Set Decorator:* R.A. Gausman. *Associate:* A.J. Gilmore. *Assistant Director:* Joseph McDonough. *Dance Director:* Carlos Romeros. *Gowns:* Vera West. Universal; released March 26, 1943. 92 minutes.

Joan is spotlighted in poster art for the reissue of *He's My Guy* (1943).

Husband-and-wife vaudeville team Van and Terry Moore ("Moore and Allen—Songs You Like to Hear") are struggling to popularize their musical act, and disagreeing about how to achieve their career goals. After one disastrous performance in which some unplanned and unintended comedy relief draws a much better response than their music, Van and Terry agree to go their separate ways. Taking a cue from her friend Madge, who gave up show biz for a normal existence, Terry lands a job in a defense plant as secretary to the personnel manager, Mr. Kirk. Seeing that the plant employees are overworked and stressed, Terry concocts the idea of putting on a show to boost morale. Mr. Kirk, who quickly takes a personal interest in his pretty new assistant, agrees to the plan, though he doesn't realize that Van, who takes charge of the show, is Terry's estranged husband. When Van receives a war bond from Terry as a memento, he mistakes it for a signal that she's pregnant. After learning the truth, he grudgingly agrees to stay on and stage the defense plant's variety show, while keeping a wary eye on Terry's amorous boss.

Nearly half the film's running time is taken up with auditions for "Victory Vanities," the show within a show, and its opening night performance. Among the talents supposedly to be found among the employees of the Marsden Aircraft plant are singer Gertrude Niesen, the African American vocal quartet the Mills Brothers, and a now-obscure vaudeville comedy team, the Diamond Brothers, who perform some rough-and-tumble comedy accompanied by Joan.

Third-billed Joan has a strong featured role here as Terry's buddy Madge. Though some sources credit Joan as playing Madge Donovan in *He's My Guy*, the character is addressed onscreen more than once as "Miss Davis." Joan's romantic interest is character actor Fuzzy Knight (1901–1976), best known as a comic sidekick to Western movie and TV heroes Gene Autry, Buster Crabbe, and Johnny Mack Brown. Playing Sparks, a theatrical electrician who's fired after he and Madge accidentally disrupt Moore and Allen's musical act, he's regarded with bemusement by his lady, who says, "He's now giving me the neglect to which I'm accustomed." Knight shares a funny scene with Joan in which she hurriedly sits on him to hide him from an intruder, and then tries to match her conversation and facial expressions to his wildly flailing hands protruding from behind her. As self-deprecating as most 1940s Joan Davis characters, Madge looks herself over in the mirror and asks Terry, "Do you think this style of face will ever come back in?" If that's not sufficient comment on her alleged homeliness, the film's opening scene finds Madge entering a theater where Universal's *The Wolf Man* (1941) is playing; when Madge says "boo" to him, the hairy beast runs in terror.

The idea of Joan Davis going to work with the machinery and assembly lines of a factory is a natural, and it's a pity that the screenwriters don't take more advantage of it. She does have a couple of funny bits involving the punching of a time clock ("I don't know why I always expect gum to come out!") and a very acrobatic routine in which she turns somersaults down a corridor after getting her hand stuck in a hose that someone's reeling in.

Gene de Paul and Don Raye's "He's My Guy" gets quite a workout here, sung twice by Terry, heard behind the opening titles, and used as background music in a couple of other scenes. Joan also performs her version of it during "Victory Vanities," accompanied by a comic monologue.

According to a Universal press release, Joan's growing fame and popularity were acknowledged during production of *He's My Guy*, when she received a questionnaire to complete so that she could be listed in a forthcoming edition of *Who's Who in America*.

The *Hollywood Reporter's He's My Guy* review (March 19, 1943) noted, "Joan Davis is again due to be rediscovered. This grand comedienne slipped into a secondary role in *He's My Guy* ... and promptly swiped the show. The story isn't about her; in fact, she performs an extremely incidental part of it. Yet she is the one the audience comes out talking about, so completely does she wrap up proceedings with her expert clowning." *Daily Variety* (March 19, 1943) concurred, saying Davis "turns in one of her cleverest performances as an ex-hoofer currently working in defense.... Picture is low-budgeted offering, but should rate high at the box office."

The *New York Times'* Edwin Schallert reported in May that Joan would team up with comedian Joe E. Brown in a comedy to be called *Return to Casanova*, but this didn't pan out. Brown's picture was ultimately released in 1944 as *Casanova in Burlesque*, with June Havoc and Dale Evans playing the lead female roles.

Two Senoritas from Chicago (1943)

Joan Davis (*Daisy Baker*), Jinx Falkenburg (*Gloria*), Ann Savage (*Maria*), Leslie Brooks (*Lena Worth*), Ramsay Ames (*Louise Hotchkiss*), Bob Haymes (*Jeff Kenyon*), Emory Parnell (*Rupert Shannon*), Douglas Levitt (*Sam Grohman*), Muni Seroff (*Gilberto Garcia*), Max Willenz (*Armando Silva*), Stanley Brown (*Mike*), Frank Sully (*Bruiser*), Charles C. Wilson (*Chester T. Allgood*), Romaine Callender (*Mr. Miffins*), Johnny Mitchell (*Reporter*), Harrison Greene (*Sam Gribble*), Eddie Laughton (*Western Union Clerk*), Wilbur Mack (*Harry*), Harry Strang (*Electrician*), George McKay (*Gus*), Sam Ash (*Jack*), Ann Loos (*Designer*)

Director: Frank Woodruff. *Producer:* Wallace MacDonald. *Screenplay:* Stanley Rubin, Maurice Tombragel. *Story:* Steven Vas. *Additional Dialogue:* John P. Medbury. *Photography:* L.W. O'Connell. *Art Director:* Lionel Banks. *Associate:* Perry Smith. *Film Editor:* Jerome Thoms. *Set Decorator:* William Kiernan. *Assistant Director:* William O'Connor. *Dance Director:* Nick Castle. *Costumes:* Travilla. *Musical Director:* M.W. Stoloff. Columbia Pictures; released June 10, 1943. 68 minutes.

Aspiring talent agent Daisy Baker has a day job as a refuse collector at Chicago's Hotel Brinkley, where her only two clients, singers Gloria and Maria, are employed as maids. When two Portuguese playwrights staying at the hotel impulsively discard the musical script of their latest work, Daisy retrieves it from the trash and sends it to Broadway producer Rupert Shannon. Shannon likes it and summons Daisy to New York to discuss a deal. Gloria and Maria, assuming Latin-tinged accents to pose as the sisters of the playwright, stipulate that they will sell Mr. Shannon the theatrical rights only if they are cast in the lead female roles. Impressed by their audition, Mr. Shannon agrees and puts the play into rehearsals at the Embassy Theatre.

Daisy and her friends can't believe their good fortune, but their charade quickly begins to fall apart. Two rivals of Gloria and Maria turn up at the theater during rehearsals and blackmail their way into playing featured roles in the show. Even worse, Daisy soon learns that another Broadway producer, Sam Grohman, is rehearsing the exact same play, which he bought legitimately from the actual playwrights. Their attempts to talk Mr. Shannon out of opening his show, or co-producing Grohman's version, fail, and so Daisy, Maria, and Gloria find themselves facing a prison term for fraud. With only 24 hours until opening night, the songwriting talents of Shannon's young assistant Jeff Kenyon offer a last-minute chance to make things right.

The film's plot is, to say the least, far-fetched. However, the role of Daisy provides Joan with some genuinely funny moments, including her losing battle with the garbage chute in the hotel basement, as well as her fainting spell that lands her head-first in a trash can. Another of Davis' patented man-hungry characters, Daisy negotiates an endorsement deal calling for her Broadway-bound clients to have their likenesses on cans of shaving cream, then comments, "Why can't some man squeeze *me* every morning before he shaves?"

Joan is reunited here with Jinx Falkenburg, her co-star in *Two Latins from Manhattan*, in a story much the same as that of their first teaming. Lovely Ann Savage (1921–2008), best known for her iconic noir role in 1945's *Detour*, fills the role assigned to Joan Woodbury in the two previous Davis-Falkenburg films, doing a nice job with the least of the three female lead roles. Fresh-faced Bob Haymes (1923–1989), younger brother of actor-singer Dick Haymes, will work with Joan a second time in *Beautiful But Broke*. This is an early credit for costume designer Travilla (1920–1990), whose career will last into the 1980s with work on TV's *Dallas* and *Knots Landing*.

According to *Variety* (June 23, 1943), "Joan Davis' solid comedy characterization helps sell an otherwise third-rate film about show biz.... [T]he other cast members merely play straight man for Miss Davis, whose burlesque is broad and whose antics get the laughs."

Around the World (1943)

Kay Kyser and His Band, Mischa Auer, Joan Davis, Marcy McGuire (*Themselves*), Wally Brown (*Clipper Pilot*), Alan Carney (*Joe Gimpus*), Philip Ahn (*Foo*), Joan Valerie

(*Countess Olga*), Shirley O'Hara (*Shirley*), Chester Conklin (*Waiter*), Claire Carleton (*Lt. Spencer*), Peter Chong (*Mr. Wong*), Barbara Hale (*Barbara*), Norman Mayes (*Orderly*), Robert Armstrong (*General*), Mary MacLaren (*Nurse*)

   Director-Producer: Allan Dwan. *Original Story and Screenplay:* Ralph Spence. *Special Material:* Carl Herzinger. *Photography:* Russell Metty. *Special Effects:* Vernon L. Walker. *Art Directors:* Albert S. D'Agostino, Al Herman. *Set Decorators:* Darrell Silvera, Claude Carpenter. *Musical Director:* C. Bakaleinikoff. *Musical and Vocal Arrangements:* George Duning. *Music:* Jimmy McHugh. *Lyrics:* Harold Adamson. *Choreographer:* Nick Castle. *Gowns:* Renié. *Recording:* Jean L. Speak. *Rerecording:* James G. Stewart. *Film Editor:* Theron Warth. *Assistant Director:* Harry Scott. RKO Radio Pictures; released November 27, 1943. 80 minutes.

Bandleader Kay Kyser, accompanied by his troupe as well as comedians Mischa Auer and Joan Davis, is on a tour to entertain American troops around the world, with stops including Australia, India, China, and Africa. In Australia, they're joined by young singer Marcy McGuire, who stows away on their trip so as to be reunited with her father in America.

   Around the World doesn't have much of a plot, but there's plenty to enjoy here for fans of Joan's physical comedy. In the course of the film's fairly brief running time, she takes a dive face-first into an orchestra pit, goes flying out of a Jeep as it traverses rough terrain, and mixes it up with trained dogs in a scene that finds her sliding across a stage on her belly. Little wonder that she remarks, after one of her more strenuous routines, "Oh, there must be an easier way to make a living!"

   Although jokes about Joan's looks had long been a staple of her act, they're taken to new heights—or depths—here. Not only does Joan diss herself ("Even ermine looks like vermin on me!"), but so do Mischa Auer (telling her she has a face that would stop clocks), bit players (the soldiers who make a steady retreat when she shows an interest in them), and even a talking bird.

   One bit of dialogue references Joan's old co-stars from *Hold That Ghost.* Doing a "Who's on First?"–type routine with Mc-Guire, who doesn't understand that something is Auer's, not ours, Joan asides, "Boy, how Abbott and Costello could kick this one around!"

   When a vignette about a

That's bandleader Kay Kyser sporting wispy whiskers as Joan's co-star in *Around the World* (1943).

ring containing a secret map shows signs of developing into a genuine subplot, Kyser takes the ring from Auer and tosses it firmly off-screen, saying, "Now, wait a minute. If you think you're going to drop a plot into this clambake, you're screwy!"

Wally Brown (1904–1961), seen here as one of Joan's erstwhile beaux, would later be a regular on radio's *The Joan Davis Show* and play a recurring role during the final season of *I Married Joan*. Pretty Barbara Hale (born 1922), nearly fifteen years before she became the coolly competent Della Street on TV's *Perry Mason*, is very noticeable in a bit role as a WAAC. Poor Philip Ahn (1905–1978) is onscreen for less than a minute, just long enough to be made the butt of a weak joke about egg foo yung.

Released at the height of World War II, *Around the World* is presented as a tribute to America's fighting men and women; Kyser and his troupe perform an upbeat song called "Great News Is on the Way." *Variety* (November 24, 1943) reported, "Story threads are started at a couple of points, but left dangling when the gang moves on, and the result is an episodic, crazy-quilt tour.... Joan Davis goes all-out with her broad comedy display for good reaction."

Beautiful but Broke (1944)

Joan Davis (*Dottie Duncan*), John Hubbard (*Bill Drake*), Jane Frazee (*Sally Richards*), Judy Clark (*Sue Ford*), Bob Haymes (*Jack Foster*), Willie West and McGinty (*Carpenters*), Danny Mummert (*Rollo*), Byron Foulger (*Maxwell McKay*), George McKay (*Station Master*), Ferris Taylor (*Mayor*), Isabel Withers (*Mrs. Grayson*), John Eldredge (*Waldo Main*), Grace Hayle (*Birdie Benson*), John Dilson (*Putnam*), The Bryan Sisters (*Trio*), Emmett Vogan (*Hotel Manager*), Gary Gray (*Boy in Nursery*), Gerald Pierce (*Elevator Boy*), Robert Williams (*Conductor*), Joe King (*Tom Martin*)

    Director: Charles Barton. *Producer:* Irving Briskin. *Screenplay:* Monte Brice. *Story:* Arthur Housman. *Adaptation:* Manny Seff. *Photography:* L.W. O'Connell. *Film Editor:* Richard Fantl. *Art Director:* Lionel Banks. *Associate:* Victor Greene. *Set Decorator:* Louis Diage. *Musical Director:* M.W. Stoloff. Columbia Pictures; released January 28, 1944. 66 minutes.

Los Angeles talent agent Dottie Duncan, profiting from the wartime shortage of male musicians, makes a great deal for an all-girl band to play the opening of a Cleveland nightclub. Having bluffed her way into booking the band by playing the nightclub manager a phonograph record over the telephone, augmented by singing from her friends Sally and Sue, Dottie scrambles to find the additional musicians she needs for the gig. Appointing herself manager of the cobbled-together troupe, Dottie books passage for the ladies on an Eastern-bound train toward their $2,500-a-week engagement.

The twelve band members are forced to make a stopover in a small Nevada town, San Madero. Thanks to Dottie, who lost their train tickets, the girls are stranded, penniless, far short of Ohio. They're befriended by Bill Drake, who works at the local defense plant. Because so many of the town's women are employed at the plant, there's a desperate need for a baby nursery, and Bill asks his new friends to play a benefit to raise money. Dottie and her friends are happy to support the war effort, especially since there are so many eligible young men at the plant. Once the successful fundraiser has been held, and the mix-up over train tickets has been straightened out, it's time for the ladies to bid Nevada goodbye—but they have grown more attached than anyone expected.

In one of the film's funniest set pieces, Dottie and her friends spend the night at what

The ladies of 1944's *Beautiful but Broke* (Jane Frazee, Joan Davis, and Judy Clark) wash dishes to earn their keep.

seems to be a deserted house on the outskirts of San Madero, unaware that it has been designated as a test site for new weaponry. Waking the next morning to find the house shaken to the rafters as missiles are fired at them, Dottie and her pals take refuge in a closet, only to emerge and find the remainder of the house demolished. Dottie steps confidently out into what used to be the main part of the house, only to take an unexpected plunge into thin air. "Watch that first step," she warns the other girls as she picks herself up and brushes herself off.

When an angry Bill confronts Dottie about their unauthorized stay in the house, saying, "Do you know you're liable to a fine of $10,000?" she responds, "Do you know you're liable not to get it?" The comedic climax finds Joan's character, Dottie, vainly seeking some peace and quiet during her lunch hour at the defense plant, but instead finding a band of slaphappy carpenters (played by the vaudeville team of Willie West and McGinty). Even with a defense plant full of eligible men, Dottie doesn't make a love connection. She does, however, attract the attention of a slightly younger fellow, namely a mischievous little boy named Rollo, played by Danny Mummert.

The film was shot during the fall of 1943. Syndicated columnist Virginia Vale reported that Joan had quite the busy schedule in November, working on her NBC radio show simultaneously with shooting *Beautiful but Broke* and *Show Business*. "How she's going to get from NBC to Universal and back to RKO and still have time to eat and sleep is a problem that's causing quite a bit of worry for everybody but Miss Davis."[27]

Said *The Hollywood Reporter* (January 28, 1944), "Topflight comedienne Joan Davis, aided by a couple of good torch singers, a galaxy of pretty girls and a lot of extremely hot jive music, combine to provide considerable entertainment in this small scale filmusical. Miss Davis presents an apparently inexhaustible capacity for evoking laughter in a single-handed job which is unflaggingly strenuous and successful." *Variety* (March 1, 1944) said, "Miss Davis does a workmanlike job with her funny antics and facial gyrations but she can't overcome the familiar fable of the stranded theatrical act."

Show Business (1944)

Eddie Cantor (*Eddie Martin*), George Murphy (*George Doane*), Joan Davis (*Joan Mason*), Nancy Kelly (*Nancy Gay*), Constance Moore (*Constance Ford*), Don Douglas (*Charles Lucas*), Claire Carleton (*Nurse*), Kit Guard (*Heckler*), Margie Stewart (*Mary*), Dick Elliott (*Man with Binoculars*), Robert Homans (*Joe*), Andrew Tombes (*Judge*), Ann Codee (*French Modiste*)

Director: Edwin L. Marin. *Producer:* Eddie Cantor. *Screenplay:* Joseph Quillan, Dorothy Bennett. *Additional Dialogue:* Irving Elinson. *Story:* Bert Granet. *Musical Director:* C. Bakaleinikoff. *Vocal Directors:* Ken Darby, George Duning. *Orchestra Arrangements:* Gene Rose. *Choreographer:* Nick Castle. *Photography:* Robert de Grasse. *Special Effects:* Vernon L. Walker. *Art Directors:* Albert S. D'Agostino, Jack Okey. *Set Decorators:* Darrell Silvera, Al Fields. *Makeup Artist:* Mel Berns. *Montage:* Harold Palmer. *Editor:* Theron Warth. *Gowns:* Edward Stevenson. *Recording:* Jean L. Speak. *Rerecording:* James G. Stewart. *Assistant Director:* Clem Beauchamp. RKO Radio Pictures; released May 10, 1944. 92 minutes.

A few years prior to World War I, handsome, outgoing singer and dancer George Doane is an up-and-coming performer in burlesque. When he sees promising amateur Eddie Martin perform at an amateur night showcase, he coaches the newcomer and casts him in a supporting role in his new show. The two men make the acquaintance of pretty singer Connie Ford and her friend Joan Mason, a not-very-successful duo in vaudeville. When the foursome teams professionally, they enjoy a new level of success and, after a profitable road tour, open to widespread acclaim at the Palace.

George, who has quite a reputation as a playboy, falls in love with Connie, much to the displeasure of his co-star and girlfriend Nancy Gay. Shy, awkward Eddie is unsuccessfully pursued by the lively Joan, who explains to him, "I don't want a man. I want you!" The romances of both couples eventually heat up, and George and Connie are married. When Connie becomes pregnant and takes a hiatus from performing, Nancy schemes to get George into her clutches again. Thanks to Nancy's manipulations, George is late to the hospital when his daughter is born. When the infant doesn't survive, a heartbroken Connie files for divorce.

With the advent of World War I and the breakup of the Doanes, George and Eddie busy themselves entertaining the troops overseas, while Connie accepts a marriage proposal from her friend and agent Charlie Lucas. Eddie and Joan, their own relationship now solid, plot to bring their friends back together by any means necessary.

According to the *New York Times*, Joan was signed for the film in October 1943. She took the place of June Havoc, who gave up the part after being offered a role in a Broadway show.

Show Business provides one of the regrettably rare opportunities to see Joan play a sizable role in an A picture. It also offers the first of two chances for her to team with popular comedian Eddie Cantor, who starred *and* produced the somewhat autobiographical film spanning thirty years. As noted in an RKO press release, "Much of the story is based on Cantor's life with a beginning in burlesque and a trail through vaudeville, tank towns, Broadway and an end in pictures and radio."[28] Among the real-life veterans of the vaudeville era who filmed scenes for *Show Business* were Bert Gordon, Pat Rooney (Mickey's father), and George Jessel; all their footage wound up on the cutting room floor.

Both adept at an active, visual style of comedy, Davis and Cantor work beautifully together, and *Show Business* gives each of them plenty of opportunities to shine. Chock-full of musical standards, notably "It Had to Be You" (the love theme for Connie and George), *Show Business* allots equal time for comedy sketches and blackouts. Particular standouts are Joan's routine as Cleopatra, with Eddie as her Mark Antony, and an operatic sketch featuring the foursome lip-synching none too successfully to a malfunctioning record.

There's also plenty of wry dialogue for Joan to deliver. When we first meet Joan and Connie, discouraged by their difficulty getting ahead in vaudeville, Joan says of their inconsistent bookings, "The last stage we were on was held up by Jesse James." She also garners laughs with her periodic asides to the camera concerning the status of her romance with Eddie. Early on, when he's proving a bit resistant to her charms, she confides to us, "I love that boy! Love him, I tell you." Later, she reiterates, "I love that boy! Well, I do." She even gets the last words in the film's closing moments.

Irene Thirer of the *New York Post* (May 11, 1944) gave *Show Business* a "Good" rating on the paper's "Movie Meter." She termed it "a solid package of musical film fare," and noted that producer-star Cantor "throws plenty of footage the way of Joan Davis, whose rowdy wisecracks roll 'em in the aisles...." The *New York Sun*'s Eileen Creelman (May 11, 1944) found "a subdued Joan Davis much funnier than the usual slapstick one." Columnist Frank Morriss, who also credited Cantor for his generosity toward his talented co-stars, said, "*Show Business* is not a musical spectacle on a big scale, but it's a darn satisfying little movie. I think you'll like it."[29]

Kansas City Kitty (1944)

Joan Davis (*Polly Jasper*), Bob Crosby (*Jimmy*), Jane Frazee (*Eileen Hasbrook*), Erik Rolf (*Dr. Henry Talbot*), Tim Ryan (*Dave Clark*), Robert Emmett Keane (*Joe Lathim*), The Williams Brothers (*Themselves*), Matt Willis (*Oscar Lee*), Les Gotcher (*Ali Ben Ali*), Edward Earle (*Burgess*), Darwood Kaye (*Keller*), Johnny Bond (*Chaps Williker*), Andrew Tombes (*Judge*), William Newell (*Gas Man*), Victor Potel (*Painter*), Vernon Dent, Bud Jamison (*Repo Men*), John Tyrrell (*Clerk*), Forbes Murray (*P.U. Keller, Sr.*), Ray Walker (*Roy Simpson*), Charles C. Wilson (*Mr. Hugo*), Doodles Weaver (*Joe*), Donald Kerr (*Woodie*), Kenneth Brown (*Student*), Alfred Paix (*Headwaiter*), Charles Williams (*George W. Pivet*)

Director: Del Lord. Producer: Ted Richmond. Screenplay: Manny Seff. Additional Dialogue: Monte Brice. Photography: Burnett Guffey. Film Editor: Gene Havlick. Art Directors: Lionel Banks, Carl Anderson. Set Decorator: Joseph Kish. Musical Director:

Marlin Skiles. *Assistant Director:* Rex Bailey. *Song,* "Kansas City Kitty": Walter Donaldson, Edgar Leslie. Columbia Pictures; released August 24, 1944. 71 minutes.

Pianist Polly Jasper takes a job as a song plugger at the fly-by-night music publishing firm of Lathim and Clark, primarily because their office window affords a good view of her inamorata, shy dentist Dr. Henry Talbot. Lathim and Clark is on its last legs until South Dakota cowboy Chaps Williker walks in off the street and offers them a chance to publish his original composition, "Kansas City Kitty."

Polly's bosses write a rubber check to finance publication of the song, sure it will reap big rewards. As it turns out, "Kansas City Kitty" is a phenomenal success, but the company's windfall is threatened when an attorney's letter advises that the song is plagiarized from his client Oscar Lee's 1929 song "Minnesota Minnie." Sensing that the jig is up, Mr. Lathim and Mr. Clark hastily sell the business to Polly and her roommate, nightclub singer Eileen Hasbrook, without mentioning the impending lawsuit. Initially Eileen's fiancé Jimmy thinks the ladies made a smart investment, but when he learns that the lawsuit may cost them the money the young couple saved for furniture in their new home, he and Eileen have a falling-out. Polly resolves to woo and charm goofy Oscar Lee out of suing the company, but their "romantic" dinner goes awry when Dr. Talbot unexpectedly shows up on the same evening. On the witness stand, Polly is going down for the third time when she gets some unexpected help from her man, who's been writing a book called *American Popular Music: Its Origin and Development.*

Songwriter Oscar Lee (Matt Willis) strikes the wrong chord with Polly Jasper (Joan Davis) in *Kansas City Kitty* **(1944).**

A lengthy set-piece here revolves around Polly's attempts to entertain two different dinner guests at the same time, in different rooms, each man unaware of the other's presence. The routine would be adapted some years later for an early episode of *I Married Joan*. Of her preferred man, bashful Dr. Talbot, Polly complains, "The only attention he pays me is dental—anything else is accidental." Later she comments, "Youth must have its fling—wish somebody'd fling a youth at me."

"Radio or screen, she's a scream!" promised ads for this low-budget Columbia release. Joan co-stars for the second time with singer-actress Jane Frazee, following *Beautiful but Broke*. She's also reunited with actor Tim Ryan, who had appeared with her in *Sweetheart of the Fleet*. Joan's handsome leading man Erik Rolf (1911–1957) may be best remembered for his brief role in *Song of the South*. Popular singer Andy Williams (1927–2012), at this time a teenager singing with his siblings as the Williams Brothers, is seen briefly as the boys use Polly's office as a rehearsal hall. The film's director Del Lord was a veteran of numerous comedy shorts featuring the Three Stooges and Charley Chase.

The Hollywood Reporter's review of *Kansas City Kitty* (August 25, 1944) said, "It is a pity that as gifted a comedienne as Joan Davis should have to appear in a vehicle so far short of her capabilities as this one. In it, she knocks herself out, converting sub-mediocre material into laughs. That she succeeds to the remarkable degree she does is a distinct tribute to Miss Davis, not to anyone else connected with the making of this picture."

She Gets Her Man (1945)

Joan Davis (*Jane "Pilky" Pilkington*), William Gargan (*"Breezy" Barton*), Leon Errol (*Officer Mulligan*), Vivian Austin (*Maybelle Clark*), Milburn Stone (*"Tommy Gun" Tucker*), Russell Hicks (*Mayor*), Donald MacBride (*Henry Wright*), Paul Stanton (*Dr. Bleaker*), Cy Kendall (*Police Chief Brodie*), Emmett Vogan (*Hatch*), Eddie Acuff (*Boze*), Virginia Sale (*Phoebe*), Ian Keith (*Oliver McQuestion*), Maurice Cass (*Mr. Pudge*), Chester Clute (*Charlie*), Arthur Loft (*Waldron*), Sidney Miller (*Boy*), Pierre Watkin (*Johnson*), Al Kikume (*Joe*), Leslie Denison (*Barnsdale*), Claire Whitney (*Landlady*), Bob Allen (*Song Specialty*), Olin Howlin (*Hank*), Richard Herbe (*Newsboy*), Syd Saylor (*Waiter*), Vernon Dent (*Doorman*), Howard Mitchell (*Train Announcer*), Hank Bell (*Clem*)

Director: Erle C. Kenton. *Producer:* Warren Wilson. *Screenplay:* Warren Wilson, Clyde Bruckman. *Additional Dialogue:* Ray Singer, Dick Chevillat. *Photography:* Jerome Ash. *Musical Director:* Frank Skinner. *Art Directors:* John B. Goodman, Robert Clatworthy. *Director of Sound:* Bernard B. Brown. *Technician:* Jess Moulin. *Set Decorators:* Russell A. Gausman, Leigh Smith. *Film Editor:* Paul Landres. *Assistant Director:* Seward Webb. *Gowns:* Vera West. Universal; released January 12, 1945. 72 minutes.

The small town of Clayton is being terrorized by a murderer using a blowgun and poisonous darts. A headline in the *Clayton Eagle* blares, "Fiend Threatens Again," reporting that the killer has challenged city fathers to come to the Neptune Club that evening to witness his latest crime. When another citizen dies at the nightclub, right under the noses of local leaders, angry citizens demand the resignation of Police Chief Brodie. Still viewed as a local hero is the late "Ma" Pilkington, described by one resident as "the greatest chief of police Clayton ever had." With public confidence in the police investigation dwindling, Henry Wright, managing editor of the *Clayton Eagle*, sends his ace reporter "Breezy" Barton to Horsetroft,

Nevada, to track down "Ma" Pilkington's daughter Jane and convince her to take charge of the case.

"Pilky" accepts the assignment but proves to be something less than the cunning investigator her mother was. Chief Brodie, resentful at having his authority usurped, assigns her his dimmest officer, hapless Mulligan. With Mulligan's help, "Pilky" proceeds to muff the investigation thoroughly, accusing the mayor of the crime after he's already dead, proposing various solutions that don't hold water, and disrupting a live theater performance of *The Voodoo Prince*, a mystery drama in which "Breezy"'s girlfriend Maybelle is starring. Mulligan loses his job, and Jane is on her way back to Horsetroft in disgrace—until there's a last-minute development in the case.

Before we catch our first glimpse of Joan as "Pilky," about eight minutes into the film, there's an amusing sequence in which we experience second-hand her dubious version of helpfulness, as various denizens of Horsetroft assure "Breezy" that she's "a great gal." That's what one fellow says about her auto repair skills, right before his jalopy falls to pieces, and it's reiterated when she sets out to help someone else (off-screen) move his piano, followed shortly by the sight of the instrument careening madly down the street at top speed.

Perhaps the film's funniest set piece takes place when "Pilky" and Mulligan wreak havoc at the Miracle Theater. On the lam from a bad guy, "Pilky" tries to dim the backstage lights, unaware that her monkeying with the control panel is interrupting the dramatic tropical scene onstage with rain and snow. Moments later, trying to prevent a loaded blowgun from being used in the play's murder scene, "Pilky" dashes onstage in the midst of the performance, improvising a character for herself to fit into the disrupted drama and throwing leading man Barnsdale (whom she calls "Barnsmell") into conniptions. Joan's timing is impeccable in a scene in which "Pilky" searches a theater dressing room, having several near-misses with seeing the skeleton dangling outside the window until she finally meets it face-to-skull and erupts in an ear-splitting shriek. She also makes the most of some good dialogue exchanges, including one in which she tries to bluff her way through a series of daunting questions about her investigation. "That's a very intelligent question," she says cheerfully to one inquisitor. "Has anybody got a stupid one?"

Veteran comedian Leon Errol (1881–1951) works well with Joan; both were adept at a loose-limbed form of physical comedy. Having just wrapped his recurring roles in the "Mexican Spitfire" series a couple of years earlier, Errol is still able to keep up with the demands of slapstick, though he was well into his sixties when he filmed his pratfall-filled scenes for *She Gets Her Man*. William Gargan (1905–1979) provides Joan's love interest here; like Joan, he would be an early convert to television with his *Martin Kane, Private Eye* series.

Character actor Ian Keith (1899–1960) has an amusing cameo as pompous radio star Oliver McQuestion, who's called into to consult on the blowgun murders after "Pilky" proves disappointing. McQuestion, full of bluster and confidence as he arrives in Clayton to cheering crowds, runs shrieking like a pre-teen girl when he witnesses an actual murder. Future movie star Ruth Roman (1922–1999) appears in a bit as a sexy lady in a tight-fitting gown who shows she's got "nothing to hide" when police are searching incoming customers for weapons at the Neptune Club.

Joan is directed here by the comedy veteran Erle C. Kenton (1896–1980), who also worked with Abbott and Costello. Kenton was given one of his first career breaks by the great Mack Sennett, but just as capably helmed horror favorites like *Island of Lost Souls* and *The Ghost of Frankenstein*.

She Gets Her Man bore the same title as another film released ten years earlier, which

1425-57.

In *She Gets Her Man* (1945), Pilky (Joan Davis) nearly turns a tropical melodrama into "Singin' in the Rain" with her backstage meddling. Mulligan (Leon Errol) isn't much help.

starred comedienne ZaSu Pitts, although the similarity didn't really extend beyond the name. The reuse of the title evidently wasn't a problem, since both were Universal Pictures productions. They even shared a common cast member: character actor Emmett Vogan was seen briefly in both versions.

While the recycling of an old title caused no difficulties, it was another matter when some familiar material surfaced in the screenplay of the second *She Gets Her Man*. Through no fault of its star, Davis' film became the subject of a plagiarism suit filed on behalf of comedian Harold Lloyd. The suit alleged that screenwriters Warren Wilson and Clyde Bruckman, previously employed by Lloyd, lifted material from his film *Welcome Danger* (1929), which Bruckman directed. Lloyd's action originally called not only for substantial damages, but also asked that all prints of *She Gets Her Man* be destroyed. The resulting settlement wasn't quite that extreme, but did make Bruckman *persona non grata* in the industry.

An item in the *She Gets Her Man* pressbook described the execution of the scene in which "Pilky"'s incompetent automotive repair causes a car to practically self-destruct. "The car used in the sequence was an ancient Pontiac convertible roadster, purchased by Universal's property department from a Hollywood junk yard. Under the supervision of Willie Cook, head of the studio's special effects department, the fenders, wheels, running boards, hood, radiator, steering wheels and doors were removed, then attached to a system of wires connected to a release mechanism operating the whole thing, and put back. When [the driver] stepped on the starter and slammed the door shut, he released a spring which made the various parts fly in every direction." Since automobiles were scarce in wartime, the publicity piece went on to assure readers that the car was then reassembled and put to work elsewhere on the Universal lot.

The *Washington Post*'s Nelson B. Bell was dubious about murders being treated so lightheartedly, but conceded, "[T]hose who prefer nonsense to sense will find an agreeable outlet for their hilarities in the grotesque sleuthing.... This is primarily due to the energetic and unfailingly good-natured clowning of Joan Davis, one of the more reliable of the cinema's high-voltage comediennes, and the group of experienced buffoons in her immediate support—most notably the veteran Leon Errol.... [T]he lusty talents of these two in combination are sufficiently amusing for all practical rough-and-tumble purposes."[30]

New York critics were less kindly disposed, several of them seeming to feel that a movie of this type had no business playing to urban audiences. In the *Journal-American* (February 9, 1945), Rose Pelswick wrote, "Joan Davis tries hard to get laughs. As a matter of fact, she tries so very hard that one wishes the director and the four scenarists and dialogue writers credited with the item had been a little more helpful and given her more material to work with." Added *PM*'s John T. McManus (February 9, 1945), "On the radio Joan Davis, along with Jack Haley, is a $1,000,000 a year comedy 'package' for Sealtest dairy products. In the movies she is not so prizable a package, being mainly remarkable for a certain case-hardened ability to endure the hard knocks and dramatic privations of micro-trivial comedy." Still, as the *New York Herald-Tribune*'s Otis L. Guernsey, Jr. (February 9, 1945), concluded, "Depending on whether or not you can still take this old-time stage business, the film is either pure amusement or pure nonsense."

George White's Scandals (1945)

Joan Davis (*Joan Mason*), Jack Haley (*Jack Evans*), Phillip Terry (*Tom McGrath*), Martha Holliday (*Jill Martin*), Ethel Smith (*Swing Organist*), Margaret Hamilton (*Clarabelle Evans*), Glenn Tryon (*George White*), Bettejane [Jane] Greer (*Billie Randall*), Audrey Young (*Maxine*), Rose Murphy (*Hilda*), Fritz Feld (*Montescu*), Beverly Wills (*Young Joan*), Gene Krupa and His Band, Larry Wheat (*Pop*), Carmel Myers (*Leslie*), Tommy Noonan (*Joe*), Eddie Dunn (*Gus*), Holmes Herbert (*Lord Asbury*), Dorothy Christy (*Lady Asbury*), Sam Ash (*Nightclub Manager*), Neely Edwards (*Lord Quimby*), Sammy Blum (*Harry*), Mary Currier (*Barbara Willis*), Rosemary La Planche (*Showgirl*), Herbert Evans (*Butler*)

Director: Felix E. Feist. *Executive Producers:* Jack J. Gross, Nat Holt. *Producer:* George White. *Screenplay:* Hugh Wedlock, Jr., Howard Snyder, Parke Levy, Howard Green. *Original Story:* Hugh Wedlock, Jr., Howard Snyder. *Musical Director:* C. Bakaleinikoff. *Musical Associate:* Norman Bennett. *Songs:* Jack Yellen, Sammy Fain. *Ballet*, "Bouquet and Lace": Leigh Harline. *Song*, "Life Is Just a Bowl of Cherries": Lew Brown, Ray Henderson. *Choreographer:* Ernst Matray. *Photography:* Robert de Grasse. *Film Editor:* Joseph Noriega. *Special Effects:* Vernon L. Walker. *Art Directors:* Albert S. D'Agostino, Ralph Berger. *Gowns:* Edward Stevenson. *Musical Settings:* Carroll Clark. *Set Decorators:* Darrell Silvera, Harley Miller. *Recording:* Jean L. Speak. *Editor:* Joseph Noriega. *Assistant Directors:* Fred A. Fleck, Clem Beauchamp. *Re-Recording:* James G.

Stewart. *Montage:* Harold Palmer. RKO-Radio Pictures; released October 10, 1945. 95 minutes.

Comic Joan Mason, a veteran of George White's annual *Scandals* revue, is enjoying a reunion with women who appeared in previous editions. Dropping by to say hello is pretty Jill, whose mother was a *Scandals* showgirl before marrying English nobility and retiring. Mistaken for an auditioning showgirl, Jill plays along with the gag, largely because she takes a liking to producer Tom McGrath, and soon finds herself added to the cast.

Joan and her partner Jack Evans, lead comics in the soon-to-open new edition of the *Scandals*, are in love, but face an obstacle to their romance: Jack's homely, overprotective sister Clarabelle, who reminds him of his promise not to get married until she does. Trying to introduce some romance into Clarabelle's life, Jack hires a $10 per hour gigolo who gamely woos the reluctant spinster, but accidentally reveals his "professional escort" status just as he seems to be making some headway.

When Mr. White sees Jill dance, he arranges to feature her in a ballet number that will be one of the show stoppers of his new production. Opening night is thrown into chaos when Jill's real identity is revealed to her guardian, Lord Quimby, and she disappears. Meanwhile, Joan and Jack are on the outs, his sister having triumphed in her desire to keep them apart. A backstage accident proves to have an unexpected benefit for the couple's stalled romance.

This was the third film to bear the name of impresario George White's popular stage shows. The original *George White's Scandals* (1934), spotlighting Rudy Vallee, Jimmy Durante, and Alice Faye, was followed a year later by *George White's 1935 Scandals*, again with Faye. In that installment, White played himself; in the 1945 version, actor Glenn Tryon plays him onscreen, while the real White takes a producer credit.

Syndicated columnist Jimmie Fidler visited the set and watched in admiration as director Felix E. Feist shepherded the cast through a tricky scene:

> The setting was the dressing room of a great stage star [Davis, who] has such a horror of mice that she scatters traps throughout the room. Take after take failed to jell and the cast developed nervous jitters. Director Felix Feist, aware of the tension, took heroic measures. "I'll show you how to play the scene," he said, and midway through his demonstration, "accidentally" put a finger in one of the traps. There was a roar of laughter—and immediate relaxation. Feist, on his next try, filmed a perfect scene.[31]

This is Joan's best onscreen teaming with her frequent film and radio co-star Jack Haley. Their "Who Killed Vaudeville?" routine, seen near the end, provides multiple opportunities for laughs.

As always, Joan provides peerless physical comedy, whether she's taking a face-forward tumble into a frosted birthday cake, narrowly ducking an axe thrown at her by an angry Clarabelle, or being tossed over the swinging doors of a saloon. Her melodramatic farewell scene with Jack, after she has resigned herself to the end of her romance with Jack, is also quite funny, with Joan mimicking a Tallulah Bankhead–style over-the-top performance.

Joan's young daughter Beverly appears as her mother's character in a flashback sequence, with Joan Mason reminiscing about her debut season with the *Scandals* 26 years earlier. Beverly capable performs a comic routine to the tune of "Life Is Just a Bowl of Cherries," with her voice dubbed by Joan. Thanks perhaps to her proud mom, Beverly receives prominent billing in the opening credits.

Screenwriters Hugh Wedlock, Jr., and Howard Snyder would later contribute scripts

Tom (Phillip Terry) tries to make a love connection for Joan in *George White's Scandals* (1945).

to *I Married Joan.* Playing himself here is the famed bandleader Gene Krupa (1909–1973). Co-star Phillip Terry (1909–1993), a solid actor who never quite reached top stardom, may be best-remembered today as the third husband of Joan Crawford. The talented character actress Margaret Hamilton (1902–1985), immortalized as the Wicked Witch in *The Wizard of Oz* (1939), plays Clarabelle. She makes a fine foil for Joan Davis, and is also quite effective paired with character actor Fritz Feld (1900–1993), cast as the paid escort who plies her with liquor and compliments. Actress Jane Greer (1924–2001), here still billed by her birth name Bettejane, appears as Jill's nasty rival Billie. Seen as one of the *Scandals* showgirls is Miss America 1941 Rosemary La Planche (1923–1979), who went on to play lead roles in two schlocky horror favorites, *Strangler of the Swamp* and *Devil Bat's Daughter*, both released in 1946.

Writing in the *New York World-Telegram* (October 10, 1945), Alton Cook said, "Everything they could think of is packed into *George White's Scandals*, but evidently it was a day when they were not thinking very hard around the RKO studios.... Miss Davis and Mr. Haley punctuate their share of the romantic tasks with joke and slapstick routines, which seem to have been written by gagsters entirely unfamiliar with what was going into other part of the picture. They show great familiarity, however, with comic material heard on the radio and in other pictures lately."

Critic Frank Morriss said Davis and Haley "do the very best with the material at hand, and have some amusing moments. Joan, in particular, is a knockabout comedienne who can sometimes make third-rate material seem first-rate.... But *George White's Scandals* doesn't give her enough to work on."[32] The *Christian Science Monitor* (October 26, 1945) said Joan "has a disarmingly good-natured manner that makes her material seem better than it might in other hands."

She Wrote the Book (1946)

Joan Davis (*Jane Featherstone aka Lulu Winters*), Jack Oakie (*Jerry Marlowe*), Mischa Auer (*Joe aka Count Boris*), Kirby Grant (*Eddie Caldwell*), Jacqueline deWit (*Millicent Van Cleve*), Gloria Stuart (*Phyllis Fowler*), Thurston Hall (*Horace Van Cleve*), John Litel (*Dean Fowler*), Lewis Russell (*George Dixon*), Cora Witherspoon (*Carrothers*), Selmer Jackson (*Fielding*), Frank Dae (*Professor*), Victoria Horne (*Maid*), Dick Elliott (*Fat Man*), Edgar Dearing (*Motorcycle Cop*), Chester Conklin (*Man at Bar*), Gladys Blake (*Miss Donovan*), Ralph Brooks (*Coach*), Gus Glassmire (*Mr. Forbes*), Verna Felton (*Mrs. Kilgour*), Olin Howland (*Baggage Master*), Jimmy Clark (*Willoughby*), Broderick O'Farrell (*Doctor*)

Director: Charles Lamont. *Producer:* Warren Wilson. *Executive Producer:* Joseph Gershenson. *Screenplay:* Oscar Brodney, Warren Wilson. *Photography:* George Robinson. *Film Editor:* Fred R. Feitshans Jr. *Art Directors:* Jack Otterson, Richard H. Riedel. *Set Decorators:* Russell A. Gausman, Ted Offenbecker. *Musical Director:* Edgar Fairchild. *Dialogue Director:* Monty F. Collins. *Sound Director:* Bernard B. Brown. *Makeup Artist:* Jack P. Pierce. *Assistant Director:* William Tummel. Universal Pictures; released May 31, 1946. 80 minutes.

Shy, bookish Jane Featherstone teaches math at Croyden College in a small Midwestern town. Jane's friend Phyllis, under a pseudonym, wrote a sizzling book called *Always Lulu*, which has become a runaway bestseller. Phyllis, wife of a college dean, hopes to use the proceeds to benefit the financially struggling school, but hits a snag when the publishers insist on meeting her in person. Unable to be publicly identified with her book, Phyllis cajoles her friend Jane into making the trip to New York and collecting the royalty check.

Unbeknownst to either of the ladies, the publisher's PR man, Jerry Marlowe, intends to take advantage of Lulu's trip to New York to make her the centerpiece of a publicity campaign for the book. Before she can extricate herself from the awkward situation, Jane sustains a bump on the head that wipes out her memory, both of her own identity as well as that of Eddie Caldwell, the prospective suitor she met on her train trip. Unaware that their "author" never wrote the first book, Jerry and his boss cajole her to write another one quickly, but the

Joan and Jack Oakie strive for elegance in *She Wrote the Book* (1946), billed as an image-changing role for her.

still-befuddled Jane balks. Wanting her back at the typewriter, the sneaky publishers hire a bartender named Joe to impersonate Lulu's lover Count Boris, and siphon off all her money so that she will have to go back to work.

Early publicity for this film gave it the title *Love Takes a Holiday*, and depicted it as an image-changing role for the leading lady. The Associated Press' Gene Handsaker, visiting the set, described Joan's new look: "The tall, collapsible comedienne was wearing a low-necked, low-backed, strapless evening gown.... The tight black gown was, well, admirably filled. A jeweled sunburst gleamed from Joan's bosom, smaller ones from her ears. A spike-feathered black aigret clung to sculptured mountains of blond hair."[33]

According to syndicated columnist Harrison Carroll, Joan sustained an injury during shooting when she "backed into a wall heater in a Universal fitting room and had to be given first aid.... She didn't have to do a single comedy fall in the film and was finishing, for once, without bruise or injury."[34]

Joan's leading man Kirby Grant (1911–1985), perhaps the most attractive, personable man to play opposite her onscreen, appeared in dozens of movies, many of them B films, but is probably best known as the star of TV's *Sky King*. This was the last significant role played by Gloria Stuart (1910–2010) before she took a long hiatus from acting. Mischa Auer is making his third film with Joan, after *Hold That Ghost* and *Around the World*. Verna Felton (1890–1966), a key featured player on Joan's radio show in the mid–1940s, has an uncredited bit as the governor's wife in the climactic party scene.

Variety (May 15, 1946) enthused, "Here's an example of the way a light-budgeted film can be turned into solid entertainment via a good script, consistently good acting and top direction and technical work.... Miss Davis gets a chance to ham up her role with a portrayal for two-thirds of the film of a sedate calculus instructor in a hick Midwestern college. Comedienne plays it well and is appealing in the more serious moments."

If You Knew Susie (1948)

Eddie Cantor (*Sam Parker*), Joan Davis (*Susie Parker*), Allyn Joslyn (*Mike Garrett*), Charles Dingle (*Mr. Whitley*), Phil Brown (*Joe Collins*), Bobby Driscoll (*Junior Parker*), Sheldon Leonard (*Steve Garland*), Joe Sawyer (*Zero Zantini*), Douglas Fowley (*Marty*), Margaret Kerry (*Marjorie Parker*), Dick Humphreys (*Handy Clinton*), Howard Freeman (*Mr. Clinton*), Mabel Paige (*Grandma*), Sig Ruman (*Count Alexis*), Fritz Feld (*Chez Henri*), Isabel Randolph (*Mrs. Clinton*), Gail Davis (*Miss Gail*), Charles Halton (*Pringle*), Jason Robards (*Ogleby*), Harry Harvey (*Sedley*), Claire Carleton (*Vicki Vale*), Joe Devlin (*Silent Cy*), Mary Field (*Telephone Operator*), Earle Hodgins (*Auctioneer*), Addison Richards (*Senator*), Sammy Stein (*Wee Willie*), Norma Drury (*Countess Ligorio*), Marion Martin (*Steve's Date*), Frank Marlowe (*Bennie*), William Newell (*Janitor*), Joe Hinds (*Martin*), Warren Jackson (*Radio Operator*), J. Farrell MacDonald (*Police Sergeant*), Robert Bray (*Reporter*)

Director: Gordon Douglas. *Executive Producer:* Jack J. Gross. *Associate Producer:* Warren Wilson. *Producer:* Eddie Cantor. *Original Screenplay:* Warren Wilson, Oscar Brodney. *Additional Dialogue:* Bud Pearson, Lester A. White. *Musical Score:* Edgar "Cookie" Fairchild. *Photography:* Frank Redman. *Film Editor:* Philip Martin. *Art Directors:* Ralph Berger, Albert S. D'Agostino. *Set Decorators:* James E. Altwies, Darrell Silvera. *Makeup Supervisor:* Gordon Bau. *Sound:* Clem Portman, Jean L. Speak. *Music Supervisor:* C. Bakaleinikoff. *Assistant Director:* Maxwell Henry. *Gowns:* Renié. RKO-Radio Pictures; released February 7, 1948. 90 minutes.

Successful musical-comedy performers Sam and Susie Parker retire from the stage in order to fulfill a longtime dream: They plan to take up residence in the town of Brookford, where Sam intends to convert the old family homestead into an inn. Their Colonial Inn gets off to a disastrous start when their snobbish neighbors boycott it. The Parkers' house and furniture are soon up for auction. As their furniture is being hauled away, the Parkers find a long-hidden wall safe that contains an unexpected treasure: a letter purportedly from George Washington, signed also by Thomas Jefferson and Benjamin Franklin, thanking Sam's ancestor Jonathan Parker for his heroic role in the American Revolution.

In Washington to verify the letter's authenticity, Sam and Susie are befriended by fast-talking newspaper reporter Mike Garrett, who hopes to repay his gambling debts with their help. Thanks to Mike, the Parkers learn that not only is the letter authentic, but it's accompanied by an I.O.U. from the Continental Congress that has been accruing interest for many years. A newspaper headline soon proclaims, "U.S. Owes Parkers 7 Billion Dollars!"

Due to receive such a windfall, the Parkers attract the attention of gangster Steve Garland, who kidnaps them. Although the government finally agrees to pay the debt to the Parkers, Sam and Susie have realized that they were happier when they were an ordinary family, and refuse the money they're owed.

Four years after their successful teaming in *Show Business* (1944), Joan again co-stars with Eddie Cantor, though she's showcased less effectively here. This was Cantor's last major film role; his energetic performance of the title song gets quite a workout here.

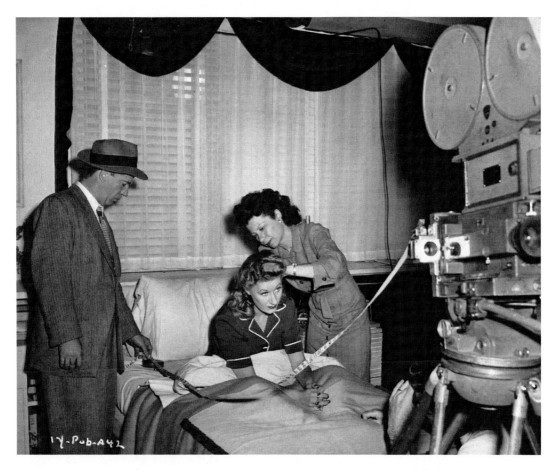

A studio hairdresser gives Joan a touch-up between scenes of *If You Knew Susie* (1948). Looking on is featured player Wallace Scott.

The fine character actor Allyn Joslyn (1901–1981) is strongly featured, taking a break from his many stuffed-shirt roles to play a conniving schemer. Child actor Bobby Driscoll (1937–1968), loaned out from Walt Disney to play the Parkers' young son, gets a prominent billing card in the opening titles that his smallish role doesn't really merit.

Said the *Washington Post*'s Orval Hopkins, in his April 16, 1948, review, "Joan Davis seems to be working hard and it may be that she has a nice sense of comedy. If she has, it's well concealed here." A slightly more positive reaction came from *Variety* (February 4, 1948), whose reviewer wasn't wowed by the picture but predicted that it "should do well enough in the family houses. There's nothing here of really sock value, but the family aura of this comedy ... should help it do business.... Miss Davis mugs as only she knows how—so what more can one ask?"

The Traveling Saleswoman (1950)

Joan Davis (*Mabel King*), Andy Devine (*Waldo*), Adele Jergens (*Lilly*), Joe Sawyer (*Cactus Jack*), Dean Riesner (*Tom*), John Cason (*Fred*), Chief Thundercloud (*Running Deer*), Minerva Urecal (*Mrs. Owen*), Eddy Waller (*Mr. Owen*), Stanley Andrews (*Dr. Stephen Monroe*), Ethan Laidlaw (*Mike Jenkins*), Charles Halton (*Mr. Clumhill*), Robert Cherry (*Simon Owen*), Harry Tyler (*Jasper North*), William Newell (*Bartender*), Harry Hayden (*J.L. King*), Jessie Arnold (*Customer*), Al Bridge (*Mr. Carter*)

Director: Charles F. Reisner. *Producer:* Tony Owen. *Story and Screenplay:* Howard Dimsdale. *Photography:* George E. Diskant. *Art Director:* Carl Anderson. *Film Editor:* Viola Lawrence. *Set Decorator:* George Montgomery. *Gowns:* Jean Louis. *Special Effects:* Fred Wolff. *Assistant Director:* Jack Corrick. *Musical Director:* Mischa Bakaleinikoff. *Songs:* Allan Roberts, Lester Lee. Columbia Pictures; released February 15, 1950. 75 minutes.

In 1889, Mabel King, who helps her father run the family-owned business, King's Independent Soap Company, tries in vain to secure a bank loan to finance their struggling operation. The banker, Mr. Clumhill, likes their product but refuses to extend them further credit unless he can be assured that the company's soap is selling. Since their only salesman, incompetent Waldo, has just returned from a sales trip empty-handed, Mabel decides to take to the road herself. Mabel's father says, "There never was a King who wasn't a born traveling salesman," but disapproves of his daughter taking on such an assignment.

Armed with a book called *Principles of Salesmanship*, Mabel heads west on her first business trip. Waldo, who's sweet on her, decides to come along. While on a sales call in a saloon, Mabel unknowingly picks up a phony bill of sale that can convict Cactus Jack and his men of cattle rustling. They follow her to the next town, Powder Creek, but before arriving she is taken hostage by an Indian tribe led by Chief Running Deer. When Running Deer learns that King Soap helps his itchy scalp, he smokes the peace pipe with Mabel and sets her free. Back in Powder Creek, Waldo takes part in a storekeeper's plot to sell his large stock of King Soap by spreading a rumor that a diamond ring fell into one of the boxes. Mabel hears about the ring and buys up all the soap, which proves unexpectedly useful when the townspeople learn that Chief Running Deer and his three thousand braves are planning an attack on Powder Creek.

Providing a coherent synopsis of *The Traveling Saleswoman* is made more difficult by the fact that the story is really just a series of loosely connected comic set pieces. In the course of the film's seventy-five minutes, Joan clowns her way through an array of slapstick involving mountains of soap suds, factory machines run amok, and shattering glass, while having fun with a variety of Western movie clichés. When her character Mabel, trying to fit in at the saloon, takes a drink too many, there's a funny scene as an inebriated, bleary-eyed Joan can't pick up a nickel off the bar. Another sequence is an extended riff on the age-old jokes about traveling salesmen and farmer's daughters, as Mabel is eyed with suspicion by a couple that allows her to spend the night despite the presence of their gawky son. She wrings laughs from some comic dialogue as well. When stuffy banker Clumhill tells Mabel that his bank "is not in the habit of lending money to people who are broke," she retorts, "Who else needs it?" She's even given an opportunity to sing a comic love song, "He Died with His Boots On," about her troubled love life.

Joan's love interest is played by comic actor Andy Devine (1905–1977), who already had plenty of experience riding the cinematic sagebrush, with the classic *Stagecoach* (1939) among his credits. Lovely Adele Jergens (1917–2002), atypically a brunette here, is featured as saloon singer Lilly, who is involved with Cactus Jack's gang, and tries to cozy up to Waldo in the mistaken belief that he may have the incriminating bill of sale. Jergens would later essay the role of Helen Cavanaugh in *I Married Joan*. Busy character actress Minerva Urecal (1894–1966) is unbilled here for her relatively sizable featured role as Mrs. Owen, whose family takes in Mabel overnight but fears that a traveling saleswoman will be a bad influence on their impressionable son. Urecal supported Joan again in *Harem Girl*, and will turn up on *I Married Joan*.

Joan and her leading man Andy Devine yelp for help in *The Traveling Saleswoman* (1950).

Screenwriter Howard Dimsdale contributed two Old West comedies to movie screens in 1950, having also written *Curtain Call at Cactus Creek*. Charles F. Reisner had previously directed a comedy feature for the Marx Brothers (*The Big Store*) as well as Abbott and Costello (*Lost in a Harem*).

According to the *New York Times*, Joan and producer Tony Owen signed the deal for the film with Columbia executives in late 1948. Though she did not take an on-screen producer credit, she would later describe the experience of taking the reins behind the scenes on *The Traveling Saleswoman* as one of the highlights of her career. Casting presented a few problems. In the spring of 1949, Hedda Hopper reported, "Joan Davis is after Rudy Vallee to co-star with her in *The Traveling Saleswoman*...."[35] After a few more false starts, Devine was ultimately chosen as her leading man. The film was shot during August 1949, for release by Columbia the following January. *Daily Variety* (October 14, 1949) reported that Joan and producer Owen hoped to promote the film with a novelty tune titled "The Traveling Saleswoman," which Joan herself would record, but apparently nothing came of this.

Columnist Darr Smith caught up with the star and unofficial producer at a sneak preview in October 1949, and wrote, "She'd seen this sneak preview in Huntington Park, then talked over how to improve the picture with everybody else connected with it, then she'd gone home and stayed awake all night long worrying about it."[36]

According to *Variety* (December 28, 1949), "*Traveling Saleswoman* is a badly contrived piece of hoke that will need all the help Joan Davis' familiar name can give it.... Miss Davis works hard to put it over but only manages spotty results." The *Oakland Tribune*'s Theresa Loeb (February 22, 1950) concurred: "Despite Miss Davis' frantic efforts to inject a few bona fide laughs into a worse than mediocre film, *The Traveling Saleswoman* emerges as a good [deal] less funny than even the dullest of the comedienne's radio shows."

Love That Brute (1950)

Paul Douglas (*E.L. "Big Ed" Hanley*), Jean Peters (*Ruth Manning*), Cesar Romero (*"Pretty Willie" Wetzchahofsky*), Keenan Wynn (*Bugsy Welch*), Joan Davis (*Mamie Sage*), Arthur Treacher (*Quentin*), Peter Price (*Harry the Kid, Jr.*), Jay C. Flippen (*Biff Sage*), Barry Kelley (*Charlie*), Leon Belasco (*Francois "Frenchy" Ducray*), Clara Blandick (*Landlady*), Charles Lane (*Joe Evans*), Edwin Max (*Lippy Lane*), Sid Tomack (*Baldy*), Dick Wessel (*Fats Leslie*), Jimmy Hawkins (*Freddy Van Zandt*), Robert Gist (*Officer Wilson*), Don Garner (*Page Boy*), Jack Elam (*Gangster*), Bill Chaney (*Butch*), Gail Bonney (*Passenger with Necklace*), Lester Allen (*Al Allen*), Leif Erickson (*Commandant*), Mary Meade (*Babe White*), Mauritz Hugo (*Ship's Purser*), Tiny Timbrell (*Santa Claus*), Nedrick Young (*Rocky*), Arthur O'Connell (*Reporter*), Grayce Hampton (*Dowager*)
Director: Alexander Hall. *Producer:* Fred Kohlmar. *Screenplay:* Karl Tunberg, Darrell Ware, John Lee Mahin. *Photography:* Lloyd Ahern. *Music:* Cyril Mockridge. *Art Directors:* Lyle Wheeler, Richard Irvine. *Set Decorators:* Thomas Little, Stuart Reiss. *Film Editor:* Nick De Maggio. *Wardrobe:* Charles LeMaire. *Costume Designer:* Rene Hubert. *Musical Director:* Lionel Newman. *Orchestration:* Earle Hagen. *Choreographer:* Billy Daniel. *Makeup Artist:* Ben Nye. *Special Photographic Effects:* Fred Sersen. *Sound:* Arthur Kirbach, Harry M. Leonard. 20th Century–Fox; released June 6, 1950. 86 minutes.

In 1928 Chicago, at the height of Prohibition, "Big Ed" Hanley is a powerful gangster who controls all the action on the city's South Side. Successful and confident, Ed is nonetheless restless, searching for meaning in life. When he meets pretty governess Ruth Manning in a city park, he is immediately smitten with her. Taking custody of a neglected kid, Harry, Ed passes the rough-hewn youngster off as his son, and engages Ruth to care for him. Completing the picture at Ed's mansion are his loyal butler, Quentin, and Mamie Sage, who temporarily gives up her work at Ed's nightclub, the Paradise Club, to pose as the housekeeper.

Initially charmed by Ed, and interested in helping Harry, Ruth is horrified when she learns she's working for a gangster. After placing Harry in a strict military school, Ruth refuses to have anything further to do with Ed, leaving his employ to pursue her career as

Mamie (Joan Davis, left) clues in the naïve Ruth (Jean Peters) in *Love That Brute* (1950).

an aspiring singer. Tricked by a *Variety* headline into believing that Ed has sold his interest in the Paradise Club, Ruth accepts an engagement singing there, and is an immediate success. Beautiful Ruth attracts the attention of Ed's chief rival, fellow gangster "Pretty Willie" Wetzchahofsky, who fails to win her heart but informs her that she is still working for Ed. Desperate to win Ruth's affections, Ed devises a scheme to end his involvement in the gang world and begin a new life with her and Harry.

Nearly a decade after her contract with 20th Century–Fox came to an end, Joan returned for a strong featured role in this likable comedy, a remake of that studio's 1941 *Tall, Dark, and Handsome.* Afforded only fifth billing here, Joan nonetheless makes an impression with her role as Mamie, Ed's less-than-elegant friend who takes his rough-and-tumble lifestyle in stride until the moment when it appears that bullets are about to fly. It's Mamie who finally clues Ruth in on the man for whom she's developing romantic feelings: "You're working for a killer, sister. He's got the whole town trembling." Among the many men reported "offed" by Ed and his gang is Mamie's "worm" of a husband Biff, about whom she says, "I heard they dropped him in a cement mixer when they were building the new Wilson Avenue school. Poor Biff, he finally got educated—the hard way." Taking her widowhood in stride, Mamie picks out her next man, "Frenchy" Ducray, only to receive some surprising news that sends her into a dead faint.

Joan inherits the role played by comic actress Charlotte Greenwood in the original Fox film. Although her physical comedy here is limited, there is a hint of the old Joan when she makes a mad dash up the stairs of Ed's lavish mansion.

Production of what ultimately became *Love That Brute* was announced in mid–1949, under the working title *Turned Up Toes.* Cesar Romero (1907–1994), who played the lead role in *Tall, Dark, and Handsome,* was cast as rival gangster "Pretty Willie" in the remake. Joan joined the company by late summer, her first film assignment in more than a year, and was described by columnist Erskine Johnson as "a slick click"[37] in her supporting role as Mamie. Upon completing her work, she went directly into production on *The Traveling Saleswoman,* which would be released earlier than this film.

Leading man Paul Douglas (1907–1959) enjoyed a successful, if brief, Hollywood career, brought to an untimely end by his death of a heart attack at the age of 52. Jean Peters (1926–2000) is remembered today less for her acting career than for her 1957 marriage to billionaire Howard Hughes. While a bit young to be Douglas' love interest, and all too obviously dubbed in her singing, she makes a pleasant female lead, playing her scenes with a bit of ladylike formality that contrasts nicely with Douglas' amiable tough guy persona.

Critic Virginia Mansfield, in the *Cedar Rapids Gazette* (September 9, 1950), called *Love That Brute* "a welcome relief" from the glut of serious gangster films on movie screens: "[It's] a light-hearted, fantastic piece of nonsense with characters that only Hollywood could contrive." Added the *Boston Globe*'s Marjory Adams (June 8, 1950), "Joan Davis as a gangster's widow is most amusing."

The Groom Wore Spurs (1951)

Ginger Rogers (*Abigail Jane "A.J." Furnival*), Jack Carson (*Ben Castle*), Joan Davis (*Alice Dean*), Stanley Ridges (*Harry Kallen*), John Litel (*Uncle George*), James Brown (*Steve Hall*), Victor Sen Yung (*Ignacio*), Mira McKinney (*Mrs. Forbes*), Gordon Nelson (*Ricky*), George Meader (*Bellboy*), Kemp Niver (*Killer*), Robert B. Williams (*Jake*

Harris), John Eldredge (*J.N. Bergen*), Ross Hunter (*Austin Tinsdale*), George Pembroke (*Fred Hillman*), Robert Carson (*Desk Clerk*), Jess Kirkpatrick (*Policeman*)
  Director: Richard Whorf. *Producer:* Howard Welsch. *Screenplay:* Robert Libott, Frank Burt, based on the story "Legal Bride" by Robert Carson. *Photography:* Peverell Marley. *Production Supervisor:* Ben Hersch. *Film Editor:* Otto Ludwig. *Production Designer:* Perry Ferguson. *Music:* Emil Newman, Arthur Lange. *Song,* "No More Wandrin' Around": Emil Newman, Leon Pober. *Set Decorator:* Julia Heron. *Makeup Artist:* Frank Westmore. *Hair Stylist:* Louise Miehle. *Assistant Director:* Tom Andre. *Sound:* Victor Appel, Mac Dalgleish. *Airplane Sequences Director:* Ralph Ceder. *Costumer for Miss Rogers:* Jacie. *Miss Rogers' Hats:* Rex, Inc. *Costumer for Miss Davis:* Eloise Jenssen. Universal-International; released March 14, 1951. 80 minutes.

Female attorney A.J. Furnival's newest client is Western movie actor Ben Castle, who hires her to resolve a $60,000 gambling debt he owes to shady Las Vegas type Harry Kallen. A longtime fan of Ben's movies like *Danger Pass* and *Sheriff of Dead Man's Gulch*, A.J. falls in love with him during their business trip to Vegas, and accepts his impulsive marriage proposal. When Kallen learns of the marriage to A.J., whose late father was Kallen's longtime attorney, he cancels Ben's gambling debt. Believing that Ben married her just as "a planned, cheap trick" to save $60,000, A.J. flies home to Los Angeles, intending to have her marriage annulled the next day.

Encouraged by her roommate Alice, who recognizes that A.J. really does love Ben, the lady lawyer takes up residence in her new spouse's home, determined to set him straight. She's dismayed to realize that most of Ben's movie mystique is phony: He can't ride a horse, his musical numbers are dubbed, and he's hardly the strong, noble type he plays onscreen. Successfully renegotiating her husband's movie contract so that he can pay off his debt, A.J. intends to bow out of his life until she finds herself unexpectedly defending him against a murder charge.

Not a career high point for anyone involved, least of all Joan Davis, *The Groom Wore Spurs* is nonetheless an amiable, enjoyable comedy that goes down easy. The film was adapted from a short story, "Legal Bride," first published in *Collier's* magazine, and during the early stages of production was known as *Illegal Bride*. Billed under the title, at the head of the supporting cast, Joan has only three scenes as Ginger Rogers' friend and confidante. She's once again the single girl with a job (this time in a beauty salon) who's on the prowl for a good man. Advising A.J. not to give up on her marriage so easily, Alice asks, "Don't you know the one way a woman can really get even with a man is by living with him?" She might almost have had more fun playing the role of Ben's lazy, obnoxious housekeeper Mrs. Forbes, who flies into a rage when A.J. coolly discharges her.

This is Joan's only film with popular leading lady Ginger Rogers (1911–1995), apparently not a match made in Heaven off-screen. Hollywood columnist Bob Thomas gossiped during the film's summer 1950 production that Rogers and Davis "were reported feuding on the set ... but both deny it."[38]

Joan does get a brief romantic interlude with a rather unexpected man. An unbilled Ross Hunter (1920–1996), on the verge of transitioning from a forgettable career as an actor to a far more successful stint as a producer, appears as Alice's date, shy bank clerk Austin Tinsdale. She has a couple of nice physical bits with a hairpiece, especially when she mistakes it for a creepy-crawly and beats it with a stick. It's hard to say why Joan needed her own costume designer (*I Love Lucy's* Elois Jenssen) for this role, as she wears only one attractive dress and is otherwise clad in either her work uniform or a nightgown.

Rarely the center of attention in the film itself, Joan (center) gives Jack Carson the once-over in *The Groom Wore Spurs* (1951), as Ginger Rogers looks on.

In the *Cedar Rapids Gazette* (May 23, 1951), critic Nadine Subotnik wrote, "*The Groom Wore Spurs* has three of the screen's top comedians and little else.... [T]he star trio deserves better than this. Considerably better." The *Los Angeles Times'* Philip K. Scheuer (April 14, 1951) concurred, saying of the trio, "I doubt if they have ever been implicated in a weaker effort.... Miss Davis' comedic gifts are almost entirely wasted." Syndicated columnist Walter Winchell (April 2, 1951) called Joan a "skillful femmedian" who "deserves more room to romp" than the film allowed.

Harem Girl (1952)

Joan Davis (*Susie Perkins*), Peggie Castle (*Princess Shareen*), Arthur Blake (*Abdul Nassib*), Paul Marion (*Majeed*), Donald Randolph (*Jamal*), Henry Brandon (*Hassan Ali*), Minerva Urecal (*Aniseh*), Peter Mamakos (*Sarab*), John Dehner (*Khalil*), Peter Brocco (*Ameen*), Rus Conklin (*Sami*), Wilson Millar (*Habib*), Ric Roman (*Hamad*), Nick Thompson (*Ben Ahmed*), Alan Foster (*Suleman*), Robert Tafur (*Captain LeBlanc*), Shepard Menken (*Major Blanchard*), George Khoury (*Ben Gali*), Emil Sitka (*Servant*), William Vedder (*Yusef*), Peter Virgo (*Maleen*), Guy Teague (*Messenger*), Eric Colmar (*Mustapha*)

  Director: Edward Bernds. *Producer:* Wallace MacDonald. *Screenplay:* Edward Bernds, Elwood Ullman. *Story:* Edward Bernds. *Photography:* Lester White. *Art Direc-

tor: Paul Palmentola. *Film Editor:* Richard Fantl. *Set Decorator:* Louis Diage. *Dance Director:* Lee Scott. *Musical Director:* Mischa Bakaleinikoff. Columbia Pictures; released January 21, 1952. 70 minutes.

In search of romance and adventure, Susie Perkins takes a job as traveling companion to beautiful Princess Shareen, who pays a return visit to the "divided, unhappy" Middle Eastern country her late father once ruled. Evil Jamal, who has usurped the throne, plots to get Shareen out of his way by marrying her off to Abdul Nassib, a wealthy potentate from a neighboring land. But Shareen is betrothed to heroic Majeed, leader of the rebel force trying to regain control of her country.

The rebels' best chance for victory over Jamal's regime lies with a hidden arsenal of guns. Susie manages to get hold of the keys to the arsenal, which is secured at an ancient dungeon said to be haunted by a headless ghost. Once the guns have been successfully retrieved by the rebel forces, Susie returns to the palace to stall for time, preventing Shareen's shotgun wedding from taking place. After inciting the ruler's dancing girls to go on strike, demanding collective bargaining, Susie takes part in the final showdown between Jamal's guards and her friends.

Joan played the title role in *Harem Girl* (1952), her final feature film.

"Joan gives those Egyptians conniptions," promised Columbia publicity for *Harem Girl*, with ads proclaiming her "America's Funniest Woman." Joan is directed here by Edward Bernds (1905–2000), who may be best known for his work with the Three Stooges; he also co-authored the screenplay. *Harem Girl* was filmed in the fall of 1951. Once initial photography was complete, *Variety* reported that additional scenes were shot in November 1951, though no reason was specified for the extra shooting days. *Harem Girl* arrived in movie houses in 1952, only a few months before the television premiere of *I Married Joan*.

Lovely Peggie Castle (1927–1973) slaps a black wig on her head to play Shareen, a more sympathetic role than many she would play; she later co-starred in the Western series *Lawman* (ABC, 1958–62). Veteran character actor John Dehner (1915–1992) was often cast as villainous types; he may be most recognizable for his role as Cy Bennett in the later seasons of *The Doris Day Show* (CBS, 1968–73). Arthur Blake, seen as the amorous but cowardly Abdul Nassib, worked occasionally in films, but his main vocation was a nightclub act in which he did impersonations of celebrities such as Katharine Hepburn and Tallulah Bankhead—as well as Joan Davis. Also to be found among the cast is actor and voice artist Shepard Menken (1921–1999), previously one of Joan's supporting players in radio's *Leave It to Joan*.

Though the laughs slow a little in the film's final third, this is an enjoyable romp that provides Joan with one of her better screen roles. She plays the lowbrow hijinks with verve and skill, whether she's taking a dive into a bathtub, squirming in agony as a mouse crawls up the leg of her pantaloons, or blowing a large flower pot wide open with the force of her sneeze. The film's title alludes to her comedic dance routine, posing as an awkward harem girl named Fatima, which comes at about the midway point. This must have been a fun movie for kids to see at a Saturday matinee in 1952, and still evokes laughs today.

Variety (January 16, 1952) termed this "a weak comedy ... familiar slapstick with few genuine audience chuckles." *The Motion Picture Guide* reported, "Not what you'd call a comedy classic, though Davis does a decent job with the poorly written script."

It was initially reported that Joan would follow this picture with another Columbia comedy, to be titled *Jungle Joan*. The *Los Angeles Times'* Edwin Schallert described the picture as "a burlesque on the jungle type of pictures at Columbia, which has made a number of these in the more serious vein."[39] Not longer after this announcement, however, Joan's weekly TV series sold, and nothing further came of *Jungle Joan*, making *Harem Girl* her last theatrical release.

Additional Film Appearances

Nancy Steele Is Missing! (20th Century–Fox, 1937). Joan listed this among her Fox film credits in a 1939 interview with *Screen Book* magazine, but she is nowhere to be found in the final print.

You Can't Have Everything (20th Century–Fox, 1937). According to the Internet Movie Database, Joan appears unbilled here as "Girl in YWCA," but isn't readily apparent in the prints currently in circulation. The *AFI Catalog* describes her appearance in the finished film as "doubtful."

Hollywood Hobbies (1939). Includes footage of a charity baseball game pitting Hollywood leading man against comedians. Joan is seen sitting in the bleachers with Cesar Romero.

Skinny the Moocher (Columbia, 1939). The Internet Movie Database has erroneously credited

Joan with the role of a maid in this Charley Chase comedy short. The unbilled actress playing Hildegarde does resemble Joan slightly, though the voice is quite different.

Screen Snapshots, Series 21, #1 (1941). Ken Murray emcees this installment, in which Joan is one of several 20th Century–Fox players seen briefly.

Hedda Hopper's Hollywood, #6 (1942). Joan is among the stars seen in footage from two wartime fundraisers held at Mary Pickford's home, Pickfair.

Make Mine Laughs (1949). The ad campaign termed this "A new musical revue including highlights from RKO film hits!" In other words, it's a collection of clips tied together with a minimal amount of new material; Joan's one-time radio co-star Gil Lamb served as master of ceremonies. Joan and Jack Haley are seen in a routine from *Show Business*.

Screen Snapshots: Motion Picture Mothers Inc. (1949) This short depicts a square dance held to commemorate the tenth anniversary of the nonprofit organization Motion Picture Mothers, Inc. Pat O'Brien is the host, with guests in attendance including Joan, Fred Mac-Murray, Bud Abbott, and Jane Powell.

The Sound of Laughter (1963). Another clipfest, narrated by Ed Wynn, with Joan seen in excerpts from *Way Up Thar*.

III

RADIOGRAPHY

Radio was one of Joan Davis' primary professional activities in the 1940s, beginning as a featured player and ultimately moving up to star of her own series. Because Joan's movie work relied heavily on sight gags, as well as her mobile and expressive face, many thought radio wouldn't be the right medium for her. By 1945, however, when Joan was debuting her own CBS comedy show, columnist Chuck Hilton wrote, "In the movies Joan Davis was considered a 'good' comedienne. She produced her quota of laughs, but it was in radio that she really became a star. At first her type of humor—based on grimaces, flops, falls and pantomime—was considered too visual by radio producers. But when her chance came she soared."[1] Between 1945 and 1950, Joan would be the top-billed star of three radio comedy series, beginning with *The Joan Davis Show*.

Unfortunately, much of Davis' radio work is inaccessible to the modern audience. Recordings from the 1945-46 season of *The Joan Davis Show* are still readily available from Old Time Radio dealers, but other shows such as *Leave It to Joan* have all but vanished.

The Rudy Vallee Sealtest Show and *The Sealtest Village Store*

Cast: Rudy Vallee, John Barrymore, Joan Davis, Jack Haley, Verna Felton, Shirley Mitchell, Sharon Douglas, Gil Lamb.
Producers: Ed Gardner, Dick Mack, Tom McAvity. *Directors*: Dick Mack, Robert L. Redd. *Writers*: Abe Burrows, Dick Chevillat, Bill Demling, Paul Henning, Jess Oppenheimer, Ray Singer, Bob Weiskopf, Si Wills, Ray Singer, Dick Chevillat, Syd Zelinka. *Music*: Eliot Daniel, Joe Lilley, Dave Street, Eddie Paul and His Orchestra. *Announcer*: John Laing.
Sponsor: National Dairies. Aired Thursdays at 9:30 p.m. on NBC, then Thursdays at 10:00 p.m. (from July 1940), then Thursdays at 9:30 p.m. (from January 1943). First aired March 7, 1940; last aired (as *The Sealtest Village Store*) September 2, 1948. Joan Davis last appeared on the June 28, 1945, broadcast.

Joan Davis was heard occasionally on radio during the early years of her motion picture days; it was a guest appearance on this popular series that truly launched her radio career. Within the space of two years, Joan would go from guest star to series regular and ultimately to top-billed star of this Thursday night variety show, on which she appeared from 1941 to 1945.

Crooner Rudy Vallee (1901–1986) had been a radio fixture since the late 1920s. He began with a local broadcast in New York City but was soon given nationwide exposure with his popular NBC show, *The Fleischmann's Yeast Hour* (later called *The Royal Gelatin Hour*, still for sponsor Standard Brands). His first show finally came to an end in 1939, after a successful ten-year association with Standard Brands. Riffing on his well-known theme song, Vallee told listeners in his final broadcast, "My time has been your time for ten solid years, and it will be yours once more after my time has been my time for a little while."[2]

Vallee returned to the airwaves in the spring of 1940 with a new, streamlined 30-minute variety show on the NBC Blue network. This time sponsorship was provided by the National Dairy Products Corporation, promoting its Sealtest products. Public response to the new show was lukewarm, so format changes were needed. Given the responsibility for sprucing up the show was new producer Ed Gardner (1901–1963); he took on the assignment shortly before achieving his own radio stardom with *Duffy's Tavern*. Among Gardner's ideas was adding matinee idol John Barrymore to the cast. His career on the downslide, Barrymore accepted the offer, and much of the comedy written for Barrymore played off his public image for carousing. In early 1941, Dick Mack replaced Gardner as producer; Mack would prove to be an important figure in Joan's radio career.

Although Vallee had made his reputation as a singer, comedy sketches were pivotal to the show's format. One of the show's writers, Jess Oppenheimer (later the creator-producer of *I Love Lucy*), remembered that Rudy's skills as a comedian were distinctly limited. "He did a decent job with the gag lines we gave him," Oppenheimer wrote, "but he never seemed to grasp what it was that made them funny. At the run-throughs he was always one beat late laughing at each gag."[3]

Over the course of his radio career, Vallee had developed a reputation for nurturing and showcasing new talent. It was, according to some, a reputation he didn't completely earn; even the star himself conceded that he had not been personally responsible for selecting some of the guest performers who appeared with him.

Each episode opened with a rendition of Vallee's longtime theme song, "My Time Is Your Time." The show had a patriotic side during World War II, with listeners frequently urged to buy war bonds and the star delivering uplifting messages about the fight for freedom taking place overseas.

Joan's first guest appearance came in the fall of 1941, at around the time moviegoers were enjoying her featured performance in *Hold That Ghost*. Joan fit in well with the show's anything-goes comic style and was soon invited back. After two well-received guest appearances, the *Atlanta Constitution* reported that Joan had been booked to appear in all of the series' November 1941 broadcasts.

In January 1942, syndicated columnist Virginia Vale reported, "Joan Davis, the film comedienne, has become a permanent member of Rudy Vallee's Thursday evening radio show.... [S]he's headed for the top, if she follows in the footsteps of other Vallee discoveries."[4] By the end of Joan's first season, radio columnist Joe Rathbun said, "After several months of ether horseplay with Rudy, [Joan] is now firmly established as a microphone star of the first magnitude."[5]

With Vallee, Barrymore, and Davis as its mainstays, the highly rated show presented a weekly comedy skit that occupied the bulk of the running time, usually with the help of a guest star. Staff writer Bob Weiskopf remembered Joan as a demanding performer who wasn't easily satisfied. Recalling a time when he accompanied fellow writer Paul Henning to a meeting with Joan, Weiskopf said, "[W]e were there all night to get six jokes. 'Cause she would laugh like hell; two minutes later she'd say, 'I think we can do better than that.' Drove me crazy."[6]

Though Barrymore's participation in the show boosted its popularity, the actor's failing health was an ongoing concern during the 1941-42 season. On some broadcasts, when he was unable to appear, brother Lionel took his place. On May 29, 1942, the veteran star died hours after taking part in a radio show rehearsal. According to *Daily Variety* (June 4, 1942), Barrymore would be given a tribute by the Vallee company on that night's broadcast: "Rudy Vallee will pay the last respects just before close of the program."

In early June, reporters were speculating as to who might replace Barrymore. Groucho Marx, who'd worked well with the group as a guest star, was said to be among the leading candidates. Ultimately, Vallee and his producer stated that rotating guest stars would fill the late Barrymore's slot, with Joan to continue as an important part of the show. Without Barrymore, Joan received billing second to Vallee. That summer, columnists reported, "Option on Joan Davis was picked up by her Rudy Vallee sponsors several weeks in advance and the program renewal carries her well into the fall."[7] Joan, however, received a month or so off to vacation, and she was absent from several mid-summer broadcasts. She relaxed in St. Paul with her family before heading back to California to start a new radio season.

With Vallee and Joan still the series' stars, the producer and writers began to build up a supporting cast for the 1942-43 season to fill the gap left by the loss of Barrymore. The new format focused on Rudy's activities as proprietor of a village store, with Joan to be found among his sales staff.

A new regular that season was character actress Verna Felton (1890–1966), beginning what would prove to be a five-year run supporting Joan. Initially, she was cast as Mrs. Two-Ton Greenbacker, but by mid-season settled into playing the coy, romantically inclined matron Blossom Blimp. Like many popular supporting players, Felton juggled duties on several shows simultaneously; she was also heard with some regularity on *The Jack Benny Program* (as Dennis Day's caustic mother) and other series. One columnist described the energetic Miss Felton as "one of the few supporting performers whose work each week draws a burst of hand-clapping from the audience without any cueing from the announcer."[8]

Comedian Gil Lamb was a regular on the show when the season began. He played Homer Clinker, who was romantically interested in Joan's character, and also did a warm-up routine for each week's studio audience. He left the show in early 1943 to complete a film assignment and never returned. Shirley Mitchell essayed the role of the "village belle," Shirley Anne.

Columnist Charles G. Sampas remarked, "A really amazing comeback has been made by Rudy Vallee, to our way of thinking. The Connecticut Yankee band is no more, but Rudy heads one of the funniest radio shows aired today. Aided and abetted by Joan Davis, who was never *that* funny in pictures!"[9] Added Dorothy Kilgallen, "Have you heard Joan Davis on the Rudy Vallee show, and isn't she funny?"[10]

Just as the show seemed to be settling into a winning pattern without Barrymore, Vallee enlisted in the Coast Guard. For a time, he would juggle his military responsibilities with his radio stardom.

Attending a rehearsal of *The Rudy Vallee Show* at NBC's West Coast studio in late 1942, columnist May Mann observed from the sponsor's booth as enlisted men in uniform rehearsed a musical number with Vallee, now chief petty officer and bandmaster in the Coast Guard. Also on hand were Joan and her daughter Beverly. "Penelope, the kid sister of Joan Davis on the air, is none other than her daughter Beverly Wills, nine years of age, and a clever youngster full of Joan's inimitable mimic antics." After the rehearsal was completed to the sponsor's satisfaction, "Joan calls in the producer of the show and the script men. They go into a huddle in her dressing room to revamp some of their lines in the script."[11]

In June 1943 came word that Vallee was taking a leave of absence from the show in order to devote more time to his Coast Guard activities, with Joan to step in as lead comic. "Joan Davis is to run the Rudy Vallee show for the duration," reported the Associated Press. "For the time being she will have the help of Jack Haley, who has been guest of the program several times."[12] As it turned out, Haley would be a series regular for the next few years, even after Joan herself left the cast. Joan would work without a break through the summer of 1943, as Vallee's show transitioned into *The Sealtest Village Store*.

Joan began the 1943-44 radio season as the top-billed star of *The Sealtest Village Store*, barely two years after her first guest appearance. Taking up the vocal slack in Vallee's absence was singer Dave Street (1917–1971). Although network executives and sponsors had been unsure how the show would fare without Vallee, they needn't have worried. By August 1943, Hedda Hopper reported in her widely syndicated column that "the show's rating is rising like the temperature."[13] *Variety* (August 4, 1943), looking in on the show a few weeks after Vallee's departure, reported, "Sealtest's Thursday evening contribution on NBC continues to be one of the merriest events of the week.... As ever, Joan Davis functions as a dynamic hub for the output of high and low tomfoolery.... [Jack Haley] is at his best when he refrains from trying too hard and when he synchronizes the tempo of his lines with those of Miss Davis."

Variety (January 24, 1945) gave Joan credit for giving female stars new opportunities in radio. "Up until very recently Kate Smith was the lone femme headlining a nighttime commercial series and for a long time it was thought she was the only gal strong enough to headline a top network production. However, after Rudy Vallee exited the Sealtest show, Joan Davis, teamed with Jack Haley, took over and in a remarkably short time, all things considered, Hooper survey figures disclosed that she was a definite click." Davis' success, the trade paper noted, opened the door for shows starring Dinah Shore, Judy Canova, Arlene Francis, Charlotte Greenwood, and others. In the summer of 1943 Joan was reported to have the #2 rated show on the air.

Now officially a star on radio, Joan wielded considerable power behind the scenes of *The Sealtest Village Store*, and didn't hesitate to exercise it for what she considered the good of the show. *Daily Variety* (May 18, 1944) reported that tensions between Joan and her producer, Tom McAvity, "threaten a crisis and bring James McFadden, radio head of McKee & Albright agency, running from other end of the country.... McAvity had offered to resign rather than impair success of the program, which now rates with the leaders." In late spring, *Variety* reported that McAvity would be leaving the show "after a series of tiffs with Miss Davis."[14] Robert Redd was signed to take his place.

A promotional gimmick during the spring of 1944 was the publication of Joan's "autobiography," *The Life and Loves of Joan Davis*. The booklet was comprised primarily of comedy routines used on the radio show. In March 1944, Joan and her troupe traveled by train to New York, where they would broadcast four shows, while also touring camps and hospitals in the area.

Trade papers reported that Joan was tinkering with her show's format as the season wound down, trying out a situation comedy approach. According to *Variety*, "Getting those yaks and boffs every week is too tough; look how well Fibber & Molly, the Aldrich Family and others get along when they have a good situation wherein to present their comedy."[15] They added in a later issue, "Joke shows on the air next fall will be fewer and fewer and the 'story line' will be the thing."[16] Some were surprised to see *The Sealtest Village Store* jump aboard the bandwagon, as its top ratings might have suggested that the show wasn't broken and shouldn't be fixed.

Rather than working through the summer, as Joan usually did, she took a vacation as the 1943-44 season wound down. "Joan's first vacation in four years was spent obeying doctor's orders to lie in the sun, munch on vitamins and build up her strength for a heavy fall radio and picture schedule," reported one journalist.[17]

She soon plunged back into work, preparing for the 1944-45 season of *The Sealtest Village Store*. *Variety* (September 6, 1944) found Joan's season opener unimpressive despite a stellar guest star lineup that offered listeners Vallee, Eddie Cantor, Johnny Mercer, Kenny Baker, and Arthur Lake. Describing missed cues, weak scripting, and a failure to properly showcase the big names present, the reviewer concluded, "Future shows can't help but improve."

The show continued to edge closer to a situation comedy format as the 1944-45 season progressed, lessening the reliance on guest stars. One article reported that Davis and her writers planned a new storyline wrinkle for the fall season. "Everybody knows Joan Davis as the top-ranking comedienne who built her reputation as a wallflower specializing in making unsuccessful passes at men.... But now her fans want her to have a man. So the famous 'fall' girl, who last spring was voted by 600 radio editors as the top-ranking female comic on the air, may return to her listeners a seductive siren. Penny Cartwright had better be on her guard!"[18]

Joan and co-star Jack Haley enjoy dinner at the Brown Derby in the spring of 1945, just prior to a broadcast of *The Sealtest Village Store*. By this time, it was already known in the industry that she would be leaving the show.

However, it soon became evident that even bigger changes were in the offing. As early as December 1944, *Variety* radio columnist Jack Hellman told his readers, "Don't be surprised if Joan Davis appears under new commercial auspices next season. It'll be her own package, at more coin than Sealtest will want to pay."[19]

By early 1945, Joan was near the peak of her radio popularity, with the highest ratings of any comedienne. Her contract with National Dairies was nearing an end, and her representatives let it be known that she would entertain offers from other sponsors. It was soon clear that this would be Joan's last season on *The Sealtest Village Store*. She was angered when told she could not say goodbye to her longtime listeners in her final broadcast on June 28, 1945, as departing radio stars were customarily allowed to do. Not only did her sponsors not wish to give a free plug for her new show, but there was apparently bad feeling over her choice to accept a contract with a rival. Joan protested the restriction, unsuccessfully, as *Variety* reported: "There was but one alternative, that of ad libbing it [during the live broadcast], but Miss Davis chose to abide by the official dictum."[20] Jack Haley would take over the lead spot on *The Sealtest Village Store* for the coming season. Comedienne Jean Carroll took Joan's place for the summer 1945 broadcasts, with Eve Arden taking over that fall for the 1945-46 season.

Although Joan left the show in mid–1945, *The Sealtest Village Store* did not close up shop, continuing its regular run through the summer of 1948. Meanwhile, Rudy Vallee, his wartime service completed, returned to the airwaves as well, though not for the same sponsor. But his subsequent shows never reclaimed the popularity he'd previously enjoyed.

Episode Guide

These listings for *The Rudy Vallee Sealtest Show* and *The Sealtest Village Store* include only those episodes in which Joan Davis appeared. She was a frequent guest star during the later months of 1941, signed on as a regular in 1942, and last appeared on the broadcast of June 28, 1945.

The symbol † at the end of a listing indicates that the synopsis is based on an extant recording of the original broadcast. Copies of many of these episodes are available from one or more Old Time Radio vendors.

Synopses for other episodes were taken from newspaper program logs or advertisements taken out in those newspapers by the sponsor or local radio station. Whenever possible, they were confirmed via multiple printed sources. The following abbreviations are used to indicate the publication in which direct quotes appeared:

AC	*The Atlanta Constitution*, Atlanta, Georgia
BDG	*The Berkeley Daily Gazette*, Berkeley, California
BDS	*The Beatrice Daily Sun*, Beatrice, Nebraska
CG	*The Charleston Gazette*, Charleston, West Virginia
ChT	*The Chester Times*, Chester, Pennsylvania
CT	*The Capitol Times*, Madison, Wisconsin
KT	*The Kingsport Times*, Kingsport, Tennessee
LBI	*The Long Beach Independent*, Long Beach, California
LN	*The Lima News*, Lima, Ohio
SS	*The Sitka Sentinel*, Sitka, Alaska
ST	*The Salisbury Times*, Salisbury, Maryland
WSJ	*The Wisconsin State Journal*, Madison, Wisconsin
ZS	*The Zanesville Signal*, Zanesville, Ohio

Unless otherwise noted, the date of the issue in which the information appeared was the same as the program's air date.

The notation "No synopsis available" indicates that newspaper radio logs confirmed that the show aired on that date, but did not yield any information about content or guest stars.

....

August 28, 1941. "The Night Club Mystery." Guests, Joan Davis, Nat Pendleton. "John Barrymore is cast in the role of night club owner with Miss Davis as an entertainer. Rudy will be head of the detective squad assigned to the mystery and Pendleton will play the part of assistant sleuth." *CG*

October 9, 1941. Guests, Joan Davis and Mischa Auer. "Miss Davis and Auer will bounce through a comedy sketch titled 'Rudy's Barber Shop,' in which Rudy turns up as proprietor of the hair-cutting emporium, Barrymore as an irascible customer, Auer as chief shear man, and Miss Davis as a quip-happy manicurist." *AC*

November 6, 1941. Joan, in the first of several consecutive appearances, plays in a sketch called "The Haunted House," spoofing her movie role in *Hold That Ghost*. Also appearing is Oscar-winning actress Hattie McDaniel (*Gone with the Wind*).

November 13, 1941. "Hotel Heigh Ho." Guest, Edward Everett Horton. "Rudy will be heard in the role of the proprietor of the hostelry, Horton as the manager, Joan as the switchboard operator and Barrymore as the wealthy guest of the hotel." *CG*

November 20, 1941. Guest, Marjorie Main. Main plays Joan's mother, "a wealthy diamond in the rough. Joan is back from finishing school, where she didn't quite get finished. Rudy ... owns a yacht and stuff and Joan wants to marry him.... John Barrymore steps in and counsels Rudy against taking such a step, speaking from wide and varied experience." *CT*

November 27, 1941. "Tournament of Noses." Guests, Jimmy Durante, Lionel Barrymore. "The Rudy Vallee program will stage its own Nose Bowl game as its contribution to the ending of the football season...." *CT*

December 4, 1941. "Tin Pan Vallee." "Ginny Simms and Joan Davis make love to Rudy while Lionel Barrymore grumbles." *WSJ*

December 11, 1941. "Football Game." Guests, Jack Oakie, Lionel Barrymore (substituting for his "ailing" brother). "Barrymore is cast as the devilish dean of Barrymore Tech, while Vallee and Oakie are the terrors of the Tech football team, which can't manage to schedule games. Tech finally schedules a game, only to discover too late that it is a girls' [team] captained by Joan Davis." *CG*

December 18, 1941. "Reunion at Max Oliver's." Guest, Edna May Oliver. John Barrymore returns to the broadcast after an absence of several weeks.

December 25, 1941. "Lionel Barrymore, distinguished actor whose annual recital of Charles Dickens' *Christmas Carol* has become a radio tradition, will be heard in his famous recital...." *CG*

January 1, 1942. "New Year's Party at Rudy Vallee's." Guest, Gene Lockhart. "The erstwhile screen bad man will be accompanied [to the party by] Joan Davis, rubbery-legged screen comedienne." *CG*

January 8, 1942. Guest, Groucho Marx. John Barrymore plays the curator of a museum, with Rudy as his assistant. "Joan Davis ... is the museum's handy-woman—handy enough, at least, for this wax works, which is run by its pieces. Marx arrives to deliver a lecture. What follows deserves a setting in a different kind of institution." Groucho sings a novelty song, "Captain G. Spaulding Marx." *AC*

January 15, 1942. Guest Hedda Hopper "joins Rudy, John Barrymore, and Joan Davis in a comedy sketch set in a newspaper office." *CT*

January 22, 1942. Guest, Edna May Oliver.

January 29, 1942. Guests, Diana Barrymore, Hattie McDaniel.

February 5, 1942. Guest, Kay Kyser. "Kyser and Vallee, as rival bandleaders, find themselves booked for the same night in the Town Hall of a hamlet which is run by the local politic [*sic*] John Barrymore. Through his press agent, Joan Davis, Rudy tries to edge Kyser out of the picture...." *CT*

February 12, 1942. "Jane Withers joins John Barrymore and Joan Davis while the Navy pins Rudy...." *WSJ*

February 19, 1942. "The Big Hold-Up." Guest, Humphrey Bogart. "Bogart keeps Big Money Barrymore, paying teller Vallee and assistant Joan Davis with their backs to the wall as he proceeds to rifle the company's safe. He suffers the greatest let-down of his career, however, when he finds that the only content of the safe is a solitary hair. But leave it to the trio of obliging victims to bolster the bad man's pride...." *CT*

February 26, 1942. Guest, Robert Benchley. "As the absent-minded head of an advertising office ... Bob will be featured in a comedy sketch which burlesques the two years of experience he once had in the advertising department of a publishing company. Vallee appears as the go-getting radio contact man, hot on the trail of a big sponsor, John Barrymore himself. Joan Davis, as Benchley's secretary, commits her usual quota of carefree faux-pas." *CT*, February 22, 1942

March 5, 1942. "The Great Profile, long starred with Rudy Vallee on their notable Thursday evening program, his brother, Lionel, and his daughter, Diana, will be on the program together...." *LN*

March 12, 1942. Guest, Akim Tamiroff. "The imaginary town of Hicksville will be the scene of a hot political campaign...." *LN*

March 19, 1942. Guest, Charles Laughton. "Besides delivering his famous recitation of Lincoln's Gettysburg Address, Laughton will appear in a comedy sketch as a bungling butler in the employ of Rudy Vallee. John Barrymore, Rudy's crusty 'boss,' is invited to dinner in the hope that he may give Rudy a raise. Jeeves, however, turns the drawing room into a madhouse by indulging in every 'don't' in the Butler's Handbook. Joan Davis, portraying Rudy's 'wife,' adds to the general confusion." *LN*

March 26, 1942. Guest, The Great Gildersleeve (Harold Peary). "In a skit featuring Cesare [*sic*] Romero as a night-club proprietor, Rudy Vallee as the hick orchestra leader, Joan Davis as his country sweetheart and John Barrymore as the farmer girl's papa, Gildy will be featured as a night club patron." *LN*

April 2, 1942. "Return Engagement." Guest, Constance Bennett. Rudy plots to give Joan an entrée into high society by presenting her with "the biggest engagement ring in the world" at a lavish party. A phony count and countess (Barrymore and Bennett), "frayed members of the light-fingered gentry[,] plan to take over the 'ice' for themselves. Once at the reception, Countess Connie sets out to tutor Joan in the ways of society, while Count John goes about the delicate business of snatching the ring." *LN*

April 9, 1942. Guests, Gloria Warren, Hattie McDaniel, Nicodemus [Nick Stewart].

April 16, 1942. "Edna May Oliver, comedienne and grand old lady of the screen, tosses a swank party for her friends and hires Rudy to croon and John to act. Just what Joan Davis will be called on to do is anyone's guess." *LN*

April 23, 1942. Guest, Bert Lahr.

April 30, 1942. Guest, Reginald Gardiner. Vallee and Barrymore play prospective investors in a sanitarium operated by Gardiner. "'In the pink' when they arrive, the two would-be investors acquire a definite tinge of green around the gills before the health fanatic gets through with them. The only saving grace is the presence of Joan Davis, nurse of the screwy institution, with whom Vallee falls in love." *CT*

May 7, 1942. Guest, Gracie Fields.

May 14, 1942. "The Big Gusher." A lucrative oil well, "according to the terms of a departed relative's will, belongs to comedienne Joan Davis, but as long as John Barrymore remains her guardian, he is in full control. John uses his power to keep fortune-hunter Rudy Vallee away from Joan and her oil." *CT*

May 21, 1942. Guest, Stuart Erwin. Joan and Rudy play employees of the John Barrymore Investment Company, who have been engaged for 12 years. The unexpected arrival of Joan's long-ago boyfriend, "barnyard Romeo" Stu Erwin, sets up a rivalry between the two suitors. This was Barrymore's final broadcast prior to his death on May 29, 1942.†

May 28, 1942. Guest, Bert Gordon ("The Mad Russian"). A circus sketch spotlights Joan as "star performer of the saw-dust ring ... the amazing trapeze artist." *CT*

June 4, 1942. "How Green Was Vallee?" Guest, Sara Allgood. The Irish actress who received a Best Supporting Actress Oscar nomination for *How Green Was My Valley* appears in a sketch spoofing the picture. "Rudy and Joan wander far afield from the paths trod by the simple folk of the Richard Llewellyn classic, and 'Mother Allgood' finds herself attending the opening of a Hollywood nitery with the young couple." *CT*

June 11, 1942. Guests, Joe E. Brown, Constance Bennett.

June 18, 1942. Guests, Billie Burke, Oscar Levant.

June 25, 1942. "The Lodge on the Lake." Guest, Groucho Marx. Vallee and his friends are at summer camp, with "Joan Davis still man-hunting and Groucho a not unwilling prey." *CT*

July 9, 1942. "Groucho Marx will continue his role as matchmaker in [*sic*] behalf of Joan Davis, and Rudy Vallee will continue to dodge the issue.... To divert his companion's attention from thoughts of matrimony, Rudy decides to toss a barbecue party for his Camp Castaway cohorts...." *CT*

July 30, 1942. "Constance Bennett and Bill 'Old Timer' Thompson will make return guest appearances and join Joan Davis, who has been AWOL for several weeks." *WSJ*

August 6, 1942. "Sparks and laughs can be expected to fly when lowbrow Joan Davis ... meets up with Mrs. Uppington, the society dowager who has been trying (in vain) for years to keep Fibber McGee and Molly in their place." Actor Alan Reed and singer Gloria Warren also appear. *CT*

August 13, 1942. It's the grand opening of Rudy Vallee's village store, with his friend Reginald Gardiner in attendance and Joan as the store's "dainty dietician." The character of Shirley Anne, the village belle, is introduced, and Verna Felton is heard as a matronly customer who tangles with Joan.†

August 20, 1942. Guest Billie Burke "decides to interior decorate the Vallee emporium. Joan, who is busy clerking in the store, is one of the fixtures that doesn't meet with Miss Burke's approval." *LN*

August 27, 1942. Rudy, "in financial trouble at his village store, visits a hard-hearted banker." *WSJ*

September 3, 1942. Guest, Jack Haley.

September 10, 1942. Guest, Jack Haley.

September 17, 1942. Guest, Billie Burke.

September 24, 1942. Guest, Ned Sparks.

October 1, 1942. Guest, Ransom Sherman.

October 8, 1942. Guest Bert Lahr finds himself "badgered by the overly romantic Joan Davis. Nor does Joan have a free rein in following her romantic designs, for her corn-fed swain, one Homer Clinker (Gil Lamb), will still be there to adore her distantly." *ZS*, October 4, 1942

October 15, 1942. Guest, Ransom Sherman.

October 22, 1942. Guest, Arthur Treacher.

October 29, 1942. "The Life of the Party." Guest, Joe E. Brown. "The scene is a Hallowe'en fiesta that Vallee, Joan Davis, Homer Clinker, and Shirley Anne are staging at the village store, and Brown is called in to make the arrangements. Joe E. arranges everything in his usual manner—including a house especially haunted for the occasion!" *ZS*, October 25, 1942

November 5, 1942. Guest, Akim Tamiroff.

November 12, 1942. "There's [to] be considerable monkey business in the air when Ransom Sherman, the glib, gay, and goofy appears again.... He'll be there to answer court charges of selling Rudy's country store customers dubiously made stuff bearing the Sherman label. Vallee will hale Ransom into court and the latter will do his utmost to fix the witnesses, said witnesses [including] the uninhibited Joan Davis...." *WSJ*

November 19, 1942. Guest, Lucille Ball. "Miss Ball will take a job in Rudy's country store to gain 'practical experience' for a movie role. But Joan Davis, who chases Rudy, and Shirley Mitchell, whom Rudy chases, will have plenty of reasons to doubt her motives, and the green-eyed monster of jealousy will rear his head." *WSJ*

November 26, 1942. No synopsis available.

December 3, 1942. Guest, Bert Lahr.

December 10, 1942. No synopsis available.

December 17, 1942. Guest, Alan Mowbray.

December 24, 1942. Guest, Lionel Barrymore. "Radio's Yuletide tradition, Lionel Barrymore's portrayal of Scrooge, will be heard...." *KT*, December 20, 1942

December 31, 1942. Guest, Elsie Janis.

January 7, 1943. "Portraying the role of a detective solving a major crime in Rudy's village store, Joe E. Brown, canyon mouth comedian, will pay a return visit to Vallee's program...." *LBI*

January 14, 1943. Guest, Sydney Greenstreet.

January 21, 1943. Guest, Bert Lahr.

January 28, 1943. No synopsis available.

February 4, 1943. "Roy Rogers, handsome cowboy star, will attempt to corral the feminine hearts on the Rudy Vallee program...." *LN*

February 11, 1943. Guest, William Bendix.

February 18, 1943. "Rudy Vallee's village store will be all agog ... when Reginald Lovelight, alleged author of *Moon Mad*, makes a guest appearance to autograph first edition copies of his romantic novel." *LN*

February 25, 1943. "Hedda Hopper, noted for her daffy hats and movieland column, will drop in.... Looking for glamour girls, Hedda will interview Joan Davis, Blossom Blimp Felton and Shirley Mitchell." *LBI*

March 4, 1943. Guest, Bert Lahr.

March 11, 1943. "Charlie Butterworth turns out to be the matrimonial bureau's answer to Joan Davis' prayer...." *WSJ*

March 18, 1943. Guest, Charles Butterworth. "Joan, it seems, has been corresponding with Butterworth through a matrimonial bureau. And the comedian was smart enough to send another man's picture. However, he's not smart enough to avoid meeting his 'dream girl' and the meeting ought to prove somewhat of a shock to both parties." *LBI*

March 25, 1943. Guest, Betty Hutton. "Rudy Vallee and his cast of daffy bumpkins, Joan Davis in particular, will be in for some glamour treatment as well as the famous Hutton brand of gymnastics...." *KT*, March 21, 1943

April 1, 1943. Guest, Basil Rathbone. "The screen star visits Vallee's village and Joan Davis gets the idea that she, too, should be a screen star. So the wacky dame writes a screenplay and casts herself as Hedy Lamarr, Rudy as William Powell, Blossom Blimp Felton as Jane Darwell and Shirley Mitchell as Marjorie Main. She allows Rathbone to play himself." *LN*

April 8, 1943. Guest, Adolphe Menjou.

April 15, 1943. Guest, William Bendix. Trying to demonstrate that he is "a mild-mannered, soft-spoken gentleman of the best drawing rooms of society, [Bendix] makes his second guest visit ... to return to his home town, which turns out to be Vallee's village." *LN*

April 22, 1943. Guest, Bert Lahr. Noted Walter Winchell in his syndicated column (April 27, 1943), "Joan Davis' screwball antics on the Vallee menu were ably abetted by Bert Lahr and Rudy."

April 29, 1943. "With the help of Joan Davis, [Blossom] will again try to raise the cultural level of Rudy Vallee's program ... when she imports a symphonic genius by the name of George Tobias to give a concert in the village. The fact that Tobias is the movie comic currently appearing in *Air Force* doesn't bother Blossom." *WSJ*

May 6, 1943. No synopsis available.

May 13, 1943. Guest, Donald Meek "as Shirley Mitchell's slightly wacky uncle." *LN*

May 20, 1943. Guest, Joe E. Brown. "Joe comes to Rudy's village to organize a baseball team, but Joan Davis convinces him he ought to form a women's team instead, with games for the benefit of the U.S.O." *ZS*, May 16, 1943

May 27, 1943. Guest, Bert Lahr.

June 3, 1943. "Ransom Sherman, goggle-eyed comedian, makes a return visit to Vallee's village store in his favorite role of salesman.... Joan Davis, who always had a weakness for the chubby dispenser of useless wares, will stage a gala reception with Shirley Mitchell and Verna Felton competing for Sherman's attention." *CG*, May 30, 1943

June 10, 1943. Guest, Jack Haley.

June 17, 1943. Guest, Jack Haley.

June 24, 1943. "A great psychoanalyst wends his way to the Rudy Vallee program ... to have a go at the minds of the Vallee Village store habitués. The mental medico, in the person of Bert Lahr, will probably develop a mild aberration or two when he comes up against the complexities of Rudy Vallee, Joan Davis, Shirley Mitchell, and Verna Felton." *CG*, June 20, 1943

July 1, 1943. Rudy Vallee makes his final appearance as a series regular.

July 8, 1943. Dennis Day is the guest for Joan and Jack Haley's first outing without Vallee. Joan invites Dennis over to dinner, hoping to trap the naïve bachelor into a marriage proposal.

July 15, 1943. Guest, John Conte. "Conte, an innocent bystander, comes to the village on a vacation looking for peace and sunlight. Happening into the village store in search of a few knickknacks, he runs afoul of Joan Davis, intent on showing off her expert salesman-ship to her store partner, Jack Haley.... Conte becomes the guinea pig in the great battle to determine who is the better salesman, and will undoubtedly emerge bewildered but unenlightened." *CG*, July 11, 1943

July 22, 1943. "Joan decides to take legal recourse against Blossom Blimp. She imports none other than Screen Star Basil Rathbone, who seems to be a high-powered detective and lawyer, to take the matter into court and charge Blossom with slander, libel, assault and battery, or something." *LN*

July 29, 1943. "Gene Kelly ... will set the collective hearts of Joan Davis and Verna (Blossom Blimp) Felton aflutter during their broadcast with Jack Haley tonight...." *LBI*, July 30, 1943

August 5, 1943. Guest, Frank Parker.

August 12, 1943. "The Santa Claus with the rancid disposition, Monty Woolley, white beard and all, will more or less meet his match in insulting repartee when he meets Joan Davis and Blossom (Verna Felton) Blimp...." *LBI* "Woolley will play the part of an old man who capitalizes on his dignified appearance by posing as Joan Davis' 'father'—at her request—to help her candidacy for Village Treasurer." *KT*, August 8, 1943

August 19, 1943. "William Bendix, an old boy friend of Joan Davis (according to Joan), will visit the Village Store tonight...." *LBI*

August 26, 1943. Guest, John Carradine.

September 2, 1943. Guest, Reginald Gardiner.

September 9, 1943. Joan and the other women in town are excited about the impending visit of crooner Frank Sinatra. Wanting to make herself stand out from the crowd of feminine admirers, Joan takes Jack's suggestion that she attract Sinatra's interest by acting aloof. When that fails to register, Jack tries to convince the visitor of Joan's class, sophistication, and wealth. Sinatra sings "Close to You."†

> JOAN: See this new dress I got on? I bought it just for Frankie.
> JACK: Well, I hope it looks better on him than it does on you.

September 16, 1943. "Basil Rathbone, the screen's master-minding Sherlock Holmes, will jug-gle elusive clues and fantastic facts in an effort to find out what makes Joan Davis tick...." *BDS*, September 12, 1943

September 23, 1943. "Joe E. Brown, billed as the Walking Grand Canyon Ad, will be the guest of Joan Davis and Jack Haley...." *CG*

September 30, 1943. Guests, George Murphy, Fred MacMurray.

October 7, 1943. Guest, Brian Aherne. "Jack Haley will have to run a protective ring around Brian Aherne when the smooth-talking screen star takes his life in his hands to visit man-chasing Joan Davis...." *LBI*, October 8, 1943

October 14, 1943. Guest, Edward Everett Horton.

October 21, 1943. Guest, Paul Lukas. "Lukas, who faced countless terrors in *Watch on the Rhine*, will really learn about the horrors of life when he faces Joan Davis...." *LN*

October 28, 1943. "Lieut. Rudy Vallee of the Coast Guard becomes Rudy Vallee, broadcaster, again.... Rudy's visit will be his first since he turned over the show to Joan Davis...." *ST*, October 22, 1943

November 4, 1943. Actress Mary Boland, the scheduled program guest, became ill and was replaced shortly before the broadcast by character actress Florence Bates.

November 11, 1943. Guest Edward Everett Horton "will return to the scene of his crime ...

'And what happened to me on that show several weeks ago really was a crime,' Horton says." *KT*, November 7, 1943

November 18, 1943. Guest, Herbert Marshall. "Marshall, usually a highly controlled gentleman, will be a duck out of water when the earthy Miss Davis starts her chummy routine." *CG*

November 25, 1943. Guest, Basil Rathbone.

December 2, 1943. Guest, George Jessel.

December 9, 1943. Guest, Edward Everett Horton. "Horton will be making his third guest appearance on the show in six weeks. It seems that Joan has some unfinished business with the comic. Jack Haley will be on hand to restore order...." *KT*, December 5, 1943

December 16, 1943. "Joan Davis, if you can imagine it, will be elegant, simply elegant.... The reason for Miss Davis' sudden refinement will be that screen smoothie, Herbert Marshall, who will saunter into her village store.... Verna (Blossom Blimp) Felton and Sharon (Penny) Douglas will do their best to cut in on Joan...." *CG*, December 12, 1943

December 23, 1943. Guest, Monty Woolley.

December 30, 1943. Guest, George Jessel. "[T]he comedian returns to assist in a hilarious celebration of New Year's Eve. Enthusiastic Joan has a few unique resolutions she's eager to try out, which, curiously enough, mostly involve Blossom Blimp (Verna Felton) and Penny Cartwright (Sharon Douglas)." *LN*

January 6, 1944. Guest, Charlie Ruggles.

January 13, 1944. Guest, Arthur Treacher.

January 20, 1944. Guest, Preston Foster.

January 27, 1944. "When Joan Davis tries to get a job as a riveter on the swing shift she encounters an efficiency expert in Edward Everett Horton.... This special performance for 3,500 employees of Douglas Aircraft Co. will originate at the Philharmonic Auditorium, Los Angeles." *CG*, January 23, 1944

February 3, 1944. Guest, Adolphe Menjou.

February 10, 1944. Guest, Basil Rathbone.

February 17, 1944. Guest, Charles Ruggles.

February 24, 1944. "Eddie Cantor will begin a search for 'G.I. Joe,' the typical U.S. fighting man, when he appears as a guest on the Joan Davis and Jack Haley show tonight.... When the search is ended, 'G.I. Joe' will find in trust for him $5,000 to use as he sees fit to re-adapt himself to a world at peace." *WSJ*

March 2, 1944. Guest, Mischa Auer.

March 9, 1944. Guest, Edward Everett Horton.

March 16, 1944. Guest, Alan Ladd.

March 23, 1944. Guest, George Raft. This episode was broadcast from Mitchell Field on Long Island, an Air Force base.

March 30, 1944. Guest, Akim Tamiroff; broadcast from the United States Merchant Marine Academy, Long Island.

April 6, 1944. Guest, Roland Young, performed for an audience at Hunter College, made up largely of future Navy WAVEs in training.

April 13, 1944. Guest, Edward Everett Horton. Joan needs help with her income taxes.

April 20, 1944. Joan "finds that Alan Hale has bought her village store...." *WSJ*

April 27, 1944. Guest, Charlie Ruggles. Joan tells listeners how to obtain a copy of her new book, *The Life and Loves of Joan Davis*.

May 4, 1944. Guest, Preston Foster.

May 11, 1944. Guest, "Jimmy Gleason, who upsets Joan's movie producing plans." *WSJ*

May 18, 1944. Guest, Adolphe Menjou, from the Army Air Forces Base, March Field in California. Joan "receives an invitation to appear with Menjou only to find that the invitation should have gone to Bette Davis...." *LN*

May 25, 1944. Guest, Edward Everett Horton.

June 1, 1944. "Joan tries out her new-found charm on Charles Ruggles." *WSJ*

June 8, 1944. Joan "will try to sell a war bond quota in 30 minutes." *WSJ*

June 15, 1944. "[A]nnual rose festival presents a problem for Joan." *WSJ*

June 22, 1944. "[D]ressmaking contest...." *WSJ*

June 29, 1944. Joan is given by a surprise birthday party. Joan and Jack Haley make their last appearance in this segment before embarking on an eight-week vacation, during which Edward Everett Horton will run the *Village Store*.

August 31, 1944. "Joan gives an August Christmas party, with Jimmy Durante, Kenny Baker, Arthur (Dagwood) Lake, Johnny Mercer, and Eddie Cantor as guests." *WSJ*

September 7, 1944. "Joan Davis encounters the housing problem." *WSJ*

September 14, 1944. "Joan Davis starts redecorating the store attic for living quarters." *WSJ*

September 21, 1944. "Joan Davis launches campaign for election as village fire chief." *WSJ*

September 28, 1944. "Joan Davis persuades Jack Haley to go deep-sea fishing." *WSJ*

October 12, 1944. "Joan Davis finds a bundle from heaven, and Jack Haley finds a blonde doll from Georgia." *WSJ*

October 19, 1944. No synopsis available.

October 26, 1944. Blossom Blimp recruits Joan to replace Penny as chair of the Women's Auxiliary fundraising efforts for a new public park. After Penny and Joan have words at the beauty parlor, Joan disguises herself as the assistant to Southern-accented beautician Scarlett O'Harrigan (Shirley Mitchell), so that she can take her rival out of commission.†

November 2, 1944. "Joan Davis is sure she has finally landed her man when she receives a romantic note from a subscriber to a Lonely Hearts bureau...." *LN*

November 9, 1944. No synopsis available.

November 16, 1944. "Joan Davis invents new ways to crash a football game." *WSJ*

November 23, 1944. Joan prepares Thanksgiving dinner.

November 30, 1944. "[W]ar bond selling contest inspires Joan Davis to new feats of salesmanship." *WSJ*

December 7, 1944. Joan "has difficulty finding unusual Christmas gifts." *WSJ*

December 14, 1944. According to *Variety* (December 14, 1944), Joan entertained 300 wounded war veterans at her broadcast, and at a party held afterwards at Slapsie Maxie's nightclub.

December 21, 1944. "When a new beauty parlor opens in the village, Joan Davis drafts Jack Haley to aid in her own beauty problems.... Blossom Blimp, who has a few beauty problems of her own, is around, as is Penny Cartwright, the village belle." *SS*, December 20, 1944

December 28, 1944. No synopsis available.

January 4, 1945. "Joan Davis discovers there's more to getting a job with Uncle Sam than filling out an application." *WSJ*

January 11, 1945. No synopsis available.

January 18, 1945. "Love and hypnotism don't mix, as Joan Davis will discover...." *BDG*, January 12, 1945

January 25, 1945. No synopsis available.

February 1, 1945. Joan "performs with a small town circus." *WSJ*

February 8, 1945. "Joan Davis braves terrors of a 'radio audition.'" *WSJ*

February 15, 1945. Eddie Cantor filled in for an ailing Jack Haley, ill with an eye infection.

March 1, 1945. "Jack goes to night school and Joan to a fortune teller." *WSJ*

March 8, 1945. Joan "takes Jack Haley for a winter swim." *WSJ*

March 15, 1945. No synopsis available.

March 22, 1945. "Joan Davis wants a part in Jack Haley's revival of his old vaudeville act." *WSJ*

March 29, 1945. No synopsis available.

April 5, 1945. "Joan Davis meets a ghost." *WSJ*

The Sealtest Village Store continued to air weekly, toplined by Joan and Jack Haley, through June 28, 1945. However, no recordings or scripts of episodes from this period from mid–April through mid–June appear to have survived, and newspaper publicity concerning storylines was scant. The season's two final episodes were synopsized as follows:

June 21, 1945. "Joan Davis decides whether to continue operating her village store or head for a career in the big city...." *ChT*

June 28, 1945. "Joan and Jack plan celebration for returning war hero; Dave Street sings 'The More I See You.'" *WSJ*

The Joan Davis Show

Cast: Joan Davis (*Joan Davis*), Andy Russell (*Andy Russell*, season 1), Harry Von Zell (*Harry Von Zell*, season 1), Verna Felton (*Rosella Hipperton III*, season 1, *Cousin Cornelia*, season 2), Shirley Mitchell (*Barbara Weatherby*, season 1), Sharon Douglas (*Barbara Weatherby*, season 2), Si Wills (*Serenus*), Wally Brown (*Wally Brown*, season 2), Ben Gage (*Dr. Ronald Crenshaw*, season 2),

Producers: Dave Titus, Dick Mack. *Director*: Dick Mack. *Writers*: Harry Crane, Larry Gelbart, Nat Linden, Bob O'Brien, Joe Quillan, Jay Sommers, Jack Harvey, Si Wills, David Victor, Herbert Little. *Music*: Paul Weston and His Orchestra (season 1) Andy Russell (season 1), Jack Meakin and His Orchestra (season 2). *Announcers*: Harry Von Zell (season 1), Ben Gage (season 2)

Sponsor: Lever Brothers Company. Aired Mondays at 8:30 p.m. on CBS. First aired September 3, 1945; last aired June 23, 1947.

With her commitment to Sealtest complete, Joan and her agents had big plans for her own show, to premiere in the fall of 1945. Initially Joan signed with United Drug, in a lucrative deal said to be worth approximately $1 million per year. The plan was to place her on either NBC or CBS, in a time slot still to be determined when the deal was closed. (The less successful Blue network, subsequently to become ABC, was deemed unacceptable to the star and the sponsor.) Before a suitable time slot could be found, however, the drug company's sixty-day option on Joan's show expired.

The show was ultimately sold to Lever Brothers, then sponsoring George Burns and Gracie Allen's Monday night show on CBS. Joan's new sponsor and advertising agency (the powerful Young and Rubicam), anticipating higher ratings than Burns and Allen had drawn, launched an expensive advertising campaign spread across various popular magazines to alert her fans that they could now hear her on a new network and new night. The main product being promoted was Swan Soap, whose ad campaign depicted it as "four soaps in one."

Having her own show provided Joan with a degree of creative control she had not enjoyed on the Sealtest program, and she formed her own company, Joan Davis Enterprises, to oversee the project. Husband Si Wills would take an active role in the writing, as well as playing the minor role of Joan's annoying cousin (sometimes brother-in-law) Serenus.

In June, *Variety* announced that Dick Mack was expected to be chosen to produce Joan's new show. Mack, most recently producer of the New York–based *Pabst Blue Ribbon Town* on CBS, was fielding multiple offers since resigning that post in favor of working in California. "Naturally Joan Davis gets first call," the trade journal reported, "largely for sentimental reasons. It was Mack who first put the comedienne on the Sealtest exhibit and realizing her potentialities gave her a steady berth with Rudy Vallee and John Barrymore. It is now radio history that she eventually inherited sole stardom and lifted the show into the upper strata of the elite..."[21]

As late as August, *Variety* reported that the show's format was not yet set, with the September 3 premiere looming. The concept of Joan as a storekeeper could not be used, as that format belonged to Sealtest. "Suggestion for placing locale in a laundry was archly sneered at as not befitting a highly Hooperated scrubwoman who might be mistaken for a scrubwoman. Tea shop format was being considered last week ... but some execs connected with the show were not too happy about that idea either, fearing that audience would think that the star was plugging tea instead of soap."[22]

Joan's new format did ultimately cast her as the proprietress of Joanie's Tea Room in Swanville (allowing for an unsubtle sponsor plug). Joshua P. Weatherby was the stodgy local banker whose snooty, self-important daughter Barbara is Joan's chief rival.

Serving as Joan's announcer, but also a featured comic player in the program, was Harry Von Zell, familiar to radio listeners from his appearances with Fred Allen, Dinah Shore, and Burns and Allen, among others. Originally hired as a straight announcer, Von Zell had evolved into a comic presence on these shows after finding his role on the Allen show changing, as he explained to an interviewer in 1945. "I don't know how it happened," Von Zell said. "I didn't start it and Fred didn't start it. But first thing I knew, there I was cracking jokes right along with Allen."[23] Each broadcast of *The Joan Davis Show*, opened with Von Zell warbling a derisive little ditty: "Poor Joan ain't got nobody; she's nobody's sweetheart now." This was followed by a chortle that let the listeners know not to take her plight too seriously.

Joan's music director was Paul Weston (1912–1996). Filling the slot of vocalist that Dave Street had occupied on the Sealtest show was singer Andy Russell (1920–1992), then a rising star especially popular with younger fans. Born Andres Rabago, Russell drew on his Mexican-American heritage, often singing songs that combined lyrics in English and Spanish. "His way of sliding into a husky chorus in Spanish—after going through the English version—has all the slick chicks swooning like crazy," reported columnist Virginia MacPherson.[24] Andy would receive $2,500 per week for his *Joan Davis Show* chores.

As with her previous radio comedy, much of the action centered on Joan's status as a reluctantly eligible female. Indeed, unrequited love constituted the main story element of Joan's show, and not only for its star. Joan pined away for Andy Russell, who had eyes only for Barbara Weatherby, played with a haughty air by Shirley Mitchell. Mitchell, one of radio's busiest actresses, was also known to listeners as Leila Ransome on *The Great Gildersleeve* and Alice Darling on *Fibber McGee and Molly*. Harry Von Zell offered his romantic attentions to Joan, who repeatedly spurned him, though Verna Felton's Rosella Hipperton found Harry quite the catch. Verna Felton, a carryover from the Sealtest show, continued as Joan's foil, playing a new character not much different from Blossom Blimp. Unlike the Sealtest show, *The Joan Davis Show* would largely eschew guest stars, emphasizing instead the ensemble cast in a situation comedy–type format.

Harry Von Zell was Joan's announcer and comic foil in CBS's *The Joan Davis Show*.

A week before her fall debut, Joan warmed up with an appearance on Ray Bolger's show. Meanwhile, Swan Soap had arranged to sponsor the final episode (August 27) of Mary Astor's sustaining show *The Life of Mary Christmas*, being heard that summer in the Monday night slot to be occupied by Joan, so that a plug for the upcoming series could be inserted.

Variety (September 5, 1945) thought the opening installment of *The Joan Davis Show* was a winner. "Initial script hit the right tempo and pattern, with the switchover of Miss Davis from the Sealtest village store to the Swanville tea shop neatly effected via capsule dramatizations and a documentary reportage technique linking all the characters for their converging on 'Joanie's Tea Room.' From here on in, depending on the scripting talents of the quintet of writers assigned to the show, it should be smooth sailing."

In October, columnists reported that Joan's orchestra leader Paul Weston and featured actress Shirley Mitchell would soon be married, but the ceremony did not take place. In the summer of 1946, Shirley instead announced plans to marry Dr. Julian Frieden and retire from radio. As it turned out, her retirement would be short-lived, and she would work often with Joan in *I Married Joan.*

Hooper ratings surveys that fall placed *The Joan Davis Show* as radio's ninth most popular show. In January 1946, Joan took out a full-page ad in *Variety* to publicly thank "the six hundred ladies and gentlemen of the press for electing me 'Queen of Comedy' for the third consecutive year."

After a few months on the air in her new format, however, early 1946 ratings found Joan no longer among radio's top 15 shows, though she continued to be the most popular female star on radio, followed closely by Dinah Shore. Noted the *Chicago Tribune's* Larry Wolters of her 15.8 Hooper rating, "Miss Davis in the past has actually had higher ratings. But this season she launched a new show changing days and networks and she has not had the advantage of a good position."[25] Her show was renewed for the 1946-47 season, but there was already talk that the sponsor was disenchanted with the show for which he had paid so richly.

The featured vocalist during the first season of *The Joan Davis Show* was Latin heartthrob Andy Russell.

When *The Joan Davis Show* returned for a second season, cast changes were the name of the game. Andy Russell had left the series, taking a regular role on *Your Hit Parade.* Shirley Mitchell had gotten married and retired (at least for the time being) from her radio work. Harry Von Zell was out as well, replaced as announcer by Ben Gage. Gage (1914–1978), busy as both a singer and announcer on radio, was then the real-life husband of movie actress Esther Williams.

Only Verna Felton remained from the previous season's cast, but her role changed in the new format. Instead of playing Rosella Hipperton, she was cast as Joan's caustic Cousin Cornelia, giving her new opportunities to berate and deride the star. According to Joan, Cornelia's been married so many times that "the last time she went to the altar, instead of 'Oh, Promise Me,' the choir sang 'I Love a Parade!'"

New to the cast as a regular was

comedian Wally Brown, who'd previously appeared opposite Joan in her film *Around the World*. Brown basically took the place of Von Zell in the cast, playing the man who pines away for Joan while she pursues another. Along with his announcing chores, Gage was assigned the role of Dr. Ronald Crenshaw, who would become the object of Joan's (initially) unrequited love. Sharon Douglas replaced the departed Mitchell as Joan's nemesis Barbara Weatherby. Jack Meakin's orchestra provided music, with the help of the Delta Rhythm Boys.

Of the season opener, *Variety* (October 9, 1946) commented, "[She] was fast, funny, and entertaining.... [S]he turned in a flock of laughs that were really deserved.... [It was] a good show all the way around." Later in the season, a less enthused Walter Winchell wrote of Joan's "brash hijinks," "The jesting consists of insults being flung at Joan by a cluster of stooges. Some of the jokes are funny; more are hoary. But Joan doesn't make any pretense at sophistication. She is selling a pie-in-the-face brand of tomfoolery. And if you are interested in that type of product, there it is week after week after week after week..."[26]

One gimmick Joan and producer Dick Mack wanted to try that fall was firmly nixed by CBS. The idea called for distributing five one-dollar bills to various spots around the country, with a winning serial number to be read aloud weekly on *The Joan Davis Show*. A listener holding that bill would win $1,000. After scripts had been drafted and Joan's husband Si made several trips to plant the cash in various cities, the network cracked down shortly before the season began, "stating it is contrary to its policy to allow air-show giveaways in cases where no skill is involved on the part of the winner."[27] *Variety* explained the concept, and the ensuing clash between Davis and the network, in more detail:

> Joan Davis [the character] came back from her vacation suffering from amnesia but by a queer quirk of memory retained in her mind only the serial numbers on five one-dollar bills.... When the first of the seven scripts was submitted to continuity acceptance, the boom was lowered and the chief censor upheld right up to the top.... CBS made it plain that it would accept contests of merit with some skill attached but the mere giveaway of money through the lucky device of finding a serial number on a greenback is not their idea of entertainment.[28]

Billboard speculated that the stunt, which had to be scrapped altogether when CBS refused to budge, was aimed at improving Joan's ratings before she went into negotiations for the 1947-48 radio season. Joan's amnesia remained a story point in the first several episodes of the season, but her writing team was left to make some hasty revisions.

Midway through the season, Wally Brown left the cast. Jack Oakie and Lionel Stander were among the comics who made guest appearances in his wake; according to *Variety* columnist Jack Hellman, "Others also get a crack at the spot vacated by Wally Brown and whoever rates the nod from Miss Davis and producer Dick Mack wins a permanent berth...."[29] As it turned out, not until the following fall would a final decision be made.

Longtime Davis listeners were surprised that spring when it appeared that Joan (the character) might finally lead an eligible man to the altar, as her romance with Dr. Crenshaw blossomed. Initially, their relationship seemed to be of a type long familiar to Davis fans, as when she complains, "In the two years I've known him, he's ignored me, he's never held my hand, he's never kissed me, never proposed to me, never paid any attention to me—so I've finally come to a decision. I'm gonna jilt him." In a late March broadcast, however, Dr. Crenshaw finally proposed, and subsequent programs focused on Joan's preparation for a June wedding.

The new development may have been a last-ditch effort to spark the show's ratings, which were no longer high enough to justify the sponsor's reported weekly $17,000 outlay.

In the spring of 1947, trade papers were reporting that Joan's chances of being renewed by Lever Brothers for a third season were slim. Ultimately, Lever Brothers opted not to renew, instead sponsoring the more modestly budgeted new sitcom *My Friend Irma* starring Marie Wilson and Cathy Lewis. During negotiations with other potential sponsors, Davis' team offered a cut to $15,000 per show. One report had Joan possibly taking an early Monday night slot on ABC, where she would inherit the audience of *The Lone Ranger.* A prospective deal with R.J. Reynolds Tobacco, according to *Billboard*, went awry when Davis "insisted on complete package control," refusing "some form of agency supervision."[30]

In 1947, deep-pocketed national sponsors were no longer easy to come by, and when no satisfactory deal emerged, Joan turned her attention to a new option that looked promising: the cooperatively sponsored show.

Episode Guide

The symbol † indicates that the synopsis is based on an extant recording of the original broadcast. Copies of many of these episodes, including numerous segments from the 1945-46 season, are available from one or more Old Time Radio vendors.

The symbol ‡ indicates that the synopsis is based on a script held in the Harry Crane Papers at UCLA. In some cases, the extant script is marked "Preview," and may have undergone modifications prior to the air show.

Synopses for other episodes were taken from newspaper program logs or advertisements taken out in those newspapers by the sponsor or local radio station. Whenever possible, they were confirmed via multiple printed sources. The following abbreviations are used to indicate the publication in which direct quotes appeared:

CRT	*The Cedar Rapids Tribune*, Cedar Rapids, Iowa
FRC	*The Findlay Republican-Courier*, Findlay, Ohio
LN	*The Lima News*, Lima, Ohio
MCGG	*The Mason City Globe-Gazette*, Mason City, Iowa
SAE	*The San Antonio Express*, San Antonio, Texas
WSJ	*The Wisconsin State Journal*, Madison, Wisconsin

Unless otherwise noted, the date of the issue in which the information appeared was the same as the program's air date.

The notation "No synopsis available" indicates that newspaper radio logs confirmed that the show aired on that date, but did not yield any information about content or guest stars.

September 3, 1945. "Joan Davis has some nervous moments as she prepares to open a tea room, with crooner Andy Russell coming to her aid as a youth working his way through college...." *CRT*, August 30, 1945

September 10, 1945. "Posing as a fortune teller, Joan Davis gives some tea-leaf reading that almost ruins the local bank and sends Wall Street into a tailspin...." *MCGG*

September 17, 1945. "Bloodhounds? No, but she might have ... a pair of handcuffs stuffed in her pocketbook. For Joan Davis is off on another man hunt...." *SAE*

September 24, 1945. "When Swanville goes all out to celebrate its 100th birthday, vivacious Joan Davis goes just as far for the title 'Queen of the Swanville Centennial,' very largely because the winner also gets Andy Russell for king...." *MCGG*

October 1, 1945. "His current salary too small to see him through Swanville College, Andy

Russell ... strikes his boss for a raise.... Instead of giving him the raise, Joan helps Andy get a job in the Swanville bank, which is owned by the father of Barbara Weatherby, Joan's arch-rival for Andy's affections." *MCGG*, September 29, 1945

October 8, 1945. "Joan Davis observes Fire Prevention Week" *WSJ*

October 15, 1945. "Joan Davis gets engulfed in a local crime wave when a bank robber hides out in her tea room and holds Joan as hostage to foil pursuing police...." *MCGG*

October 22, 1945. Reading in a movie magazine that Atomic Film Studios is seeking a new singing movie star, Joan decides this is the perfect opportunity for Andy Russell to make it in Hollywood. When director Vladimir Vestoff arrives in Swanville to shoot Andy's screen test, Joan can't conceal her jealousy that Barbara Weatherby is asked to play his love interest. Andy sings "How Deep Is the Ocean."†

October 29, 1945. "Election time rolls around in Swanville and finds Joan Davis setting her bonnet for the mayoralty.... When both political parties are unanimous in wanting banker Weatherby for mayor, Joanie goes all out with some fancy electioneering." *LN*, October 28, 1945

November 5, 1945. Guest, George Jessel. Harry is running for mayor of Swanville, and Joan enlists George Jessel to write his keynote speech. Andy sings "I'll Buy That Dream."

November 12, 1945. "Joan Davis invents new ways to crash the gate when football hits Swanville.... Joanie's rival ... Barbara Weatherby snags Andy to escort her to Swanville's big annual football dance and how to recover the tea room's handsome hired man for herself is the boss-lady's problem." *LN*, November 11, 1945

November 19, 1945. "Joan Davis sets out with all good intentions to sell Thanksgiving turkeys.... But some helpful citizen reads between the lines a diabolic plot that makes Joanie out less than the dauntless darling she really is." *MCGG*

November 26, 1945. "Joan Davis inherits an estate in the nick of time to give the wolf at the door the brushoff.... Banker Weatherby puts the bee on the 'Queen of Comedy' when the quarterly payment on her tea room comes due and she has no money to pay up." *LN*

December 3, 1945. "Going Hunting." Joan and the gang visit the Weatherbys' hunting lodge. Andy sings "Love Letters."†

> HARRY: What's the matter, Miss Weatherby?
> BARBARA: Oh, I cut my finger on a nail. I hope it doesn't get infected. What'll I do?
> JOAN: Well, run it through your hair, Babs. The peroxide'll sterilize it.

December 10, 1945. Tea room customer Mr. Havemeyer enlists Joan, Harry, and Andy to help out at his department store, which is busy with Christmas shoppers. Andy, embarrassed to make the purchase himself, asks Joan to buy his mother's present, a suit of red flannel underwear. Joan manages to confuse Andy's package with one containing the new dress Hippy bought for her appearance in the holiday parade. Andy sings "Nancy." Joan does a promo for Christmas Seals.†

> JOAN: Oh, boy, what a Christmas this is going to be! I can just see it—Andy's mother milking the cows in a white sequined evening gown, while Mrs. Hipperton leads the Grand March in a suit of red flannel underwear.

December 17, 1945. "[H]olidays bring a rush of trade to Joan's tea room." *WSJ*

December 24, 1945. Joan and her friends host a holiday party for underprivileged kids from the local settlement house. Mr. Weatherby initially agrees to play Santa Claus, but then rescinds his offer at the last minute. Joan's fall from a ladder knocks her out cold, and she dreams of meeting childhood versions of her friends. Andy sings "White Christmas" and a Spanish version of "Silent Night."†

> HARRY: Joan, listen, stop chasing the band around the studio with that piece of mistletoe! They won't kiss you—they've got a strong union.

December 31, 1945. "An invitation to a New Year's ball at Swanville's swanky country club leaves Joan Davis crying blues.... The Queen of Comedy has no formal and it looks as tho [sic] she'll have to pass the bid by. But when rival Barbara Weatherby snares Andy Russell for the big event, Joanie has a brainstorm and rents an outfit from the local hock shop...." *LN*

January 7, 1946. "Fighting Over Andy Russell." It's opening night of the opera season in Swanville, and Joan is jealous that Andy escorted Barbara there. Barbara tells Joan that she and Andy are engaged, and gives her a phone number to call that should help her get over Andy. Little does Joan realize that Barbara has given her not the number of the local Lonely Hearts Club, but that of the Swanville Zoo. Joan decides to get even by posing as the French-born opera star with whom Barbara's father is infatuated. Andy sings "As Long as I Live."†

> HARRY: Stop kidding yourself, Joan. She'll never give him up.
> JOAN: Yeah, but maybe we can compromise and share Andy's company 50–50.
> HARRY: 50–50?
> JOAN: Yeah, when I'm fifty, she can have him.

January 14, 1946. "An amateur fencing contest sponsored by Swanville University provides Joan Davis and Barbara Weatherby with a good excuse to fight a duel over Andy Russell.... The winner takes Andy to a buffet dinner ... so the battle is raged with due regard for keeping the scratches where they won't show." *LN*

January 21, 1946. "Andy Russell Gets a Letter." Joan gets a bright idea from a *True Heartthrob* magazine story called "I Got Rid of My Rival by Mail." With Hippy's help, she forges a letter that convinces Barbara that her boyfriend Andy has a wife and three kids in Peoria. Once Harry and Andy catch on to the gag, they decide to turn the tables on Joan. Andy sings "Love Me."†

January 28, 1946. "Joan Joins Literacy Society." "Joan Davis is called upon to mend the breach when famed George Bernard Schwartz fails to show up before the annual meeting of the Swanville Literacy Society.... The red letter affair takes place in Joanie's tea room, and it's up to the 'Queen of Comedy' to keep the customers happy. She proffers a reasonable facsimile of George Bernard Schwartz and everything is lyrically lovely until Barbara Weatherby unmasks the deception and reveals Harry Von Zell as the man behind the long white beard." *MCGG*

February 4, 1946. "Gold Found in Swanville." When news breaks of a gold rush in Swanville, Joan and her friends decide to tunnel under the tea room in search of the abandoned Lucky Nugget Mine. A cave-in leaves the gang trapped, until Serenus finds some light at the end of the tunnel—literally. Andy sings "Slowly."†

February 11, 1946. "Birthday Party for Joan." Joan's friends are planning a surprise birthday party for her, but to keep the secret they tell her it's a party for Barbara Weatherby. Annoyed, Joan replaces Barbara's cake with one guaranteed to result in an explosive celebration. Jack Carson makes a cameo appearance. Andy sings "If I Had a Wishing Ring."†

February 18, 1946. Joan's missing $300 from her cash register just as all of her friends suddenly seem strangely affluent: Hippy bought a purebred Irish setter puppy, Andy hired a famous vocal coach who charges $30 a lesson, Barbara discusses her $300 nest egg, and Harry has a new motorcycle. Meanwhile, Mr. Weatherby and his staff try to figure out why there's a $300 surplus at the bank. Andy sings "Without You."†

> ANDY: Thanks, Miss Davis. I'm glad you trust me. You know I wouldn't do anything to harm you. After all, you're the one who gave me so many opportunities.
> JOAN: Yeah, and you're the one who never took any!

February 25, 1946. "U.N.O. Banquet." When the tea room is booked for a U.N.O. affair, Joan's friends assume she's hosting important dignitaries from the United Nations, but she's actually been hired to entertain members of the Umpires National Organization. Thinking there's an opportunity to have the United Nations settle permanently in Swanville, Mr. Weatherby does his best to make friends with Joan, and insists that Barbara do the same. Andy sings "Laughing on the Outside (Crying on the Inside)."†

> WEATHERBY: Come, come, Miss Davis, let's get to the point. I'm a practical man, and you're a practical woman. Isn't that so?
> JOAN: Well, I'm practically a woman.

March 4, 1946. "'Hippy' Hipperton confides that the way she got her third husband was by playing on his sympathy, whereupon Joanie decides to do a Camille to win Andy Russell away from rival Barbara Weatherby. She goes to a doctor for X-rays and when the plates show that she has only one more day to live, Andy agrees to marry Joanie and make her last hours happy." *MCGG*

March 11, 1946. "Joan Has Insomnia." Unable to sleep for a week, Joan resists taking the sleeping pills she's offered by Hippy. Thanks to her well-meaning friends, Joan accidentally takes too many pills, and has to be driven home by Harry. En route, Harry is involved in a traffic accident with Mr. Weatherby, who threatens to sue, believing that drowsy Joan was at the wheel. Unfortunately, the wreck left Harry with amnesia, and unable to defend Joan in court. Andy sings "Let It Snow."†

March 18, 1946. "Counterfeiter Visits Tea Room." "Prosperity comes to the 'Queen of Comedy' when flashy out-of-towners rent her basement and pay her off in brand new $10 bills. Counterfeit money that floods the town is traced back to Joanie, and she's in a spot trying to explain away the bundles of fresh bills that clutter up her cellar." *MCGG*

March 25, 1946. Joan "decides to turn her tea room into a hacienda" complete with rhumba band. *WSJ*

April 1, 1946. "Joan Davis ... sets up a chocolate éclair business as a tea room sideline." *WSJ*

April 8, 1946. "Joan Davis impersonates Madam Zaza, seeress, and advises Mrs. Hipperton to lend her $2,000 to save the tea room from being condemned by the fire department.... During the séance, 'Hippy' insists on consulting her three husbands, all deceased, about the financial matter. Joanie does some fast thinking...." *LN*

April 15, 1946. "Joan Davis finds herself in her musical teacups when the 'Queen of Comedy' enters the Swanville songwriting contest.... Barbara Weatherby, what with her extensive musical background and a well-stacked jury, figures to win the contest.... But Harry Von Zell has other ideas and he connives with Serenus to change names on the songs so Barbara's contribution is switched to Joanie. Naturally, the switch backfires." *LN*

April 22, 1946. "Mrs. 'Hippy' Hipperton plans a charity circus, and when 'Goona' and his trainer fail to arrive, Andy Russell, in a rented costume, impersonates the gorilla—with 'trainer' Joanie putting him through his paces. Meanwhile, the real gorilla puts in an appearance in Joanie's darkened tea room and the 'Queen of Comedy,' on her return from the circus, finds herself in an intriguing situation—until Andy comes along and turns on the lights." *MCGG*

April 29, 1946. "Joan Davis ... goes on a treasure hunt." *FRC*

May 6, 1946. "Joanie wants to be selected as 'Queen of the May' but she hasn't a chance against Barbara Weatherby, whose pater is the judge. Serenus sends a false telegram to get rid of Mr. Weatherby, but the ruse is discovered at the last minute, and Joan is elected low woman on the Maypole." *MCGG*

May 13, 1946. "Joan Davis finds her cupboard as bare as Mother Hubbard's when the meat shortage hits Swanville...." *MCGG*

May 20, 1946. "Andy Russell saves the day for Joan 'Love in Bloom' Davis when the comedienne takes up fiddle-playing for the Swanville musical festival...." *MCGG*

May 27, 1946. In the season finale, Joan and the gang accept Hippy's invitation to spend two weeks at her desert ranch. After Joan loads up on Western wear at Havemeyer's Department Store, plans change—and change again, leaving Joan up to her ears in mountain gear, beachwear, and multiple bales of hay. Andy sings "They Say That Falling in Love Is Wonderful." At the end of the broadcast, Joan thanks her cast and listeners for their support.†

....

September 30, 1946. In the second season opener, "Joanie returns to the air suffering from a loss of memory and Babs Weatherby seizes the opportunity to take Joanie's tea room away from her, but Cousin Cornelia intervenes by being appointed Joan's guardian. Wally Brown appears, and one look at him brings Joanie back to her rather sparse senses." *MCGG*

October 7, 1946. Cousin Cornelia goes AWOL right after an argument with Joan, and is nowhere to be found. Meanwhile, Wally hears that Joan "cut Cornelia with a knife," and then finds the soup bones she buried in the backyard. Before Cornelia turns up alive and well, Joan herself is beginning to wonder if she killed her annoying aunt while in an amnesiac haze.‡

> CORNELIA: Judge Lottkas phoned to remind you about your mental incompetence trial. He said you must be prepared to answer questions concerning your family background.
> JOAN: Oh, yeah. He wanted me to check up and see if there was ever any sanity in my family.

October 14, 1946. "Joanie and Babs Weatherby finally fight it out for complete control of the tea room.... Babs is trying to take over the tea room from Joan, claiming that the latter is incompetent." *MCGG*

October 21, 1946. Joan's on trial, defending her mental competence after being afflicted with amnesia, but the testimony of friends like Wally and Cousin Cornelia isn't helping much. A mysterious benefactor chooses an odd method (messages attached to rocks thrown through the window) to assure Joan that she will emerge victorious.‡

> WALLY: Well, I was just sitting there when suddenly I looked up, and there before me was a beautiful, gorgeous young lady.
> JOAN (softly): Isn't he sweet?
> WALLY: And then this beautiful, gorgeous young lady stepped aside, and there behind her was Joan Davis.

October 28, 1946. "As the tea room proprietress who has been suffering from amnesia, Joan Davis recovers her lost memory and promptly wishes for her former state of blissful ignorance.... Trying to get rid of her visiting cousin Cornelia forms the basis of comic devel-

opments.... Jack Meakin and the Delta Rhythm Boys add musical variation to the show."
MCGG

November 4, 1946. Barbara Weatherby is running for a seat on the county welfare committee, and her father thinks Joan is the perfect opponent to insure his daughter's win. Joan
isn't sure she wants to run, until she learns that the winner will have the chance to work
closely with handsome Dr. Crenshaw. As the votes come in, Joan slips into a fantasy world
where gender roles are reversed, and women hold all the important positions in the community.‡

> JOAN: Why, Serenus, you're wearing six buttons that say "Vote for Joan Davis"—are you try-
> ing to keep my morale up?
> SERENUS: No, I'm trying to keep my pants up.

November 11, 1946. Cousin Cornelia advises Joan to win Dr. Crenshaw's affections with her
cooking skills. Joan invites him to dinner, determined to outdo the lavish meal her rival
Babs served him. Unbeknownst to Joan, a jealous Wally gives her crows to serve for dinner,
telling her they're pheasants, while Babs plots to get Joan into trouble with the game warden for hunting pheasant out of season.†

November 18, 1946. "Joan Davis, who thinks the white line in the middle of highways is for
bicycles, enters a safe-driving contest to win a new car...." *LN*

November 25, 1946. "Wally Brown and Serenus immerse a ticking package in water, only to
have Joanie tell them they've ruined an antique clock instead of a time bomb. The clock
belongs to Joanie's heart-throb, Dr. Ronald Crenshaw, and her efforts to have it repaired
result in hilarious consequences." *MCGG*

December 2, 1946. "The problem of rehashing the turkey hash besets Joanie's Tea Room....
Wally Brown is elected chief taster of the tea room while his rival, Dr. Crenshaw, drools
over Joanie's culinary cuteness." *MCGG*

December 9, 1946. "With less than three weeks left before the holiday, Joanie gets started
on her Christmas shopping. Her burning problem is a present for Dr. Crenshaw, who has
everything except the right viewpoint toward Joanie." *MCGG*

December 16, 1946. "'Babs' Weatherby and Joanie battle it out for the affections of Dr.
Ronald Crenshaw. Things look grim until Joanie's dimwitted brother [*sic*] Serenus casts
his shadow upon the scene of honor." *MCGG*

December 23, 1946. "Zany preparations for Christmas in Joanie's Tea Room provide the
basis for the evening's comedy." *MCGG*

December 30, 1946. "Joan Davis redeems a pawn ticket...." *WSJ*

January 6, 1947. Joan wants to attend the upcoming Winter Carnival with Dr. Crenshaw.
After outfitting herself with skis and ski wear, she learns that the event is held in Palm
Springs, where the weather will be sunny. Further complications ensue when the doctor's
car breaks down, and Joan offers to drive him—although she doesn't have a license. Frank
Nelson appears as a store clerk akin to the ones he so often played for Jack Benny. Asked
by Joan if he's a salesman, he snaps, "I'm not standing behind this counter because I forgot
my pants."‡

January 13, 1947. Guest, Jack Oakie. Joan signs up for a $20 beauty treatment in hopes of
dazzling Dr. Crenshaw. A mix-up results in Joan obtaining the services of a trainer (played
by Oakie) from the Mammoth Muscle School, while Serenus gets her makeover. After
getting the works from the muscleman, Joan is in no shape to attend a dance, but Barbara
is more than happy to be the doctor's escort.‡

> JOAN: Say, Babs, do you think I should have my face lifted?
> BARBARA: Certainly not, it's sticking out far enough now!

January 20, 1947. "Joan Davis continues her efforts to arouse romantic interest in Dr. Crenshaw.... However, her efforts to direct Cupid's aim produce an interesting backfire." *MCGG*

January 27, 1947. Guest, Walter O'Keefe. "Called in to solve the mystery of the missing baby, the glib Walter manages to put Joanie directly behind the eight ball." *MCGG*

February 3, 1947. Guest, Walter O'Keefe. An Internal Revenue Service inspector informs Joan that she is due a $2,000 rebate because of an error on her 1944 tax returns. Feeling financially flush, Joan consults a financial adviser, who inspires her to save money by throwing Cousin Cornelia out of the house. No sooner has Joan done so than she learns that her tax windfall was dependent on claiming Cornelia as a dependent, leaving Joan trying to mend fences with her outspoken cousin.‡

> JOAN: Who would lie to a government that sponsors the three freedoms?
> INSPECTOR: The three freedoms?
> JOAN: Yeah—life, liberty, and the pursuit of Gregory Peck.

February 10, 1947. Guest, Richard Lane. Sprucing up her tea room in preparation for meeting with her landlord, Joan falls victim to a paint salesman, who runs amok spattering blue paint from floor to ceiling. Dropping by to brag about her movie date with Dr. Crenshaw, Barbara sits in a freshly painted chair, and can't get up. Luckily for Joan, she's invited to take her rival's place on the date. The paint salesman poses as a famous interior decorator who tells Joan's landlord how much he loves the chaotic new look of the tea room.‡

February 17, 1947. Reading a newspaper announcement of Dr. Crenshaw's engagement to Barbara Weatherby, a discouraged Joan wants to leave Swanville. But when she finds what appears to be a previously unknown Shakespeare manuscript, she's suddenly of great interest to Hollywood producers, and to actor Joel McCrea, who sees her as his inside path to winning the lead role.‡

February 24, 1947. Guest, Allyn Joslyn. Ali Bey, an Arabian prince with 28 wives, comes to Swanville to inspect a precious ruby owned by the Weatherbys. Joan, hired to cater the Weatherbys' dinner for the visiting potentate, hires an undercover reporter as a waiter, leading to complications when the ruby vanishes during the party.‡

March 3, 1947. Guest, Ransom Sherman. Heartsick over Dr. Crenshaw's impending marriage to Barbara Weatherby, Joan writes to the newspaper's lovelorn columnist. The column is actually written by a man who takes a fancy to Joan, and decides to pursue her for himself, while leading Joan to believe he's helping her win Dr. Crenshaw away from Barbara.‡

March 10, 1947. A tea room customer comes up short on his bill, and settles the debt by giving Joan "a genuine, antique, fourteen-carat, solid gold, Oriental good luck ring." Joan tests the ring's powers of luck by betting on a horse race, and tosses it away in disgust when she wrongly believes her horse lost. Once she learns of her racetrack windfall, Joan places a newspaper lost-and-found ad, offering $5 for the ring's return. Its previous owner starts selling 50-cent replicas which they can then sell to Joan for a tidy profit. Barbara Weatherby sneers at Joan's foolishness, but lives to regret it when Dr. Crenshaw overhears and promptly breaks their engagement.‡

March 17, 1947. Joan, who's been suffering from amnesia, unwittingly takes too many of the pills Dr. Crenshaw prescribed. When the good doctor takes her for a drive, and winds up in a traffic accident, he gets amnesia, and suddenly thinks he's Joan's brother-in-law Serenus. Barbara Weatherby sues Joan, claiming she caused the accident by driving under the influence. At the courthouse, Serenus falls and hits his head, leaving him thinking he's Cousin Cornelia. This is a remake of the March 11, 1946 episode.‡

> JOAN: Whatcha gonna do over at the gym, Doc?
> CRENSHAW: Well, you know I always believe in keeping in condition, so twice a week I spend a lot of time at the parallel bars.
> JOAN: My Uncle Sylvester spent a lot of time at the parallel bars. One was at Ninth Avenue, and one was on Tenth.
> CRENSHAW: Miss Davis, the bars I'm talking about are horizontal.
> JOAN: That's just the way Uncle Sylvester came out, horizontal!

March 24, 1947. Guest, Bill Thompson (of *Fibber McGee and Molly*). Barbara Weatherby's father offers a $1,000 reward for information leading to the capture of the burglar who's been targeting Swanville. When a man visits the tea room claiming to be a friend of Dr. Crenshaw's, and asks Joan to hold $500 for him, she decides she needs a guard dog. Despite the presence of her new Saint Bernard, Joan is paid a visit that night by the burglar, who looks quite familiar.‡

March 31, 1947. "Prodded by the guest appearance of promoter Dick Lane, radio's fastest-talking human, Dr. Crenshaw finally proposes to Joan.... Will Joan accept the marriage offer? The answer will be given at the end of the program." *MCGG*

April 7, 1947. "Alan Reed's 'Falstaff Openshaw' comes back to life long enough to pour potions of poesy over the romantic souls of Joan Davis and her new [fiancé] Dr. Crenshaw. Reed deals out copious doses of advice and the newly engaged couple shop for a wedding site." *MCGG*

April 14, 1947. Guest, Billy De Wolfe. Given Dr. Crenshaw's busy schedule, his marriage to Joan is scheduled for June 2, and he entrusts her with finding them a new home. With a little help from Cousin Cornelia, Joan manages to buy a rundown mansion whose previous owners have all been murdered.‡

> CORNELIA: Well, the way to a man's heart is through his stomach.
> JOAN: That sounds kinda messy...

April 21, 1947. Joan is happily making plans for her wedding to Dr. Crenshaw, until Barbara maliciously tells her she is not good enough or wealthy enough to deserve him. Hoping to win a fancy trousseau, Joan enters herself and Dr. Crenshaw in a radio contest for the most exciting tale of romance. Though they don't win the contest, Dr. Crenshaw persuades Joan that she does not need fancy things in order to keep his love.‡

April 28, 1947. Holding down the fort at Dr. Crenshaw's office while he makes a house call, Joan accidentally inhales a blast of ether, resulting in a woozy dream where she has become a famous surgeon.‡

May 5, 1947. Guest, Billy De Wolfe. Wanting to fix up their dream house, Joan consults an interior decorator who coaxes her into mortgaging the house to the tune of $2,000. Dr. Crenshaw takes exception to the expensive redecorating plan, and insists that his fiancée return all the new furniture.‡

May 12, 1947. Guest, Lionel Stander. With her wedding imminent, Joan unexpectedly receives visits from two men who are members of a lonely-hearts club to which she once applied, cowhand Cactus Carraway and sailor Duke Stander. She has some fast talking to do when Dr. Crenshaw arrives on the scene to see his fiancée surrounded by admirers.‡

May 19, 1947. Dr. Crenshaw doesn't want his wife to work and encourages Joan to sell her tea room. Comedian Phil Silvers is interested in buying the business, until Joan's old neme-sis Mr. Weatherby, who still holds a mortgage on the property, threatens to queer the deal.‡

May 26, 1947. "With Joan preparing to be a June bride, scriptly speaking, Alan Reed and Lionel Stander turn up to supervise the wedding rehearsal." *MCGG*

June 2, 1947. The day has come for Joan's dream wedding to Dr. Crenshaw, but fate intervenes when one of his patients gives birth to sextuplets. Amidst the ensuing media fuss, with radio reporters covering the babies' arrival, Dr. Crenshaw tells Joan they should postpone the ceremony.‡

> JOAN: Something old, something new, something borrowed, something blue.... Well, for something old, I've got my grandma's old lace veil. Something new? My wedding outfit, the gown, the shoes. Something blue? Well, I just bought a new blue sapphire bracelet and earrings. Something borrowed? The money to pay for everything!

June 9, 1947. Blue because her wedding was postponed, Joan receives a visit from her old frenemy Barbara Weatherby. With less than altruistic motives, Barbara tells Joan she should let Dr. Crenshaw go, so as not to stand in the way of his promising medical career. When her would-be suitor Cactus Carraway resurfaces, Joan agrees to go on a date with him, which doesn't sit well with the good doctor.‡

June 16, 1947. Joan is asked to host an official dinner in honor of the two-week birthday of Mrs. Johnson's sextuplets. Barbara and Cousin Cornelia spar over who will get to sit next to the mayor at the dinner, and Barbara takes the opportunity to make Joan feel inadequate to serve as the wife of a prominent doctor. Asked to treat the tea room with DDT to avoid flies, Joan finds herself unexpectedly on the dais after unwittingly serving a dinner coated with insect repellent.‡

June 23, 1947. Guest, Lionel Stander. In the season finale, Joan is overjoyed that she's finally marrying the man of her dreams. When her Uncle Sylvester's former prison cellmate, Lefty Stander, turns up unexpectedly, Joan fears that Dr. Crenshaw will not want a wife who has such a disreputable family. Caught by surprise when Dr. Crenshaw meets Lefty at the tea room, Joan tells an impulsive lie that puts her happy marital ending in jeopardy.‡

Joan Davis Time

Cast: Joan Davis (*Joan Davis*), Lionel Stander (*Lionel*); with Mary Jane Croft, Hans Conried, Doris Singleton.

Producer-Director: Dick Mack. *Writers:* Abe Burrows, Harry Crane, Larry Marks, Arthur Stander. *Music:* John Rarig and His Orchestra, The Choral-Aires. *Announcer:* Ben Gage. Aired Saturdays at 9:00 p.m. on CBS. Multiple sponsors. First broadcast, October 4, 1947; last broadcast, July 3, 1948.

By the summer of 1947, with Lever Brothers out of the picture after two years, Joan was looking to get back into the radio game for the fall season. Finally, in September, trade papers reported that CBS programming vice-president Hubbell Robinson had struck a deal to put *Joan Davis Time* on the web's Saturday night schedule.

"CBS said yes to Joan Davis' $7,000-a-week co-op show deal late last week," *Variety* reported in mid–September, "just before the net's option expired."[31] The new deal did not provide as lavish a budget for Joan's show as she had once enjoyed, forcing her to cut costs on performers and behind-the-scenes talent.

Heading Joan's supporting cast was comic actor Lionel Stander (1908–1994), playing a character who shared his name. Stander, who'd clicked with Joan as a guest star during the previous season, was cast as the rough-hewn manager she employs for her tea room. Character actor Hans Conried (1917–1982) was assigned no regular character, but was heard frequently in support. Also intended to be a regular was Florence Halop (1923–1986); after two broadcasts, however, *Variety* (October 15, 1947) reported, "Doris Singleton has replaced Florence Halop as a character stooge ... effective this week...." Guest stars were heard with more frequency than in Joan's previous show for Swan Soap, with Danny Thomas and Garry Moore clocking multiple visits to the series.

Episodes typically opened with an exchange like this one, featuring announcer Ben Gage:

GAGE: Operator! [Sound of nervously clicking phone receiver]. Operator, will you give me the correct time?

OPERATOR: Certainly, sir! It's *Joan Davis Time.*

GAGE : Well, friends, you can set your watches for a half-hour of fun, because from coast to coast, it's *Joan Davis Time!*

Not involved in this series, as either writer or performer, was Joan's husband Si Wills, from whom she had recently filed for divorce. Well-regarded radio writer Abe Burrows, who had previously worked with Joan on the Sealtest show, took the reins, steering Joan's comedy in a new direction. *Joan Davis Time* was markedly different from its predecessor, as *Daily Variety* (October 13, 1947) noted in its review of the series opener:

The tea room's situation premise of seasons past has been discarded and it's more joke and hoke, the possible effect of pleasing her multi-sponsorship. For a first show in new habilaments [*sic*] it paid off well, with punchy gags by Abe Burrows, Artie Stander and Larry Marks and to the credit of producer Dick Mack, the smoothest running yet of any of the co-ops.

Most observers thought Burrows had improved the show. Said the *Washington Post,* "The impact of Mr. Burrows' humor on that noisy, bewildered lady has had an effect not much different from that of Flo Ziegfeld, after Ziegfeld dredged Miss Brice out of burlesque. Burrows has succeeded in softening some of her bleaker outlines and, more importantly, in demonstrating that the Davis talent consists of something more than the ability to open her mouth a great distance and make loud noises."[32] The *New York Times'* Jack Gould concurred: "Joan Davis, whose comic efforts last season reached a rather low ebb, has bounced back with engaging éclat in her new program.... Thus far it has proved a half-hour which gets away from the usual hackneyed routines and strikes out spiritedly in the direction of absurd situations with a novel twist."[33] According to syndicated columnist John Crosby, "The Joan Davis show is situation and, in a sketchy way, character comedy of a sort that will remind you strongly of Mack Sennett. Most of the characters might have walked right out of the Sennett comedies."[34]

Variety's reviewer (October 15, 1947) opined, "In reconverting her into co-op programming, CBS has remedied one of the major flaws in the Davis shows of recent vintage—that of giving her a proper scripting assist. The fact that Abe Burrows now heads up a three-way writing team is the best thing that could have happened to the comedienne."

Not being bankrolled by a single sponsor, Joan's new show was funded under a cooperative program that was new to radio. According to Jack Gould, *Joan Davis Time* "would be the first major evening comedy offering to be sponsored over CBS by a different advertiser in each city."[35] Each local station broadcasting *Joan Davis Time* could sell the commercial time to any interested company. Those stations that didn't secure a sponsor filled the time with network promos or public service announcements instead. As *Newsweek* explained, "Under the cooperative setup, the network puts on the show and charges each station according to its potential audience.... For example, 50,000-watt WCBS, New York, pays $810 for Miss Davis's half-hour of high jinks, and charges White Rose Quality Foods $1,000 to sponsor it. But 250-watt WMBR, Jacksonville, Fla., pays only $78 for the program and lets it go to the Jax Brewing Co. for the same amount."[36] In December, CBS placed an ad in *Variety* noting that local sponsorship of "radio's best comedienne" was still available "in a few cities."

Because the American Federation of Musicians would not permit its members to perform on co-op shows, believing that to do so would hurt the employment opportunities for musicians working outside New York and Los Angeles, Joan hired an *a cappella* choir, the Choral-Aires, to provide musical interludes. They also led into commercial breaks and scene changes with musical segues like, "And in the meantime, lend an ear to this...." Although the networks resolved the union dispute midway through the radio season, Joan still did not add studio musicians to the cast, primarily for budgetary reasons.

Despite her conversion to a new format, some familiar voices from Joan's radio past turned up as guest stars on *Joan Davis Time*, among them Rudy Vallee and her *Joan Davis Show* co-stars Andy Russell and Harry Von Zell.

Joan faced competition from two popular programs, *Gangbusters* on ABC and *Your Hit Parade* on NBC, which translated into disappointing ratings in most markets for *Joan Davis Time*. In June 1948, CBS canceled *Joan Davis Time*. For a time, it appeared that Joan might be coming back for the fall season under the auspices of her previous sponsor, National Dairies (Sealtest). *Billboard* reported that Joan was in negotiations for a new show in which her pay would be tied directly to the show's ratings, "asking $10,000 for the package for the first year against a Hooperating of eight to ten. In addition, she is to get $500 for each additional Hooper point over ten."[37] Since her *Joan Davis Time* ratings had been not much more than half of the quoted figure, it was an ambitious goal, and Joan was reportedly asking for a two-year contract to reward her efforts. Ultimately, the deal fell through, and the fall of 1948 would be the first radio season in several years with Joan nowhere to be heard. Joan was nothing if not tenacious, though, and her radio career wasn't over yet.

EPISODE GUIDE

The symbol † indicates that the synopsis is based on an extant recording of the original broadcast. Copies of many of these episodes are available from one or more Old Time Radio vendors.

The symbol ‡ indicates that the synopsis is based on a script held in the Harry Crane Papers at UCLA. In some cases, the extant script is marked "Preview," and may have undergone some modifications prior to the air show.

Synopses for other episodes were compiled from newspaper program logs or advertisements taken out in those newspapers by the sponsor or local radio station. Whenever possible, they were confirmed via multiple printed sources. The following abbreviations are used to indicate the publication in which direct quotes appeared:

BC   *Bakersfield Californian*
MCGG   *The Mason City Globe-Gazette*, Mason City, Iowa

October 4, 1947. Guest, Danny Thomas; with Florence Halop. Frustrated by her lack of romantic success with Dr. Crenshaw, Joan decides to give up men and concentrate on her career. Her debutante friend, Gloria Newsome, advises her that a spiffed-up wardrobe is critical to her career goals. With the help of Danny Thomas, "Tailor to the Elite," Joan tries to assemble a fashionable wardrobe at a cut-rate price. Meanwhile, Joan wants to hire a hostess for the tea room, but somehow winds up with Lionel instead.†

> JOAN: What's wrong with the way I look?
> GLORIA: Darling, that dress you're wearing is miles too short. You look simply outlandish.
> JOAN: What do you mean, outlandish? My landish isn't out any more than yours is.

October 11, 1947. Guest, Victor Borge.

October 18, 1947. Guest, Danny Thomas. Having not yet found her ideal career, Joan accepts Lionel's suggestion that she apply for the job of "social secret'ry" to a wealthy society couple, the Billingtons. When that doesn't pan out, Joan meets a man who needs investors in his cold cream company. Dreaming that her $100 investment has netted her both fortune and the love of her new friend, Joan awakens to a more prosaic reality.‡

October 25, 1947. Guest, Danny Thomas. Joan and Lionel are asked to pose as the parents of Lionel's brilliant ten-year-old nephew, who's in trouble at school. When the teacher sends Lionel's "parents" to see the school principal, it seems that he remembers Joan quite well as a former pupil, and now understands the boy's problems.‡

November 1, 1947. "Joan Davis' search for an exciting career becomes even more complicated when those two unpredictable characters, [Bob] Sweeney and [Hal] March, drop in to see the comedy Queen...." *BC*

November 8, 1947. Guest, Garry Moore; with Florence Halop, Gail Bonney. Joan has been taking a $25 nursing course by correspondence, and is ready to launch her career in health care. After an unsuccessful job interview with Dr. Schnitzel at the city hospital, Joan is advised to seek help from "Honest Garry Moore," the most powerful man in local politics.†

> JOAN (describing her training): The Acme Correspondence School would send a letter with the symptoms, and we'd rush a letter back with the treatment we thought the patient should get. Unfortunately, my patient died.
> LIONEL: Yeah, what'd he die of?
> JOAN: Insufficient postage!

November 15, 1947. Joan tries to earn money by becoming a contestant on various radio quiz shows. Trying to infiltrate *Take It or Leave It*, hosted by Garry Moore, Joan poses as a reporter writing a story about the show from a contestant's point of view, and soon finds the answer to the $64 question.‡

> JOAN: Oh, stop worrying, Lionel. You'll get every cent of your back salary. Every week I don't pay you, it mounts up. Someday you'll have a nice little nest egg.
> LIONEL: Boss, I'm a workin' man, not an Easter bunny!

November 22, 1947. Guests, Bob Sweeney, Hal March. Joan thinks she's interviewing for the job of City Insect Exterminator, but she's actually talking to the City Playground Director. Her interview less than a success, she learns from Lionel that she has a secret admirer, and hires a detective to smoke him out. When it develops that Bob Sweeney is her bashful beau, and wants to marry her, his partner Hal March intervenes to prevent the union.‡

JOAN: Being broke wouldn't be so bad if only I had a little money. Gee, I wish I had a rich uncle with one foot in the grave. Boy, would I trip him!

November 29, 1947. Guest, Danny Kaye. Joan and Lionel have two free passes to the local movie theater, where Danny Kaye is making a personal appearance. After meeting the star backstage, Joan fantasizes that he falls in love with her.‡

JOAN: Y'know, Lionel, when Danny came out on stage in person, I could have sworn he looked right at me!
LIONEL: Yeah?
JOAN: Yeah, he gave me a sort of come-hither look, and boy, I hithered!

December 5, 1947. Guest, Garry Moore; with Jerry Hausner, Maxine Marx. Joan pawns Lionel's watch in order to pay for lessons at Jerome's Dancing School. But when that doesn't cover her $200 tuition, Joan has a backup plan. Seems she's accidentally invented a cleaning fluid that's worth $10,000 to a chemical company run by Garry Moore. It's made of four ingredients—boric acid, vinegar, rose water, and—one that suddenly Joan can't remember.†

LIONEL: But, gee, boss, you shouldn't've hocked that watch. It has such sentimental value.
JOAN: Sentimental value?
LIONEL: Yeah, I stole it from my father.

December 12, 1947. Guest, Rudy Vallee; with Florence Halop. Expecting a visit from her old boss Rudy Vallee, Joan wants to impress him with how successful she is. After a failed attempt to buy some new finery on credit, Joan enlists Lionel to pose as her would-be beau, a Harvard man. Little does she know that she's setting the stage for a rivalry with proud Yale graduate Rudy.‡

JOAN: Well, Lionel, I admit I used to be crazy about Rudy. But I happen to be very particular, and there was one annoying little habit Rudy had, that I absolutely refused to put up with.
LIONEL: What was that?
JOAN: He wouldn't have anything to do with me!

December 20, 1947. "Hal March intervenes with Santa to get his fellow comedian Bob Sweeney the Christmas present he covets most, to wit: the entrancing Joan Davis...." *MCGG*

December 27, 1947. Guest, Danny Thomas. Wanting to enjoy a night on the town on New Year's Eve, Joan and Lionel tell her Uncle Sylvester they're engaged, so that he will reward them with a cash gift. When that plan falls through, Joan suggests they attend Danny Thomas' nightclub act, thinking he is an old childhood acquaintance of hers who will remember the good old days and pick up her check.‡

JOAN: Danny, it's me, it's me.
THOMAS: Oh, I knew it was you the minute I saw you.
JOAN: No fooling, you did?
THOMAS: Sure, there's only one thing that puzzles me.
JOAN: What's that?
THOMAS: Who's you?

January 3, 1948. "Joan Davis attempts to snare Bill Goodwin in her romantic web.... Needless to say, Joanie loses out again but amidst plenty of laughs...." *BC*

January 10, 1948. Guest, Charles Cantor. When Lionel gambles away a day's worth of income from the tea room, Joan fires him and replaces him with Clifton Finnegan (Cantor's character from *Duffy's Tavern*). To get his job back, Lionel tells Joan that Finnegan is actually "Clifton the Bluebeard," who marries women for their money and then kills them.‡

LIONEL: But, boss, you can't mean you'd really fire me. Why, we've been so close to each other ... like brother and sister, mother and daughter, father and son.
JOAN: Yeah, but now we're like powder and cannon.
LIONEL: Powder and cannon?
JOAN: Yeah, you're fired. Goodbye!

January 17, 1948. Guest, Chico Marx. An insurance policy taken out by Joan's parents has matured, resulting in a $500 payout. Joan considers various options, including investments through a bank, and financing eccentric inventor Ludwig von Himmelstrasser. She finally decides to buy a songwriting business run by Chico Marx. When her new venture proves unprofitable, Joan devises a scheme to get her money back from the cagey chiseler.‡

CHICO: Wait a minute, you want to buy the company—but you're a woman.
JOAN: Sure.
CHICO: Sure, I can tell by the nail polish.
JOAN: That has nothing to do with it. I'm interested in getting a business.
CHICO: Lady, if you're interested in getting the business, you come to the right place!

January 24, 1948. Guest, Howard Duff; with Bob Jellison. Joan glamorizes herself as a *femme fatale* for her date with timid Freddie Hartzfelder, but the new look only scares him off. Disappointed, Joan dreams that she's the newest client of radio detective Sam Spade (Howard Duff), whom she hired to defend her against accusations of murdering her husband Reginald (Lionel Stander). Unfortunately, the results of Spade's investigation lead Joan holding the bag.‡

REGINALD: I say, you're not sorry you married me, are you, old heifer?
JOAN: Why, Reginald, what makes you say that?
REGINALD: Oh, I don't know. You seem to be cooling off towards me lately.
JOAN: Cooling off?
REGINALD: Yes, I felt it yesterday when you tried to knife me.

January 31, 1948. Guest, Billy De Wolfe. Joan manages to elicit a marriage proposal from her boyfriend Freddie Hartzfelder (Bob Jellison), and decides to have his apartment redecorated to make a suitable home for the happy couple.‡

JOAN: I want a decorating job to fit the personality of a young, glamorous, attractive woman.
DECORATOR: A young, glamorous, attractive woman?
JOAN: Yes, after all, what am I?
DECORATOR: Miss Davis, I hate riddles! Now, this room is furnished horribly –miserably— that chair over there, that's simply got to go, and that thingamajig over there, that definitely has to go.
JOAN: That's Freddie, my fiancé.
DECORATOR: Well, the very least we can do is have him repainted.

February 7, 1948. Guest, Bob Crosby; with Jean Vander Pyl. Joan tries to drum up business at the tea room by making it the meeting spot for women's clubs. The clubwomen want music at their luncheons, so Joan tries to hire swing singer Bob Crosby to entertain them. When he balks at taking the gig, Joan blackmails him with the embarrassing fact that he actually prefers opera to the latest Hit Parade songs.‡

February 14, 1948. "Joan Davis faces Valentine's Day without a sweetie but Garry Moore shows up ... in answer to Joanie's prayer." *BC*

February 21, 1948. Guests, Bob Sweeney, Hal March.

February 28, 1948. Guest, Kenny Baker. Joan wants to get into show business, so Lionel introduces her to his friend Mr. Murphy, owner of a talent agency. When she hears that the agency's clients include singer Kenny Baker, she buys out Mr. Murphy for $200, and proceeds to get Baker a $100-a-week singing job. Too bad Kenny has never heard of Murphy, or the agency.‡

March 6, 1948. "Howard Duff brings his character of Sam Spade to the show to help Joanie in her search for a man." *BC*

March 13, 1948. Guests, Bob Sweeney, Hal March.

March 20, 1948. No synopsis available.

March 27, 1948. Guest, Xavier Cugat; with Sylvia Syms. The Choral-Aires sing "When You're Smiling." Joan has taken an advertising course from the Acme School of Advertising, and is going door-to-door selling classified ads for the local newspaper. When that doesn't pan out, she decides to open her own advertising agency, seeking to win the account of Latin bandleader Xavier Cugat for his candy company, Cugat's Nougats. Joan proposes a new radio show to compete with *Queen for a Day*, called *King for a Week*, which Cugat can sponsor.†

April 3, 1948. Guest, John Payne. Joan has bragged to her old school friend Cynthia that she's married to movie star John Payne. When Cynthia visits the tea room, however, Joan tries to cover by admitting that she and John have recently separated—after four days of marriage. But when she and Cynthia run into Payne at a restaurant, Joan convinces the actor to help her save face by corroborating her stories. Mention is made of Payne's real-life marriage to actress Gloria DeHaven, allowing for a joke in which Joan alludes to the popular radio soap opera *John's Other Wife*.†

April 10, 1948. Bob Sweeney and Hal March pay a return visit, with Bob in pursuit of Joan romantically. He invites her to a dance, where he plans to pop the question, but Joan won't go—she thinks the occasion calls for a fur coat, and she doesn't have one. Hal, who was on his way to take his neighbor Mrs. Hammerschlog's fur coat to a storage vault, lends it to Bob, so that can impress Joan. But when Mrs. Hammerschlog unexpectedly wants her coat back, Bob tries to finesse the awkward situation by telling Joan about an impending attack of "mink weevils."‡

> BOB: I was hoping you'd go to the dance with me so that maybe I could kiss you ... and then maybe we could become engaged.
> JOAN: Engaged? But that means marriage ... if we ever did get married, how could we manage? You have nothing ... how would we live?
> BOB: Don't worry, I'm sure something would come along.
> JOAN: Yeah, and then we'd have to feed that, too!

April 17, 1948. Dropping by the tea room on her way to a movie, Joan learns that she missed a visit from her old pal Rudy Vallee. When Rudy returns, he asks Joan to marry him: He wants to adopt a little girl, but the authorities won't let him unless he has a wife to help care for her. After applying for a marriage license, Joan goes back to the tea room, where she has a dream about what marriage to Rudy might really be like.‡

April 24, 1948. Returning from her pal Mazie's wedding, Joan is depressed that she's still single. When her old boyfriend Harry Von Zell stops by, Joan is impressed that he's come up in the world since she dated him, having launched a movie career. Looks like Joan might finally have hooked a husband, but there's a problem: Harry's father opposes the marriage. Joan tries to impress her prospective father-in-law by cooking him a pheasant dinner. But Lionel, who's jealous of her relationship with Harry, gives her the wrong birds, and Joan's crow dinner leaves a bad taste in the mouths of the Von Zells.‡

May 1, 1948. Guest, Peter Lind Hayes. Suffering from insomnia, Joan decides to take up ballet, so that she will be tired enough to fall asleep every night. When that doesn't work, she visits a hobby shop to find another strenuous activity, but comes up empty-handed. Joan places herself in the care of psychiatrist Dr. Hayes, who thinks the answer to her sleepless nights can be found by examining her love life.‡

May 8, 1948. Joan doesn't have enough money to take the vacation she wants with her pal Mabel. When she hears about a contest sponsored by Herman's Department Store, offering $100 for the best original idea for a radio show, Joan leaps into action. Mr. Herman doesn't care for her first few ideas, but he's intrigued when she proposes a panel discussion show featuring well-known academics such as Professor Cavendish and Professor Schultz. When she's unable to get the real eggheads to appear, Joan tries to make do with rough-hewn Lionel and his bird-brained buddy.‡

> HERMAN: You mean you really know Schultz, the famous physicist?
> JOAN: Sure, I knew him before he even learned to fizz!

May 15, 1948. Guest, Alan Young. Needing vacation money, Joan tries selling Dr. Schultz's Health Tonic door to door. When that venture doesn't pan out, Joan takes the advice of her friend Alan Young, who suggests she try to break into the movies. Joan decides to make her Hollywood splash with a story showing the dark underbelly of Los Angeles life.‡

> JOAN: Gee, I hope I can sell enough of this stuff to earn some vacation money.... They told me it was a great rejuvenator. One bottle of Schultz's Health Tonic is supposed to make you ten years younger. In fact, any customer who buys eight bottles gets a set of diapers free!

May 22, 1948. Guest, Andy Russell. Still on the prowl for vacation funds, Joan tries selling insurance. Boarding a Hollywood tour bus, Joan stops at the home of her old pal Andy Russell, who agrees to insure his singing voice. Joan's boss, Mr. Nelson, doesn't approve of the deal, and wants her to cancel the policy. But in the meantime, it seems Andy has developed a cold that threatens to interfere with his next gig.‡

May 31, 1948. Guest, Constance Bennett; with Frank Nelson. Joan's latest moonlighting gig finds her working as a reporter for the *Daily Bugle*. Her man-on-the-street interviews at the corner of Hollywood and Vine don't produce anything newsworthy, so her editor sends her to interview movie star Constance Bennett.‡

> JOAN: Gee, Constance Bennett! Let's see, what should I talk to her about?
> EDITOR: I don't know. What is the conversation usually about when two women talk?
> JOAN: Two men!

June 5, 1948. Joan and Mabel buy a rundown private detective agency for $100. Their first client is a man who wants them to shadow his girlfriend, but balks at the $300 price Joan quotes him—and asks her for a date instead. Next up is singer Bob Crosby, who calls the office and says he has a case for them. Awaiting his arrival, Joan dozes off and dreams she's helping Crosby investigate a murder.‡

MABEL: Joan, that [bathing] suit was terribly loose on you.

JOAN: That's true, it was a little loose. The first time I went in swimming, I caught ten pounds of tuna!

June 12, 1948. Guest, Pat O'Brien. Joan's Irish great-uncle Timothy O'Davis sends her a letter expressing his dying wish—that she find and marry a member of the O'Brien clan, thus ending the "bitter feud" that existed between the two families. With the help of a friendly leprechaun (Hans Conried), Joan tries to awaken the ardor of movie star Pat O'Brien.‡

JOAN (yawning): Oh, gosh, what a nightmare I just had. I was dreaming that Cary Grant was making love to me, and smothering me with kisses, and more kisses, and more...

GAGE: Joanie, wait a minute, how could that turn into a nightmare?

JOAN: I woke up, didn't I?

June 19, 1948. Guests, Frances Langford, Jon Hall. A con artist soaks Joan for $200, leading her to believe she has bought her own airline. The real owners turn out to be movie stars Langford and Hall, who help Joan out of her predicament.‡

JOAN (to Hall): Gee, my boyfriend Freddie took me to see one of your pictures last night. Wow, what love scenes. Every other minute you were kissing the leading lady. I never saw so much kissing. Three solid hours.

HALL: Three hours? Just the picture couldn't have run much more than an hour.

JOAN: I know but when the picture stopped, Freddie didn't....

June 26, 1948. Joan is jealous: Mabel has accepted a marriage proposal from a man named Harry Krub. When Joan takes out a newspaper ad announcing her availability as a wife for $10,000, actress Marjorie Main shows up to see if she can snag one of Joan's rejects for herself. Both ladies take an interest in a horticulturist named Herbert. Miss Main tries to undercut Joan's price by offering to marry Herbert for $9,500, and soon the bidding war is on.‡

Note: This synopsis was taken from a preview script dated June 23, 1948, in the Harry Crane Papers. However, Miss Main, who previously worked with Joan on the Sealtest show, did not ultimately appear in the broadcast three days later, and syndicated columnist Erskine Johnson (July 22, 1948) reported "rumors that Joan Davis cancelled Marjorie Main's guest appearance ... because of Marjorie's comedy-stealing tricks."

Leave It to Joan

Cast: Joan Davis (*Joan Davis*), Joseph Kearns (*"Pops" Davis*), Willard Waterman (*Simon L. Hackaday*), Shirley Mitchell (*Penny Prentiss*), Shepard Menken (*Tom Hinkle*)

Producer-Director: Dick Mack. *Writers*: Harry Crane, Al Gordon, Jesse Goldstein, Jack Harvey, Lee Karson, Marvin Marx. *Music*: Lyn Murray and His Orchestra. *Announcers*: Bob Lemond, Ken Niles, Bob Stevenson.

Sponsor: American Tobacco Company. Aired Mondays at 9:00 p.m. (through August 1949), then Fridays at 9:00 p.m. (through March 1950), then Mondays at 10:00 p.m. on CBS. First aired on July 4, 1949; last aired on August 21, 1950.

Off the air for nearly a year after the demise of *Joan Davis Time*, the star wouldn't get another opportunity for a weekly series until mid–1949. *Billboard* reported in September 1948 that Joan was near to striking a sponsorship deal with the Chrysler Corporation, but this didn't pan out. Not until the following May did *Billboard* announce that Joan was on the way back to the CBS airwaves with her new show, despite some bumps along the road. "The chief difficulty was that CBS felt it had the right to an audition record of the contemplated program, while Miss Davis believed her years on radio were sufficient guarantee of a competent performance." Joan was ultimately signed by American Tobacco for a weekly tab of $8,500, with a guarantee of 21 weeks on the air; as *Billboard* noted, "A click on her new radio show would put her on her feet in the TV picture."[38] *Leave It to Joan* premiered as an eight-week summer replacement for *The Lux Radio Theater*, with the hope that it would be sufficiently popular to warrant a regular, sponsored run for the 1949-50 season.

In the series opener, Joan played a young woman wrongly arrested for shoplifting at a department store by her own father, a policeman newly promoted. To avoid litigation over the incident, Joan is offered a job at Willock's Department Store. Joan's sponsor, the American Tobacco Company, had a longtime association with Jack Benny's Sunday night show, plugging its Lucky Strike cigarettes, but the chief product advertised here was its Roi-Tan cigar—"the cigar that breathes." Though some observers found it odd to have a female star plugging cigar sales, especially one who readily admitted she didn't smoke them, American Tobacco's copywriters did their best to take advantage of Joan's comedic skills. Brandishing a tomahawk, moccasins, and a feathered headdress, Joan's image took the place of the traditional cigar store Indian in stores across the country, and graced the cover of millions of Roi-Tan cigar boxes. "I really don't know why the Roi-Tan company should think of me as a cigar store Indian," Joan told a reporter shortly after the show's premiere. "I guess it's because I'm good at selling to men."[39]

As one CBS press release described *Leave It to Joan*, "Her new comedy series stars Miss Davis as a saleslady with romantic inclinations in Willock's Department Store. However, it seems that Joan devotes more time to Mr. Hinkle, the store detective, than she does to the customers. This, of course, causes considerable anguish to the store's manager, Simon L. Hackaday. Joan's misadventure[s] across the counter make *Leave It to Joan* one of the most popular comedies on the air."[40]

Chief among Joan's supporting players was veteran character actor Joseph Kearns (1907–1962), cast as "Pops" Davis, her father. Perhaps most recognizable as the original Mr. Wilson on TV's *Dennis the Menace* (CBS, 1959–63), Kearns enjoyed a busy radio career supporting comedians such as Jack Benny and Burns and Allen, but also appeared on radio dramatic shows such as *Suspense*. Willard Waterman (1914–1995) was heard in the role of Simon Hackaday, Joan's constantly frustrated and fuming manager. Waterman had not yet assumed his most famous radio role, replacing Harold Peary as the star of NBC's *The Great Gildersleeve*.

There was usually a good role in Joan's radio shows for an actress to play her prettier, smarter rival, and here Shirley Mitchell (veteran of *The Joan Davis Show*) once again did the honors, playing Mr. Hackaday's assistant Penny Prentiss. Romantic interest was provided by Shepard Menken (1921–1999) as co-worker Tom Hinkle. Also heard in the initial broadcast were seasoned radio performers Lou Merrill, Elvia Allman, Sara Berner, Herb Vigran, and Bob Jellison.

Segments often opened with Joan (the character) at the breakfast table with "Pops." The writers could mine humor from items read aloud from the morning newspaper, as in this exchange from the November 4, 1949, episode:

> JOAN: Say, here's another unusual news item. In Pocatello, Idaho, a farmer named Jensen went into his barn one night. He reached up for the light switch, pulled it, and flooded the room.

"Pops" Davis (Joseph Kearns) lays down the law to his zany daughter (Joan) in CBS' *Leave It to Joan* (1949-50). Joan used Kearns again in her 1950 television pilot *Let's Join Joanie* and in guest roles on *I Married Joan*.

"POPS": With light?

JOAN: No, with milk! ... Jensen's a midget and he had a tall cow!

These sequences also allowed an opportunity for the writers to crack wise about current events, with various episodes alluding to movie queen Rita Hayworth's recent marriage to Prince Aly Khan, and the baby they were expecting, or President Harry Truman's controversial decision to award $15 million in foreign aid to France.

Writing in *Billboard* (July 16, 1949), reviewer Sam Chase wasn't dazzled by the series opener. "As a comedienne, Miss Davis has her points," Chase conceded, "but they are not particularly well brought out in this show, just as her past few series have had difficulties. The situations are just plain contrived and tired, and some of the gags left even the studio audience cold." According to the *New York Times'* Jack Gould, *Leave It to Joan* "does not differ perceptibly from the comedienne's past efforts. She still hits a line with shrill vehemence and the gag lines in the script are overweighted with the man-crazy motif. Perhaps the commercials will prove to be new."[41]

Audiences enjoyed the show, judging from its ratings. *Variety* (August 29, 1949) reported that Joan's Hooper rating of 9.2 made her show the most popular half-hour program on the Monday or Tuesday night airwaves. "CBS moved her to Friday nights for its last two sustainers previous to sponsorship Sept. 9 to break audiences into Friday night listening."

By January 1950, after only a few months on the air, the trades were reporting that American Tobacco wanted out, dissatisfied with the numbers Joan's show had been drawing. The growing popularity of television, and radio's declining ratings, were making it more difficult to keep sponsors bankrolling shows. By the end of the month came an announcement that Joan's deal with her current sponsor would come to a close in March. *Daily Variety* (January 23, 1950) reported that the decision was a puzzler in the eyes of industry observers: "Insiders can't figure cancellation since rating of 11.6 was best Hooper of any Friday night CBS show during the past year." The show went on hiatus after Joan declined a CBS offer to keep it on the air as a sustaining show, but it returned for a brief summer run in July and August, replacing *My Friend Irma*. The summertime slot found her part of a trio of short-run CBS comedies, following on the heels of *Too Many Cooks*, a family comedy starring Hal March, and *Granby's Green Acres*, a predecessor to television's *Green Acres*, with Gale Gordon as the blustery character who would be taken over on TV by Eddie Albert.

Upon the show's revival in July, *Variety* (July 5, 1950) called it "an enjoyable situation comedy with a heaping helping of gags.... Miss Davis is reviving her bungling department store salesgirl who snared a CBS sponsor last season. She still makes an appealing character. And there's a frank, down-to-earth quality in the humorous handling of the gal who is candidly after a man—any man."

With the conclusion of *Leave It to Joan* that summer, Joan's starring career as a radio comedienne was over, though she would continue to make guest appearances into the early 1950s. As Joan herself had realized, it was time to give serious consideration to a television career.

Said *Variety* (July 5, 1950), "This eight-week stint is just a stop-gap for the madcap miss. CBS has ambitious television plans for the lady, perhaps feeling that the end of the line isn't far off for her sound antics and that she'll even grow in stature as a sight act.... We'll be seein' you, Joanie."

EPISODE GUIDE

The January 20, 1950, episode of *Leave It to Joan*, with guest star Al Jolson, is the only one (as of this writing) in general circulation among Old Time Radio collectors.

The symbol ‡ indicates that the synopsis is based on a script held in the Harry Crane Papers at UCLA. In some cases, the extant script is marked "Preview," and may have undergone modifications prior to the air show.

Synopses for other episodes were compiled from newspaper program logs or advertisements taken out in those newspapers by the sponsor or local radio station. Whenever possible, they were confirmed via multiple printed sources. The following abbreviations are used to indicate the publication in which direct quotes appeared:

MCGG   *The Mason City Globe-Gazette*, Mason City, Iowa
PT   *The Portsmouth Times*, Portsmouth, Ohio
SAE   *The San Antonio Express*, San Antonio, Texas
WSJ   *The Wisconsin State Journal*, Madison, Wisconsin

The notation "No synopsis available" indicates that newspaper radio logs confirmed that the show aired on that date, but did not yield any information about content or guest stars.

....

July 4, 1949. "Joan is back for the summer as a day-dreaming department store clerk...." *MCGG*

July 11, 1949. "Joan Davis muddles up the exchange department of Willock's Department Store...." *MCGG*

July 18, 1949. No synopsis available.

July 26, 1949. "Joan bags two thieves the hard way...." *MCGG*

August 1, 1949. No synopsis available.

August 8, 1949. "There's a picnic for Willock's Department Store employees and Joan Davis manages to get lost on a treasure hunt on Catalina Island...." *PT*

August 15, 1949. Joan is on probation at the store due to her latest blunders. Mr. Hackaday assigns her to work in the book department, expecting little business there because a popular author will be signing his books at Tracy's, the rival store across the street. Joan decides to help out by persuading the author to change his plans, but it doesn't soothe the situation when she encounters him, and mistakes him for a janitor.‡

August 22, 1949. No synopsis available.

September 2, 1949. Working in the Lost and Found department, Joan takes in an Irish setter who's been separated from his owner. Once the dog has broken an expensive vase Joan uses to give him drinking water, and bitten Mr. Hackaday, Joan is out $90 and unemployed to boot. "Pops" tells Joan about a $100 reward posted by the dog's owner, and she scrambles to retrieve the valuable pooch from the store where he's been locked up overnight.‡

   JOAN: Uh-oh! He smashed up that valuable vase! Or is it vahse? I better look that up.

September 9, 1949. "Pops" gives Joan two tickets to a wrestling match, and she invites her college-aged co-worker, Roy Douglas, to accompany her. Joan's rival Penny, who wants Roy for herself, persuades Mr. Hackaday to make Joan stay late and work on inventory so that her plans will be disrupted. Trying to retrieve the inventory lists she accidentally discarded, Joan visits the Main Street Mission, where she makes another find that proves unexpectedly beneficial.‡

   HACKADAY: Miss Davis, I'm tired of this jabber. Your stupidity has finally reached an apex.
   JOAN: A who-pex?
   HACKADAY: Apex. Surely you know what an apex is.
   JOAN: Oh, yeah. When two apes get married, they have a little apex!

September 16, 1949. Willock's is sponsoring a radio show, in which callers who correctly name a song being played win cash prizes. Joan learns that the consultant hired to put on the radio show has arranged for a friend of his to call in and win the $15,000 grand prize, but she unwittingly fouls up his scheme when she plays the wrong side of the record during the broadcast.‡

> JOAN (reading the newspaper): Gee, look, "Pops," this page is just full of pictures of kids and teachers hurrying back to public school and high school. The only ones who are taking their time are the college professors.
>
> "POPS": College professors?
>
> JOAN: Sure, you know—college professors—the guys who get what's left after the football coaches are paid off!

September 23, 1949. Joan tries to help Mr. Hackaday settle his traffic ticket. "Trying to impress the boss, Joanie takes the ticket to her father to fix, but because of the commotion over an unknown car-smashing violator called 'Flat Fender Philip,' she not only fails to fix the ticket, but causes the swearing out of a warrant for her boss as 'Flat Fender.'" *PT,* September 14, 1949

September 30, 1949. "Joan Davis and the boss' nephew give their opinions of modern art...." *MCGG*

October 7, 1949. Joan's working in Willock's campus shop department, selling fashions for college girls. The department is overstocked, thanks to Joan's faulty ordering, so Mr. Hackaday sends her and Penny Prentiss to UCLA, where Penny can model the clothes. At the university, Joan hits her head on a fountain, and while out cold dreams that she's a smart, pretty college student. Reviving, she finds that all the co-eds covet the Willock's outfit she's wearing, which luckily happens to be the skirt and blouse she over-ordered.‡

> PENNY: I think we're going to sell a lot of campus clothes here, Mr. Hackaday.
>
> HACKADAY: We certainly should, Miss Prentiss. There's a very large student body here.
>
> JOAN: Hey, maybe if that student's body is too large, we won't be able to fit it!

October 14, 1949. An important client, Mr. Donaldson, is coming to Joan's department to buy furniture for his Las Vegas hotel, the Flamingo. Joan's worried that her recent bout of insomnia will get her into trouble at work, so Mr. Hinkle gives her a soda laced with sleeping pills. Penny drinks the soda and passes out while she and Mr. Hackaday are entertaining Mr. Donaldson at a nightclub. Summoned by Mr. Hackaday to fill in for Penny, Joan too has been doped with pills (by a well-meaning "Pops"), and winds up unconscious on the nightclub floor. The club's patrons are held up by robbers, but they trip over Joan's prone body and are caught, making her a heroine in the client's eyes.‡

October 21, 1949. The proud new owner of two shares of stock in Willock's Department Store, Joan decides to implement some improvements in the store's operation, angering her boss. Fired by Mr. Hackaday, Joan turns up at the stockholders' meeting where he's running for chairman of the board of directors. A takeover attempt by the owners of Willock's rival store, Tracy's, makes Joan's vote, as a minority stockholder, critical to the outcome. With Joan now working as a clerk at Tracy's, Mr. Hackaday and his rivals find themselves bidding for her services.‡

> HACKADAY: There's a stockholders' meeting today and ...
>
> JOAN: You want me to attend?
>
> HACKADAY: No, no. But I would like you to give me your proxy.
>
> JOAN: My who-xy?
>
> HACKADAY: Proxy. Surely you know what a proxy is.
>
> JOAN: Oh, sure. When two bottles of peroxide get married, they have a little proxy. That's one subject I'm an expert on.

October 28, 1949. Joan, wanting to get America's youth "off of the streets and out of the pool rooms," is sponsoring a youth football team, coached by her Willock's co-worker Roy Douglas. For their game against the Beverly Hills Broncos, Joan orders new uniforms from Willock's, planning to use $250 "Pops" raised from his colleagues at the precinct. When the money turns up missing, Mr. Hackaday wants the uniforms returned. Having placed a bet with Penny as to the game's outcome, Joan lets her boys wear them anyway. They win, but Joan loses (when Mr. Hackaday fires her), until an unexpected savior appears on the scene.‡

> ROY: Personally, I'll be satisfied if our boys just make a good showing. They're liable to get the pants beat off them.
>
> JOAN: If they get the pants beat off them, they're *bound* to make a good showing!

November 4, 1949. While driving Joan to work in Mr. Hackaday's car, Tom Hinkle gets a traffic ticket. Because Mr. Hackaday received a ticket the night before, Joan's irascible boss is now expected to appear in court, per a new state law. Tom poses as Mr. Hackaday in court, but he and Joan can't raise enough money to pay the fines. When the judge deduces that Joan and her pal are trying to cover for their boss, Mr. Hackaday himself is hauled in front of the bench, leaving Joan's continued employment at Willock's in jeopardy.‡

November 11, 1949. Willock's is sponsoring a float in the Chamber of Commerce's parade, using the slogan "Willock's customers look like this." The Willock's float theme is a secret, until a detective from their rival store, Tracy's, worms it out of Joan, causing Penny to cancel the store's entry. Driving the float to observe the parade in progress, Joan and Tom pick up two hoboes who make themselves at home atop the float, barbecuing "weenies" and taking a dip in the swimming pool. When the Willock's float, complete with ragged hoboes, accidentally joins the parade route, onlookers see the sign, "Willock's customers look like this," followed by the Tracy's float, which reads, "Since they switched to Tracy's."‡

November 18, 1949. Mr. Hackaday assigns Joan to perform an in-store demonstration of cooking a Thanksgiving turkey. Thanks to a misprint in the cookbook, Joan prepares her bird with varnish instead of garnish, resulting in an explosive situation. With her job at stake (again), Joan and Tom crash a party at the home of the cookbook's author, Susie Schuyler, to enlist her help.‡

> JOAN (offering a holiday jingle her boss can use with customers in arrears):
>> Here's a wish from Willock's Department Store,
>> May you have Thanksgiving cheer galore,
>> And while you eat your turkey and your candied yams,
>> Don't forget you owe us thirty clams!

November 25, 1949. When movie star Mayra Martin shops for maternity items at Willock's, Joan writes a story for the department store's new newsletter, the *Willock's Weekly*. Penny sends Joan's story to be published, but attaches her own byline. Informed that the movie actress is not pregnant, and was only shopping for her sister, Mr. Hackaday holds Penny accountable for the error. But a follow-up visit from Mayra reveals that she has been secretly married, and is in fact expecting a blessed event.‡

December 2, 1949. "Courtesy week" at Willock's goes awry for Joan, who's fired after a new employee, Penny's sister Cynthia—wearing Joan's smock and nametag—is rude to a customer. When unemployed Joan tries to cheer herself up with a shopping expedition to Willock's, she too experiences Cynthia's brand of customer service, and files a complaint with Mr. Hackaday.‡

JOAN: Well, "Pops," it's about Willock's. I'm not working there any more.
"POPS": You mean you lost your job?
JOAN: No, "Pops," I didn't lose it—they took it away from me!

December 9, 1949. Working in the credit department, Joan tries to collect the balance on the account of Mr. and Mrs. Taylor. Joan makes matters worse by accepting a rubber check from the Taylors, and allowing them to place a large order for furniture. When Joan and Tom Hinkle pay a follow-up visit to the Taylors, they find only an empty lot where the house previously stood, and a shoebox containing $5,000 in cash.‡

December 16, 1949. Joan's new friend Steve Martin has been "out for five years," which she takes to mean that he's an ex-convict (he's actually been out of the Navy for that time). Trying to "rehabilitate" Steve, she gets him a job at the store, then panics when a robbery is committed. With Steve's help, the real crook is apprehended and Joan's job at Willock's is safe for another week. Gerald Mohr plays Steve.‡

JOAN (flattered by Steve's compliments): Beautiful? Do you really think I'm beautiful?
STEVE: I sure do, baby!
JOAN: Oh, you must've been in for more than five years!

December 23, 1949. Joan is hosting a Christmas party for poor children at the local settlement house, but her gift-giving plans are thwarted when Mr. Hackaday refuses to extend her credit. Learning that the Willocks' spoiled son Myron has $50 in store credit that he doesn't need, Joan tells him the story of *A Christmas Carol* in hopes of inspiring the boy to give those less fortunate a happy holiday.‡

January 13, 1950. "Joan Davis escorts two visitors through Willock's Department Store.... The first man on the Davis tour is a possible investor, for whom Joanie runs down the store. The second visitor gets a buildup, and turns out to be the tax assessor." *SAE*

January 20, 1950. Guest, Al Jolson. It's the 25th anniversary of Willock's Department Store, to be commemorated with a party attended by Al Jolson and featuring entertainment by store employees. Joan, who just saw *Jolson Sings Again* (with Larry Parks playing Jolson), doesn't recognize the real star when she sees him, and assumes her new friend is just a Jolson impersonator.†

Leave It to Joan continued to air weekly through March 3, 1950. It returned on July 3, 1950, for an eight-week summer run that concluded with the final series episode on August 21, 1950.

None of the episodes from this period are currently in circulation, nor are scripts held in the Crane Papers at UCLA. Newspaper listings indicated that guest stars during this period included Art Linkletter (February 2, 1950) and Garry Moore (February 18, 1950). Only the briefest of synopses could be extracted from newspaper listings:

January 27, 1950. "Joan is more interested in the store detective than her job as a clerk." *MCGG*

March 3, 1950. Joan "finds that the police commissioner's snooty wife is an ex-strip tease artist...." *SAE*

July 24, 1950. "[D]epartment store's Western promotion turns into a stampede." *WSJ*

According to *Variety* (July 5, 1950), the first episode of the summer run "dealt with Miss Davis' posing as an heiress to impress a chauffeur posing as his multi-millionaire boss."

Selected Guest Appearances

The Shell Chateau. NBC, May 30, 1936. "John Barrymore, Madame Ernestine Schumann-Heink, comedian Robert Wildhack, Frank Shields, tennis star turned screen actor, and Joan Davis, Hollywood comedy singer, will join Smith Ballew and Victor Young...." (*Carroll* [IA] *Daily Herald*, May 29, 1936)

Command Performance. August 18, 1942. Host Cary Grant welcomes "that Yankee Doodle dumbbell" Joan, along with singer Virginia O'Brien and Bert Lahr. Grant challenges Joan to join him in "a serious love scene." Flattered by his attentions, Joan declares, "What's Betty Grable got that I couldn't have straightened?"

Command Performance. October 7, 1942. Host Cary Grant introduces "that old corny favorite," Joan, who sings her novelty song, "Jim." Also appearing are Spike Jones and the City Slickers, Abbott and Costello, Ethel Waters, and Rise Stevens.

Command Performance. January 6, 1943. Host Robert Taylor introduces Joan and additional guests the King Sisters and Lum and Abner. Joan does a flirtation scene with Taylor, and performs her specialty version of "He's My Guy." Taylor asks if there's "a particular guy" in Joan's life, to which she responds, "Well, he's not *too* particular!" Of working opposite Taylor, Joan later told a reporter, "What actress wouldn't enjoy that assignment? What *woman* wouldn't?"

Soldiers with Wings. January 23, 1943. This patriotic program, broadcast from the West Coast Air Force Training Center, featured Joan as guest star, along with Preston Foster and Dona Drake.

The Camel Comedy Caravan. CBS, March 19, 1943. "Rudy Vallee and Joan Davis contribute a laugh-filled sketch.... Their portion of the program comes from Hollywood." (*San Antonio Light*)

The Camel Comedy Caravan. CBS, March 26, 1943. Host Jack Carson welcomes Joan as guest in the show's first broadcast after relocating from New York to Hollywood.

People Are Funny. NBC, December 10, 1943. Joan begins her week of guest appearances on multiple shows, searching for a mysterious package. Taking part in one of host Art Linkletter's stunts, Joan plays a love scene with an audience member.

The National Barn Dance. NBC, December 11, 1943. The program features a winter party of Christmas carols, with Joan and Donald Novis as guests.

Blondie. CBS, December 13, 1943.

Duffy's Tavern. NBC Blue, December 14, 1943. Guest, Dinah Shore. Joan visits the tavern looking for her package, but goes home empty-handed. Archie suggests she look for a straitjacket instead, but she replies, "Oh, no, I got one of those!" Series star Ed Gardner (Archie) was previously Joan's Sealtest show producer.

Time to Smile. NBC, December 15, 1943. "Roy Rogers, movieland's 'King of the Cowboys,' and Joan Davis, screenland's daffiest comedienne, ride herd on Eddie Cantor and his ... troupe...." (*Findlay* [OH] *Republican-Courier*)

The Kraft Music Hall. NBC, December 16, 1943. Joan and Phil Silvers are the guests of host Bing Crosby.

Mail Call. March 8, 1944. Joan appears alongside Eddie Cantor, Lionel Barrymore, and the Pied Pipers.

Time to Smile. NBC, February 2, 1944. Joan pays a return visit to Eddie Cantor's program.

Storyteller. ABC, September 13, 1944. Joan is guest narrator.

Time to Smile. NBC, September 27, 1944. Joan is the guest star on Eddie Cantor's season premiere.

The Rudy Vallee Show. NBC, October 7, 1944. Rudy and Joan exchange badinage while he sings "For Me and My Gal." Joan claims she's been offered an MGM contract to appear opposite a major star: "By the way, who is Lassie?"

The Silver Theater. CBS, August 5, 1945. "A Charmed Life." Host Conrad Nagel introduces a drama starring Joan and Harry von Zell.

Command Performance. August 23, 1945. Host Franchot Tone introduces Joan, Edgar Bergen and Charlie McCarthy, and Margaret Whiting.

The Bob Hope Show. NBC, January 8, 1946. Joan is crowned "Queen of Comedy," based on a national magazine poll, and Bob as King.

Joan is crowned "Queen of Comedy" by the star of *The Bob Hope Show.*

Birds Eye Open House. NBC, March 21, 1946. Joan guests on Dinah Shore's program. A ladies' organization, GOOPLEFINC, "a sister organization of Gracie Allen's Beverly Hills Uplift Society," recommends Dinah and Joan as new members of the Chamber of Commerce. Joan's performance, which includes a novelty song called "T'isn't Rain" (to the tune of "Let It Snow"), reduces Dinah to giggles during the broadcast.

Stars in the Afternoon. CBS, September 29, 1946. Joan and her new supporting player Wally Brown are among the guests in this preview of CBS's 1946-47 radio season, hosted by Ozzie Nelson and Harriet Hilliard.

Command Performance. July 15, 1947. Host Eddie Cantor welcomes Joan as guest star, along with singer Imogene Carpenter and Bert Gordon ("The Mad Russian"). Eddie is dismayed to find that, after they played a wedding scene together in *If You Knew Susie*, Joan claims they are married for real.

Red Cross Program. CBS, June 12, 1948. Joan and her former radio co-star Andy Russell were among the celebrities heard in a 45-minute program saluting the American Red Cross. Bob Hope and Phil Baker emceed the broadcast, which also featured Jack Benny, Dinah Shore, Betty Hutton, and Danny Kaye.

Command Performance. November 30, 1948. Host Vincent Price introduces Joan and singer Kay Starr.

The Sealtest Variety Theatre. NBC, February 3, 1949. Host: Dorothy Lamour. Joan and Robert Cummings are the guests in this episode, marking a return for Joan to the (revamped) show in which she once starred. In a sketch, Joan plays an aggressive *Daily Bugle* newspaper reporter, determined to interview Dorothy Lamour and ask her pressing questions such as, "Do you think television will ever replace necking?" Given the bum's rush at Lamour's home, Joan turns up in disguise everywhere the star goes that day, posing as her French hairdresser, a Swedish masseuse, and an English-accented fellow guest at an elegant party.

The Kraft Music Hall. NBC, February 17, 1949. Joan is the guest of series star Al Jolson, with pianist Oscar Levant also featured.

The Sealtest Variety Theatre. NBC, May 12, 1949. Host: Dorothy Lamour. Joan and Eddie Bracken are the guests. In a sketch, Joan tries to make a love match with Eddie.

The Edgar Bergen-Charlie McCarthy Show. CBS, December 4, 1949. "Joan Davis will try to show Charlie McCarthy some of the fine—and rough—points of door-to-door selling.... Miss Davis throws herself into this project with her usual hilarious abandon." (*Long Beach Press-Telegram*, November 29, 1949)

Duffy's Tavern. NBC, May 4, 1950. Davis "finds herself cast as the star of a western play written by manager Ed (Archie) Gardner, who promises to make her as famous as Hopalong Cassidy." (*La Crosse* [WI] *Tribune*)

The Big Show. NBC, December 3, 1950. This top-budgeted ($100,000 per week) 90-minute variety show hosted by stage and film star Tallulah Bankhead represented one of the networks' last major efforts to compete with television. Each episode featured multiple top-name guest stars ("the most scintillating personalities in the entertainment world"). Joan would return frequently to the show throughout its nearly two-year run, until she began working on the fall 1952 premiere of her TV show *I Married Joan*. Davis and Bankhead trade insults in an early scene, until the latter says in frustration:

> TALLULAH: I don't know why I beat my head against the wall talking to you!
> JOAN: Well, maybe you're trying to get a shape you like!

After imitating Bankhead's smoky voice, Joan remarks, "One of us ought to quit gargling with Drano!"

The Big Show. NBC, February 11, 1951. Guests, Joan, Groucho Marx, Judy Garland, Dean Martin, Jerry Lewis, The Andrews Sisters. *Variety* (February 14, 1951) termed this installment "one of the smoothest and funniest in the hep series, with an impressive array of talent delivering to the hilt."

The Bob Hope Show. NBC, March 13, 1951. Joan and singer Johnny Desmond are Bob's guests in a segment broadcast from the Hollywood USO Canteen.

The Big Show. NBC, April 1, 1951. This segment originates from Hollywood. Joan exchanges banter with Bankhead and fellow guest Ethel Barrymore, before launching into a calypso number, "Happiness." Serving as Joan's backup singers are Ezio Pinza, Groucho Marx, Van Johnson, and Bob Hope.

The Big Show. NBC, April 22, 1951. Tallulah complains of her recent illnesses, but an undaunted Joan is determined to top her.

> JOAN: Did you know I have a silver plate in my head?
> TALLULAH: I have a service for six! Top *that*.
> JOAN: Five years ago, I died!
> TALLULAH: Well, I died *ten* years ago.
> JOAN: Yeah, I saw you in *Lifeboat*!

The Big Show. NBC, November 4, 1951. Guest Stars: Joan, Groucho Marx, George Sanders, Evelyn Knight. According to *Variety* (November 7, 1951), "The show held to a pretty good comedy level, for a program par or above, even though a certain magic spark that gave the airer its initial zip was missing.... [C]omedy takeoff by Groucho and Miss Davis was weak."

The Martin and Lewis Show. NBC, December 7, 1951. Joan joins the boys for "an original operatic melodrama, *The Curse of the Aching Heartburn*," with "the enchanting voice of our contralto, Joan Davis" as the heroine, Theodora. This show was produced by Joan's own longtime producer, Dick Mack.

The Big Show. NBC, December 30, 1951. Joan, Fred Allen, Georgia Gibbs, Gertrude Berg.

The Big Show. NBC, January 6, 1952. Joan, Claude Rains, and Vera-Lynn are Bankhead's guests. Columnist Earl Wilson reported (January 11, 1952) of this broadcast, "Tallulah Bankhead hauled off and gave Joan Davis a playful kick on the derriere when Joan forgot a lyric."

The Big Show. NBC, February 10, 1952. Joan, Claude Rains, and Phil Foster are featured in this installment.

The Big Show. NBC, February 17, 1952. Guests are Joan, Fred Allen, Hoagy Carmichael, and Vera-Lynn.

The Martin and Lewis Show. NBC, October 28, 1952. Joan appears in a sketch about the Martin Escort Bureau.

IV

VIDEOGRAPHY

By the late 1940s, it was apparent to most radio stars that the emerging medium of television lay in their future. Many were not eager to give up the relative ease of performing on radio for what they knew would be a significantly more demanding routine of memorizing lines, blocking scenes, and other requirements that the purely aural medium did not present. Some knew that they would be unable to carry their radio roles over to the new medium, as they had to not only sound but look the part they played. However, as early as 1948, while still the well-paid star of her own weekly radio show, Joan publicly expressed herself interested in TV work. "Television is being added to the other activities in entertainment," she said in a newspaper interview. "That is something I want to be identified with, because I believe that anyone who has had experience in vaudeville just naturally will take to television."[1]

In late 1949, *Billboard* reported that CBS had agreed to do a test kinescope of Joan's radio show *Leave It to Joan*, with an eye to moving it to television. "If Miss Davis is not successful in a video copy of her AM situation comedy," the journal noted, "the web plans to build a variety show around her."[2]

Joan's first attempt to launch a television series came in 1950, when she signed to star in a CBS pilot called *Let's Join Joanie*. The format was similar to that of her most recent radio program, *Leave It to Joan*, and would feature her radio supporting player Joe Kearns. Not part of the deal, however, was her longtime colleague Dick Mack. Orchestra leader Lyn Murray noted, "CBS is producing it and Dick Mack, who produced and wrote her radio program, has been aced out." Of the modest fee he was paid to provide music for the audition show, Murray noted wryly, "I thought TV was where the money was, but not in California."[3] The pilot episode was recorded on kinescope in January 1951 and taken to New York for previewing with advertising agencies.

Ready to tackle what she knew would be a challenge, Joan told syndicated columnist Erskine Johnson, "This is going to take stamina. When you do a weekly show for television, every night's like opening night on Broadway. I'm going to miss that little script I used to hold in my hand. But I always knew they'd catch up with us sooner or later and make us do the work."[4] Though Joan was right about the rigors of a weekly series, she was worrying prematurely. *Let's Join Joanie* failed to attract a sponsor, and her radio show soon ended its run as well.

When her initial television venture failed to catch on, Joan spent much of the next two years working out a new formula, while keeping active as a performer with her last feature film, *Harem Girl*, and guest stints on radio's *The Big Show*. Another raucous, visually oriented comedienne, Martha Raye, found television success in the variety show format, and there was interest in making Joan one of the rotating stars of NBC's *The Colgate Comedy Hour*, though nothing came of this. In early 1952, columnist Erskine Johnson reported that Joan "will depart from her radio comedy style to dance and sing in her series for NBC-TV...."[5] But the format that ultimately emerged, while indeed a departure from her radio programs, seemed to take its inspiration chiefly from *I Love Lucy*.

The enormous popularity of *I Love Lucy*, which premiered on CBS in the fall of 1951, may well have eased the way for Joan's selling another show about a zany housewife. If so, it wasn't alone; *Lucy* historian Bart Andrews counted "fourteen new sitcoms" premiering in the fall of 1952 that were "all trying to copy the basic *I Love Lucy* formula."[6]

According to *Variety* (August 6, 1952), the completed pilot for *I Married Joan* had no trouble finding an interested sponsor. "Already two agencies and their respective clients are in a hassle as to 'who got there first' and insisting on recognition of their option priorities. NBC-TV meanwhile sits back smiling—the Davis situation comedy heads thataway." The Young and Rubicam agency was interested in matching Joan's new show with General Electric's appliance division, while Chrysler, via the Ruthrauff & Ryan agency, was also a hot contender. The latter was thought to have an edge, since GE preferred only an alternate-week sponsorship. Much would change in the weeks ahead.

Ultimately, General Electric signed on to sponsor Joan's new show, *I Married Joan*, which would premiere on NBC in the fall of 1952. In addition to her profit participation in the series, Joan would earn a weekly salary of $7,500. Cast as her husband was actor Jim Backus (1913–1989), best known for his featured roles on radio shows like Alan Young's. Playing a featured role in a popular TV sitcom would take Backus' career to a new level, as *TV Guide* noted in a 1953 profile of the actor: "[U]ntil his entrance into television as husband to Joan Davis in NBC-TV's *I Married Joan*, Backus was president and founder of Character Actors Anonymous.... [H]is radio career ... brought laughs and money but no fame to one Jim Backus."[7]

The show was scheduled for a Wednesday evening slot conducive to family viewing on the sixty-odd affiliates that then comprised the NBC television network. According to an NBC press release, "Spotlighted as the wife of a judge of the Court of Domestic Relations, Miss Davis will portray a lady whose well-meaning antics invariably result in complications almost too great for her husband to bear. Many times he is on the verge of going to court to seek advice on how to cope with his ever-loving spouse."[8]

Backus told reporters that he owed his casting in roles such as Judge Stevens to a suit that he had acquired some years earlier, after wearing it in a movie. "It was tailored for my exact measurements, so the studio let me have it for $25 after the picture was finished. So far I have worn it on 22 different interviews and screen tests. It always gets me those distinguished parts."[9]

Aside from Davis and Backus, there were no other series regulars during the show's early episodes. Seen the most often over the course of the series' run was actress Geraldine Carr (1914–1954), cast as Joan's buddy Mabel Henderson. Carr, a stage actress whose credits included *The Voice of the Turtle*, also appeared in a few motion pictures. Among them were *The Sniper* (1952), featuring Carr's strong performance as the protagonist's unsympathetic supervisor, and *The Long, Long Trailer* (1954), in an uncredited minor role as one of Tacy's pals and bridesmaids. She made two *Joan* appearances in non-recurring roles before being offered the part of Mabel.

Joan also made use of an informal stock company of character players who popped up repeatedly, playing various roles. Among the most frequently seen were Jerry Hausner, Shirley Mitchell, Bob Sweeney, and Dick Elliott. Several ladies recurred as members of Joan's club, among them Sandra Gould (1916–1999) as Mildred Webster and Myra Marsh (1894–1964) as Clara Foster. Even Backus' real-life wife Henny made a few appearances as one of Joan Stevens' pals. Joan was also loyal to her old friends and colleagues, and a number of players who worked alongside her in films or her radio shows would turn up in the series as well.

The show's memorable theme song was performed by the Roger Wagner Chorale. Named after its founder, the group performed frequently with the Los Angeles Philharmonic Orchestra and was under contract for a number of years with Capitol Records. They contributed musical bridges and segues to every *I Married Joan* segment. During the original network run, the opening titles found Joan (the character) standing happily alongside a car, streamers and confetti being tossed in her direction, as she gestures to a sign affixed to the vehicle that reads, "Just Married." Pointing to herself and grinning, she then turns over the sign to reveal the flipside, which says, "And It Wasn't Easy!!"

A trio of writers who joined the series for its first season created much of the material Joan Davis performed over the next three years. Phil Sharp (1911–1980) was credited as co-scripter of dozens of episodes. After *I Married Joan*, he worked steadily in TV sitcoms until his death of a heart attack some twenty-five years later, contributing scripts to *The Donna Reed Show*, *Bewitched*, *Hogan's Heroes*, *The Doris Day Show*, *All in the Family*, and *Maude*, among others, while also functioning as a producer. Sherwood Schwartz (1916–2011) was a radio veteran later to be famous as the creator-producer of *Gilligan's Island* and *The Brady Bunch*. Jesse Goldstein (1915–1959), also with a radio background, had his career cut short by a fatal illness in his forties, but in addition to collaborating on numerous *Joan* scripts, wrote for Red Skelton and Burns and Allen. Goldstein had previously worked on Joan's radio series *Leave It to Joan*, as well as the pilot script for *Let's Join Joanie*. Also on the writing staff that first year was Arthur Stander (1917–1963), who went to enjoy a long stint on *Make Room for Daddy* (later retitled *The Danny Thomas Show*).

Early episodes of *I Married Joan* were directed by Hal Walker (1896–1972), a motion picture veteran whose recent credits included the Hope-Crosby comedy *Road to Bali*. Walker readily admitted that not every movie director would be happy working in television. "Some directors, including some of the best ones in the business, should never get into television," he told columnist John Crosby. "Some of these guys require four days before they even start to think. In four days, we have to have two pictures in the can."[10] Joan also had the able assistance of veteran cinematographer Hal Mohr (1894–1974), an Oscar winner for *A Midsummer Night's Dream* (Warners, 1935) and *Phantom of the Opera* (Universal, 1943). Of his work on *I Married Joan* and other popular 1950s shows, Mohr said, "I enjoyed them; they were quick money, and we made them fast. Of course, you don't do your best work on television shows."[11]

Backus admitted that the working hours on a TV sitcom were long. "You know, this is like being married to this woman," Backus commented. "We live on the set together, eat together, work together. I see much more of Joan than of my own wife."[12] Davis concurred, adding, "I get home so seldom now that my dogs bite me when I come in. They don't recognize me any more."[13]

Shortly before the show's October 1952 premiere, advertising agency Young and Rubicam hosted a group of prominent television journalists in a junket to Hollywood, where they were invited to review early episodes of the show. The trip also included social activities such as a party hosted by Joan at her home, in the hopes that favorable coverage for *I Married Joan* would follow in their widely read newspapers.

Reviewing the series opener, syndicated columnist Jack O'Brian said, "It is at its best when the pace gets hysterical; like all farce, if you stop to reason things out they seem pretty ridiculous. Taken headlong, they're mighty funny.... All considered it would seem Joan Davis has a suitable vehicle for the season."[14] Invited to a screening of the first two episodes, columnist Bob Foster was likewise enthusiastic. "The Joan Davis type of comedy is unique and is particularly well adapted for television use. It has plenty of sparkle, and the writers have not telegraphed their gags as so many other writers have done in television."[15] Foster believed the show could provide some serious competition for CBS's *I Love Lucy*.

The *New York Times'* Jack Gould, not always a hardcore fan of Joan's radio work, had a positive reaction to *I Married Joan*'s pilot episode: "On television Miss Davis is infinitely more diverting than she was in radio. Her style is much less brittle and she has a good intuitive sense of timing for visual make-believe. Her depiction of the hostess trying to wait on the passengers during a storm was broad horseplay done with a professional know-how."[16] Gould likewise thought Davis' new series could prove to be as successful as *I Love Lucy*. Columnist Peg Simpson gave the show another thumbs-up, saying that it "may lack the skillful characterizations of the *Lucy* show but gives every sign of gaining a large audience."[17]

Joan herself was happy with the show's format, saying, "*I Married Joan* is patterned after believable situations that might be found in any home. The producers feel that with this homey formula, the series can go on forever. And that's all right with me."[18]

Aside from demonstrating the popularity of comediennes, *I Love Lucy* also made it acceptable for stars to refuse the live performances usually favored by networks in the early days of television. Each *Joan* segment was produced in four days, beginning with rehearsals on Tuesday mornings and concluding with a Friday filming. Joan described the mayhem that ensued to columnist Ellis Walker:

> We read straight through the first time without trying any changes. Then we begin to work on each scene as it is to be played. Lines may be changed. And this always makes the writers a little unhappy. Hah! Put that down on paper and you'll get credit for quoting the understatement of the season. By the end of the day we know pretty well what we're going to shoot on Friday.
> Wednesday is devoted to memorizing and walking through the business.... Thursday is always the day for someone to come up with a bright new idea. Course I can't complain too much. Occasionally—or oftener—I'm the one with the idea.[19]

After blocking the show for three cameras on Thursday afternoons, the cast and crew reassembled for a Friday filming that often took twelve hours or more.

A set visitor during the shooting of a first-season episode observed a few tense moments as star, producer, director, and writers hashed out a solution to a scene that didn't work. Afterwards, Joan told him, "Honestly, we're not mad at each other. These are the birth pangs of a show. This is the sweating out. In the movies they take weeks to film an hour and a half show. We shoot ours in two days. Television is the toughest of them all."[20] Columnist Buddy Mason, another early visitor to the *Joan* set, wrote, "Not since the days of two-reel comedies have we seen a company go about playing the craft of comedy construction like the Joan Davis unit at General Service Studios. It gives you the feeling of watching a lost art being revived.... Joan Davis herself is a perfectionist. She'll toy with a spoken line until it gains a maximum of meaning and comic impact."[21]

Not everyone in the 1950s, of course, adjusted easily to a workplace in which a woman held such a powerful position. "I guess it's tough to work for a woman," Joan acknowledged. "I am tough, but I'm also just. Anybody who ever left the show has always asked to come back."[22]

Though several members of Joan's production staff were hired away from *I Love Lucy*, the methods used on Lucille Ball and Desi Arnaz's show were not replicated fully. Joan preferred not to perform in front of a studio audience; instead, the final show was played for an audience and their reactions recorded for the soundtrack. Among the former *Lucy* colleagues hired was Marc Daniels (1912–1989), who directed most of the show's first season. "My director, Marc Daniels, bless him, is as close to a slave-driver as I would ever want to be," Davis told a fan magazine. "Talk about snapping the whip—he even puts knots in the rawhide. If I'm not on the set ready to tackle the script of the week at 9 o'clock, I'm fined $5."[23] Credited as *Joan's* associate producer, Al Simon brought his production expertise in using multiple cameras to film a comedy show.

Although the show was originally produced by Dick Mack, who had guided most of Joan's radio efforts in the 1940s, he left the production after only a few weeks (*Variety* reporting his resignation in late September 1952), and was quickly replaced by producer Pincus J. "P.J." Wolfson (1903–1979). Wolfson, known to friends as "Pinky," was a pulp fiction writer as well as a Hollywood writer-producer, with credits dating back to the early days of sound motion pictures. He was most prolific as a screenwriter, and was no stranger to working with strong women, having toiled on scripts for Joan Crawford (*They All Kissed the Bride*, 1942), Betty Hutton (*The Perils of Pauline*, 1947), and Barbara Stanwyck (*The Bride Walks Out*, 1936), among others. After working on *I Married Joan* for the remainder of its run, Wolfson produced the unsuccessful sitcom *Love and Marriage* (NBC, 1959–60). While Mack's association with *I Married Joan* was brief, one of his contributions left its mark on the show in perpetuity: his lyrics for the theme song, written to accompany music by Lyn Murray.

Looking in on the show again several weeks into the season, *Variety* (December 12, 1952) declared that all seemed fine: "*I Married Joan* has hit on a happy format for comedienne Joan Davis who registers solidly as the scatterbrained but thoroughly appealing wife of Jim Backus. Miss Davis manages not to overact in situations that must be tempting for her to do just that.... Backus somehow manages never to look ridiculous. He makes a perfect partner for the lively Miss Davis."

Joan told columnist Erskine Johnson, "It's the toughest thing in the world for a woman to be funny. A woman comic has to have a certain warmth like Marie Dressler had, and it must come over. Otherwise the audience doesn't give a darn. You have to make them want to root for you."[24] Johnson praised Davis, calling her "right up there with Lucille Ball as a skillful, inventive comedienne."[25]

Unlike radio or film work, a weekly television series required performers to quickly memorize a substantial amount of dialogue. "I've become a crammer," Joan confessed of the weekly struggle to learn a 50-page script. "It's tough for me. I wish I could take a dialogue pill."[26] Gone were the days of vaudeville, where Wills and Davis could perform the same routine in different cities for months on end, delighting new audiences at each stop. During the four days a television episode was in production, additional dialogue or bits of business were often created, adding to the difficulty of delivering a polished performance. TV also presented visual challenges that radio didn't. "I always have a smart outfit on," said Joan of her TV wardrobe, "unless I've just fallen in a mud puddle or something. This makes it hard on the wardrobe mistress, because I sometimes have six or eight changes. I don't have time for fittings; the dresses are tried on a dummy.... I held out for three years against doing live TV. One of the main reasons I wanted to film was that you can look better."[27]

Joan received a nomination as Best Comedienne when the 1952 Emmy Awards were announced. Not yet broadcast nationally, the awards, presented in a ballroom at the Statler

Hotel on February 5, 1953, were telecast in Los Angeles by KLAC-TV, and emceed by Art Linkletter. Competing with Eve Arden (*Our Miss Brooks*), Imogene Coca (*Your Show of Shows*), Martha Raye, and Lucille Ball (*I Love Lucy*), Joan lost out to Ball, in her second year of *I Love Lucy*. It was to be Joan's only nomination. Her co-star Jim Backus later said of Joan's lack of recognition from the Academy, "[I]t's always irritated me. I feel it's totally unfair."[28]

Her series successfully launched, Joan told columnist Hal Humphrey, "My only problem now is getting my dad to watch the show. He lives in St. Paul, Minnesota, and it seems the fights are on another channel at the same time. When I write and ask him how he liked the show that week, he comes back with, 'Well, Joanie, you looked pretty good in the first four rounds, but after that you forgot to use your left.' I'll either have to come on the show with gloves some night, or try to bribe one of those fighters to take a dive in the first round so Dad will get a chance to see me."[29]

Now that Joan was playing a married woman, she and her colleagues dreamed up a promotional gimmick—a contest to determine where single ladies could best meet their mate. Though Joan said she got a kick out of the mail that resulted, "I don't know any more now than when I started. Not that I haven't received hundreds of letters, but, brother, the next time anyone says anything about a television or movie script being too slapstick or unbelievable, I've got a sack of Uncle Sam's mail to prove that this stuff really happens." After plowing through accounts of women who found romance while attending wakes, falling into swimming pools, and visiting the ladies' room, Joan noted that some 30 percent of her correspondents reported meeting Mr. Right on a bus. "Maybe that's what they mean by the 'Streetcar Named Desire,'" Joan cracked.[30]

By the time production was winding down on the first season, Joan was understandably weary. "This television is a rough go," she told journalist Howard McClay that spring. "We're working on May's shows and we're still behind. And when we catch up we have to start thinking about next season's series."[31]

Although *I Married Joan* would never become the ratings blockbuster that *I Love Lucy* did, it drew satisfactory ratings. In the early days of television, when there were fewer stations in smaller cities, ratings in major metropolitan outlets were extremely important, and it seemed that New York City viewers didn't much take to Joan's style of comedy. "I guess I'm just not chic enough for New Yorkers," she said lightly in 1953. "New York is the place that's holding back our rating. If I had time, I'd go door to door."[32]

In June 1953, *Billboard* reported that General Electric had renewed the series, paying $1.2 million for 39 new episodes. The deal also called for thirteen summer reruns of first-season episodes, then a fairly new practice in television.

Production on the second season began in August 1953. New on board was director John Rich (1925–2012), at the beginning of a long and successful television career that would eventually encompass *The Dick Van Dyke Show*, *All in the Family*, and many others. Then still in his twenties, Rich was one of the youngest directors in television. Some older directors were expressing concern that their function was becoming increasingly mechanical with the advent of television, more involved with equipment and technical aspects than performances, but Rich begged to differ. Of working on *I Married Joan*, he told *Variety*, "Nobody tells me how to shoot a picture. It's strictly up to my imagination. Producer P.J. Wolfson and Miss Davis allow me broad latitude in direction.... I think today must be a great deal like motion pictures 25 years ago. We improvise a great deal. At all times you have a good deal of responsibility to the star, but you are never in a straitjacket from a standpoint of inventiveness."[33]

Many years later, however, Rich admitted that there were ups and downs in his relationship with Joan, writing in his memoirs, "I learned a lot about comedy from that talented but tortured woman who cursed like a longshoreman. She was given to extreme moods and sometimes bitter outbursts. I heard her ask the writers one day, 'Why can't our scripts have some of that fucking whimsy?'"[34] The show remained in its Wednesday night time slot, where it was joined by another compatible sitcom, Gale Storm's *My Little Margie.*

Having encouraged daughter Beverly's career aspirations for the past several years, Joan gave her a break when she cast the 21-year-old in a recurring role. Since Joan and Brad Stevens had already been established as childless, Beverly couldn't play her mother's daughter. Instead, young Miss Wills, whose credits included a featured role on the radio comedy *Junior Miss,* would play Joan Stevens' college-aged sister, also named Beverly, who moved in while attending school. Beverly's character was introduced in the second season's fourth aired episode, "Sister Pat." Beverly's initial appearances were sufficiently well-received to justify signing her for additional episodes.

Of being cast on her mother's show, Beverly told a journalist, "I was pretty nervous at first. Every time I fluffed a line I figured I'd get a private lecture later on. But it seems they're satisfied with me. I've been offered a regular contract to remain with the show. I guess I do

Joan's daughter Beverly played a recurring role as Joan's sister Beverly during Season Two of *I Married Joan*. Also pictured is Jim Backus as Brad.

the same things as mother—only cheaper."[35] Said columnist Bob Foster of Beverly's television work, "Joan Davis is a mighty proud mother these days."[36]

Beverly appeared frequently during the second season, her character often cast as a side-kick to Joan and collaborator in her schemes. After her marriage to Alan Grossman in the summer of 1954, however, Beverly did not continue in *I Married Joan* as a regular, making only one guest appearance in the show's third and final season.

Audiences flocked to watch when the show returned to the NBC schedule that fall. *Daily Variety* (October 15, 1953), however, wasn't overly impressed by the second-season opener, "Brad's Mustache," noting that Davis and Backus "are much better than a spotty script." The reviewer attributed much of the show's ongoing appeal to "Joan Davis' extremely fine talent as a comedienne..."

Even when taking time off, Joan found ways to further her television interests. During the 1953 Christmas break, she spent two weeks in Hawaii, accompanied by the show's cameraman Hal Mohr. Their footage of Joan clowning around the islands was later incorporated into the episode "Home Movies."

The show's popularity peaked during its second season, when it placed among television's top 25 shows. Its 30.2 rating paled in comparison to that of its competition, CBS' *Arthur Godfrey and Friends*, at 43.6, but demonstrated a substantial following nonetheless. ABC's public affairs shows, *At Issue* and *Through the Curtain*, barely registered a pulse ratings-wise, while DuMont's *Johns Hopkins Science Review* suggested the struggling fourth network had pretty well thrown in the towel trying to counter-program Godfrey.

Though Joan's show rarely raised any censorship issues, columnist Erskine Johnson reported that her sponsor, General Electric, balked at a scripted line that had Joan saying to husband Brad, "If you don't treat me right, I'll take the gas pipe."[37] Apparently only electric stoves were allowable in GE-sponsored shows, whatever their intended purpose might be.

By 1954, situation comedies were thick on the ground in television, with more and more actors struggling to demonstrate their comedic skills. "Comedy should be left to the comedians," Joan opined to columnist Hal Humphrey. "It takes more than funny lines and situations to be a comic. The real comedians in this business are being burned to death by people who just think they are funny."[38] Though Joan preferred not to name names, Humphrey was less reticent, citing Celeste Holm (whose sitcom *Honestly, Celeste!* had flopped on CBS) and June Havoc (of Desilu's *Willy*) as two actresses who lacked the chops to do broad comedy.

Just before the show's third season hit the airwaves, tragedy struck when Geraldine Carr, featured as Joan's friend Mabel, was killed in a car wreck at the age of 40. At the wheel on September 2, 1954, was *New York Herald-Tribune* correspondent Ned Russell, who suffered a fractured skull and other injuries. Carr's husband, musician (and, later, TV writer) Jess Carneol, was also injured but survived. The crash occurred on the way home from a swimming party with friends, and was attributed to a jammed accelerator which caused the car to overturn and catch fire.

According to syndicated columnist Harrison Carroll, Carr had been contracted to appear in 24 of the series' 26 third-season segments, "and was to have figured even more prominently in the series due to the withdrawal of Joan's daughter, Beverly Wills."[39] Since several third-season episodes were already in the can at the time of the actress' death, Carr would continue to be seen on the series for the next few months.

With her series renewed for a third season, Joan seemed to be thriving professionally in 1954. She featured in a story by columnist Hal Humphrey on former movie players who had found a new career vitality on TV. "Lucille Ball, Ann Sothern, Eve Arden and Joan Davis have left movie careers behind them," Humphrey noted, "but could hardly be tagged as has-beens. It might be more apt to describe them as mistakes made by the movie industry and rectified by television." Ironically, he added, their TV popularity might well have revived their silver screen careers. "Had they the time to get away from the exacting grind of their TV shows, the movie magnates are standing with open arms and contracts to welcome them."[40]

With only 26 new episodes comprising the series' third season, there was a slightly more humane shooting schedule than in previous years. Once again the show had a new director: That spring, *Variety* announced that Don Weis would helm the series' third season, and he did in fact direct the season opener and one subsequent episode. From that point forward, however, Weis gave way to actor-turned-director Ezra Stone (1917–1994). Still remembered by fans for his radio role as Henry Aldrich in *The Aldrich Family*, Stone would eventually become one of TV's busiest directors, helming multiple episodes of *The Munsters*, *The Flying Nun*, and *Lost in Space*.

Recruited to play a recurring role in the third season was comic actor Wally Brown, previously a regular on the 1946-47 season of radio's *The Joan Davis Show*. Added to the writing staff were scribes Hugh Wedlock, Jr., and Howard Snyder, who had worked with Joan as far back as *George White's Scandals* (1945).

Variety (October 13, 1954) welcomed the show back for its third year with a positive review that gave due credit to its hardworking star: "It's Miss Davis' show for the complete footage and not for more than seconds was she off camera. Her type of comedy seems to have caught fire and not alone from the violence of physical exertions. She handles a line with skill and can wring a laugh by a mere grimace."

Posing a serious threat to Joan's television show was the popularity of *Disneyland*, which premiered that fall on ABC. With its 7:30 p.m. start, *Disneyland* had much of the younger audience already transfixed half an hour before Joan's show began. The ratings for Davis' show, which had previously benefited from a strong appeal to families, plummeted accordingly, as did those of Arthur Godfrey's on CBS. By November, *Variety* was reporting a 49.5 percent audience share for ABC's new hit, one of the highest ratings ever on the perennial third-place network, putting a serious dent in the competition's ratings.

The stakes in TV had only grown since Joan's series began three years earlier, as had the attention sponsors paid to ratings. "A respectable rating is not enough," *TV Guide* reported in the spring of 1955. "A constant theme among sponsors and ad agencies is 'Higher, higher, higher!'"[41] With nearly 50 million viewers tuned in to *Disneyland*, its sponsors were happy as clams. The competition's? Not so much.

In February 1955, newspapers reported that Joan had asked to be released from her contract with General Electric, saying she needed a rest. As most insiders realized, this was likely Joan's effort to beat her sponsors to the punch before they could pull the plug. Naturally, some journalists couldn't resist poking holes in Joan's plan to make a graceful exit. Said columnist Robert L. Sokolsky, "The fact of the matter is that the show was in real trouble anyway. It probably would have been axed in any event.... [T]he enormous ratings of the ABC *Disneyland* have cut sharply into the opposing [Arthur] *Godfrey and Friends* and [*I Married*] *Joan*."[42] *I Married Joan* aired its last first-run episode on NBC in March; also consigned to the Dumpster was the show that followed it, *My Little Margie*. The show chosen to replace Davis in the fall, *Screen Directors' Playhouse*, didn't do much better and was dropped after its first year.

Though it was certainly true that Joan had found the making of nearly 100 *I Married Joan* episodes stressful and tiring, she was by no means ready to retire in her early forties. As early as November 1955, only months after *Joan* ceased production, columnist Peg Simpson reported that Joan was plotting a TV comeback. "The format would have Joan traveling Europe and visiting fashion centers."[43]

In early 1956, Joan signed a long-term deal with ABC, expected to result in a new series that would appear on the network's schedule that fall. *Billboard* reported that actor Mark Stevens' new company would oversee technical production. According to columnist Faye Emerson, Beverly too would have a role in the show, this time playing Joan's daughter instead of her sister as she had in *I Married Joan*.[44] Joan's creative collaborator on the *Joan Davis Show* pilot for ABC was producer-screenwriter Stanley Shapiro (1925–1990), who had previously produced the first season of Ray Bolger's TV sitcom, *Where's Raymond* (CBS, 1953–55). Together they devised a show that presented a fictionalized version of Joan's life as a comedienne, with daughter Beverly, son-in-law (here called Tony), and a small grandson named Stevie.

According to columnist Dick Kleiner, Joan was "excited about her new show" after more than a year of relative inactivity: "TV is like childbirth. My last show, *I Married Joan*, was so hard, it took me months to recover. But after a while you forget the pain and you just enjoy the product—my weekly checks—and you say to yourself, 'Gee, this is pretty good; let's do it again.'"[45]

ABC took out a three-page *Variety* ad to announce the availability of "twelve excellent new fall properties," among them *The Joan Davis Show*—"May well be the season's big comedy hit." Joan's pilot was described in the ad as "A brand new comedy half hour with an old favorite of TV audiences! Joan Davis plays the starring role, of course. But to make the package even more surefire, Joan produces the series, too. Each show will be on film ... and, almost surely, on most TV screens next fall." Unfortunately, Joan's show was dropped from ABC's fall 1956 schedule, where it had been destined for a Thursday time slot, when network executives were unable to nail down sponsorship.

In May 1957, *Billboard* reported that the pilot was still being shopped around, and was being considered by NBC for a fall time slot. Later that year, however, columnist Eve Starr reported that this version "has finally been junked" and that Joan was now in collaboration with writer-producer Philip Rapp on a new concept.[46]

Meanwhile, her first series continued to be widely seen. Original plans were for *I Married Joan* reruns to be sold to local stations through syndicator Interstate Television, but the show was withdrawn from that market when a deal was reached with NBC. In the spring of 1956, reruns were added to NBC's daytime schedule, and proved immediately popular. Reported one observer, "NBC took her filmed series and threw it into a dead afternoon spot which they had hanging around. Miss Davis immediately knocked off the opposition, including ABC's omnipotent *Mickey Mouse Club* which had been considered impregnable."[47] Ratings surveys reported that the audience watching the afternoon reruns was comprised of 60 percent children, and 40 percent adults. *Joan* was soon tied with *Queen for a Day* for highest-rated show in daytime, demonstrating that Davis still had a loyal following that might well watch her in a new prime time series. The show's popularity in reruns also resulted in a financial windfall for its star, whose 50 percent ownership of the property dropped an estimated $1 million in her bank account.

Having moved on to other projects in the wake of the sitcom's demise, co-star Jim Backus nonetheless expected *I Married Joan* to play for years to come, not always for reasons pertaining to its quality. "You know there was no booze on that show," he pointed out in 1957. "You'd have a whole roomful of people and you'd offer them a bowl of fruit. There's nothing in it that could possibly offend anyone. Those far-sighted producers, thinking of residuals, never had us use an auto or smoke, because of possible sponsors they might go after at some time. We never even mentioned anyone living because he might be dead later and that would date the series."[48] Signed to host a daily show on ABC radio that year, Backus

Radio's King and Queen of Comedy, Bob Hope and Joan Davis, were reunited with her 1956 guest appearance on his NBC television show.

complained that his sitcom work had typecast him. "A series like *I Married Joan* dissipates you as a personality. I played a judge on the show and after awhile, every time my name would come up, everyone would think of me as just that—that kindly judge on the Joan Davis show."[49]

In late 1957, Joan told columnist Vernon Scott she was optimistic about the prospects for her new sitcom, which would be called *Joan of Arkansas*. Joan was hoping to trade on widespread public interest in space exploration, though real-life developments such as the launch of the *Sputnik I* in October 1957 threatened to date the comedy. Written and directed by Rapp, who had recently completed Wally Cox's single-season NBC sitcom *The Adventures of Hiram Holliday*, the pilot was shot in early 1958 at a reported cost of $60,000. When Scott pointed out to Joan that top TV stars like Cox, Eve Arden, and Imogene Coca had failed to capture audience attention in their second series efforts, she conceded, "I realize I'm in for a rough time. It's always tough to grind out 39 shows in a season. But I've got faith in this one and the energy to make it a hit."[50] The show was being pitched by NBC as a candidate for the fall 1958 schedule, but was not picked up.

Though she no longer had her own series, Joan continued to turn up now and then as a guest star on the popular variety shows of Bob Hope, Dinah Shore, Steve Allen, and others. In November 1956, she was in New York rehearsing for her appearance on Hope's NBC show. When a journalist noted that she seemed nervous about the broadcast, Joan said, "Wouldn't you be? Oh, well, if I'm not any good, I'll blame the script. I'm going to sing and dance and everything, and I don't even know what the script's going to be. About 7 o'clock this morning somebody rang the bell. When I opened the door, he shoved in three pages of the script and said, 'Here's some of the jokes.' Bob Hope is used to this sort of thing—but I'd like a little time to get ready."[51] Joan made her last guest appearance in mid–1959, then vanished from the television scene.

Comedy shows starring women were at an all-time low in the early 1960s, with Ann Sothern one of the few comediennes still holding on to her weekly series amid a flood of Westerns. After two successful shows, Gale Storm's sitcom career was essentially over, and Lucille Ball had forsaken TV for the time being in the wake of her impending divorce from Desi Arnaz. "It's a man's world on TV now," Sothern complained. "It's populated mostly with broad shoulders and slim hips, and apparently the women in the audience like it that way."[52] It was hard to argue Sothern's point, especially after her own show was canceled a year or so later.

Joan's 1960 pilot for a *Joan Davis Show* failed to sell, and by that time she had also stopped turning up in TV guest appearances.

Reruns of *I Married Joan* continued to be a staple of local TV schedules well into the 1960s, as did many of Joan's films, but eventually faded away as the demand increased for shows in color. A new generation discovered Joan's television work when the Christian Broadcasting Network licensed the show in the 1980s, adding daily reruns to its daytime schedule alongside other vintage shows such as *My Little Margie* and *The Farmer's Daughter*. To date, there has been no authorized DVD release of Joan's series.

I Married Joan

Cast: Joan Davis (*Joan Stevens*), Jim Backus (*Judge Bradley Stevens*)
Producers: Dick Mack, P.J. Wolfson. *Directors:* Marc Daniels, John Rich, Philip

Rapp, Ezra Stone, Don Weis. *Writers:* Lou Derman, Bob Fisher, Jesse Goldstein, Alan Lipscott, Richard Powell, Sol Saks, Al Schwartz, Sherwood Schwartz, Phil Sharp, Howard Snyder, Arthur Stander, Ben Starr, Frank Tarloff, Hugh Wedlock, Jr. *Associate Producer:* Al Simon. *Production:* Herbert Browar. *Photography:* Clyde De Vinna, Alfred C. Gilks, Sam Leavitt, Hal Mohr, James Van Trees. *Production Supervisor:* Dewey Starkey. *Assistant Directors:* Tom Connors, Joseph Depew. *Art Director:* Al Goodman. *Set Decorators:* Jack Mills, Anthony C. Montenaro. *Supervising Editors:* Marvin Coil, Stanley Frazen. *Editors:* Marsh Hendry, Ernie Leadlay, Robert Stafford. *Sound:* Hugh McDowell. *Music:* Roger Wagner Chorale. *Music Editor:* Robert Stafford. *Casual Wear for Miss Davis:* DeDe Johnson. *Mr. Backus' Wardrobe:* Louis Roth Clothes, House of Worsted-Tex. *Filmed by* Volcano Pictures, Inc. Aired Wednesdays at 8 p.m. on NBC-TV. 98 episodes.

First Season

The Fur Coat

Air Date: October 15, 1952. *Writers:* Arthur Stander, Phil Sharp. *Director:* Philip Rapp
   Cast: Hal March (*Mr. Mitchell*), Shirley Mitchell (*Mrs. Mitchell*), Hope Emerson (*Minerva Parker*), Shepard Menken (*Ground Officer*), Marjorie Riordan (*Marilyn*), Phil Arnold (*Bald Passenger*)

Summary: Counseling a married couple on the verge of divorce, Brad tells them that maintaining a sense of humor is the key to a happy marriage. To illustrate his point, he recalls meeting Joan, on her maiden flight as a stewardess, where her nervousness and some turbulence resulted in chaos. Later, learning that Joan has bought a fur coat without his permission, Brad purposely arrives home in time for the delivery to take place, forcing her to hide her new coat in the freezer.
   Note: According to this episode, the maiden name of Joan (the character) was Davis. Shirley Mitchell, a regular player on Joan's 1940s radio shows, makes her *I Married Joan* debut here, and will make three more appearances during the show's first season. Shepard Menken, seen here as a member of the flight crew, was a veteran of Joan's radio comedy *Leave It to Joan.*

Career

Air Date: October 22, 1952. *Writers:* Arthur Stander, Phil Sharp. *Director:* Hal Walker
   Cast: Sheldon Leonard (*Mr. Magruder*), Sandra Gould (*Mrs. Magruder*), Margie Liszt (*Miss Burton*), Shepard Menken (*Fred*), Bob Sweeney (*Al*), Jane Easton (*Model*), Earle Ross (*George Chester*), Howard Freeman (*Martin Bishop*)

Summary: Once again advising a quarreling married couple in his chambers, Brad tells them about the time Joan decided she wanted a career. In a flashback, Joan's ambition to become an actress is squelched when she is cast in a wearying role as a floor-scrubbing housewife. Later, at home, Brad is dismayed to learn that two of his biggest political supporters—who despise each other—have both been invited to dinner.
   Note: Character actress Sandra Gould (1916–1999), best-known for her role as Gladys Kravitz in the color episodes of *Bewitched*, makes her series debut with this episode. She will

later be cast in a recurring role as Joan's friend, called Elsie in early appearances, and then later Mildred Webster. Actor Sheldon Leonard had previously worked with Joan in the film *If You Knew Susie*. He will make several *I Married Joan* appearances.

Ballet

Air Date: October 29, 1952. *Writers:* Arthur Stander, Phil Sharp. *Director:* Hal Walker

Cast: Florence Bates (*Mrs. Turner*), Bob Jellison (*Mr. Fisher*), Doris Singleton (*Mrs. Fisher*), Russell Hicks (*Mr. Fletcher*), Teddy Hart (*Gangster*)

Summary: Noticing that Joan seems listless, Brad suggests that she needs regular exercise. She undergoes instruction in ballet at Mrs. Turner's school, but struggles to keep up with the little girls who are fellow members of the beginner's class. Later, Brad is entertaining an important guest from the Bar Association. Because Mr. Fletcher saw Brad buying a new dress for a pretty young woman (whose clothes he ruined by splashing her with mud), Brad decides to bring the woman home and have her pose as his wife.

Note: More than almost any other early episode, this segment basically consists of two unrelated stories. No mention is made at all of Joan's ballet lessons in Act Two. Lucille Ball had already done "The Ballet," her classic episode of *I Love Lucy*, earlier in 1952. This episode features the first of several appearances in the series by character actor Bob Jellison (1908–1980), who also made multiple appearances on *I Love Lucy*, often as a bellboy. Jellison previously played Joan's erstwhile boyfriend Freddie Hartzfelder on *Joan Davis Time*. Russell Hicks, seen as Mr. Fletcher, was a veteran of Joan's movies *Bunker Bean* and *Hold That Ghost*.

Quote: BRAD: Did you make dinner?
JOAN: No, dear, I'm afraid we'll have to eat out.
BRAD: Did you make the beds?
JOAN: We'll have to sleep out, too.

Jitterbug

Air Date: November 5, 1952. *Writers:* Arthur Stander, Philip Sharp, Richard Powell. *Director:* Hal Walker

Cast: Leon Tyler (*Alvin*), Betty Hart (*Sally*), Peter Leeds (*Repairman*), Phil Arnold (*George*), Janice Carroll (*Sally*), Teddy Hart (*Wesley Newkirk*), Rolfe Sedan (*Mr. Robinson*), Florence Ravenel (*Mrs. Robinson*)

Summary: Joan takes offense when she is summoned to traffic court and receives no special treatment from the presiding judge, Brad. Determined to recoup the $50 she was fined, Joan begins charging Brad for his meals at home, offers hungry repairmen a $1 all-you-can-eat special in her kitchen, and takes the place of a teenage girl as a babysitter at 50 cents per hour.

Note: This is the first episode credited to producer P.J. Wolfson. Under his guidance, the format changes to that of a more typical sitcom, with a single story that runs throughout the half-hour show.

Quote: BRAD (to Joan in traffic court): Mrs. Stevens, will you please be reasonable? Who committed this offense? You did!
JOAN: Who taught me how to drive? You did!

Crime Panel

Air Date: November 12, 1952. *Writers:* Arthur Stander, Philip Sharp, Frank Tarloff. *Director:* Hal Walker

Cast: Anne Chaffey (*Betty Cosgrove*), Tom Duggan, Jim Hayward (*Policemen*), Jock George (*Dr. Thaddeus Wartell*), Hal Taggart (*Dr. Johnson*), Gil Frye, Jesse Simberg, George Neise (*Radio Voices*)

Summary: Brad and Joan are going to appear as panelists discussing crime on a TV show, *America Speaks.* Joan tries to bone up on the topic by listening to radio mystery shows and hanging out among the criminal element at a pool hall. But by the time she appears on the live broadcast, her capers leave her so exhausted that she can't keep her eyes open.

Note: Joan and Brad's bedroom, as seen here, looks different than it will in most subsequent episodes, with the doorway across the room from their beds. Actor-announcer George Neise (1917–1996), who previously played Jim Benson in Joan's CBS television pilot *Let's Join Joanie,* provides the radio voices of Inspector Harrigan and Mr. Twilight. He will make multiple appearances on *I Married Joan,* often playing a television host or emcee.

Joan explains the latest predicament at the Stevens home to policemen Jim Hayward (left) and Tom Duggan in "Crime Panel," the fifth aired episode of *I Married Joan.* At her feet is Jim Backus.

Brad's Class Reunion

Air Date: November 19, 1952. *Writers:* Arthur Stander, Phil Sharp. *Director:* Marc Daniels

Cast: Hal Smith (*Charlie Henderson*), Elvia Allman (*Aunt Vera*)

Summary: Brad is looking forward to his Stanford class reunion, while Joan plans to stay home with Aunt Vera to keep her company. But when Joan finds an essay Brad wrote in college, describing his ideal woman, she concludes that he's still carrying a torch for his former classmate Jeannie Richards. Joan and Vera pull out every stop to try to prevent Brad from going to the reunion.

Notes: For the purposes of this episode, Joan is said not to have known Brad in his college days; later episodes will contradict this. Actor Hal Smith makes his debut as Charlie, said to be a classmate of Brad's from Stanford. Smith will later be given a recurring role as the husband of Joan's pal Mabel. Character actress Elvia Allman makes the first of her several appearances as Joan's Aunt Vera. She previously worked with Joan in *Sweetheart of the Fleet.*

Hunting

Air Date: November 26, 1952. *Writers:* Arthur Stander, Phil Sharp. *Director:* Marc Daniels

Cast: Elvia Allman (*Aunt Vera*), Margie Liszt (*Miss Bromley*)

Summary: When Brad tells Joan that he's planned a camping trip with two pals, she wants to go along, but he insists a woman would be out of place. In order to prove her abilities, Joan takes horse riding lessons and sets up a makeshift camp in the Stevenses' living room. Calling her bluff, Brad puts her camping skills to the test, seeing how his wife copes with cold, insects, rain (from a watering can), and the need to pitch a tent.

Note: According to this script, Brad's middle name is Jerome.

Joan's Curiosity

Air Date: December 3, 1952. *Writers:* Arthur Stander, Phil Sharp, Frank Tarloff. *Director:* Marc Daniels

Cast: Elvia Allman (*Aunt Vera*), Bob Sweeney (*Joe Perkins*)

Summary: Brad dislikes Joan's habit of opening his mail and decides to teach her a lesson. When an intriguing package addressed to her husband arrives by post, Joan can't resist opening it, letting loose a self-inflating rubber rowboat that quickly engulfs her. When Brad tells a chastened Joan that curiosity is "a feminine characteristic" from which he does not suffer, she sends him a series of odd parcels and crates in hopes of proving otherwise.

Note: Scriptwriter Frank Tarloff, under his pseudonym David Adler, later wrote "The Curious Thing About Women," a well-remembered episode of *The Dick Van Dyke Show* in which Laura Petrie suffered a similar fate.

Birthday

Air Date: December 10, 1952. *Writers:* Arthur Stander, Phil Sharp, Frank Tarloff. *Director:* Marc Daniels

Cast: Elvia Allman (*Aunt Vera*), Richard Reeves (*Attorney*), Maurice Cass (*Attorney*), Kathleen Freeman (*Dress Shop Customer*), Kay Wiley (*Saleslady*)

Summary: Disgusted by Joan's inability to manage money, Brad cuts off her charge accounts. When she sees a "Birthday" notation in his calendar, she finds a unique way to finance his surprise party. Now if she can just get him home from a hockey game in time to attend it.

Quote: JOAN: I've got a perfect right to go over on my budget. I'm a woman.

Bazaar Pie

Air Date: December 17, 1952. *Writers:* Arthur Stander, Phil Sharp, Frank Tarloff. *Director:* Marc Daniels

Cast: Elvia Allman (*Aunt Vera*), Jerry Hausner (*Arthur*), Maurice Marsac (*Señor Rodriguez*), Harvey B. Dunn (*Man at Bazaar*), Myra Marsh (*Clara Foster*), Geraldine Carr (*Edna*)

Summary: When Aunt Vera admits she'd like a little romance in her life, Joan decides the perfect candidate is their new neighbor, a wealthy, retired diamond broker. So that Señor Rodriguez won't think Vera is a fortune hunter, Joan decks her out in a borrowed fur coat and a $5,000 diamond ring she charged, intending to return it the next day. When the ring goes missing, Joan and Brad conclude that it must have fallen into one of the several dozen pies Joan and Vera baked for a charity bazaar.

Note: French-born actor Maurice Marsac (1915–2007), best-known for playing Mr. LeBlanche on *Our Miss Brooks*, plays the wealthy Spaniard. Geraldine Carr, later to assume the recurring role of Mabel Henderson, makes her *Joan* debut here as a member of the Women's Welfare League.

Quote: BRAD (chiding Joan for matchmaking): When are you going to learn to let nature take its course?

JOAN: Wherever a man is concerned, there never was a woman who didn't give nature a helping kick in the pants.

Dreams

Air Date: December 24, 1952. *Writers:* Arthur Stander, Phil Sharp, Frank Tarloff. *Director:* Marc Daniels

Summary: Joan is looking forward to seeing her old high school friends at a reunion, sure they'll be impressed that she married a prominent judge. Her news is overshadowed by the accomplishments of her pals, who have highly successful careers of their own. Fantasizing that she is a famous athlete like Gloria, a cosmetics magnate like Minnie, or a diplomat like Marcia, Joan suddenly finds that her life as a housewife no longer satisfies her.

Note: Backus does a classic spit take in response to Joan's insistence that, of her circle of friends, "I was the normal one."

Acrobats

Air Date: December 31, 1952. *Writers:* Arthur Stander, Sol Saks, Richard Powell. *Director:* Marc Daniels

Cast: Elvia Allman (*Aunt Vera*), Geraldine Carr (*Mrs. Gilmore*), Joe DeRita (*Waiter*), Henny Backus (*Saleslady*)

Summary: Preparing to attend an important social evening with a law school dean and his wife, Joan goes to a hat shop and gets into a tussle with another customer. When she realizes that the woman with whom she had a spat was the dean's wife, Joan tries to back out of the dinner engagement, but Brad won't let her. Disguising herself in a wig and costume from a charity play, Joan plans to attend the dinner incognito, but loses the wig just as Brad and the other couple arrive. Joan's efforts to make a fast getaway find her caught in the clutches of an acrobatic troupe, who assume she's with the show and act accordingly.

Note: Actress Geraldine Carr, as the dean's wife, makes a fine partner for Joan in the very physical fight sequence in the hat shop. She will return to the series a few months later as Joan's buddy Mabel Henderson. This is Elvia Allman's final appearance in the series as Aunt Vera.

Bad Boy

Air Date: January 7, 1953. *Writers:* Arthur Stander, Sol Saks. *Director:* Marc Daniels
Cast: Danny Richards, Jr. (*Tommy*), Sandra Gould (*Bernard's Mother*), Frank Jaquet (*Vegetable Truck Owner*), Bill McKenzie (*Child*)

Summary: Before sentencing a ten-year-old delinquent, Brad takes the boy home to observe him for a week. After trying unsuccessfully to rehabilitate the boy with love and kindness, Joan decides to try a different approach.

Note: Child actor Danny Richards, Jr. (born 1942), would be a busy performer in early TV, racking up guest appearances on *My Little Margie*, *Private Secretary*, and *The Millionaire*, among many others, as well as a featured role in the short-lived comedy series *Willy* (CBS, 1954–55).

Circumstantial Evidence

Air Date: January 14, 1953. *Writers:* Arthur Stander, Sol Saks, Richard Powell. *Director:* Marc Daniels
Cast: Shirley Mitchell (*Mrs. Slattery*), Rusty Hamer (*Boy*), Joe Devlin (*Rocky Slattery*), Vince Barnett (*Fancy Farney*), Harry Guardino (*Joe*)

Summary: Brad takes offense when Joan is less interested in his work than in reading lurid newspaper accounts of a lady crook nicknamed the "Blonde Bandit." Trying to make amends, Joan visits her husband's courtroom, where she befriends the wife of defendant Rocky Slattery and decides he's innocent. When Brad doesn't accept her explanation that all the evidence against Slattery is circumstantial, Joan decides to prove her point by planting evidence that she's the Blonde Bandit.

Note: In the scene where Joan brings in kids to pose as the Slattery family, the first boy to speak is child actor Rusty Hamer (1947–1990), soon to be cast as Rusty Williams on *Make Room for Daddy*.

Uncle Edgar

Air Date: January 21, 1953. *Writers:* Arthur Stander, Sol Saks, Richard Powell. *Director:* Marc Daniels
Cast: Robert Sweeney (*Edgar Stevens*), Dorothy Adams (*Agatha Peterson*), Bob Jellison (*Club Manager*), Richard Keene (*Mr. Hodgkiss*), Kathleen Freeman (*Betty*), Robert Pike (*Judge Peterson*)

Summary: Brad's elderly uncle, a relentless womanizer, pays a visit. Trying to keep him out of trouble, Brad and Joan resolve not to let him leave the house. When he sneaks out and joins a lonely-hearts club, Joan devises a scheme to keep him distracted by posing as her own Aunt Susie.

Moosehead

Air Date: January 28, 1953. *Writers:* Arthur Stander, Frank Tarloff, Ben Starr. *Director:* Marc Daniels

Cast: Kathleen Freeman (*Betty*), Sheldon Leonard (*Auctioneer*), Lurene Tuttle (*Mrs. Bunker*), Henny Backus (*Woman at Auction*), Philip Tonge (*Judge Bunker*), Bernard Gorcey (*Joe*), Billy Benedict (*Deliveryman*)

Summary: Short on cash after buying a new hat, Joan is delighted when Brad gives her $50 to buy a housewarming gift for a colleague. At the suggestion of her neighbor Betty, Joan attends an auction hoping to bag a bargain gift, but mistakenly buys a moose head instead. Holding her own auction in order to unload the white elephant, Joan manages to sell off her own furniture instead.

Note: Jim Backus' wife Henny makes her second series appearance. Actor Billy Benedict (1917–1999), seen here and in several subsequent episodes as a delivery boy, played some of his earliest roles at Fox in the 1930s, as did Joan. Both appeared in *Hold That Co-Ed*.

Fireman

Air Date: February 4, 1953. *Writers:* Arthur Stander, Frank Tarloff, Ben Starr. *Director:* Marc Daniels

Cast: Geraldine Carr (*Mabel*), Hal March (*Tom Regan*), Mary Ellen Kaye (*Louise Regan*), Phil Arnold, Robert Spencer (*Firemen*)

Summary: After getting unwittingly involved in Mabel's quarrel with her husband, Joan is warned by Brad not to interfere in the affairs of married couples. But when she pays a visit to Tom and Louise, the newlywed couple that just moved in down the street, Joan's innocent reminiscences of her own Las Vegas honeymoon spark a fight between the Regans. While Louise camps out at the Stevens house, declaring she will go to Reno and get a divorce, Joan tracks down fireman Tom at his job. When the firemen are called out on an emergency, Joan tags along in order to get Tom reunited with his wife.

Note: In this episode, Mabel's (unseen) husband is named Harvey. Later he will be called Charlie.

Memory

Air Date: February 11, 1953. *Writers:* Arthur Stander, Ben Starr. *Director:* Marc Daniels

Cast: Kay Wiley (*Mrs. Trotter*), Gail Bonney (*Polly Saddler*), Don Brodie (*Pete Saddler*), Edward Earle (*Mr. Trotter*), Frank Jaquet (*Store Owner*)

Summary: Joan forgets a telephone message concerning a dinner date, causing her and Brad to have three spaghetti dinners in one evening—first at home, then at the house of some friends who *didn't* invite them over, and finally at the site of the original invitation. Brad urges Joan to write messages down, but when she leaves an important one in the pocket of a jacket she sold to a second-hand man, she finds herself plowing through the merchandise at his store after hours.

Notes: In this episode's funniest scene, Joan poses as a store window mannequin to avoid being seen by a patrolman walking his beat. Seen in this episode is an exchange that will be repeated occasionally throughout the series. Brad, horrified by Joan's latest escapade, says hopefully, "Tell me you didn't do it." Joan sweetly answers, "I didn't do it," but nods in shame when he adds, "But you did."

Draft Board

Air Date: February 18, 1953. Writers: Arthur Stander, Frank Tarloff, Ben Starr. Director: Marc Daniels
Cast: Mary Treen (*Harriet*), Charles Smith (*George Burton*), Arthur Lovejoy, George Eldredge, Herbert Lytton (*Draft Board Members*)

Summary: Brad is asked to serve on the local Selective Service Board, but when he receives the letter, Joan assumes he's been drafted. She tries unsuccessfully to persuade Brad that he's too out of shape for life in the service. But by the time that mix-up is resolved, she has a bigger problem: She just rented out the house for a year.
Note: According to this script, Brad was at one time an officer in the U.S. Navy.

Opera

Air Date: February 25, 1953. Writers: Phil Sharp, Sherwood Schwartz, Jesse Goldstein. Director: John Rich
Cast: Myra Marsh (*Clara Foster*), Geraldine Carr (*Mabel Henderson*), Edith Leslie (*Mme. Cortini*), Bing Crosby (*Neighbor*), Dorothy Adams, Kay Wiley (*Clubwomen*), Connie Van (*Maid*)

Summary: As chair of the Women's Welfare League's Entertainment Committee, Joan is put in charge of the opera being staged as a fundraiser. The show seems destined for success when retired opera singer Mme. Cortini agrees to take the lead role of Brünnhilde. But the temperamental star quarrels with her producer on opening night and Joan is forced to take her place onstage, lip-synching to records as she stumbles through the star part.
Note: Bing Crosby makes a cameo appearance in the closing moments, playing a new neighbor who denies being a certain famous singer, saying, "He'll never be on television." General Electric, Joan's TV sponsor, was also sponsoring Crosby's show on CBS radio.

Shopping

Air Date: March 4, 1953. Writers: Arthur Stander, Frank Tarloff, Ben Starr. Director: Marc Daniels
Cast: Bob Sweeney (*Mr. Harris*), Jerry Hausner (*Charlie*), Bernard Gorcey (*Bailiff*)

Summary: Always craving new clothes, Joan promises she'll buy no more until Brad, who has only two suits, gets something for himself. Joan accompanies Brad to a menswear store to buy a new suit, and talks him into a garish plaid one. When he sees a cheap crook wearing the same suit, however, he insists that Joan return his. Because Brad's suit has been altered, the store won't take it back, so Joan decides to sell it to another customer to get her $85 back. When some alterations are needed to make the suit fit its diminutive new owner, Joan promptly takes scissors in hand.

The Stamp

Air Date: March 11, 1953. *Writers:* Arthur Stander, Frank Tarloff, Ben Starr. *Director:* Marc Daniels
    Cast: Bernard Gorcey (*Joe*), Frank Jaquet (*Postman*)

Summary: Joan prepares to butter Brad up before breaking the news that she's dented the fender on the car yet again. It turns out Brad has something of his own to confess: He just spent $350 on a collectible Mozambique Purple stamp. Too bad Joan just used his rare stamp to mail a letter. A guilt-ridden Joan has a nightmare in which she's put on trial for goofiness, with a judge, prosecutor, defense attorney, and bailiff who all look strangely like Brad.
    Note: The dream sequence allows not only Backus but also Joan to play multiple characters. She plays both an elderly woman and a young girl who try with limited success to serve as character witnesses.

Little Girl

Air Date: March 18, 1953. *Writers:* Arthur Stander, Frank Tarloff, Ben Starr. *Director:* Marc Daniels
    Cast: Anne Whitfield (*Janet Whitmore*), Leon Tyler (*Harold Miller*), Frank Fenton (*Mr. Miller*), Florence Ravenel (*Mrs. Miller*)

Summary: Joan and Brad's 16-year-old houseguest, Janet Whitmore, is a shy young lady who is afraid of boys. Joan decides to fix her up with an equally timid neighborhood boy, Harold Miller. When the match proves more successful than they could have envisioned, Joan and Brad try to persuade the teenagers that they can't afford to get married on Harold's salary of $20 a week.
    Note: This episode presents yet another scenario of how Joan and Brad first met. Each of them tells the story of getting acquainted at their junior prom, though they remember the incident a bit differently.
    Quote: JOAN: Well, how would you like to be all alone in the world? Too shy, even, to get a husband? You wouldn't like it!
        BRAD: I wouldn't like it even if I got a husband.

Diet

Air Date: March 25, 1953. *Writers:* Arthur Stander, Frank Tarloff, Ben Starr. *Director:* Marc Daniels
    Cast: Myra Marsh (*Clara Foster*), Geraldine Carr (*Mabel Henderson*), Henny Backus (*Harriet Brown*), George Neise (*Harry Martin*), Don Brodie (*Pharmacist*), Billy Benedict (*Deliveryman*), Kay Wiley (*Clubwoman*)

Summary: On her ninth wedding anniversary, Joan is dismayed to realize that she now weighs nine pounds more than she did when she married Brad. In only three days, Joan is scheduled to do a live TV endorsement for Gruber's non-fattening salad dressing, for which she will earn a $200 donation to her club's children's aid fund. Determined to lose the extra weight in three days, Joan enlists the help of her fellow club members, who move into the house to monitor her eating night and day. On the day of her television performance, Joan's successful diet leaves her dangerously hungry when she's placed in front of a table full of fattening food to deliver her spiel.

Note: When Brad comes home to find all the clubwomen in his house, he mistakes two of them for Joan and tries to kiss them. The second of the two is played by Backus' real-life wife, Henny.

Model

Air Date: April 1, 1953. *Writers:* Arthur Stander, Frank Tarloff, Ben Starr. *Director:* Marc Daniels

Cast: Shirley Mitchell (*Elsie*), Geraldine Carr (*Mabel Henderson*), Fay Baker (*Nancy*), Bernard Gorcey (*Joe*), Margie Liszt (*Miss Bromley*), Jane Easton (*Model*)

Summary: When Brad tries to settle an argument with his wife by asserting his authority as the breadwinner in the Stevens household, Joan resolves to find a job. At Armand's dress shop she works as a stock clerk, but tries to impress Brad by telling him she's a designer. When Brad shows up at the salon unexpectedly, what's a girl to do but tie up her boss and take his place at an impromptu fashion show?

Note: Shirley Mitchell, making her third guest appearance of the show's first season, plays Joan's cynical co-worker Elsie.

Lateness

Air Date: April 8, 1953. *Writers:* Arthur Stander, Sherwood Schwartz, Frank Tarloff. *Director:* Marc Daniels

Cast: Geraldine Carr (*Mabel Henderson*), Bob Jellison, George Pirrone (*Shoe Salesmen*), Dave Alpert (*Ticket Agent*), Robert Spencer (*Mailman*)

Summary: Joan and Brad have theater tickets to see a whodunit called *Summer Hotel.* She arrives late, causing them to miss the first act. Promising to curb her tendency to tardiness, Joan agrees to pick up their tickets by 4:00 the next day, right after she runs a quick errand at the shoe store.

Quote: JOAN (to Brad, who's angry about missing the beginning of the play): You'll still find out whodunit, you just won't know what he done.

The Eviction Show

Air Date: April 15, 1953. *Writers:* Arthur Stander, Sherwood Schwartz. *Director:* Marc Daniels

Cast: Myra Marsh (*Clara Foster*), Geraldine Carr (*Mabel Henderson*), Fay Baker (*Nancy*), Henny Backus (*Harriet*), Joanne Jordan (*Barbara*), Bernard Gorcey (*Joe*), James Nusser (*Phil*), Don Brodie (*Harold*), Arthur Lovejoy (*Jim Randolph*)

Summary: Joan's club, the Women's Welfare League, is being evicted from its headquarters due to a zoning violation. Because Brad signed the eviction notice, the other members are all angry with Joan. She tries convincing Brad to rescind the eviction—first by evicting him from the bedroom, and then by using some strategically placed onions to make him believe his decision has reduced her friends to tears. When all else fails, Joan decides that a nice, loud, boisterous club meeting held in her own living room will give Brad ample cause to reconsider.

The Recipe

Air Date: April 22, 1953. *Writers:* Arthur Stander, Sherwood Schwartz. *Director:* Marc Daniels

Cast: Myra Marsh (*Clara Foster*), Geraldine Carr (*Mabel Henderson*), Alan DeWitt (*Alfonso*), Cosmo Sardo (*Headwaiter*), Emlen Davies (*Helen Cavanaugh*), Ross Elliott (*Harry Cavanaugh*), Fay Baker (*Nancy*)

Summary: The women's club is entering a cooking competition, and everyone assumes that Helen Cavanaugh will win in the soup category, as she has previously. Joan decides to give her rival some competition, and wants to make oxtail soup, which both ladies have learned is the favorite of the contest judge. Unable to get the temperamental chef Alfonso to divulge his soup recipe, Joan poses as his sous-chef to gain entrée to his kitchen while he makes a batch to serve 500 people.

Note: This fondly remembered episode builds to a memorable scene in which Joan hides in an enormous soup tureen to spy on Alfonso, and learns the recipe the hard way, as each ingredient is dumped over her head. Introduced here is the character of Joan's frenemy Helen Cavanaugh, played by Emlen Davies. Adele Jergens will assume the role in subsequent appearances.

Repairs

Air Date: April 29, 1953. *Writers:* Arthur Stander, Sherwood Schwartz. *Director:* Marc Daniels

Cast: Myra Marsh (*Clara Foster*), Robert Foulk (*Mr. Johnson*)

Summary: A rainy night and a leaky roof result in some plaster falling from the ceiling of Joan and Brad's bedroom. Because she neglected to have the roof checked, as he had asked, Brad insists that Joan should pay the $20 for repairing the ceiling. At the suggestion of her buddy Clara, Joan decides to do the work herself, but only makes the problem worse. Faced with a $119 repair bill she can't pay, Joan scouts through the attic for items she can sell.

Notes: Sight gags are the order of the day in this very funny episode: Joan getting a faceful of falling plaster, sneezing the sleeves off Brad's decrepit raccoon coat, and getting her head stuck between the strings of a harp. Myra Marsh has one of her largest roles here, giving the second act a real Lucy-and-Ethel feel as she helps Joan sort through junk in the attic.

Secrets

Air Date: May 6, 1953. *Writers:* Arthur Stander, Sherwood Schwartz. *Director:* Marc Daniels

Cast: Myra Marsh (*Clara Foster*), Sandra Gould (*Elsie*), Bernard Gorcey (*Joe*), Fay Baker (*Nancy*), Richard Bartell (*Frank*), Don Brodie (*Harold*), Joanne Jordan (*Barbara*)

Summary: When Brad confides in Joan that he's being considered for a federal judgeship, his wife can't resist spreading the news. Later, when Brad comes into $1,500 unexpectedly, he decides to buy Joan a fur coat, using this as an opportunity to see if she's learned her lesson about keeping secrets. Told half the secret (that someone she knows will be getting a fur coat), Joan lets slip more than she should to the members of the Women's Welfare League.

Notes: According to this episode, Joan and Brad's telephone number is Dunbar 3-1232. The show's highlight is a scene in which Joan, forbidden to tell her friends about the fur coat for the next 24 hours, can't resist acting out the news in charades using lettuce, ice trays, frankfurters and other items from her kitchen.

The Artist Show

Air Date: May 13, 1953. *Writers:* Sherwood Schwartz, Arthur Stander. *Director:* Marc Daniels

Cast: Myra Marsh (*Clara Foster*), Geraldine Carr (*Mabel Henderson*), Lee Patrick (*Mrs. Adams*), Fritz Feld (*M. LeTouche*), Sandra Gould (*Elsie*), Joanne Jordan (*Barbara*)

Summary: At Brad's behest, Joan takes an interest in civic affairs, inviting Senator Adams to address her club luncheon. After Joan offends him by inadvertently stripping off his toupee, Brad fears he'll never get the federal judgeship. Determined to make amends, Joan learns that Mrs. Adams is an enthusiastic painter, and enrolls in art class to bone up on the subject, unaware of the identity of her fellow student.

Notes: Not until well past the halfway point is this episode's title elucidated, when Joan turns up in art class. The first act's comic highlight involves Joan's clumsy efforts to replace the Senator's toupee without his noticing. Even better is her slapstick scene in the art studio with Lee Patrick, involving free-flying paint and a hapless male artist's model caught in the line of fire.

The Threat

Air Date: May 20, 1953. *Writers:* Arthur Stander, Sherwood Schwartz. *Director:* Marc Daniels

Cast: Geraldine Carr (*Mabel Henderson*), Bob Sweeney (*Doctor*), Joe Devlin (*Rocky Collins*), Tony Michaels (*Deliveryman*)

Summary: Joan and Brad go to see a movie that leaves her convinced that some violent criminal will inevitably want to exact murderous revenge on her judge spouse. After reading in the newspaper that felon Rocky Collins, who vowed vengeance against Brad, has been released, Joan panics. Brad summons a doctor to treat his hysterical wife, not knowing that Rocky Collins is soon to arrive on the Stevenses' doorstep.

Notes: This episode's comic highlight finds Joan, who's disguised as a heavyset Swedish cleaning lady to keep an eye on Brad at work, trying to simultaneously carry out her impersonation in his office, while also seemingly talking to him (as herself) from home. Also noteworthy is the opening scene in which Backus, as Brad, does an impersonation of Mr. Magoo—easy enough, since he voiced that famous cartoon character for many years.

Country Club

Air Date: May 27, 1953. *Writers:* Arthur Stander, Sherwood Schwartz. *Director:* Marc Daniels

Cast: Sheldon Leonard (*Joe Edwards*), Geraldine Carr (*Mabel*), Frank Gerstle (*Tom*), Emlen Davies (*Alice*), Kay Wiley (*Mrs. Kenworthy*), Hal Taggart (*Mr. Kenworthy*), Jock George

Summary: So that they can join the country club, Joan tries to complete twelve golf lessons in one day. When they receive a home visit to determine if they're suitable club members,

Joan does her best to convince their guests that she and Brad come from a "conservative, dignified" background. She rents family heirlooms from an antique store, and tries to seal the deal with an old family recipe for salt water taffy.

Note: In real life, Joan Davis was an accomplished and enthusiastic golfer.

Quote: JOAN: You and I share a very serious problem.

BRAD: We do? What?

JOAN: Me!

Theatrical Can-Can

Air Date: June 3, 1953. *Writers:* Arthur Stander, Sherwood Schwartz. *Director:* Marc Daniels

Cast: Myra Marsh (*Clara Foster*), Geraldine Carr (*Mabel Henderson*), Sandra Gould (*Elsie*), Joanne Jordan (*Barbara*), Richard Keene (*Milkman*)

Summary: The Women's Welfare League is staging an original historical drama, *The Colonel's Daughter*, as a fundraiser. Expenses exceed ticket sales, leaving the ladies in a bind. Learning that Brad has a $250 entertainment budget for the upcoming Lawyers' Club banquet, Joan tries to persuade him to book a performance of the play, but Brad prefers to hire chorus girls. At the last moment, Brad learns that some staid city officials will be in attendance at his event, and decides *The Colonel's Daughter* would be more appropriate. Unfortunately, Joan gives her friends the wrong directions to the hotel, leaving her to play all the roles in the costume drama.

Neighbors

Air Date: June 10, 1953. *Writers:* Arthur Stander, Sherwood Schwartz. *Director:* Marc Daniels

Cast: Lee Patrick (*Agatha Murdoch*), Myra Marsh (*Clara Foster*), Geraldine Carr (*Mabel Henderson*), Sandra Gould (*Clubwoman*), Joanne Jordan (*Barbara*), George Milan (*Officer Kilpatrick*), Jerome Sheldon (*Dr. Schaefer*)

Summary: Relieved to hear that their noisiest neighbors, the Carstairs, are moving away, Joan decides to make sure the new owners are satisfactory. She's happy when the house is sold to a quiet older couple—until she learns that they own two purebred dogs that bark all night. Advised by a veterinarian that the dogs are probably lonesome, Joan spends the night in their doghouse so as to insure that Brad gets a good night's sleep.

Note: Actress Lee Patrick (1901–1982), seen here as Mrs. Murdoch, is a veteran character actress who was soon after cast as Henrietta Topper on *Topper*. She returned to *Joan* a few weeks later, in the episode "Brad's Broken Toe," and played a featured role in Joan's 1958 television pilot *Joan of Arkansas*.

Talent Scout

Air Date: June 17, 1953. *Writers:* Arthur Stander, Hy Freedman, Ed Tyler. *Director:* Marc Daniels

Cast: Barney Phillips (*Jim*), Jerry Hausner (*Joe*), Geraldine Carr (*Mabel Henderson*), George Neise (*Mervin*), Bob Sweeney (*Harry*), Sandra Gould (*Mildred Webster*), Myra Marsh (*Clara Foster*), Joanne Jordan (*Barbara*)

Summary: Brad's friend from the district attorney's office is trying to track down some phony talent scouts who prey on bored housewives. When Brad learns that their newest pigeon is Joan, he encourages her to enroll in their $500 course and entrap them. Joan finds herself playing her big audition for the movies with a temperamental chimpanzee as her leading man.

Note: Fantasizing about her imminent rise to stardom, Joan does a bit as the downtrodden housewife from *Come Back, Little Sheba*, a role that netted Shirley Booth an Oscar in 1953.

Honeymoon

Air Date: June 24, 1953. *Writers:* Arthur Stander, Phil Sharp. *Director:* Hal Walker
Cast: Herb Vigran, Paul Dubov (*Handymen*), Betty Lou Gerson (*Betty*), Tim Graham (*George Anderson*), George Perroni (*Bellboy*)

Summary: Counseling yet another quarrelsome married couple, Brad relates two episodes from his own married life. He tells the story of his honeymoon, when Joan accidentally locked him in a hotel closet. Later, he discusses the time he reneged on a promise to give Joan a diamond bracelet in exchange for six months of keeping a neat house.

Note: This episode's last act, in which Brad brings home important guests only to find his home transformed into a pig sty, is similar to the *I Love Lucy* segment "Men Are Messy." Filmed several months earlier, while Dick Mack was still the show's producer, this episode was held back.

Business Executive

Air Date: July 1, 1953. *Writers:* Arthur Stander, Alan Lipscott, Bob Fisher. *Director:* Marc Daniels
Cast: Shirley Mitchell (*Agnes*), Joe Besser (*Harry*), Margie Liszt (*Miss Bromley*), Robert Foulk (*Dave Butterworth*), Ross Elliott (*Steve Harper*), Jerome Sheldon (*Bill Morrison*), Henny Backus (*Saleslady*)

Summary: Brad is reunited with two old fraternity brothers who gave up practicing law for lucrative careers in the business world. Feeling that he owes it to Joan, Brad agrees to accept a $25,000 per year job with a soup company. After Joan's nightmare about Brad's stressful new job, she tries to talk him out of it, but has no luck until they visit a fur salon, where he insists on buying his wife a mink.

Quote: JOAN (bragging for the benefit of the other wives): Brad and I take a trip
         every year. Last year, we took a trip around the world. This year, we're
         going to try somewhere else.

Brad's Broken Toe

Air Date: July 8, 1953. *Writers:* Arthur Stander, Ben Starr. *Director:* Marc Daniels
Cast: Frank Gerstle (*Dr. Griswold*), Geraldine Carr (*Mabel Henderson*), Lee Patrick (*Miss Everett*), Alan DeWitt (*Orderly*), Barney Phillips (*Doctor*), Almira Sessions (*Miss Hodgkiss*)

Summary: Brad laughs at Joan's hypochondriac hysterics over a simple cold. When he slips on a banana peel at the zoo, she returns the favor by pooh-poohing his injury. But Brad's

X-rays show that he has three broken toes and he's admitted to the hospital, much to Joan's shame. Feeling the need to be at Brad's side, Joan tries in vain to gain admittance to his room after visiting hours. When all else fails, she poses as a patient, only to find herself in danger of being taken directly to surgery.

Note: A funny, lively episode that features several of Joan's favorite recurring players, this was a strong finale to the series' first season.

SECOND SEASON

Brad's Mustache

Air Date: October 14, 1953. *Writers:* Sherwood Schwartz, Al Schwartz, Jesse Goldstein. *Director:* John Rich

Cast: Lewis Russell (*Mr. Fitzgerald*), Norma Varden (*Mrs. Fitzgerald*), Griff Barnett (*Ed Rushmore*), Martha Wentworth (*Mrs. Rushmore*), Pattee Chapman (*Amy*), Joe Besser (*Wig Shop Clerk*)

Summary: Hoping to be appointed judge of Superior Court, Brad grows a mustache to give himself a look of distinction and maturity, with Joan's approval. But when Joan realizes that her man's new facial hair makes him more appealing to other women, she takes scissors in hand for some drastic action while Brad's asleep. Too bad he just received that Superior Court nomination, forcing Joan to substitute a $5 wiglet for the missing mustache before Brad wakes up and realizes it's gone.

    Quote: BRAD (when Joan easily "shaves" off the fake mustache in one stroke): This is the closest shave I've ever had!
        JOAN (relieved): You and me both!

First Lie

Air Date: October 21, 1953. *Writers:* Sherwood Schwartz, Jesse Goldstein, Lou Derman. *Director:* John Rich

Cast: Barney Phillips (*Tom Randolph*), Fay Baker (*Nancy*)

Summary: Joan buys a new dress even though she is already over her budget. Her pals Nancy and Helen convince her that she should avoid an argument by telling Brad it's an old dress with a new belt. Though Brad seems to accept the lie, Joan is wracked with guilt. Ready to confess as one of the masked guests on a TV panel show called *Marriage Clinic*, Joan chickens out when she sees that one of the expert panelists is none other than Brad. To teach her a lesson, Brad has his friend Tom bring home a lie detector machine and puts Joan through a test.

Furniture Quick Changes

Air Date: October 28, 1953. *Writers:* Sherwood Schwartz, Al Schwartz, Jesse Goldstein. *Director:* John Rich

Cast: Geraldine Carr (*Mabel Henderson*), Evelyn Scott (*Dr. Laura Hammond*), Harvey B. Dunn (*Edgar*), Richard Keene (*Carnival Ring Toss Man*), Frank Mitchell (*Carnival Oil Can Man*), Sheila Connolly, George Norris (*Couple at Carnival*)

Summary: With Mabel's help, Joan spends a busy afternoon repeatedly rearranging her living room furniture. Brad, tired and stressed from overwork, thinks he's seeing things, and consults a pretty psychologist, Dr. Hammond, who has eyes for Brad and manipulates him into taking her out for the evening without telling his wife. Joan proves to be nobody's pushover when she sees that someone has designs on her man.

Note: This episode's high point is a very funny routine in which Joan, following Brad and Laura to a carnival, impersonates the mechanical fortuneteller in a vending machine to spy on them.

Sister Pat

Air Date: November 4, 1953. *Writers:* Sherwood Schwartz, Al Schwartz, Jesse Goldstein. *Director:* John Rich
Cast: Beverly Wills (*Beverly*), Jerry Hausner (*Sam*), Ron Kennedy (*Dave*), James Cronin (*Jack*), Paul Grant (*Fred*)

Summary: Joan receives a letter from her parents asking if her kid sister Beverly can move in with the Stevenses while she attends nearby Southside Junior College. Brad acquiesces, but has a difficult time adjusting to living with a teenager. When Joan claims she would have welcomed any member of Brad's family who needed to move in, he decides to put her to the test with a few phony cousins.

Tropical Fish

Air Date: November 11, 1953. *Writers:* Sherwood Schwartz, Jesse Goldstein, Lou Derman. *Director:* John Rich
Cast: Beverly Wills (*Beverly*), Robert Foulk (*Store Owner*), Tom Peters (*Biff*), Alan DeWitt (*Professor Pemberton*), Marjorie Bennett (*Visitor*), Leon Tyler (*Doorman*)

Summary: Trying to share Brad's newfound interest in tropical fish, Joan buys him a fish and puts it into his tank, not knowing it's a cannibal that will eat all his other fish. Desperate to replace his rare "Tropicana Africanus," Joan sneaks into the Aquarium Society to find a replacement. Caught in the act, she's mistaken for Miss Fisher of *Fish Fancier's Digest* and asked to deliver a talk to the membership—including Brad.

Note: In one of this episode's funniest bits, Joan tries to stuff a wriggling fish into a slender-necked soda bottle, and then is forced to hide it in her sweater when she's apprehended.

Missing Food

Air Date: November 18, 1953. *Writers:* Jesse Goldstein, Sherwood Schwartz, Lou Derman. *Director:* John Rich
Cast: Beverly Wills (*Beverly*), Dick Elliott (*Bill Manners*), Martha Wentworth (*Mrs. Manners*), Robert Easton (*Joey*)

Summary: Joan's intimate dinner with Brad goes awry when he unexpectedly invites Mr. Manners, publisher of the *Legal Review*, his wife, and other guests to join them. Trying in vain to stretch the meager food to accommodate so many people, Joan inflates a cream puff until it explodes, adds far too much water to her pea soup, and stuffs her Chicken El Dorado with anything she can find to make it bigger. To make amends for the disastrous meal, Joan and Brad invite Mr. and Mrs. Manners on a picnic. When a stray dog eats everything in Joan's picnic basket, she resorts to swiping food from other unsuspecting picnickers.

Initiation

Air Date: November 25, 1953. *Writers:* Sherwood Schwartz, Jesse Goldstein, Phil Sharp. *Director:* John Rich
   Cast: Beverly Wills (*Beverly*), Marjorie Bennett (*Miss Patterson*), Don Beddoe (*Calvin J. Huntington*), Tyler McVey (*Mr. Dougherty*), Eleanore Tanin, Diane Ware, Janice Carroll (*Sophomores*)

Summary: College freshman Beverly is doing her best to avoid the hazing that sophomores traditionally give to newcomers. When Joan, not taking the situation seriously, dons the tacky blazer and beanie that freshmen are expected to wear, she falls prey to a trio of nasty sophomores. Joan's hazing finds her chased through the men's locker room and forced to drink a potion.

Bev's Boyfriend

Air Date: December 2, 1953. *Writers:* Jesse Goldstein, Sherwood Schwartz, Phil Sharp. *Director:* John Rich
   Cast: Beverly Wills (*Beverly*), Tom Peters (*Tom*), Sandra Gould (*Elsie*), Billy Benedict (*Deliveryman*), Robert Spencer (*Waiter*)

Summary: Beverly is infatuated with her classmate Tom, but he only has eyes for his hot rod, Agnes. Joan invites Tom to dinner intending to fix him up with Beverly, but the young man falls for Joan instead. Joan decides to cool his ardor with a dinner date, at which she reveals her false teeth, wig, mustard plaster, and bad hip. When even this doesn't do the trick, Brad steps in to help Joan convince her young suitor that she's not only married, but the mother of several young children.
   Note: This lively episode introduces Tom Peters in his recurring role as Beverly's boyfriend Tom. According to publicity at the time, Tom was a Hollywood newcomer, transplanted from Illinois, who was spotted by Joan when he appeared on a TV talent show. He would go on to enjoy a solid career as a character actor, and was still active into the early 1980s.
   Quote: TOM (complimenting Joan): Why, she looks as bright and sparkling as a
      chrome-plated cylinder head!

Lost Check

Air Date: December 9, 1953. *Writers:* Jesse Goldstein, Phil Sharp, Sherwood Schwartz. *Director:* John Rich
   Cast: Beverly Wills (*Beverly*), Florence Bates (*Librarian*), Jane Easton (*Blonde Applicant*), Carol Brewster (*Brunette Applicant*), James Nusser (*Agent Mitchell*), William Bryant, Ed Wolff (*Library Patrons*)

Summary: Brad needs to hire a temporary legal secretary while his usual one is on vacation, and Joan thinks she's perfect for the job. Trying to show her how demanding the position is, Brad gives his wife a tryout. Joan stashes a $10,000 certified check in a library book, *The Mystery of the Three Dead Women*, which Brad unwittingly returns. Now Joan and Beverly must find the missing item amidst a mountain of books.
   Note: Ed Wolff, a former circus giant who appeared in films including *The Colossus of New York* (1958) and *Return of the Fly* (1959), plays a *very* tall patron in the library scene.

Quote: JOAN (holding the $10,000 check): This money could buy two convertibles, or one-and-a-half mink coats!

The Shotgun

Air Date: December 16, 1953. *Writers:* Phil Sharp, Sherwood Schwartz, Jesse Goldstein. *Director:* John Rich
   Cast: Beverly Wills (*Beverly*), Geraldine Carr (*Mabel*), Tom Peters (*Tom*), Harvey B. Dunn (*Mr. Jackson*), Bob Jellison (*Soda Jerk*), Joe Devlin (*Cop*)

Summary: Joan lends Brad's golf clubs to Beverly and Tom, who bring them back ruined. Brad is angry because Joan doesn't respect his personal property, but changes his tune when his wife wins a shotgun in the Women's Welfare League raffle. Claiming she wants the gun for herself, Joan totes it to the drugstore, where the nervous clerk assumes she's trying to hold him up and passes out—just before two policemen arrive on the scene.

Musical

Air Date: December 23, 1953. *Writers:* Phil Sharp, Sherwood Schwartz, Jesse Goldstein. *Director:* John Rich
   Cast: Geraldine Carr (*Mabel Henderson*), Beverly Wills (*Beverly*), Tom Peters (*Tom*), Hal Smith (*Dave*)

Summary: As entertainment chairman of the annual Ladies' Club Follies, Joan is frustrated by Brad's reluctance to play a role in the production. Persuaded to do a man-and-wife sketch with Joan, Brad finds himself playing a femme fatale in drag, while Joan dons a Groucho Marx getup to play the hubby.
   Notes: This episode nicely showcases Beverly Wills, who does a song-and-dance number with Tom Peters. The choreography is credited to Willetta Smith. Hal Smith appears here as Brad's buddy Dave, but will soon settle into the role of Mabel's husband Charlie.

Double Wedding

Air Date: December 30, 1953. *Writers:* Phil Sharp, Sherwood Schwartz, Jesse Goldstein. *Director:* John Rich
   Cast: Beverly Wills (*Beverly*), Shirley Mitchell (*Natalie Lyons Matthews*), Anthony Warde (*Bill Matthews*), Joseph Kearns (*Mr. Ferguson*), Joe Devlin (*Policeman*), James Nusser (*Attendant*)

Summary: With their tenth anniversary approaching, Joan and Brad accept Beverly's suggestion that they celebrate by renewing their wedding vows. They make arrangements to replicate the original ceremony, which was a joint wedding featuring the Stevenses and another couple, the Matthewses. A shocked Joan, however, realizes that her marriage certificate shows a major blunder: The justice of the peace married her to Bill Matthews, and Brad to Bill's fiancée Natalie. Complications ensue when Bill likes the idea of trading in his wife for Joan.
   Note: Joan and Brad last celebrated their wedding anniversary about nine months ago on the show. They'll be due for another one before the season is over. Superficially, this episode resembles the 1952 *I Love Lucy* installment "The Marriage License," but the plot developments and treatment are quite different. This episode reunites Joan with actor Joseph

Kearns, who played her father on radio's *Leave It to Joan*, as well as her boss in the *Let's Join Joanie* pilot. He will make several more appearances during the run of *I Married Joan*.

Superstition

Air Date: January 6, 1954. *Writers:* Sherwood Schwartz, Jesse Goldstein, Phil Sharp. *Director:* John Rich

Cast: Frank Nelson (*Happy Garrity*), Beverly Wills (*Beverly*), Geraldine Carr (*Mabel Henderson*), Hal Smith (*Charlie Henderson*), Billy Benedict (*Deliveryman*)

Summary: Joan is saving box tops in hopes of being chosen as a contestant on the *Hilarity with Garrity* TV show, but figures she's doomed to failure when she misplaces her lucky locket. Trying to teach her a lesson about being superstitious, Brad sends her two fake telegrams about being chosen for the show. Only after Joan shows up at the TV studio does she learn that Brad tricked her. Emcee Happy Garrity takes pity on Joan and arranges for her and Brad to appear together on the show, which involves subjecting them to a series of outlandish stunts that are mostly bad luck for the hapless judge.

Note: This episode finds Joan appearing on a fictional TV game show that greatly resembles the popular *Truth or Consequences*. Producer Ralph Edwards' long-running hit, which began on radio in the early 1940s, was revived for NBC's prime time schedule in the fall of 1954 with Jack Bailey as host. Actor Frank Nelson (1911–1986), best known for his many appearances with Jack Benny, also played smarmy game show host Freddie Fillmore on *I Love Lucy*.

Barbecue

Air Date: January 13, 1954. *Writers:* Phil Sharp, Sherwood Schwartz, Jesse Goldstein. *Director:* John Rich

Cast: Adele Jergens (*Helen Cavanaugh*), Beverly Wills (*Beverly*), Wallace Chadwell (*George Cavanaugh*), Charles Williams (*Salesman*)

Summary: After a dinner party with the Cavanaughs, Brad is raving about Helen's barbecued spare ribs. Not to be outdone by her rival, Joan buys her own $415 barbecue, but the company is too busy to build it right away. After a few false starts, Joan and Beverly manage to assemble a barbecue that looks okay—but doesn't work. With the Cavanaughs as their dinner guests, and the help of her accomplice Beverly, Joan does her best to make it look as if she's grilling steaks on their new barbecue.

Note: This episode featured a bit of product placement for Joan's sponsor, as she is seen taking a parfait out of her refrigerator and commenting, "Gee, GE appliances are wonderful." This episode precedes by three years the sixth-season episode of *I Love Lucy* entitled "Building a Bar-B-Q."

Quote: JOAN: They laughed at Edison, they laughed at Marconi, they laughed at the Wright Brothers. Well, one day they'll laugh at me!

Mothers-in-Law

Air Date: January 20, 1954. *Writers:* Phil Sharp, Sherwood Schwartz, Jesse Goldstein. *Director:* John Rich

Cast: Geraldine Carr (*Mabel Henderson*), Hal Smith (*Charlie Henderson*), Mabel Paige (*Nellie Davis*), Norma Varden (*Florrie Stevens*), Strother Martin (*Ticket Agent*)

Summary: Joan and Brad argue over where they will spend their vacation: visiting her mother in St. Paul, or his in Cleveland. Instead they find themselves hosting both ladies for a visit. The relationship between haughty Florrie, Brad's mom, and Joan's homey mother Nellie makes for some tense moments, culminating in a competition over who makes the better beef stew.

Note: This episode introduces veteran character Mabel Paige (1880–1954) as Joan's mother, Nellie Davis. Paige, who worked with Joan in *If You Knew Susie,* will reprise the role of Mrs. Davis in "Pop Retires" a few weeks later. Actor Strother Martin (1919–1980), who made additional *Joan* appearances in "Missing Witness" and "Get Rick Quick," is probably best-remembered as the prison camp boss in *Cool Hand Luke* (1967) who diagnoses "a failure to communicate."

Mabel's Dress

Air Date: January 27, 1954. *Writers:* Sherwood Schwartz, Jesse Goldstein, Phil Sharp. *Director:* John Rich
    Cast: Geraldine Carr (*Mabel Henderson*), Hal Smith (*Charlie Henderson*)

Summary: Joan finds a wrapped package containing a new dress in her bedroom closet and assumes it's a gift from Brad. She decides to restyle it, removing the bow, ruffle, and sleeves. Unfortunately, the dress was actually Mabel's birthday present, which Charlie asked Brad to hide. The resulting argument leaves Joan and Brad lonely and bored at home during the Hendersons' party. Trying to make amends, Joan bakes an orange cake and takes it to the party, not knowing that some cleaning fluid leaked into the cake batter. Mabel and her guests get a big bang out of Joan's exploding cake, not to mention the inadvertent gift of a book titled *How to Be Happy Though Fat.*

Note: According to this episode, Joan was responsible for introducing Mabel to her husband Charlie.

Quote: MABEL (to Joan): Now, don't be modest, dear! You know your orange cake is dynamite!

Monkeyshines

Air Date: February 3, 1954. *Writers:* Phil Sharp, Sherwood Schwartz, Jesse Goldstein. *Director:* John Rich
    Cast: Beverly Wills (*Beverly*), Dick Elliott (*Huntley Potter*), Martha Wentworth (*Millicent Potter*), Alan DeWitt (*Salesman*), Arthur Walsh (*Trainer*)

Summary: Marty, a two-year-old chimpanzee, has just inherited $500,000 from his late owner, making Brad concerned for his welfare and suspicious of Mr. and Mrs. Potter, the couple applying for custody of him. Brad brings the hairy heir home to Joan's mothering. Marty's day in court finds him on the verge of being sent home with the Potters, until some unexpected antics from Joan and her simian sidekick reveal his would-be guardians in their true light.

Note: According to reporter Hal Humphrey's *Los Angeles Mirror* column (November 9, 1953), it was during a lunch interview with him that Joan met Marty and his trainer, Arthur Walsh. "Cutest thing I've ever seen," Joan proclaimed, introducing Marty to her writers and signing him up for this segment. Walsh appears on-camera in the closing scene.

Bev's Mistaken Marriage

Air Date: February 10, 1954. *Writers:* Jesse Goldstein, Phil Sharp, Sherwood Schwartz.
Director: John Rich
   Cast: Beverly Wills (*Beverly*), Geraldine Carr (*Mabel Henderson*), Tom Peters (*Tom Peters*), Philip Tonge (*Judge Lionel Cushing*), Richard [Dick] Sargent (*Roy*)

Summary: Joan flies into a panic when she believes that Beverly is planning to elope with Tom. In truth, Beverly is only helping a pair of college friends, Ralph and Janet, who are getting married. There are complications when Brad persuades Joan she should pretend to be in favor of the plan. Believing that Brad's judge friend has just performed Beverly's wedding ceremony, the Stevenses plan a surprise party for the happy couple.

Notes: Seen here as one of Beverly and Tom's college chums is a young Dick Sargent, billed as "Richard," who will go on to co-star as the second Darrin on *Bewitched*. This episode has Joan planning to dine at Chasen's, a Los Angeles restaurant popular with the Hollywood crowd. In real life, Beverly had already been married and divorced, and would announce plans for her second marriage a couple of months after this episode aired.

Quote: JOAN: You know what they say: "Blood is thicker than water." And when it comes to my sister Beverly, nobody is thicker than me!

Missing Witness

Air Date: February 17, 1954. *Writers:* Sherwood Schwartz, Jesse Goldstein, Phil Sharp. *Director:* John Rich
   Cast: Geraldine Carr (*Mabel Henderson*), Charles Williams (*Harry Watts*), Strother Martin (*Reporter*), Frank Gerstle (*Detective Lt. Harrison*)

Summary: Brad is worried about his current case, the murder of a shopkeeper by gangster Curly Gordon, because the key witness, Harry Watts, has vanished. When Watts turns up on the Stevens' doorstep and narrowly escapes being shot, Brad and his friend, Detective Lt. Harrison, lay a trap for the bad guys. Reporters are told that Joan, too, can testify against Gordon, and is confined to bed at home after being shot.

Note: According to this episode, Brad's middle name is Jericho, contradicting the first-season segment "Hunting."

Anniversary Memo

Air Date: February 24, 1954. *Writers:* Phil Sharp, Sherwood Schwartz, Jesse Goldstein. *Director:* John Rich
   Cast: Beverly Wills (*Beverly*), Tom Peters (*Tom*), Anthony Warde (*Treadwell*), Beverly Garland (*Millie*), Billy Benedict (*Deliveryman*), Marilyn Gustafson (*Floral Clerk*), Jerome Sheldon (*Janitor*)

Summary: When Joan finds a note written by Brad reminding himself, "don't forget present and flowers for ann, july 5," she's convinced he's involved with another woman. In fact, the note alludes to Brad and Joan's upcoming anniversary. When a shyster lawyer threatened with disbarment tries to taint Brad's reputation by arranging a compromising photo with beautiful young Millie, Joan sees them together and assumes this is Ann.

Note: This episode features up-and-coming actress Beverly Garland (1926–2008), soon to be seen in low-budget Roger Corman movies like *Not of This Earth*, and as a policewoman in her own TV series, *Decoy* (1957–58).

Dented Fender

Air Date: March 3, 1954. *Writers:* Jesse Goldstein, Sherwood Schwartz, Phil Sharp. *Director:* John Rich

   Cast: Beverly Wills (*Beverly*), Tom Peters (*Tom Peters*), Joseph Kearns (*Morton Clark*)

Summary: Brad declares the Stevenses' car repair bills exorbitant, but Joan claims she's not the responsible party. They agree to take turns driving the car, so as to see who is more careful with it.

Mountain Lodge

Air Date: March 10, 1954. *Writers:* Sherwood Schwartz, Jesse Goldstein, Phil Sharp *Director:* John Rich

   Cast: Beverly Wills (*Beverly*), Tom Peters (*Tom Peters*), Robert Foulk (*Mr. Fenster*), Paul Keast (*Mr. Tuttle*)

Summary: Brad and Joan each spend the $1,100 in their "Life Can Be Beautiful" fund on the same day, he on a mountain cabin, she on a motorboat. Joan decides the solution to her problem is to convince Brad he doesn't really want the cabin. With help from Beverly and her boyfriend Tom, Joan proceeds to make the remote cabin unlivable—just before she and Brad become stranded there without food.

Home of the Week

Air Date: March 17, 1954. *Writers:* Jesse Goldstein, Sherwood Schwartz, Phil Sharp. *Director:* John Rich

   Cast: Adele Jergens (*Helen Cavanaugh*), Beverly Wills (*Beverly*), Tim Graham (*Judge Hammond*), James Nusser (*Albert Kellner*), Grady Sutton (*Man in Newsroom*), Richard Keene (*Photographer*), Paul Keast (*Judge*)

Summary: Joan is envious when her rival Helen's ritzy house is spotlighted in the *Gazette*'s "Home of the Week" feature. Goaded by Helen, Joan arranges for her own home to be the next one photographed, and borrows some of her friends' most elaborate furnishings to spruce it up. The *Gazette* staff eagerly shoots photos of the Ming vase, Gainsborough painting, and other valuables in the Stevenses' living room. Meanwhile, a scandal is about to break concerning a local judge who's enriching himself with bribes.

Pop Retires

Air Date: March 24, 1954. *Writers:* Jesse Goldstein, Phil Sharp, Sherwood Schwartz. *Director:* John Rich

   Cast: El Brendel (*Axel Davis*), Beverly Wills (*Beverly*), Tom Peters (*Tom*), Mabel Paige (*Nellie Davis*), George Neise (*Mr. DeMuth*)

Summary: Brad's parents, currently living in Cleveland, are ready to retire, and Joan writes a letter inviting them to come to California. Beverly mistakenly sends the letter to Joan's parents instead. Her father, a retired "wick-braider," is only too happy to take up residence at the Stevenses' home. Persuaded to take up a new career, Pop takes a job at an airplane factory, but it's Joan who gets caught in the draft.

   Note: Dialect comedian El Brendel, an ex-vaudevillian like Joan, was an old pal from their days together at 20th Century–Fox in the 1930s. Absent from the screen for some time, he told syndicated columnist Bob Foster (April 21, 1954), of his *Joan* appearance, "I guess more people saw me the first week I was on, than saw me all the time I was in movies. Joan is great to work with." He made two more appearances in weeks to come, in "Get Rich Quick" and "Masquerade." Mabel Paige makes her second and final appearance here as Joan's mother; the actress died of a heart ailment shortly after filming this episode.

> *Quote:* BRAD (coaxing Joan): Joanie, I want you to remember, I love you.
> JOAN: Okay, now what is it you want me to forget?

Changing Houses

Air Date: March 31, 1954. *Writers:* Jesse Goldstein, Phil Sharp, Sherwood Schwartz. *Director:* John Rich

Cast: Geraldine Carr (*Mabel Henderson*), Hal Smith (*Charlie Henderson*), Phil Arnold (*Joe*), Bill Kennedy (*Rug Salesman*)

Summary: Joan admires her pal Mabel's modern house design, while Mabel envies the early American charm of the Stevenses' place. The two families agree to switch houses for a week to see if they really like the others' décor. Joan and Brad quickly decide they hate the gadgets and fixtures of Mabel's house, and are ready to end the experiment after one day. But Joan spills a bottle of blue ink on Mabel's treasured white carpet, and needs time to make things right.

Note: This episode's highlights include a physical comedy sequence involving Brad and Joan struggling with the Hendersons' beds, which roll into the wall at the push of a button, and Joan's trip to the rug store, where she tries to hide in a rolled-up carpet when Mabel shows up.

> *Quote:* BRAD (to Joan, grumbling about the Hendersons' house): Might as well give up your subscription for *House Beautiful* and get one for *Popular Mechanics*.

Jealousy

Air Date: April 7, 1954. *Writers:* Jesse Goldstein, Phil Sharp, Sherwood Schwartz. *Director:* John Rich

Cast: Philip Van Zandt (*Dr. Carlos Salazar*), Geraldine Carr (*Mabel Henderson*), Hal Smith (*Charlie Henderson*), Barbara Hill (*Dr. Faversham*)

Summary: The women's club hosts a visiting lecturer, Dr. Carlos Salazar, an expert on marriage and home life. Mabel's husband Charlie is jealous of the attentions that the suave doctor pays to his wife, but Joan says Brad is "too intelligent" to be jealous. When Dr. Salazar suggests that jealousy is actually a sign of a husband's love and devotion, Joan changes her tune. The doctor accepts a dinner invitation to the Stevens house, and succeeds in arousing Brad's jealousy to the point where Joan fears her husband is in a murderous rage.

Note: Joan's writers had trouble remembering whether Mabel and Charlie's last name is Henderson or Harrison. Here, Dr. Salazar addresses her as Mrs. Harrison.

Get Rich Quick

Air Date: April 14, 1954. *Writers:* Jesse Goldstein, Phil Sharp, Sherwood Schwartz. *Director:* John Rich

Cast: El Brendel (*Axel Davis*), Frank Gerstle (*District Attorney*), Anthony Warde (*J. Farrington Randolph*), Herb Vigran, Martha Wentworth (*Stockholders*), Strother Martin (*Moving Man*)

Summary: Joan's father buys $250 worth of stock in a company that supposedly controls the biggest uranium mine in South America. Afraid her father has been fleeced, Joan visits the office of fast-talking company president J. Farrington Randolph, who not only keeps the original investment but persuades Joan to double it. Brad's friend, the district attorney, warns him privately that a crackdown on this crooked operation is imminent. But by the time that happens, Randolph has flown the coop, leaving Joan and her father as the company's newly appointed executive officers to face angry investors and the repossession of everything in the office.

Masquerade

Air Date: April 21, 1954. *Writers:* Sherwood Schwartz, Jesse Goldstein, Phil Sharp. *Director:* John Rich

Cast: Geraldine Carr (*Mabel Henderson*), El Brendel (*Axel Davis*), Hal Smith (*Charlie Henderson*), Sandra Gould (*Betty*), Dick Elliott (*Golf Player*), Tim Graham (*Golf Player*), Paula Blythe (*Club Member*)

Summary: The ladies want the annual country club dance to be a masquerade, but the men refuse to wear costumes. Joan promises her friends that she can talk Brad into dressing up, since he was a member of his college dramatic society, and that the other men will then follow suit. When the men cave in, Brad devises a scheme that he is sure will prevent their wives from ever suggesting another masquerade dance.

Note: Reviewing this segment in the *Boston Globe* (April 22, 1954), critic Mary Cremmen said, "*I Married Joan* should report for a checkup. Last night's episode failed to produce a single clever line and the story was that old chestnut about men dressed in women's clothes."

Quote: JOAN (promising her friends): I will deliver my husband lock, stock, and—
                    he might be wearing the barrel!

The Milkman Cometh

Air Date: April 28, 1954. *Writers:* Phil Sharp, Sherwood Schwartz, Jesse Goldstein. *Director:* John Rich

Cast: Geraldine Carr (*Mabel Henderson*), Hal Smith (*Charlie Henderson*)

Summary: When Joan overhears Mabel giving the milkman an earful about his poor customer service, she mistakes the conversation for an argument between Mabel and Charlie. Against Brad's advice, Joan decides to play marriage counselor and save the Hendersons' relationship. Later, Mabel accepts the milkman's apology; Joan, misunderstanding yet again, thinks the Hendersons have made up, and invites them to dinner to celebrate. Before all the misunderstandings are settled, Joan tries to bring her neighbors closer together with a live, in-person version of their favorite TV show, *This Is Your Life.*

Quote: JOAN (realizing she's goofed yet again): It could've happened to anybody.
                    BRAD: But it always happens to you!
                    JOAN: Yeah, how about that?

Predictions

Air Date: May 19, 1954. *Writers:* Jesse Goldstein, Phil Sharp, Sherwood Schwartz. *Director:* John Rich

Cast: Beverly Wills (*Beverly*), Dan Tobin (*Roger Brooks*), Herbert Ellis (*Bob Sanford*), Maura Murphy (*Melissa Sanford*), Gil Frye (*Randolph*), Barbara Hill (*Nurse*), Paul Keast (*Brooks' Associate*)

Summary: After ten years, Joan finds a list of predictions she made shortly after she and Brad were married. When Brad hears that she predicted he could become a millionaire, like her other boyfriend Roger Brooks, he feels he's failed his wife. To soothe Brad's feelings, Joan asks Roger to pay them a visit and pretend to be destitute.

Note: Around the time this episode was filmed, Joan announced Beverly's engagement to Army Second Lieutenant Alan Grossman. Beverly later said that she would give up her career. She didn't return to the series as a regular following her marriage, though she did make one guest appearance in Season 3.

Quote: BRAD: When we lived here, I was a struggling young lawyer, and we'd just gotten married.

JOAN: That's right. Even after I landed him, he was still struggling.

Brad's Initiation

Air Date: June 9, 1954. *Writers:* Sherwood Schwartz, Jesse Goldstein, Phil Sharp. *Director:* John Rich

Cast: Beverly Wills (*Beverly*), Anthony Warde (*Exalted Leader*), Joseph Kearns (*Vice-Exalted Leader*), Robert Foulk (*Sub-Vice-Exalted Leader*)

Summary: Brad's initiation into a lodge, the Loyal and Secret Order of Masquers and Frolickers, puts him a variety of embarrassing situations, chiefly the requirement that he express absolute agreement with anything and everything Joan says. His odd behavior makes Joan and Beverly worry that Brad may be the victim of an international spy ring, just like Burt Lancaster's character in a new movie Beverly just saw.

Confidence

Air Date: June 23, 1954. *Writers:* Phil Sharp, Sherwood Schwartz, Jesse Goldstein. *Director:* John Rich

Cast: Geraldine Carr (*Mabel Henderson*), Bill Kennedy (*Mr. Swanson*), Hal Smith (*Charlie Henderson*)

Summary: Brad lacks the confidence to pursue a suggestion that he run for president of the City Council. By the time Joan gets through with him, though, Brad decides he should enter the mayoral race instead. Wanting to set things right, Joan enlists a paperboy to pose as a grammar-school newspaper reporter who will flummox the blossoming candidate with tough questions.

Note: Once again, Charlie and Mabel, usually the Hendersons, seem to have changed their name to Harrison.

Joan's Haircut

Air Date: July 7, 1954. *Writers:* Sherwood Schwartz, Jesse Goldstein, Phil Sharp. *Director:* John Rich

Joan and Brad (Joan Davis and Jim Backus) argue over who got the worse coiffure in the second-season finale, "Joan's Haircut."

Cast: Alan DeWitt (*Fletcher*), Jerry Hausner (*Larry*), Hal Smith (*Charlie Henderson*), Geraldine Carr (*Mabel Henderson*), Richard Reeves (*Butch Henderson*), Billy Benedict (*Deliveryman*), Kay Wiley (*Mrs. Norman*), Barbara Hill (*Beautician*)

Summary: Joan and Brad enjoy a good laugh over a new women's hairstyle, the panda, that they both agree looks ridiculous. Unfortunately, a mix-up at the hairdresser results in Joan getting exactly that style. Meanwhile, Brad has a similar mishap at the barber shop. Embarrassed by her appearance, Joan refuses to attend their college reunion. When Brad decides he'll go anyway, Joan devises an elaborate scheme to convince him that he's suffered a blow to the head, and that the reunion took place three weeks ago.

Note: According to syndicated columnist Lawrence Witte, this episode was chosen to be the season finale so that both Joan and her co-star could "submit to weird haircuts" for maximum comedy effect without impinging on shooting of other segments.

THIRD SEASON

New House

Air Date: September 29, 1954. *Writers:* Sherwood Schwartz, Jesse Goldstein, Phil Sharp. *Director:* Don Weis

Cast: Sheila Bromley (*Janet Tobin*), Dan Tobin (*Kerwin Tobin*), Joseph Kearns (*Mr. Edwards*), Tim Graham (*Mr. Simpson*), Sidney Clute, Frank Mitchell (*Moving Men*)

Summary: Joan and Brad fall in love with a house at 345 Laurel Drive and decide to buy it. Unfortunately, two salesmen from the same company showed the house on the same day, and both accepted checks for down payments. Neither the Stevenses nor the Tobins will budge, so both couples set up an uneasy co-existence in the house.

Note: Thanks to some judicious film editing, Joan plays both her usual character and an annoying hag of a neighbor in the same scene. Actress Sheila Bromley is introduced here as new neighbor Janet Tobin, with whom Joan will continue to have a somewhat adversarial relationship.

Party Line

Air Date: October 6, 1954. *Writers:* Jesse Goldstein, Phil Sharp, Sherwood Schwartz. *Director:* Don Weis
    Cast: Sheila Bromley (*Janet Tobin*), Dan Tobin (*Kerwin Tobin*), Charles Williams (*Telephone Man*)

Summary: Joan's already prickly relationship with new neighbor Janet Tobin isn't improved when the ladies are forced to share a telephone party line. The ensuing war of one-upsmanship is interrupted when Joan and Brad mistakenly believe that Janet is terminally ill, and that her callous husband is gleefully anticipating his life insurance payoff. When the truth comes out, the result is a neighbor-vs.-neighbor free-for-all that tops all that came before.

Note: Physical comedy is the order of the day here, with Joan and her cohorts doused with garden hoses, splattered with a pile of leaves, and sprayed with a bottle of champagne.

Quote: JOAN (to Brad, after he kisses her): I know we've been married over ten years. Now you kiss me to calm me down.

Wall Safe

Air Date: October 13, 1954. *Writers:* Phil Sharp, Sherwood Schwartz, Jesse Goldstein. *Director:* Ezra Stone
    Cast: Geraldine Carr (*Mabel Henderson*), Lou Lubin (*"Light Fingers"*)

Summary: While hanging pictures in their new house, Joan finds a hidden safe installed by a previous owner. Consumed with curiosity, Joan hires a retired safecracker to open it, and finds a treasure map. As Brad watches in amusement, Joan and Mabel dig up half the Stevenses' yard in search of a buried treasure.

Alienation of Affections

Air Date: October 20, 1954. *Writers:* Jesse Goldstein, Phil Sharp, Hugh Wedlock, Jr., Howard Snyder. *Director:* Ezra Stone
    Cast: Geraldine Carr (*Mabel Henderson*), Hal Smith (*Charlie Henderson*), Hal March (*Mr. Owens*), Alan DeWitt (*Store Clerk*), Vivi Janiss (*Genevieve Fisher*), Wally Brown (*Dr. Randolph Fisher*)

Summary: Trying to help a stranger select a gift in a department store, Joan is accosted by the man's wife, who takes her for his girlfriend and threatens to sue for alienation of affections. Joan tries to set things right by inviting Mrs. Fisher to her house, enlisting Charlie to pose as Brad and demonstrate how happily married Joan is. But when Mabel decides her husband's love scene with Joan is a little too realistic and takes him home in a huff, Joan hurriedly casts the hapless milkman as her loving spouse.

Note: Wally Brown, seen here in a guest appearance, will join the show later in the season in a recurring role.

Bombay Duck

Air Date: October 27, 1954. *Writers:* Phil Sharp, Hugh Wedlock, Jr., Howard Snyder, Jesse Goldstein. *Director:* Ezra Stone
Cast: Geraldine Carr (*Mabel Henderson*), Martha Wentworth (*Miss Denton*), Emlen Davies (*Mrs. Cushing*), Jock George (*Mr. Peabody*)

Summary: Seeing how helpful Judge Cushing's wife is to her husband, Joan decides to take a six-week secretarial course at Peabody Business College. Wanting to surprise Brad with her achievement, Joan tries to combine her coursework, making a fancy dinner of Bombay Duck and stuffing 4,000 envelopes into one hectic day.

Note: Written on the blackboard in Joan's classroom are the names of her fellow students, many of them taken from members of the show's crew, including director of photography James Van Trees, director Ezra Stone, and producer P.J. Wolfson.

Clothes Budget

Air Date: November 3, 1954. *Writers:* Howard Snyder, Jesse Goldstein, Phil Sharp, Hugh Wedlock, Jr. *Director:* Ezra Stone
Cast: Adele Jergens (*Helen Cavanaugh*), Myra Marsh (*Clara Foster*), Bernard Gorcey (*Mr. Frisbee*), Fritz Feld (*Henri*), Sara Seegar (*Charity Worker*)

Summary: Joan wants to buy a new evening gown for an upcoming charity function to impress her rival Helen Cavanaugh. Brad agrees to give her $412 in one lump sum to cover her wardrobe expenses for an entire year, and Joan gleefully goes shopping. Showing off for Helen, Joan buys a gown that costs the entire $412, and then must try to retrieve her old clothes, all of which she donated to charity.

Note: Actress Sara Seegar was the real-life wife of series director Ezra Stone. She was later a regular on TV's *Dennis the Menace* (1959–63), as the wife of the second Mr. Wilson, played by Gale Gordon.

Dancing Lessons

Air Date: November 10, 1954. *Writers:* Howard Snyder, Jesse Goldstein, Phil Sharp, Hugh Wedlock, Jr. *Director:* Ezra Stone
Cast: William Forrest (*Judge Desmond Palmer*), Verna Felton (*Nora Palmer*), Tareaux Forchand (*Carlotta Carlyle*), Sara Berner (*Lulu*), Maurice Marsac (*Hernando*), Dick Reeves (*Lefty*), Sid Clute (*Dancer*)

Summary: After a dull evening at home with "old fogies" Judge and Mrs. Palmer, Joan wants more fun in her life, and persuades Brad to take dancing lessons at the Arthur Murray studios. After meeting his pretty instructor Carlotta, Brad is more than ready to sign up for a three-month course. At the suggestion of her pal Lulu, Joan decides to fight fire with fire, and signs up for lessons of her own, with suave Hernando.

Note: This episode features the only *I Married Joan* appearance by Joan's longtime radio supporting player Verna Felton, who would find TV popularity as a cast member on *December Bride* (CBS, 1954–59).

Two Saint Bernards

Air Date: November 17, 1954. *Writers:* Jesse Goldstein, Phil Sharp, Hugh Wedlock, Jr., Howard Snyder. *Director:* Ezra Stone

Cast: Jerry Hausner (*Pet Shop Owner*), Sharon Baird (*Susan*), Bill Kennedy (*Desk Sergeant*), Phil Arnold (*Police Officer*), Joe Devlin (*Second Officer*)

Summary: Meeting a little girl's new Chihuahua puppy makes Joan want her own dog, but Brad says no. Subsequent visits to the pet store result in both Joan and Brad taking home matching Saint Bernards, each trying to hide the dog from the other. When one of the dogs goes missing, Joan invades the local police station to report his disappearance.

Note: Frequent *Joan* player Jerry Hausner is spotlighted nicely here as the canny pet store owner, who uses a variety of tricks (including vocal impersonations of dogs) to make sales.

Manhole Cover

Air Date: November 24, 1954. *Writers:* Sherwood Schwartz, Jesse Goldstein, Phil Sharp. *Director:* Ezra Stone

Cast: Sig Ruman (*Professor Gottschalk*), Geraldine Carr (*Mabel Henderson*), Don Brodie (*Clerk*), Bob Jellison (*Clerk*), Dick Rich (*Workman*), Martha Wentworth (*Vocal Student*), Paula Blythe (*Chorale Member*)

Summary: Brad tells Joan emphatically that he doesn't approve of using his position as judge to gain special favors. So when a loose manhole cover keeps Joan awake at night, she goes to the city Department of Works and becomes hopelessly entangled in red tape trying to get it fixed. Frustrated, she pounds a spike into the manhole herself, causing Brad to blow out two tires when he drives over it. Only then does Brad call a commissioner and use his influence to arrange repairs. Meanwhile, Joan and her choral group long to hire a famous conductor to prepare them for an upcoming competition, but his fee is $1,000. Joan visits Professor Gottschalk, and manages to subtly disclose that she is married to the judge who will be trying his upcoming court case. Her trick gets her a free rehearsal session with the distinguished conductor—just as city workers arrive with jackhammer and blasting equipment to fix the broken manhole.

The Farm

Air Date: December 1, 1954. *Writers:* Jesse Goldstein, Phil Sharp, Hugh Wedlock, Jr., Howard Snyder. *Director:* Ezra Stone

Cast: Sam Hearn (*Mr. Bennett*), Minerva Urecal (*Mrs. Bennett*), Gladys Hurlbut (*Mrs. Fairchild*), Paul Power (*Mr. Fairchild*), Frank Gerstle (*Bill Jones*), Lillian Sayre (*Helen Jones*), Margie Liszt (*Miss Bromley*)

Summary: Joan and Brad have been invited to spend a week at the country estate of socially prominent Mrs. Fairchild, with whom he worked on a charitable project. Told to bring everything she'll need for fox hunting, tennis, riding, and a cocktail party, Joan promptly goes shopping, only to learn Brad has a different vacation in mind. He's arranged for them to visit the Bennetts' working farm, where they, like all guests, will help with the chores to earn their keep. In the midst of a tiring regimen of chopping wood, picking fruit, and the like, Joan learns that the Fairchilds will be paying a visit, having believed Joan's lie about the farm belonging to the Stevenses.

> *Quote:* JOAN (inventing a reason why she and Brad "own" a rundown farm): It's an antique—George Washington slept here.
> BRAD: Washington never saw California. It belonged to the Spanish back then.
> JOAN: Okay, then Xavier Cugat slept here!

Home Movies

Air Date: December 8, 1954. *Writers:* Sherwood Schwartz, Jesse Goldstein, Phil Sharp. *Director:* Ezra Stone
Cast: Myra Marsh (*Clara Foster*), Sandra Gould (*Mildred Webster*), Charlotte Lawrence (*Vi*), Maxine Semon (*Frieda*), William Forrest (*Judge Desmond Palmer*)

Summary: Returning home after a two-week Hawaiian vacation, Brad is annoyed to see that Joan left the back door unlocked, failed to turn off the radio, and didn't cancel the milkman's deliveries. But when he sees that she also failed to mail an important legal opinion for him, he accuses her of doing it deliberately because she disagreed with his ruling. Brad stomps out the house to stay at his club, but returns when he learns he's under consideration to replace a retiring judge in the Court of Domestic Relations. Still angry, Joan and Brad try to put on a good front while showing home movies of their trip to her friends and to the judge whose job he wants.
Note: Footage from Joan Davis' own Hawaiian vacation of the previous summer is incorporated into this episode.

Gun Moll (a.k.a. "Big Louie's Parole")

Air Date: December 15, 1954. *Writers:* Hugh Wedlock, Jr., Howard Snyder, Jesse Goldstein, Phil Sharp. *Director:* Ezra Stone
Cast: Ben Welden (*Martin Logan*), Lewis Charles (*Lefty Barker*), Barney Phillips (*Lieutenant*), Dorothy Granger (*Dorothy*), Frankie Darro (*Shorty*), Paul Baxley, Dick Crockett (*Gangsters*)

Summary: When the local newspaper reports that Brad will be the judge who decides whether gangster Big Louie is paroled, the Stevenses begin getting threatening messages from members of Louie's mob. Accompanied by Brad's actor friend Martin Logan, who's played gangsters in dozens of movies, Joan invades the mob's hideout behind a local sporting goods store. Joan's pose as gum-chewing, slangy gun moll Brainy Annie fools the mobsters for a time—until she and Martin run out of threatening dialogue from his movie *Love Is Murder*.
Note: This episode climaxes with a wild physical comedy fight scene involving a skeet shooter, collapsing tents, slide-whistle sound effects, and every other gag the writers could conceive using the props from the sporting goods store. Note that, despite the supposed threat of mobsters invading her home in the earlier scenes, one thing that never seems to occur to Joan is to lock the doors, allowing two characters to walk in on her at will. Guest player Ben Welden, cast as a movie actor who typically played gangsters, did exactly that in 1937's *Love and Hisses*, which also featured Joan Davis.

Crazy Toes Smith

Air Date: December 22, 1954. *Writers:* Jesse Goldstein, Phil Sharp, Hugh Wedlock, Jr., Howard Snyder. *Director:* Ezra Stone
    Cast: Archer MacDonald (*Ambrose "Crazy Toes" Smith*), Joseph Crehan (*Coach*), Pattee Chapman (*Gloria*), Betty Jean Hainey (*College Girl*), Chet Marshall (*College Boy*)

Summary: The star football player from Joan's alma mater, Eastside High School, is in danger of losing his eligibility to play just prior to the big game. Joan, who made a bet with Brad on the game's outcome, takes on the task of tutoring the young quarterback, but finds that the only thing that motivates him to study is food. After stuffing him full of cake and other goodies, Joan learns that the boy passed his exam, but he's now ineligible to play because of his weight. With eight days until the big game, Joan must whip him back into shape.
    Note: This is the first of two third-season episodes to feature the comic talents of up-and-coming actor Archer MacDonald (1925–1955), whose promising career will be cut short by his early death brought on by multiple ulcers. He appears again in "The Letter."

Joan Plays Cupid

Air Date: December 29, 1954. *Writers:* Jesse Goldstein, Phil Sharp, Hugh Wedlock, Jr., Howard Snyder. *Director:* Ezra Stone
    Cast: Sally Kelly (*Sally Shepherd*), Wally Brown (*Wally*), Jerry Hausner (*Joe Rollins*), Jack Kruschen (*Ted Morgan*), Alan DeWitt (*Escort Service Manager*), Harry Bartell (*Max*)

Summary: Trying to help her friend Sally land a husband, Joan decides to spread a rumor that Sally is a Texas oil heiress. The ruse brings out no one but sleazy fortune hunters, and alienates Wally, the old boyfriend with whom Sally is really in love. Joan reasons that jealousy will bring Wally around, and rents a gigolo from the Continental Escort Service. Confusion reigns when Max, the escort, mistakes Joan for Sally.
    Note: This episode introduces Joan's radio and film co-star Wally Brown in a recurring role.

The Wedding

Air Date: January 5, 1955. *Writers:* Phil Sharp, Hugh Wedlock, Jr., Howard Snyder, Jesse Goldstein. *Director:* Ezra Stone
    Cast: Sally Kelly (*Sally*), Wally Brown (*Wally*), Joseph Kearns (*Mr. Saxton*), Maxine Semon (*Frieda*), Billy Bletcher (*Justice of the Peace*)

Summary: With Joan's help, bashful Wally proposes to Sally, who promptly accepts. With only three days to arrange the ceremony, which will be held at the Stevens house, Joan enlists the help of wedding planner Mr. Saxton. Assuming that heiress Sally is footing the tab, Joan and Brad encourage Mr. Saxton to think big. But when they realize they're liable for the expenses, the Stevenses try to scale down the $1,000 event.
    Note: According to this script, Joan and Brad were married on her lunch hour, at City Hall.
    Quote: SALLY (angry at Joan): Everybody in town says you're a busybody!
    JOAN: That's ridiculous! I don't know everybody in town.

The Maid

Air Date: January 12, 1955. *Writers:* Hugh Wedlock, Jr., Howard Snyder, Jesse Goldstein, Phil Sharp. *Director:* Ezra Stone

Cast: Virginia Rose (*Tillie Jenkins*), Philip Van Zandt (*Rodney Parker*), Sheila Bromley (*Janet Tobin*), Sandra Gould (*Mildred Webster*), Margie Liszt (*Miss Bromley*)

Summary: Joan hires a new cook whose meals are so outstanding that Brad doesn't even mind the extra expense. But Tillie came to California in hopes of meeting movie stars, and is ready to quit her job after only two weeks. Brad convinces his fraternity brother, actor Rodney Parker, to meet Tillie, but the men concoct a plan to cure the cook of her ardor. When Joan turns up unexpectedly at Parker's penthouse, he mistakes her for Tillie, and proceeds to do his best to make himself obnoxious.

Note: The title of this episode is a misnomer, as Tillie is a cook, not a maid. Trying to persuade Tillie that they hobnob with the stars, Jim Backus, as Brad, does vocal impersonation of Ronald Colman and Clark Gable, while Joan (not for the first time in the series) does a brief Bette Davis routine.

Money in the Shotgun

Air Date: January 19, 1955. *Writers:* Howard Snyder, Jesse Goldstein, Phil Sharp, Hugh Wedlock, Jr. *Director:* Ezra Stone

Cast: Wally Brown (*Wally Brown*), Sally Kelly (*Sally Brown*), Anthony Warde (*Mr. Hokinson*)

Summary: Joan thinks she's made a sharp deal selling some old furniture, until Brad tells her one of the pieces was quite valuable. Rather than confessing her misdeed, Joan manages to cancel the sale and recoup her money, which she temporarily hides in the barrel of Brad's shotgun. Before she can retrieve the cash, Brad lends his gun to a pal, forcing queasy Joan to spend a miserable day aboard a boat in order to prevent her money from going up in smoke.

Notes: Stock footage of the boat in rough waters during a storm looks like it could have been taken from the same source used to show the S.S. *Minnow* being "tossed" in the opening titles of *Gilligan's Island.*

Eye Glasses

Air Date: January 26, 1955. *Writers:* Howard Snyder, Jesse Goldstein, Phil Sharp, Hugh Wedlock, Jr. *Director:* Ezra Stone

Cast: Wally Brown (*Wally Brown*), Sally Kelly (*Sally Brown*), Phil Arnold (*Waiter at Bowling Alley*), Paul Keast (*Dr. Walker*), Charlotte Lawrence (*Nancy*), Barbara Hill (*Miss Doty*)

Summary: Joan needs glasses, but is self-conscious about the way she'll look, so she tries to persuade Brad he needs them as well. A trip to the eye doctor proves otherwise, and inadvertently makes Joan's problem worse, when she's given the wrong eye drops shortly before she and Brad compete against the Browns in a bowling match.

The Allergy

Air Date: February 2, 1955. *Writers:* Jesse Goldstein, Hugh Wedlock, Jr., Howard Snyder. *Director:* Ezra Stone

Cast: Robert Foulk (*Walter Patton*), Dick Elliott (*Judge Casper T. Bennington*),

Martha Wentworth (*Mrs. Bennington*), Lewis Russell (*Dr. Smith*), George Neise (*Jimmy Dooley*)

Summary: Brad is running for Superior Court judge, and his campaign manager wants him to emphasize his happy home life. Unfortunately, Joan seems to have developed a sudden allergy to her own husband, and can't be within ten feet of Brad without breaking into a sneezing fit. When Brad and his opponent appear on the local TV show *Daily with Dooley*, the host unwittingly forces Mr. and Mrs. Stevens into some highly uncomfortable togetherness.

Note: Brad tells TV host Jim Dooley, "Joan and I have been sweethearts since we were in high school," contradicting previous versions of how they met.

Lieutenant General

Air Date: February 9, 1955. *Writers:* Jesse Goldstein, Hugh Wedlock, Jr., Howard Snyder. *Director:* Ezra Stone

Cast: Beverly Wills (*Beverly*), Alan Grossman (*Alan*), Mary Jane Croft (*Penelope Winthrop*), Wally Brown (*Wally*), Bill Kennedy (*General Peterson*), Sandra Gould (*Mildred Webster*), Jeanne Baird (*Diane*), Charlotte Lawrence (*Vi*)

Summary: Beverly returns for a visit with her new husband Alan in tow. Alan's a military man, but his rank of lieutenant isn't enough to impress Joan's snooty friend Penelope Winthrop, so Joan fibs that he's a general. At a reception for the newlyweds, Alan's uniform threatens to give away his true status, so Wally is pressed into service to pose as Beverly's high-ranking husband.

Note: Beverly Wills' real-life husband Alan Grossman makes his acting debut in this segment. This is Beverly's last appearance in the series.

Quote: BEVERLY (to Joan): You haven't changed a bit. I'm home for ten minutes and I'm already in the middle of one of your messes.

JOAN: And you haven't changed a bit. You're home for ten minutes and you're already complaining about being in the middle of one of my messes.

The Letter

Air Date: February 16, 1955. *Writers:* Phil Sharp, Hugh Wedlock, Jr., Howard Snyder, Jesse Goldstein. *Director:* Ezra Stone

Cast: Dan Tobin (*Kerwin Tobin*), Sheila Bromley (*Janet Tobin*), Frank Nelson (*Postal Supervisor*), Archer MacDonald (*Ambrose Smith*), Sid Clute (*Postal Worker*), Joe Devlin (*Security Officer*)

Summary: Joan mistakenly opens a letter from Toledo addressed to neighbor Kerwin Tobin. Knowing the Tobins will simply think she was snooping if she admits her error, Joan plots to right things by having her aunt in Toledo re-mail the letter to the right destination. After dropping the letter in the mail, however, Joan learns that she may be liable for damages if Mr. Tobin is delayed receiving the important business information contained in the letter. Rushing to the post office, Joan bluffs her way into the mailroom, where she wreaks havoc posing as a temporary employee while she searches for Tobin's letter.

Note: Joan's physical comedy in the last act of this episode is a tour-de-force, ably abetted by the strong support of character actor Frank Nelson as her nemesis. Adding to the fun are a pair of pneumatic tubes that suck in outgoing packages, and spew out incoming ones, with great force. Archer MacDonald reprises his role as Ambrose Smith from "Crazy Toes Smith."

Ladies' Prison

Air Date: February 23, 1955. *Writers:* Jesse Goldstein, Phil Sharp, Hugh Wedlock, Jr., Howard Snyder. *Director:* Ezra Stone
  Cast: Bill Baldwin (*C.O. Talbot*), Marsha [Marcia Mae] Jones (*Babe*), Harriette Tarler (*Midge Martin*), Jack Kenny (*Warden*), Beatrice Maude (*Selma*), Jameson Shade (*Second C.O.*), Sylvia Stanton (*Contortionist*)

Summary: Newly appointed to the prison board, Brad persuades Joan to go undercover as an inmate to investigate living conditions in a women's prison. Joan unwittingly switches uniforms with a cellmate, Midge Martin, who's plotting a jailbreak. Persuading the new guard they're ill with food poisoning, the prisoners are transported to the infirmary, all part of Midge's plan that Joan tries desperately to foil without blowing her cover.
  Note: This episode is a fun parody of women-in-prison films like *Caged*, a popular movie genre in the 1950s and beyond. The episode title is similar to *Women's Prison*, a Columbia picture starring Ida Lupino and Jan Sterling, which was in general release around the time the segment first aired.

The Lady and the Prizefighter

Air Date: March 2, 1955. *Writers:* Phil Sharp, Hugh Wedlock, Jr., Howard Snyder, Jesse Goldstein. *Director:* Ezra Stone
  Cast: Wally Brown (*Wally Brown*), Sally Kelly (*Sally Brown*), Mushy Callahan (*Referee*), Gregg Martell (*Dynamite Tucker*), Jim Nusser (*Mr. Rutledge*), Charles Williams (*Soapy Fenton*)

Summary: Joan and Brad attend a prizefight with their friends, the Browns. When boxer Dynamite Tucker loses the match almost immediately, Brad calls an inquiry to determine if the fight was fixed. In Brad's chambers, Tucker is accidentally punched out by Wally, giving Joan the idea of staging a rematch between the two for charity.
  Note: According to an NBC press release, Wally Brown lost ten pounds in the course of rehearsing and shooting this physically strenuous episode. Mary Jane Croft is billed in the show's closing credits, apparently for reprising her role from "Lieutenant General" as Penelope Winthrop, but only a glimpse of her remains in the syndicated cut of the episode.

How to Win Friends

Air Date: March 9, 1955. *Writers:* Sherwood Schwartz, Jesse Goldstein, Phil Sharp. *Director:* Ezra Stone
  Cast: Geraldine Carr (*Mabel Henderson*), Marjorie Bennett (*Ruth Gibson*), Anthony Warde (*Oliver Putnam*), Charlotte Lawrence (*Vi*), Dick Elliott (*Fatso*), Hal Taggart (*Waiter*)

Summary: Joan overhears her ladies' club friends planning a surprise testimonial dinner in her honor. But a schedule change causes Joan to show up at the wrong place and time, leaving her to conclude that she's been snubbed. Responding to a newspaper ad, Joan takes lessons in friendship from expert Mr. Putnam, but the techniques he teaches her only succeed in alienating her friends.

Notes: This episode features a truly odd dream sequence in which Joan, believing she is friendless, contemplates killing herself with either poison, a rifle, or a jump from the window, as her friends' voices ring in her ears ("Go ahead! Do it!"). There's also a blooper when Jim Backus, as Brad, converses with Vi by telephone concerning the upcoming luncheon, then gives Joan the message moments later, saying, "Mabel just called." This is the last aired episode featuring Geraldine Carr as Mabel: It was filmed in August 1954, but held back until several months after her death.

The Cowboy

Air Date: March 16, 1955. *Writers:* Jesse Goldstein, Phil Sharp, Howard Snyder, Hugh Wedlock, Jr. *Director:* Ezra Stone
Cast: Hoot Gibson (*Bucko Bob Brady*), Wally Brown (*Wally*), Sally Kelly (*Sally*), Danny Richards, Jr. (*Tommy*), Tyler McVey (*P.J. Foxson*)

Summary: Bucko Bob Brady, a onetime Western movie idol whose fame has faded, finds himself hauled into Brad's court for the payment of back rent he owes. Joan and Brad decide to instigate a comeback for the former leading man. Learning that Bucko Bob has a TV script he hasn't been able to peddle, Joan tries to sell it to producer P.J. Foxson. With a cast headed by Brad (as "Potshot Pete"), Wally ("Coyote Charlie"), and herself, Joan puts on an unintentionally hilarious Western saga that wins Bucko Bob a new contract.

Note: Guest star Edmund Richard "Hoot" Gibson (1892–1962) was himself a Western movie star whose career dated back to 1912. The character P.J. Foxson, the television producer, is named for *Joan*'s own producer, P.J. Wolfson.

Quote: BRAD (chiding Joan, who wants to buy an expensive pair of alligator shoes): We've got to put something away for a rainy day. Ten, twenty, twenty-five years will go by, and where will we be then?
JOAN: I don't know about you, but I'll be too old to look good in a pair of red alligator shoes.

The Jail Bird

Air Date: March 23, 1955. *Writers:* Phil Sharp, Jesse Goldstein. *Director:* Ezra Stone
Cast: Sheila Bromley (*Janet Tobin*), Barney Phillips (*Lieutenant*), Sid Tomack (*Police Detective*), Harry Guardino (*Officer Brannigan*), Harry Bartell (*Dr. Oglethorpe*)

Summary: Shortly after Joan befriends a crow that flies in the kitchen window, her neighbor Janet's pearl necklace turns up in Joan's purse. Before long, Joan has collected a stash of jewelry and doesn't know how she got it. Joan and Brad fear she's suffering from kleptomania, not realizing that the bird, a trained accomplice of a crook, has taken a liking to Joan and is bringing her gifts stolen from her neighbors.

Unsold Series Pilots

LET'S JOIN JOANIE (1950)

Producers: Frank Galen, Dick Linkroum. *Director:* Dick Linkroum. *Writers:* Frank Galen, Keith Fowler, Hal Goodman, Jesse Goldstein. *Associate Producer:* Dick Mack. *Music Director:* Lyn Murray. *Sets:* Rudi Feld. *Cast:* Joan Davis (*Joan Davis*), Joseph Kearns (*Antoine*), Hope Emerson (*Miss Emerson*), George Neise (*Jim Benson*). CBS, 1951.

Joan Davis, a salesgirl at Hats by Antoine, is infatuated with her new neighbor Jim Benson and dreams of a romantic future with him. Muscle-bound Jim is a firm proponent of physical fitness, so Joanie resolves to impress him with her own strength. At the suggestion of a customer, Mrs. Huntington, Joan makes an excuse to leave work (claiming she's contracted "the purple plague") and enrolls in the Emerson Health Farm. With only one day available in which to complete Miss Emerson's rigorous week-long program, Joan sweats her way through calisthenics, rhythmic dancing, a workout with a medicine ball, and the accompanying starvation diet that she hopes will transform her into Jim's ideal woman.

> ANTOINE (annoyed with Joan): Sometimes I don't know whether to kill you, or kill myself!
> JOAN (sweetly): May I make a suggestion?

THE JOAN DAVIS SHOW (1956)

> *Director*: John Rich. *Producer*: Stanley Shapiro. *Writers*: Bob Ross, Fred Fox, Stanley Shapiro. *Photography*: Hal Mohr. *Editor*: Frank Tessena. *Music*: MSI Spencer-Hagen. Joan Davis Enterprises, 1956.
> *Cast*: Joan Davis (*Joan*), Beverly Wills (*Beverly*), Carol Veazie (*Agnes Dunkirk*), Michael Galloway (*Tony*), Ray Ferrell (*Stevie*), Hope Summers (*Tessie*), Anthony Warde (*Jack*), Robert Carson (*Doctor*), Charles Williams (*Photographer*), William Irwin (*Appliance Man*), Joe Sanchez (*Mexican Boy*), The Blackburn Twins.

Joan plays a fictionalized version of herself, a popular television entertainer with a daughter, Beverly, a son-in-law, Tony, who's in the military, and a four-year-old grandson named Stevie. When Tony has to report to the base, accompanied by Beverly, Joan insists she can handle the job of babysitting her grandson for several days. Stevie's other grandmother, Agnes Dunkirk, is a snobbish society matron from Pasadena who thinks she should care for him instead. Says Beverly, in her mother's defense, "She may do a lot of weird things onstage, but at home she's a very normal woman!" When Joan loses Stevie in the park and brings home a little Mexican boy instead, her credentials as a caretaker are called into question. With her future babysitting privileges at risk, Joan enlists the help of two actor friends and her housekeeper Tessie to convince Agnes that Stevie is a rambunctious troublemaker who will be better off in Joan's care.

> JOAN (arguing her suitability to babysit): There's nothing that goes on in a child's mind that doesn't go on in mine!
> AGNES (trading insults with Joan): I was going to invite you to a party but I didn't think you'd like it. The place was simply crawling with intellectuals.
> JOAN (to Agnes): I like what you're doing with your hair. Orange is so much more becoming than gray.

JOAN OF ARKANSAS (1958)

> *Writer-Director*: Philip Rapp. *Producer*: Robert Stillman. *Photography*: Les White. *Production Designer*: Arthur Lonergan. *Film Editor*: Bruce Pierce. *Production Supervisor*: Charles C. Irwin, Jr. *Assistant Director*: Jack Voglin. *Set Decorator*: Alfred E. Kegerris. *Sound*: Joe L. Edmondson. *Costume Supervisors*: Byron Munson, Maria Donovan. *Script Supervisor*: Mercy Wiereter. *Music Supervisor*: Raoul Kraushaar. *Casting Supervisor*: Lynn Stalmaster. *Photographic Effects*: Jack Rabin, Louis DeWitt. Joan Davis Enterprises, in association with NBC-TV. 1958.

Cast: Joan Davis (*Joan Jones*), John Emery (*Dr. John Dolan*), Wilton Graff (*Prof. Henry Newkirk*), Lee Patrick (*Mrs. Putnam*), Paul Frees (*Dr. Ferguson*), Bob Brubaker (*Dr. Curtis Short*), Jolene Brand (*Nurse Kelly*), Olan Soulé (*Mr. Kepler*).

A team of scientists uses a computer to identify "one perfectly normal American adult" to take part in the country's first manned space flight. Chosen for the mission is scatterbrained Joan Jones, a dental technician from Hot Springs, Arkansas. Despite the skepticism of project leader Dr. John Dolan, who doubts a woman's suitability for the job, Joan undergoes a rigorous training regime in preparation for being launched into outer space. A dream sequence compares this Joan from Arkansas with Joan of Arc, also supposedly an ordinary woman who had greatness thrust upon her.

THE JOAN DAVIS SHOW (1960)

Joan played an answering service operator in this unsold pilot, her last attempt at a TV comeback, for producer Devery Freeman.

Guest Appearances

The Bob Hope Chevy Show. NBC, November 11, 1956. Guests, Perry Como, Julie London. Said syndicated columnist Jack O'Brian of the kinescoped broadcast, "Joan Davis was funnier with Bob than she ever was on TV before" (*Charleston* [WV] *Gazette*, November 22, 1956). Added *Variety* (November 19, 1956), Hope "was well seconded by Joan Davis, who proved herself equal to the mad antics and played along with Hope for the show's lustiest laughs. She also had herself a time hoofing and foiled with éclat."

The Dinah Shore Chevy Show. NBC, November 10, 1957. Guest host Tony Martin, filling in for a vacationing Dinah, welcomes Joan, Nat "King" Cole, Red Buttons, Vera-Ellen, and dancer Maria Tallchief in this live color broadcast.

The George Gobel Show. NBC, March 25, 1958. Guest star Joan is joined by Jonathan Winters, Eddie Fisher, and Pat Suzuki. "George presents his own 'Oscar Awards' show and presents them to his cast" (*Long Beach* [CA] *Press-Telegram*). "Joan Davis does her special interpretation of 'Just My Bill,' with a flashback about 'her romance with Bill'" (*Troy* [NY] *Times Record*).

The Steve Allen Show. NBC, September 28, 1958. Steve's guest stars are Davis, bandleader Ray Anthony, and Jimmie Rodgers. "Steve and Joan Davis show us how TV pilot films are made," and Joan returns for a skit called "Who's Got the Pain." (*Syracuse Herald Journal*).

The Dinah Shore Chevy Show. NBC, October 26, 1958. *Producer-Director*: William Asher. Guests, Maurice Chevalier, Joan Davis, Julius La Rosa, Elsa Lanchester. "Spooks and witches will dominate the stage in the evening's major production number. Dinah, a non-believer, discovers that old crones do ride brooms through Hallowe'en skies. Joan and Elsa do the convincing" (*Hutchinson* [KS] *News*, October 25, 1958). Joan's best moments come in a novelty song, "Don't Be a Woman If You Can," backed up by a line of elegantly attired chorus boys as she bemoans the complications of maintaining a fashionable appearance in a fast-changing world. *Variety* (October 28, 1958) commented, "Joan Davis was funny, quick-witted and nimble in a song-and-dance routine about the fashion world." Less effective, according to the reviewer, was "an elongated Hallowe'en routine that was really routine.... The special effects men had a ball, but even one of their wires went haywire, and the result was an embarrassing moment for the cast."

The Steve Allen Show. NBC, December 7, 1958. Louis Nye, Tom Poston, Don Knotts, Pat Harrington, Jr.; guest stars Joan Davis, Andre Previn, Sugar Ray Robinson. Joan plays the pregnant heroine of a live TV soap opera, *The Life of Helen Burdett*, with Steve as her loving husband. Leading into the sketch, Steve explains that the demands of a daily, live TV show require that the actors use a Teleprompter, rather than fully memorizing their lines. The first half of the sketch, representing the show performed as it was intended, shows Joan and Steve held at gunpoint by a criminal (Louis Nye), complicated by the arrival of the grocery boy (Don Knotts) and a policeman (Tom Poston). On the second go-round, the scene is played as if the Teleprompter has suddenly gone haywire. Lines are read out of order, cues are mangled, characters say each other's dialogue, and Joan's character becomes involved in a wild brawl involving collapsing scenery and a tumble out the window. The sketch ends with Steve's bewildered character kissing Tom Poston on the lips instead of Joan. In another sketch, Joan appears as a female stockbroker.

The Kraft Music Hall Starring Milton Berle. NBC, January 30, 1959. *Producer-Director*: Hal Kanter. *Writers*: Hal Goodman, Hal Kanter, Larry Klein, Milt Josefsberg. Said *Variety*, "Berle dug into his files to resurrect a takeoff on Noël Coward and Mary Martin—something he did on his hour-long show a coupla years back. Except for the fact Joan Davis was his comedy partner instead of Kay Thompson, it was the identical skit.... Miss Davis' talents were largely wasted...."

The Garry Moore Show. CBS, April 28, 1959. Guests, Joan Davis, Tommy Leonetti, Janis Paige, The Original Washboard Band. After an opening with a Wild West theme, "Miss Davis and host do a skit about foreign movies. The samba was the rage during 'That Wonderful Year—1942' as demonstrated by nightclub performer Miss Paige and dancers Garry and Miss Davis" (*Oakland Tribune*).

NOTE: Joan has been erroneously credited with a guest appearance on ABC's *The Pepsi-Cola Playhouse*, in an episode titled "The Psychophonic Nurse" (February 5, 1954). This segment actually featured actress *Joanne* Davis, opposite Lee Marvin.

Notes

Preface

1. Abe Burrows, *Honest, Abe: Is There Really No Business Like Show Business?* (Boston: Little, Brown, 1980), p. 95.
2. Fred Allen, *Treadmill to Oblivion* (Boston: Little, Brown, 1954), pp. 238–40.

I. Biography

1. Transcript, "The Justice Harry A. Blackmun Oral History Project," Library of Congress, www.loc.gov/rr/mss/, p. 52.
2. Mabel Hunt, "That Screwball, Davis!" *Screen Book*, June 1939.
3. Paul Harrison, "Joan Davis Is as Apt at Low Comedy as at Gentler Nuances of Nonsense," *Lowell* (MA) *Sun*, August 23, 1937.
4. William Lynch Vallee, "Queen of Comedy," *Silver Screen*, July 1944.
5. Joan Davis, as told to Jane Kesner Ardmore, "I'll Never Quit Now," *Woman's Home Companion*, November 1954.
6. Roy Wilkins with Tom Mathews, *Standing Fast: The Autobiography of Roy Wilkins* (New York: Da Capo Press, 1994), p. 38.
7. "'On the Jazz Boat' at Rajah," *Reading* (PA) *Eagle*, October 3, 1928.
8. "Road Show Vaude at Plaza," *Waterloo* (IA) *Evening Courier*, September 23, 1927.
9. Joan Davis, as told to Jane Kesner Ardmore, "I'll Never Quit Now," *Woman's Home Companion*, November 1954.
10. Lucie Nelville, "Is It Fun to Be Funny?" *Laredo Times*, October 9, 1938.
11. Allen Saunders, "Want Ad Bride," *Toledo News-Bee*, December 2, 1931.
12. "Five Big Acts of Orpheum Offerings at Majestic Today," *La Crosse Tribune and Leader-Press*, October 23, 1921.
13. "Pantages Bill at Majestic Will Be One of Best Ever," *Lethbridge Herald*, June 18, 1924.
14. Lupton Wilkinson, "Joan Davis, Million Dollar Wallflower," *The Woman*, October 1945.
15. Chester B. Bahn, "*Consolation Marriage* on Keith Screen," *Syracuse Herald*, November 1, 1931.
16. "Enjoyable Vaudeville," *Winnipeg Free Press*, December 29, 1931.
17. "Honey Boys Prove Real Big Timers; Singing Quintet Captures Laurels at Orpheum; Joan Davis Is Also Attraction," *Seattle Daily Times*, January 16, 1932.
18. Paul Harrison, "Joan Davis Is as Apt at Low Comedy as at Gentler Nuances of Nonsense." *Lowell* (MA) *Sun*, August 23, 1937.
19. William Lynch Vallee, "Queen of Comedy," *Silver Screen*, July 1944.
20. Anthony Slide, *The Encyclopedia of Vaudeville* (Westport, CT: Greenwood Press, 1994), p. 386.
21. Joan Davis, as told to Jane Kesner Ardmore, "I'll Never Quit Now," *Woman's Home Companion*, November 1954.
22. Hubbard Keavy, "Awkward by Design," *Hartford Courant*, November 27, 1938.
23. Mabel Hunt, "That Screwball, Davis!" *Screen Book*, June 1939.
24. Dick Kleiner, "Some TV Stars Off-Screen: Robert Young Could Use Writers at Home," *Biloxi Daily Herald*, November 23, 1956.
25. Alma Whitaker, "Madcap Girl Dancer Storms Hollywood," *Los Angeles Times*, August 29, 1937.
26. "Joan Davis Signed," *Port Arthur* (TX) *News*, April 19, 1936.
27. "Amusements," *Panama City News-Herald*, April 10, 1937.
28. Jeff Gordon, *Foxy Lady: The Authorized Biography of Lynn Bari* (Duncan, OK: BearManor Media, 2010), p. 84.
29. Alma Whitaker, "Madcap Girl Dancer Storms Hollywood," *Los Angeles Times*, August 29, 1937.
30. Harrison Carroll, "Behind the Scenes in Hollywood," *San Mateo Times*, August 13, 1937.
31. Read Kendall, "Around and About in Hollywood," *Los Angeles Times*, May 5, 1937.
32. Read Kendall, "Odd and Interesting," *Los Angeles Times*, January 15, 1939.

33. Jimmie Fidler, "Joan Davis Can't Survive Stardom, Fidler Contends," *Salt Lake Tribune*, December 20, 1939.

34. Lupton Wilkinson, "Joan Davis: Million Dollar Wallflower," *The Woman*, October 1945.

35. Jimmie Fidler, "Joan Davis Has Marital Break," *Los Angeles Times*, October 28, 1941.

36. "Tattletale Talks," *Los Angeles Times*, August 23, 1942.

37. Rudy Vallee, *Let the Chips Fall* (Harrisburg, PA: Stackpole Books, 1975), p. 130.

38. Virginia Vale, "Star Dust," *Ruthven* (IA) *Free Press*, September 2, 1942.

39. Jimmy Fidler, "Jimmy Fidler in Hollywood," *Chester* (PA) *Times*, January 20, 1945.

40. Abe Burrows, *Honest, Abe: Is There Really No Business Like Show Business?* (Boston: Little, Brown, 1980), p. 95.

41. John Crosby, "Well, Well, Joan Davis Gets Funny," *Oakland Tribune*, June 2, 1947.

42. Unidentified clipping, Joan Davis file, Minnesota Historical Society.

43. "Mom Handles Mail," *Charleston Daily Mail*, July 5, 1953.

44. Herbert G. Goldman, *Banjo Eyes: Eddie Cantor and the Birth of Modern Stardom* (New York: Oxford University Press, 1997), p. 238.

45. Harrison Carroll, "Behind the Scenes in Hollywood," *Greensburg* (IN) *Daily News*, October 11, 1947.

46. "Divorce Won by Joan Davis," *Los Angeles Times*, December 2, 1947.

47. *Newsweek*, December 15, 1947.

48. Herbert G. Goldman, *Banjo Eyes: Eddie Cantor and the Birth of Modern Stardom* (New York: Oxford University Press, 1997), p. 255.

49. Hedda Hopper, "Joan Davis' Ring Cements Rumor," *Los Angeles Times*, June 2, 1948.

50. Erskine Johnson, "In Hollywood," *Sandusky* (OH) *Register-Star-News*, August 30, 1949.

51. Dorothy Kilgallen, "Voice of Broadway," *Charleston Gazette*, May 5, 1950.

52. William Bast, *Surviving James Dean* (Fort Lee, NJ: Barricade, 2006), pp. 68–69.

53. Ibid., p. 50.

54. Erskine Johnson, "Hollywood Chatter," *Corpus Christi Times*, November 8, 1950.

55. "Joan Davis' Daughter, 18, in Elopement," *Los Angeles Times*, June 26, 1952.

56. "Comedienne Finds Romance Unfunny," *Salt Lake Tribune*, June 26, 1952.

57. Harrison Carroll, "Hollywood," *Massillon* (OH) *Evening Independent*, September 10, 1952.

58. Harrison Carroll, "Behind the Scenes in Hollywood," *Lethbridge* (Alberta) *Herald*, September 2, 1953.

59. Anton Remenih, "Audience Laugh Often Built on Tears of Star," *Chicago Tribune*, October 26, 1952.

60. Howard McClay, "Stars Who Turn to TV Should Not Forget Their Movie Fans," *Los Angeles Daily News*, April 9, 1953.

61. "Joan Davis, Col Split," *Daily Variety*, July 30, 1953.

62. Harrison Carroll, "Behind the Hollywood Scene," *New London* (CT) *Evening Day*, May 10, 1955.

63. Harrison Carroll, "Behind the Scenes in Hollywood," *Lexington* (NC) *Dispatch*, July 14, 1955.

64. Grace Lee Whitney with Jim Denney, *The Longest Trek: My Tour of the Galaxy* (Clovis, CA: Quill Driver, 1998), pp. 47–48.

65. "Judo Punch Ended Romance, Joan Davis Says," *Hartford Courant*, January 31, 1959.

66. "Joan Davis Wins $20,000 Damage Suit," *Redlands* (CA) *Daily Facts*, January 2, 1960.

67. "Actress Joan Davis Saved from Fire by Encino Man," *Van Nuys* (CA) *News*, September 8, 1960.

68. "Joan Davis, 53; TV, Film Star Dies Suddenly," *Chicago Tribune*, May 24, 1961.

69. "Joan Davis Was Greatest Comedienne, Backus Says," *Sheboygan Press*, May 24, 1961.

70. "Joan Davis Funeral Held; 100 Attend," *Los Angeles Times*, May 28, 1961.

71. Bob Foster, "TV Screenings," *San Mateo Times*, May 24, 1961.

72. Earl Wilson, "It Happened One Night," *Long Beach Press Telegram*, May 30, 1961.

73. "Joan Davis [obituary]," *Variety*, May 24, 1961.

74. Louella O. Parsons, "Actress Shirley Jones Is Expecting Baby This Fall," *Anderson* (IN) *Daily Bulletin*, May 29, 1961.

75. Lydia Lane, "Lydia Lane Interviews Second Generation 'Names,'" *Abilene Reporter-News*, October 4, 1962.

76. Charles Hillinger, "Four of Joan Davis' Family Die in Fire," *Los Angeles Times*, October 25, 1963.

77. Mike Connolly, untitled column, *Pasadena Independent Star-News*, November 10, 1963.

78. "Court Settles Joan Davis Estate Issue," *Los Angeles Times*, February 11, 1965.

79. Alex Freeman, "Sue Lyon's Romance Irks Stars," *Hartford Courant*, November 28, 1963.

80. Louella O. Parsons, "Producers Obtain Rights to Movie Story of Singing Nun," *Anderson* (IN) *Daily Bulletin*, February 20, 1964.

81. "Ask Dick," *Altoona* (PA) *Mirror*, October 3, 1985.

II. Filmography

1. William Lynch Vallee, "Queen of Comedy," *Silver Screen*, July 1944.

2. Hubbard Keavy, "Performances of Small Bit

Players Are Often Valued More Than Stars," *Sandusky* (OH) *Register*, December 29, 1935.

3. "Joan Davis Signed," *Port Arthur* (TX) *News*, April 19, 1936.

4. "If You Aren't Pretty, Says Star, Be Funny," *Chillicothe* (MO) *Constitution-Tribune*, June 12, 1937.

5. "Comedienne in Film Deserves 'Gamest' Title," *Ames* (IA) *Daily Tribune*, September 11, 1937.

6. Alma Whitaker, "Madcap Girl Dancer Storms Hollywood," *Los Angeles Times*, August 29, 1937.

7. "Comedienne in Film Deserves 'Gamest' Title," *Ames* (IA) *Daily Tribune*, September 11, 1937.

8. Phyllis Marie Arthur, "*College* Tests for Foxlets," *Daily Variety*, July 3, 1937.

9. "Joan Davis Gets Role in *Love, Hisses*," *Oakland Tribune*, August 29, 1937.

10. "Dancer Travels Many Miles in Dance Routine," *Los Angeles Times*, March 17, 1938.

11. "New Comedy Team Clicks," *Carroll* (IA) *Daily Herald*, July 8, 1938.

12. Lucie Neville, "Is It Fun to Be Funny?" *Laredo Times*, October 9, 1938.

13. John Lahr, *Notes on a Cowardly Lion: The Biography of Bert Lahr* (New York: Knopf, 1969), p. 185.

14. Harrison Carroll, "Behind the Scenes in Hollywood," *Massillon* (OH) *Evening Independent*, November 18, 1938.

15. "Hilarious Comedy Coming to Rialto," *Laredo Times*, September 1, 1940.

16. "Fun, Romance, Mystery in *For Beauty's Sake*," *Havre* (Mont.) *Daily News*, August 9, 1941.

17. "Joan Davis 'Wears' Tin Bucket in Film," *Hartford Courant*, April 30, 1941.

18. "Rip-Roaring Comedy Now at the Ritz," *Panama City News-Herald*, August 10, 1941.

19. May Mann, "Don't Depend on Glamor, Girls, Says Clever Actress," *Ogden* (UT) *Standard-Examiner*, October 19, 1941.

20. Ibid.

21. "Gay Musical *Two Latins* Coming," *Laredo* (TX) *Times*, December 14, 1941.

22. Jimmie Fidler, "Jimmie Fidler in Hollywood," *Joplin* (MO) *Globe*, February 6, 1942.

23. Gioia Diliberto, *Debutante: The Story of Brenda Frazier* (New York: Knopf, 1987), p. 153.

24. "In the Theaters," *Zanesville* (OH) *Times Recorder*, June 3, 1942.

25. Lupton A. Wilkinson, "Diamond Joan," *Los Angeles Times*, May 10, 1942.

26. Jimmie Fidler, "Jimmie Fidler in Hollywood," *Joplin* (MO) *Globe*, November 17, 1942.

27. Virginia Vale, "Star Dust," *Big Piney* (WY) *Examiner*, November 4, 1943.

28. William Lynch Vallee, "Queen of Comedy," *Silver Screen*, July 1944.

29. Frank Morriss, "Mr. Cantor Is Smart." *Winnipeg Free Press*, October 14, 1944.

30. Nelson B. Bell, "'She Gets Her Man,' and How, at the Met; Notes of the Theater," *Washington Post*, March 31, 1945.

31. "Jimmie Fidler in Hollywood," *Joplin Globe*, February 13, 1945.

32. Frank Morriss, "Here, There, and Hollywood," *Winnipeg Free Press*, April 25, 1946.

33. Gene Handsaker, "Joan Davis Is Glamorous in Her New Movie," *Portsmouth* (OH) *Times*, February 23, 1946.

34. Harrison Carroll, "Behind the Scenes in Hollywood," *Uniontown* (PA) *Morning Herald*, February 25, 1946.

35. Hedda Hopper, "Looking at Hollywood," *Portland Press-Herald*, April 18, 1949.

36. Darr Smith, untitled column, *Los Angeles Daily News*, October 7, 1949.

37. Erskine Johnson, "Hollywood," *Chester* (PA) *Times*, November 14, 1949.

38. Bob Thomas, "Hollywood News," *Indiana Evening Gazette*, July 18, 1950.

39. Edwin Schallert, "Australia Again Lures For 'Man Tracks'; Young Diva Will Act and Sing," *Los Angeles Times*, February 26, 1952.

III. Radiography

1. Chuck Hilton, "On the Beam with Chuck Hilton," *Mason City Globe-Gazette*, September 17, 1945.

2. John Dunning, *On the Air: The Encyclopedia of Old-Time Radio* (New York: Oxford University Press, 1998), p. 549.

3. Jess Oppenheimer with Gregg Oppenheimer, *Laughs, Luck, and Lucy: How I Came to Create the Most Popular Sitcom of All Time* (Syracuse: Syracuse University Press, 1996), p. 100.

4. Virginia Vale, "Star Dust," *Elma* (IA) *New Era*, January 15, 1942.

5. Joe Rathbun, "Joe's Radio Parade," *Zanesville* (OH) *Times-Signal*, June 28, 1942.

6. Jordan R. Young, *The Laugh Crafters: Comedy Writing in Radio and TV's Golden Age* (Beverly Hills: Past Times, 1999), p. 151.

7. "Ethel Clark's Radio Flashes," *Ogden* (UT) *Standard-Examiner*, June 21, 1942.

8. Joe Rathbun, "Joe's Radio Parade," *Zanesville Times-Signal*, April 4, 1943.

9. Charles G. Sampas, "Sampascoopies," *Lowell* (MS) *Sun*, November 12, 1942.

10. Dorothy Kilgallen, "Tales from Times Square," *Lowell Sun*, November 20, 1942.

11. May Mann, "Hollywood," *Ogden Standard-Examiner*, December 11, 1942.

12. "Turn the Dial," *Sandusky* (OH) *Register-Star-News*, June 24, 1943.

13. Hedda Hopper, "Chaplin, Bride Fuss in Public," *Salt Lake Tribune*, August 2, 1943.

14. "Redd in Line to Take on Joan Davis Show," *Daily Variety*, May 24, 1944.

15. "Joan's June Experiment on Situation Scripts," *Variety*, April 26, 1944.

16. "Joke Shows' Own Tag Line," *Variety*, June 7, 1944.

17. "Behind the Scenes with Radio Artists," *Charleston Gazette*, August 27, 1944.

18. "Behind the Scenes with Radio Artists," *Charleston Gazette*, July 9, 1944.

19. Jack Hellman, "Light and Airy," *Variety*, December 7, 1944.

20. "Hollywood Inside," *Daily Variety*, June 29, 1945.

21. Jack Hellman, "Light and Airy," *Variety*, June 7, 1945.

22. "Swan Soap Buying CBS Sustainer as Joan Davis Trailer," *Variety*, August 1, 1945.

23. Virginia MacPherson, "Harry Von Zell Is Ready to Be a Film Comedian," *Winnipeg Free Press*, April 24, 1945.

24. Virginia MacPherson, "Andy Russell Is Crooning Now as a Corporation," *Pittsburgh Post-Gazette*, June 26, 1945.

25. Larry Wolters, "Joan and Dinah Lead Feminine Ranks in Radio," *Chicago Tribune*, January 6, 1946.

26. Walter Winchell, "Broadway and Elsewhere," *Logansport* (IN) *Pharos-Tribune*, February 3, 1947.

27. "CBS Nixes 5G Giveaway Stunt by Joan Davis," *Billboard*, October 5, 1946.

28. "Joan Davis 'Lucky Bucks' Gets Kayo from CBS; No Shill, No Dice, No Scripts," *Variety*, October 2, 1946.

29. Jack Hellman, "Light and Airy," *Variety*, January 10, 1947.

30. "Reynolds Cancels Abbott, Costello; Replacem't Mulled," *Billboard*, July 7, 1947.

31. "CBS Picks Up Davis 7G Co-Op," *Variety*, September 17, 1947.

32. "Shore Helped Joan," *Washington Post*, June 8, 1947.

33. Jack Gould, "Programs in Review," *New York Times*, October 26, 1947.

34. John Crosby, "Girl Comic Cleans Up," *Oakland Tribune*, November 28, 1946.

35. Jack Gould, "Catholic College Federation Plans to Judge Comedies—Joan Davis Discusses Show," *New York Times*, September 16, 1947.

36. "Co-op Joan," *Newsweek*, October 20, 1947.

37. "Joan Davis, Sealtest Dicker Pay-Per-Point Package Deal," *Billboard*, June 19, 1948.

38. "Joan Davis to Cut Disk for Show on CBS," *Billboard*, May 14, 1949.

39. Patricia Clary, "Miss Joan Davis Believes in Preserving Old Traditions," *Middlesboro* (KY) *Daily News*, August 1, 1949.

40. "Best Bests for Good Listening," *Cedar Rapids Tribune*, September 22, 1949.

41. Jack Gould, "Programs in Review," *New York Times*, July 24, 1949.

IV. Videography

1. Edwin Schallert, "Joan Davis and Daughter Seen as Friendly Rivals," *Los Angeles Times*, February 29, 1948.

2. "CBS Plans Kine of Joan Davis AM Show," *Billboard*, December 17, 1949.

3. Lyn Murray, *Musician: A Hollywood Journal of Wives, Women, Writers, Lawyers, Directors, Producers and Music* (Secaucus, NJ: Lyle Stuart, 1987), p. 26.

4. Arskine [sic; Erskine] Johnson, "Joan Davis' Television Debut Takes on Proportions of Bout," *Burlington* (NC) *Daily Times-News*, August 24, 1950.

5. Erskine Johnson, "In Hollywood," *Statesville* (NC) *Daily Record*, February 9, 1952.

6. Bart Andrews, *The I Love Lucy Book* (New York: Doubleday, 1985), p. 95.

7. "The Man in the $150 Suit," *TV Guide*, October 30, 1953.

8. "Joan Davis Makes TV Debut with Belly-Rocking Comedy," *Ogden* (UT) *Standard-Examiner*, November 12, 1952.

9. "Serious Jim Backus Is 'Card' Off Screen," *Oakland Tribune*, June 28, 1953.

10. John Crosby, "Even Queen Elizabeth," unsourced clipping, ca. 1953, Joan Davis file, AMPAS.

11. Leonard Maltin, *The Art of the Cinematographer: A Survey and Interviews with Five Masters* (New York: Dover, 1978), p. 92.

12. John Crosby, "Even Queen Elizabeth," unsourced clipping, ca. 1953, Joan Davis file, AMPAS.

13. "Madcap with a Brain, Yet," *Motion Pictures*, January 1954.

14. Jack O'Brian, "A Vote for Joan Davis' New Show," *Lowell* (MS) *Sun*, October 16, 1952.

15. Bob Foster, "Joan Davis TV Series May Press 'I Love Lucy,'" *San Mateo Times*, October 14, 1952.

16. Jack Gould, "Joan Davis and Jane Froman Headline New Video Programs Over N.B.C. and C.B.S., Respectively," *New York Times*, October 20, 1952.

17. Peg Simpson, "'New' Joan Davis Will Make Debut on Video Tonight," *Syracuse Post-Standard*, October 15, 1952.

18. Walter Ames, "Comedienne Credits Homey Atmosphere for Success of 'I Married Joan' TV Show," *Los Angeles Times*, January 2, 1953.

19. Ellis Walker, "Video Notes," *Hayward* (CA) *Daily Review*, September 11, 1953.

20. Anton Remenih, "Audience Laugh Often Built on Tears of Star," *Chicago Tribune*, October 26, 1952.

21. Buddy Mason, "Behind the Movie Sets," *Algona* (IA) *Upper Des Moines*, February 12, 1953.

22. Val Adams, "Joan Davis: Physical Comedienne," *New York Times*, November 22, 1953.

23. "She's No Quitter," *TV Fan*, ca. 1953, Joan Davis file, AMPAS.

24. Erskine Johnson, "In Hollywood," *Portsmouth* (NH) *Herald*, January 3, 1953.

25. Erskine Johnson, "Movies Seeking to Best Television in 3-D Films," *Long Beach* (CA) *Independent*, February 11, 1953.

26. Wayne Oliver, "Joan Davis Crams for TV Program," *Salina* (KS) *Journal*, December 6, 1953.

27. Bob Thomas, "So That's What's Causing All These Funny Ladies," *Washington Post*, May 21, 1953.

28. Dave Kaufman, "On All Channels," *Daily Variety*, March 2, 1956.

29. Hal Humphrey, "Joan Davis Wins Chimp Role in Show," *Oakland Tribune*, November 4, 1953.

30. "And Where Did You Meet Your Husband?" *Charleston* (WV) *Daily Mail*, January 25, 1953.

31. Howard McClay, "Stars Who Turn to TV Should Not Forget Their Movie Fans," *Los Angeles Daily News*, April 9, 1953.

32. Val Adams, "Joan Davis: Physical Comedienne," *New York Times*, November 22, 1953.

33. "Praises TV's Pioneer Spirit: Yet Vidpix Megger John Rich Discerns No 'Mechanical' Age," *Daily Variety*, January 22, 1954.

34. John Rich, *Warm Up the Snake: A Hollywood Memoir* (Ann Arbor: University of Michigan Press, 2006).

35. "Beverly Wills Learns Comedy Tricks from Mom," *San Antonio Express and News*, January 31, 1954.

36. Bob Foster, "TV-Radio," *San Mateo Times*, November 10, 1953.

37. Erskine Johnson, "In Hollywood," *Redlands* (CA) *Daily Facts*, June 14, 1954.

38. Hal Humphrey, "Everybody's a Comedian," *Los Angeles Mirror*, December 30, 1954.

39. Harrison Carroll, "Behind the Scenes in Hollywood," *Lethbridge* (Alberta) *Herald*, October 12, 1954.

40. Hal Humphrey, "Movie Stars of Yesterday Shine on TV," *Oakland Tribune*, September 7, 1954.

41. "The Race for Ratings," *TV Guide*, March 12, 1955.

42. Robert L. Sokolsky, "Looking and Listening," *Syracuse Herald-Journal*, February 12, 1955.

43. Peg Simpson, "New Video Series Being Cooked Up for Joan Davis," *Syracuse Post-Standard*, November 2, 1955.

44. Faye Emerson, "Faye Emerson on TV," *San Antonio Express*, March 28, 1956.

45. Dick Kleiner, "Nothing Worries Hackett," *Lima* (OH) *News*, December 24, 1956.

46. Eve Starr, "Inside TV," *Pasadena Star-News*, December 14, 1957.

47. Milton R. Bass, "The Lively Arts," *Berkshire* (MA) *Eagle*, June 19, 1956.

48. John Crosby, "Backus on That Old Medium," *Lawrence* (KS) *Journal-World*, October 31, 1957.

49. "Jim Backus a Refugee from Television Roles," *Logansport* (IN) *Pharos-Tribune*, October 23, 1957.

50. Vernon Scott, "Joan Davis Faces Most Difficult Task," *Monessen* (PA) *Daily Independent*, December 5, 1957.

51. Tom O'Malley and Bob Cunniff, "Joan Has Her Qualms About Visit to Bob Hope Show," *Cedar Rapids Gazette*, November 13, 1956.

52. Hal Humphrey, "Last of Comediennes?" *Waterloo* (IA) *Daily Courier*, April 6, 1960.

Bibliography

Andrews, Bart. *The "I Love Lucy" Book*. New York: Doubleday, 1985.

Backus, Jim, and Henny Backus. *Forgive Us Our Digressions: An Autobiography*. New York: St. Martin's Press, 1988.

Bast, William. *Surviving James Dean*. Fort Lee, NJ: Barricade, 2006.

Brooks, Tim, and Earle Marsh. *The Complete Directory to Prime Time Network and Cable TV Shows, 1946–Present*. New York: Ballantine, 2003.

Burlingame, Jon. *TV's Biggest Hits: The Story of Television Themes from "Dragnet" to "Friends."* New York: Schirmer, 1996.

Burrows, Abe. *Honest, Abe: Is There Really No Business Like Show Business?* Boston: Little, Brown, 1980.

Cox, Jim. *Sold on Radio: Advertisers in the Golden Age of Broadcasting*. Jefferson, NC: McFarland, 2008.

De La Hoz, Cindy. *Lucy at the Movies*. Philadelphia: Running Press, 2007.

Diliberto, Gioai. *Debutante: The Story of Brenda Frazier*. New York: Knopf, 1987.

Dunning, John. *On the Air: The Encyclopedia of Old-Time Radio*. New York: Oxford University Press, 1998.

Gargan, William. *Why Me? An Autobiography*. Garden City, NY: Doubleday, 1969.

Gaver, Jack. *There's Laughter in the Air: Radio's Top Comedians and Their Best Shows*. New York: Greenberg, 1945.

Goldberg, Lee. *Unsold Television Pilots: 1955 Through 1988*. Jefferson, NC: McFarland, 1990.

Goldman, Herbert G. *Banjo Eyes: Eddie Cantor and the Birth of Modern Stardom*. New York: Oxford University Press, 1997.

Gordon, Jeff. *Foxy Lady: The Authorized Biography of Lynn Bari*. Duncan, OK: BearManor Media, 2010.

Hickerson, Jay. *The 4th Revised Ultimate History of Network Radio Programming and Guide to All Circulating Shows*. Hamden, CT: J. Hickerson, 2010.

Koseluk, Gregory. *Eddie Cantor: A Life in Show Business*. Jefferson, NC: McFarland, 1995.

Lahr, John. *Notes on a Cowardly Lion: The Biography of Bert Lahr*. New York: Knopf, 1969.

Malarcher, Jay. *The Classically American Comedy of Larry Gelbart*. Lanham, MD: Scarecrow Press, 2003.

Maltin, Leonard. *The Art of the Cinematographer: A Survey and Interviews with Five Masters*. New York: Dover, 1978.

Marc, David. *Comic Visions: Television Comedy and American Culture*, 2d ed. Malden, MA: Blackwell, 1997.

Martin, Linda, and Kerry Segrave. *Women in Comedy*. Secaucus, NJ: Citadel Press, 1986.

McClelland, Doug. *The Golden Age of B Movies*. New York: Bonanza, 1981.

Mitz, Rick. *The Great TV Sitcom Book*. New York: Perigee, 1983.

Murray, Lyn. *Musician: A Hollywood Journal of Wives, Women, Writers, Lawyers, Directors, Producers and Music*. Secaucus, NJ: Lyle Stuart, 1987.

Nash, Jay Robert, and Stanley Ralph Ross. *The Motion Picture Guide*. Chicago: Cinebooks, 1985–1987.

Nollen, Scott Allen. *Abbott and Costello on the Home Front: A Critical Study of the Wartime Films*. Jefferson, NC: McFarland, 2009.

Ohmart, Ben. *Hold That Joan: The Life, Laughs, and Films of Joan Davis*. Albany, GA: BearManor Media, 2007.

O'Neil, Thomas. *The Emmys: The Ultimate, Unofficial Guide to the Battle of TV's Best Shows and Greatest Stars*, 3d ed. New York: Perigee, 1992.

Oppenheimer, Jess, with Gregg Oppenheimer. *Laughs, Luck, and Lucy: How I Came to Create the Most Popular Sitcom of All Time*. Syracuse: Syracuse University Press, 1996.

Parish, James Robert. *The Slapstick Queens*. South Brunswick, NJ: A.S. Barnes, 1973.

_____, and William T. Leonard. *The Funsters*. New Rochelle, NY: Arlington House, 1979.

Poole, Gary. *Radio Comedy Diary: A Researcher's Guide to the Actual Jokes and Quotes of the Top Comedy Programs of 1947–1950*. Jefferson, NC: McFarland, 2001.

Rich, John. *Warm Up the Snake: A Hollywood Memoir*. Ann Arbor: University of Michigan Press, 2006.

Robbins, Jhan. *Inka Dinka Doo: The Life of Jimmy Durante*. New York: Paragon House, 1991.

Slide, Anthony. *The Encyclopedia of Vaudeville*. Westport, CT: Greenwood, 1994.

Taylor, Robert. *Fred Allen: His Life and Wit*. Boston: Little, Brown, 1989.

Terrace, Vincent. *Radio Program Openings and Closings, 1931–1972*. Jefferson, NC: McFarland, 2003.

_____. *Radio Programs, 1924–1984: A Catalog of Over 1800 Shows*. Jefferson, NC: McFarland, 1999.

Tucker, David C. *The Women Who Made Television Funny: Ten Stars of 1950s Sitcoms*. Jefferson, NC: McFarland, 2007.

Tucker, Fredrick. *Verna Felton*. Albany, GA: Bear-Manor Media, 2010.

Vallee, Rudy. *Let the Chips Fall*. Harrisburg, PA: Stackpole, 1975.

_____, and Gil McKean. *My Time Is Your Time: The Story of Rudy Vallee*. New York: I. Obolensky, 1962.

Variety Television Reviews. New York: Garland, 1989–91.

Wertheim, Arthur Frank. *Radio Comedy*. New York: Oxford University Press, 1979.

Whitney, Grace Lee, with Jim Denney. *The Longest Trek: My Tour of the Galaxy*. Clovis, CA: Quill Driver, 1998.

Wilkins, Roy, with Tom Mathews. *Standing Fast: The Autobiography of Roy Wilkins*. New York: Da Capo, 1994.

Young, Jordan R. *The Laugh Crafters: Comedy Writing in Radio and TV's Golden Age*. Beverly Hills: Past Times, 1999.

Vital Records

Josephine Donna Davis, birth certificate #45543, 1912 (amended 1944). Office of Vital Records, Minnesota Department of Health.

LeRoy Davis, death certificate #031252, December 21, 1959. Section of Vital Statistics, Minnesota Department of Health.

United States Federal Census, 1900, 1910, 1920, 1940. Provo, UT: Ancestry.com.

Archival Materials

The Cogwheel (Mechanic Arts High School, St. Paul, Minnesota). Microfilm, 1925–1930. Minnesota Historical Society, St. Paul, Minnesota.

Harry Crane Papers. Collection #203, Boxes 67–71. Performing Arts Special Collections, Charles E. Young Research Library, University of California, Los Angeles.

Joan Davis file. Margaret Herrick Library, Academy of Motion Picture Arts and Sciences, Los Angeles, California.

The Joan Davis Show. Joan Davis Enterprises, Inc., 1956. UCLA Film and Television Archive, Los Angeles, California.

The Life and Loves of Joan Davis, by Joan Davis. Sealtest, 1944.

The M. Billy Thomas, editor-in-chief. Mechanic Arts High School, St. Paul, Minnesota, June 1927.

Pupil Cards, 1920–1941, Mechanic Arts High School. Minnesota Historical Society, St. Paul, Minnesota.

Periodicals

Billboard
Daily Variety
The Hollywood Reporter
TV Guide
Variety

Websites

The American Film Institute Catalog of Feature Films (www.afi.com/members/catalog)
www.ancestry.com
www.findagrave.com
The Internet Movie Database (www.imdb.com)
www.newspaperarchive.com
www.radiogoldindex.com
www.varietyultimate.com
www.youtube.com/user/JoanDavisChannel

Index

Numbers in **bold italics** indicate pages with photographs.